W9-CAE-506

Violence against Women and Girls

SOUTH ASIA DEVELOPMENT FORUM

Violence against Women and Girls: Lessons from South Asia

Jennifer L. Solotaroff and Rohini Prabha Pande

 WORLD BANK GROUP

© 2014 International Bank for Reconstruction and Development / The World Bank
1818 H Street NW, Washington DC 20433
Telephone: 202-473-1000; Internet: www.worldbank.org

Some rights reserved

1 2 3 4 17 16 15 14

This work is a product of the staff of The World Bank with external contributions. The findings, interpretations, and conclusions expressed in this work do not necessarily reflect the views of The World Bank, its Board of Executive Directors, or the governments they represent. The World Bank does not guarantee the accuracy of the data included in this work. The boundaries, colors, denominations, and other information shown on any map in this work do not imply any judgment on the part of The World Bank concerning the legal status of any territory or the endorsement or acceptance of such boundaries.

Nothing herein shall constitute or be considered to be a limitation upon or waiver of the privileges and immunities of The World Bank, all of which are specifically reserved.

Rights and Permissions

This work is available under the Creative Commons Attribution 3.0 IGO license (CC BY 3.0 IGO) http://creativecommons.org/licenses/by/3.0/igo. Under the Creative Commons Attribution license, you are free to copy, distribute, transmit, and adapt this work, including for commercial purposes, under the following conditions:

Attribution—Please cite the work as follows: Solotaroff, Jennifer L., and Rohini Prabha Pande. 2014. *Violence against Women and Girls: Lessons from South Asia.* South Asia Development Forum. Washington, DC: World Bank. doi:10.1596/978-1-4648-0171-6. License: Creative Commons Attribution CC BY 3.0 IGO

Translations—If you create a translation of this work, please add the following disclaimer along with the attribution: *This translation was not created by The World Bank and should not be considered an official World Bank translation. The World Bank shall not be liable for any content or error in this translation.*

Adaptations—If you create an adaptation of this work, please add the following disclaimer along with the attribution: *This is an adaptation of an original work by The World Bank. Responsibility for the views and opinions expressed in the adaptation rests solely with the author or authors of the adaptation and are not endorsed by The World Bank.*

Third-party content—The World Bank does not necessarily own each component of the content contained within the work. The World Bank therefore does not warrant that the use of any third-party-owned individual component or part contained in the work will not infringe on the rights of those third parties. The risk of claims resulting from such infringement rests solely with you. If you wish to re-use a component of the work, it is your responsibility to determine whether permission is needed for that re-use and to obtain permission from the copyright owner. Examples of components can include, but are not limited to, tables, figures, or images.

All queries on rights and licenses should be addressed to the Publishing and Knowledge Division, The World Bank, 1818 H Street NW, Washington, DC 20433, USA; fax: 202-522-2625; e-mail: pubrights@worldbank.org.

ISBN (paper): 978-1-4648-0171-6
ISBN (electronic): 978-1-4648-0172-3
DOI: 10.1596/978-1-4648-0171-6

Cover photo: High school students leaving school in Suapur, Bangladesh. © Scott Wallace / World Bank. Used with the permission of Scott Wallace / World Bank. Further permission required for reuse.
Cover design: Critical Stages

Library of Congress Cataloging-in-Publication Data

Solotaroff, Jennifer L.
Violence against women and girls : lessons from South Asia / Jennifer L. Solotaroff and Rohini Prabha Pande.
    pages cm. — (South Asia development forum)
  Includes bibliographical references and index.
ISBN 978-1-4648-0171-6 (alk. paper) — ISBN 978-1-4648-0172-3 (electronic : alk. paper)
1. Women—South Asia—Social conditions. 2. Girls—South Asia—Social conditions. 3. Women—Violence against—South Asia. 4. Girls—Violence against—South Asia. I. Pande, Rohini (Rohini P.) II. World Bank. III. Title.
  HQ1735.3.S63 2014
  305.40954—dc23
                                                       2014026057

ACC LIBRARY SERVICES AUSTIN, TX

South Asia Development Forum

Home to a fifth of mankind, and to almost half of the people living in poverty, South Asia is also a region of marked contrasts: from conflict-affected areas to vibrant democracies, from demographic bulges to aging societies, from energy crises to global companies. This series explores the challenges faced by a region whose fate is critical to the success of global development in the early 21st century, and that can also make a difference for global peace. The volumes in it convey in an accessible way findings from recent research and lessons of experience, across a range of development topics. The series is intended to present new ideas and to stimulate debate among practitioners, researchers, and all those interested in public policies. In doing so, it exposes the options faced by decision makers in the region and highlights the enormous potential of this fast-changing part of the world.

South Asia Region, The World Bank

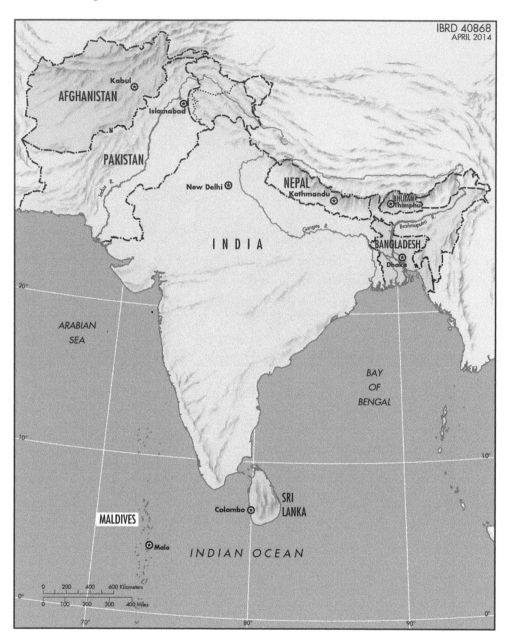

Source: World Bank (IBRD 40868, April 2014).

Contents

Boxes

Figures

Map

Tables

Foreword

For years and even decades, dedicated women and men in South Asian countries have been working to prevent and respond to violence against women and girls, often putting their own lives at risk. Their efforts in the field—together with those of researchers who seek to better understand the drivers of this violence and improve interventions—are the heart and foundation of this study. Its analysis, synthesis of lessons, and recommendations for stakeholders stand on the shoulders of these committed practitioners, many of whom are survivors of violence themselves. Their motivation is to improve the opportunities, rights, and lives of women and girls.

Such violence has economic and fiscal consequences for South Asian countries. The costs are enormous, and they are crippling to economies and societies. As detailed in the pages that follow, the human, social, and financial costs of violence against women and girls severely hamper countries' ability to achieve six of the eight Millennium Development Goals. These costs will continue to accrue unless government, the private sector, media and entertainment, and other stakeholders can coordinate and launch large-scale efforts that complement ongoing interventions in the region to address such violence and legislation to combat it, to varying degrees, in each country. By summarizing these costs and consequences, capturing ongoing efforts to address violence against South Asian women and girls in the field, and collating findings from research on risk factors and evaluations of interventions, this book is intended to serve as a reference and a policy tool. Hopefully it can help those already working on these issues in South Asia to learn more about each other's work and take advantage of synergies across actors, stakeholders, sectors, and even countries. Hopefully the recommendations it has distilled from findings of legal, government, research and other experts in the region can help guide policy makers as they prioritize and fund intervention programs.

Philippe Le Houérou
Vice President
South Asia Region
The World Bank

Acknowledgments

This book is the product of the dedicated teamwork of a core team, bolstered by the generous advice and sharing of expertise by a host of individuals working on violence against women and girls across South Asia.

The core team, in Washington DC, India, Nepal, and Thailand, was led by Jennifer L. Solotaroff (South Asia Social Development Unit, World Bank—SASDS), who also managed and prepared this report with Rohini Prabha Pande (SASDS). Tanya D'Lima (SASDS) conducted extensive field research in India and Pakistan and developed case studies and chapter drafts. Piotr Pawlak (SASDS) led field research in Bangladesh, Maldives, and Sri Lanka and developed case studies. Erisha Suwal (SASDS) led field research in Afghanistan, Bhutan, and Nepal and developed case studies. These three field-based staff members were instrumental in identifying and analyzing the interventions discussed in this study. Syed Usman Javaid (SASDS) conducted all data analysis and contributed to chapter drafts. Hiska Noemi Reyes (SASDS) developed chapters, reviewed impact evaluations, and led communications and outreach efforts. Dustin Andrew Smith (SASDS) conducted desktop research, contributed to chapter drafts, and oversaw concept note consultations in Delhi, Dhaka, Kathmandu, and Washington, DC, September 30–October 4, 2013. Gladys Lopez-Acevedo of the South Asia Chief Economist's Office (SARCE) conducted desktop research, contributed to chapter drafts, and provided strategic guidance. Muqaddisa Mehreen (SASDS) supported field research and overall communications in Pakistan. Bilgehan Gokcan (SARCE), Amir Sadeghi (SARCE), and Ayesha Raheem (SARCE) provided research support, and Indira (Mona) Edwards (SASDS) provided technical support. Neelam Chowdhry, Janet Bably Halder, Kirin Gautam, Zahin Takrim Hussein, Maya Krishnan, Sulochana Nepali, Wahida Obaidy, Abdul Qadir, Dechen Tshering, and Binny Verma provided administrative support and technical assistance on communications and event organizing. John (JD) Dawson provided editorial support.

The study also draws on a background paper, "Violence against Women in South Asia and the Limits of Law," written for this book by Ratna Kapur (2013).

The team is extremely grateful to Philippe Le Houérou (Regional Vice President, South Asia) for his contributions and overall guidance. We thank Martin Rama (Chief Economist, South Asia Region) for valuable strategic and substantive guidance throughout the study. We also thank Maria Correia (Sector Manager, SASDS) for overall guidance and critical support since the study's inception. Rachid Benmessaoud (Country Director, Pakistan), Françoise Clottes (Country Director, Sri Lanka and Maldives), Onno Ruhl (Country Director, India), Robert Saum (Country Director, Afghanistan and Bhutan), and Johannes Zutt (Country Director, Bangladesh and Nepal) graciously provided support and guidance for in-country consultative and dissemination events.

We are also grateful to Maitreyi Bordia Das (SASDS), Nata Duvvury, Mary Ellsberg, Shireen Huq, Kiersten Johnson, Matthew Morton (SASSP), Maria Beatriz Orlando (SDV), Fouzia Saeed, Julie Thekkudan, and Ravi Verma for their considerable substantive guidance throughout the year it has taken to write this report.

The research for this study draws on the contributions of hundreds of people from South Asia and experts from other regions. Several of these individuals generously devoted their time to field interviews: Pranita Achyut, Nisha Agrawal, Eknarayan Aryal, Anant Asthana, Brinda Bartaula, Parvati Basnet, Laxman Belbase, Robia Charles, Sunita Dhanuwar, Kesang Chuki Dorjee, Irada Gautam, Sushmita Gautam, Uma Gautam, Geeta (a rape survivor; this is not her real name), Selay Ghaffar, Nirmala Gupta, Sabin Gurung, Radha Gurung, Jinat Ara Haque, Angela Ison, Samjhana K.C., Noreen Khali, Ruchi Lohani, Raju Man Singh Malla, Sudha Pant, Kamala Panthi, Hajera Pasha, Aarati Pathak, Sonam Penjor, Badri Pokharel, Sitaram Prasai, Chandani Rana, Sri Ranganathan, Pramila Shah, Renu Shah, Sapna Shrestha, Ravi Verma, Chimi Wangmo, and Sangay Zam.

Our thanks go also to the following individuals who provided insightful verbal or written comments for concept note drafts, chapter drafts, or various report outlines: Yasmin Abbasi, Tahir Abdullah, Pranita Achyut, Omer Aftab, Tasneem Ahmar, Maksuda Akhter, Kohenour Akter, Bharti Ali, Uzma Altaf, Avni Amin, Sajeda Amin, Mohna Ansari, Hangama Anwari, Shohini Banerjee, Nandita Baruah, Hannana Begum, Sharifa Begum, Nadia Behboodi, Smita Bharati, Nandita Bhatla, Sarad Bista, Mohona Chatterjee, Srijana Chettri, Phintsho Choeden, Dipa Nag Chowdhury, Huma Daha, Monica Das Gupta, Amita Dey, Anju Dubey, Ishita Dutta, Irada Gautam, Margaret Greene, Asika Gunasena, Rebecca Haines, Shabana Hamid, Lucia Hanmer, Tazeen Hasan, Lubna Hawwa, Camille Hennion, Abul Hossain, Sara Hossain, Maliha Hussein, Angela Ison, Shirin Jahangeer, Vanessa Lopez Janik, Ramani Jayasundere, Shireen Jejeebhoy, Rachel Jewkes, Ratna Kapur, Shinkai Karokhail, Gurjeet Kaur, Hamrah Khan, Md. Abdur Rahim Khan, Md. Nazrul Islam Khan, Sonali Khan, Saifora Khan, Sanjaya Khanal, Sujata Khandekar, Chulani Kodikara, Suneeta Krishnan, Sangeeta Kumari, Antara Lahiri, Teresa Marchiori, Jennifer McClearly-Sills, Muqadissa Mehreen, Renuka Motihar, Homira Nassery, Sharmila Neogi, Janardan Nepal, Habibun

Nessa, Naoko Ohno, Asta Olesen, Karuna Onta, Elizaveta Perova, Rakshanda Perveen, Bahni Shikha Das Purkayastha, Md. Zahidur Rahman, Rajani Ranjan, Humaira Rasuli, Aishath Rizna, Fouzia Saeed, Niranjan Saggurti, Rekha Saha, Nina Hal Schejelderup, Sidney Schuler, Humaira Shaikh, Rabindra Kumar Shakya (Honorable Vice Chairman, National Planning Commission, Government of Nepal), Leyla Shamchiyeva, Jaya Sharma, Humaira Mumtaz Sheikh, Bandita Sijapati, Gitanjali Singh, Sudeep Bahadur Singh, Winnie Singh, Maheen Sultan, Fareeha Ummar, Bernice van Bronkhorst, Tahera Yasmin, and Kathryn Yount.

We benefited greatly from guidance and technical support on communications and outreach from a number of people; many individuals also took the time to send us a rich selection of reports, articles, and working papers to which we may otherwise not have had access: Shashi Kumary Adhikary, Nazneen Akhtar, Alana Albee, Amar B.K., Tushar Anchal, Sudarshana Anojan, Muneeb Ansari, Manizeh Bano, Babar Bashir, Lynn Bennett, Bibhusan Bista, Sarad Bista, Lauri Calhoun, Ashish Ashok Damle, Abhijit Das, Amita Dey, Emma Fulu, M. Parthapriya Ghosh, Bilge Gokcen, Passanna Gunasekera, Sophie Hardefeldt, Zainab Ibrahim, Chhaya Jha, Kamani Jinadasa, Anuj Kapilashrami, Pramila K.C., Mizanur Rahman Khan, Kalpana Khatiwada, Sveinung Kiplesund, Sunita Kishor, Pranika Koyu, Amrita Limbu, Kristi Maskey, Allison McGonagle Glinski, Stephanie Miedema, Will Muir, Poonam Muttreja, Qamar Naeem, Kamrun Nahar, Priya Nanda, Meena Narula, Indu Nepal, Habibun Nessa, Anders Öhrström, Corine Otte, Minty Pande, Anju Pandey, Ayesha Raheem, Saama Rajakaruna, Swarna Rajgopalan, Bandana Rana, Sabina Faiz Rashid, Mohamed Ghani Razaak, Diane Richardson, Trupti Shah, Ena Singh, Steve Snyder, Maheen Sultan, Shraddha Thapa, Fr. Augustine Thomas, Noor ul Ulain, Junita Upadhyay, George Varughese, Dominic de Ville, Ayesha Wadood, Sunayana Walia, Rabia Waqar, Ann Warner, Barbara Weyermann, Haidar W. Yaqub, and Muhammad Zabhi.

This book has been made possible by Trust Fund support from an AusAID grant through the South Asia Gender (SAGE) Initiative window and by Bank Budget.

About the Contributors

TANYA D'LIMA is an international development consultant who specializes in projects related to social justice, conflict resolution, and inclusive development. Prior to the World Bank, she worked for the Asia division of Search for Common Ground, an international conflict resolution organization based in Washington, DC, and John Snow Inc., a public health research and consulting firm. She has an MA in international development and social change from Clark University.

SYED USMAN JAVAID works as a consultant with the World Bank South Asia Region's Sustainable Development Department. His current primary work focus is research on violence against women and girls. He also has contributed to the Region's flagship report on urbanization in South Asia. Prior to the World Bank, he worked with the Calvert Social Investment Foundation, where he helped analyze the social impact of the Foundation's Women Investing in Women (WIN WIN) portfolio. He has an MA in Public Policy from the Kennedy School of Government at Harvard University, where he studied economic and political development, and a BA in Economics from Ohio Wesleyan University.

RATNA KAPUR is a Global Professor of Law at Jindal Global Law School, India. She is also on the Faculty of the Geneva School of Diplomacy and International Relations, in Geneva, Switzerland. After practicing law for a number of years in New Delhi, India, she now teaches and publishes extensively on issues of international law, human rights, critical legal theory, and postcolonial theory. She was the Senior Gender Advisor with the UN Mission in Nepal during the transition period from 2007–08. She has been a visiting professor at a number of distinguished law schools, including Georgetown University Law Center, NYU School of Law, the United Nations Peace University, Yale Law School, Zurich University, and a Visiting Fellow at Harvard Law School and Cambridge University. Professor Kapur also works as a human rights consultant on issues of trafficking, migration, sexuality, and equality for various international organizations.

GLADYS LOPEZ-ACEVEDO is a Lead Economist in the Office of the Chief Economist in the World Bank South Asia Region. Her research interests include poverty, inequality, labor markets, and evaluation. She is a fellow in global knowledge institutions such as the Latin America Economics Association and the International Development Research Center. Gladys has been an associate professor at the Institute Technology Autonomous of Mexico (ITAM) and a research fellow at the University of Virginia. She has a BA in Economics from ITAM and a PhD in Economics from the University of Virginia.

ROHINI PRABHA PANDE is the lead consultant for this report. She has more than 20 years of research and program experience in gender and development. Prior to this assignment, she worked at the International Center for Research on Women (ICRW) for over eight years, leading intervention research programs in South Asia that focused on adolescent reproductive health and empowerment. She also has worked with the Rockefeller and Ford Foundations, Care International and other NGOs in South Asia and West Africa, on female education, women's income generation, and women's empowerment. She has an Sc.D. from the Johns Hopkins Bloomberg School of Public Health and an MPA from Princeton University's Woodrow Wilson School of Public and International Affairs.

PIOTR PAWLAK is an independent gender consultant. He is working with the World Bank on several initiatives related to gender, masculinity, economic development and migration in South Asia, and youth and gender in the Maldives. As a Program Officer at Instituto Promundo, he led male engagement research, gender trainings, and advocacy campaigns on men, violence and gender; co-coordinated the MenEngage initiative; worked on the Men and Gender Equality Policy Project; co-authored a report, *What Men Have to Do With It*, to promote gender in public policies; and contributed to the development of the *International Men and Gender Equality Survey* (IMAGES), a study on men, women and gender equality that is being conducted in Africa, Asia, Europe, and Latin America. Mr. Pawlak is currently completing his PhD at Mahidol University in Bangkok, Thailand.

HISKA NOEMI REYES is an Operations Officer in the World Bank South Asia Region's Social Development Unit. She has worked on gender and social inclusion issues in Latin America and the Caribbean and Africa, and is currently leading a regional program on gender-based violence that will support greater attention to this issue in the World Bank's operations and analytical work in South Asia. She serves as an alternate representative for the region on the World Bank Gender and Development Board. She has an MA in international relations from the Maxwell School of Citizenship and Public Affairs at Syracuse University.

DUSTIN ANDREW SMITH is a Junior Professional Associate in the World Bank South Asia Region's Social Development Unit. His research interests include the socio-cultural norms underlying gender inequality in South Asia, as well as the relationship between women and law in the region. He has a Master of Divinity from Harvard University, where his culminating thesis sought to assess and to envision an appropri-ate response to the phenomenon of forced marriage among South Asian communities in the United States. In addition, Mr. Smith has a BS from Brandeis University in Waltham, Massachusetts.

JENNIFER LYNN SOLOTAROFF is the team leader for this report. She is a Senior Social Development Specialist and the Gender Coordinator for the World Bank South Asia Region, which she represents as a principal on the World Bank Gender and Development Board. During her 10 years at the Bank, she has led programs and analytical tasks related to gender inequality, labor force participation, and microenterprise in South Asian countries, with particular attention to Afghanistan, Bangladesh, Bhutan, India, Pakistan, and Sri Lanka. She also manages AusAid and multi-donor trust funds dedicated to work on gender in the region. Her research interests include gender and labor markets, gender-based violence, and social stratification in South Asia and East Asia. She has a PhD in sociology, an MA in economics, and an MA in East Asian studies from Stanford University.

ERISHA SUWAL is a consultant for the World Bank South Asia Region's Social Development Unit. Based in Kathmandu, Nepal, she coordinates an Information Communication Technology pilot called FightVAW to report and manage cases of violence against women and girls. Previously, she worked for Samata Foundation, a Dalit think tank that conducts research for policy advocacy in Nepal. She has an MA in public administration from Columbia University's School of International and Public Affairs and a BA in economics and South Asia studies from Wellesley College.

Executive Summary

This report examines the prevalence and the factors associated with various types of violence against women and girls in South Asia (Afghanistan, Bangladesh, Bhutan, India, Maldives, Nepal, Pakistan, and Sri Lanka). The report also highlights the gaps where intensive research or interventions might be undertaken. Its focus, themes, and organization, as well as its content and analyses, have benefited greatly from consultation, guidance, and direct inputs from experts in the public, nongovernmental organization (NGO), private, donor, and research sectors of South Asia. This report is one component of the World Bank's regional program, launched in January 2013, to attend to issues of gender-based violence in its operations, analytics, and collaborative work with other practitioners in South Asia.

Organizing Frameworks

The report's organizing framework and analysis, described in chapter 1, draw from Heise's (1998) ecological model of abuse. The ecological model posits that violence is a function of multiple factors that interact at various levels of the "social ecology," not only the level of the individual but also the levels of her household, community, and society. We combine the ecological model with a life-cycle approach to capture the fact that women and girls in South Asia face the risk of multiple forms of violence throughout their lives, from birth through old age. We examine violence faced by girls in infancy and early childhood (excess female child mortality and physical and sexual abuse), in adolescence before marriage (sexual harassment by nonmarital intimate partners), and in adolescence and adulthood once married (dowry-related violence and intimate partner and domestic violence). We also examine forms of violence that cut across life stages—namely, sexual harassment of adolescent and adult women, trafficking of women and girls, honor killings, and custodial violence.

We draw from the fields of feminist research, economics, sociology, anthropology, public health, demography, and law to review the large body of literature on all the forms of violence against women and girls in the region. We analyze data from multiple sources to provide additional information on trends over time and comparisons of South Asia with other world regions. Finally, we map the landscape of interventions to address different forms of violence across the eight South Asian countries and draw promising lessons from their evaluations.

Why Is Violence against Girls and Women in South Asia Critical to Address?

The violence that women and girls are subjected to throughout their lives prevents them from realizing their rights as human beings and as equal citizens. This fact in itself provides an imperative to act. A large literature also investigates the human, social, and economic costs and consequences of this violence. Available data and measurements capture a tiny fraction of the totality of these costs, and yet even this fraction can be a massive drain on individuals, families, communities, and societies. Women suffer direct consequences to their physical, sexual, and emotional health. Violence in childhood and later can also affect girls' and women's abilities to fully benefit from and participate in schooling and employment, thus constraining their lifetime opportunities for an education and a career. Violence not only affects the girls and women experiencing it and their families, but also can spiral across generations. Monetizing the costs of these consequences has proved challenging, and estimates of costs to individuals and households vary tremendously across studies. Still, it is clear that monetary costs are borne because of days lost to work, treatment costs of injuries, or police and judicial arrangements. Finally, violence against girls and women undermines countries' achievements of at least six of the eight United Nations Millennium Development Goals. Chapter 1 further elaborates on these points.

What Does Violence against Women and Girls in South Asia Look Like?

South Asian women and girls face a range of types of violence throughout their lives, as detailed in chapter 2. Starting with the beginning of the life cycle—that is, in childhood—South Asia has the highest levels of excess female child mortality among world regions. Within South Asia, India has the greatest excess female child mortality of all countries for which data are available; Bangladesh, Nepal, and Pakistan also show high levels. Since the early 1990s, however, excess female child mortality has declined in Nepal and Sri Lanka and dramatically in Bangladesh. Excess female child mortality in India, however, has remained firmly and largely unchanged.

FIGURE ES.1 Child Marriage Prevalence: Countries with Highest Proportion Married by Age 15

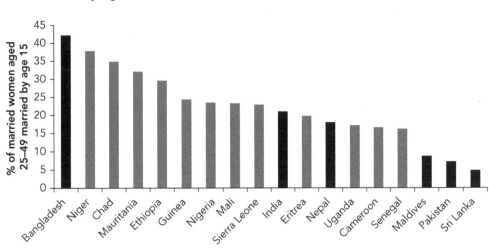

Source: DHS, multiple years.
Note: Sample size = more than 1,000 in each country. DHS data are not available for Afghanistan and Bhutan.

South Asia also has the highest rate of child marriage in the world, with 46 percent of girls married by age 18. In Bangladesh, more than 40 percent of girls are married by age 15 (figure ES.1). Analysis of data from the Demographic and Health Surveys (DHS) suggests that rates of child marriage are slowing in the region. Qualitative data provide cautious optimism that attitudes toward child marriage may also be changing. Still, a divide persists between individual desires on the one hand and perceived cultural norms and compulsions for early marriage on the other, thus contributing to the persistence of child marriage in the region.

Large surveys may inaccurately estimate prevalence of intimate partner violence. Regardless, such violence is unacceptably high: DHS data from countries whose surveys include questions about physical domestic violence show that almost one-half of surveyed married women in Bangladesh, one-third in India, and one-quarter or more in Nepal and Pakistan report physical spousal violence. A growing body of research also documents that the violence experienced by South Asian women at the hands of their husbands is frequent, severe, and of multiple forms. Married adolescents may be particularly vulnerable. Much of the marital abuse that women suffer likely occurs in the first few years of marriage. Given the early average age at marriage in much of South Asia, this finding means that a great deal of this violence is experienced by married adolescents, who may be more powerless than older married women to defend themselves. Significant proportions of men and women accept or condone spousal violence against women for many behaviors; however, some research suggests that attitudes toward domestic marital violence are not unequivocally supportive of violence, but vary by the reason and the extent of violence.

Data remain limited for several aspects of intimate partner violence in South Asia, including forms of violence other than physical and sexual—such as economic violence or controlling behavior—and intimate partner violence faced by never-married women or older women. Research on domestic violence perpetrated by other household members is limited for women at all ages and for divorced or widowed women. Reliable data are also lacking to estimate prevalence or trends in (a) physical and sexual abuse against girls, (b) sexual harassment, (c) trafficking, (d) honor killings, and (e) custodial violence. Several small-scale quantitative and qualitative studies suggest, however, that these forms of violence are persistent across many parts of South Asia and require further research.

Why Is Violence against Women and Girls in South Asia So Persistent?

Violence against women and girls in South Asia plays out in a historical, social, and political context where structures and functioning of government, social institutions, and the law all may contribute to its persistence, as analyzed in detail in chapter 3. In recent years, governments have been increasingly active in implementing policies that may contribute to preventing violence and that strengthen support services for those who experience violence. Yet, many policies and services continue to reflect a gender bias. Religious institutions and norms across the region also continue to reinforce unequal gender relations.

All eight countries in South Asia have specific constitutional provisions addressing gender equality and have signed the Convention on the Elimination of All Forms of Discrimination Against Women, albeit some with reservations. All countries also have some legal protection against several forms of violence, including female infanticide, child marriage, and intimate partner violence. Yet, legal systems contend with significant barriers to reform as well as with structural deficiencies that inhibit women's access to justice: implementation is poor, and legal awareness is limited.

A major barrier to needed legal and social reform is the continued lack of recognition that women and girls are first and foremost citizens, individuals who should be accorded the same rights and privileges as men and boys. A perception of women as victims or subjects—rather than as individuals with rights to their own identities, sexualities, and other forms of self-expression—has circumscribed the social and legal provisions for women's safety. This perception perpetuates the patriarchal belief that female household members must be protected by men and in ways that ensure female conformity to roles defined by traditional, patriarchal norms.

Patriarchy in South Asia also creates other circumstances that perpetuate social norms conducive to continuing violence against women and girls. Most critically, both women and men are prescribed numerous attributes that are tied directly to feminine and masculine social identities and enforced not only by men but also by women—for example, by mothers and mothers-in-law. The result is a cycle of violence against women and girls.

In addition to these societal- and institutional-level factors underlying violence, women and girls are vulnerable to many forms of violence because of a host of household- and individual-level risk factors. Although specific factors may vary by type of violence, some key risk factors span all forms of violence.

At the individual level, childhood exposure to violence is a key risk factor for future vulnerability to violence as adults for women, and, for men, a greater likelihood of being a perpetrator. Life stage appears to be important as well, such that young girls and adolescents are at heightened risk of many forms of violence. The ability of women and girls to negotiate with peers, parents, spouses, family members, and society at large is likely to be protective, but rigorous research unfortunately is scarce, especially regarding what kinds of negotiation skills are most useful. Secondary education is considered protective also, possibly because it provides women the opportunity to acquire skills and confidence.

In the immediate environment, a small but unequivocal body of research posits that alcohol abuse is a key risk factor triggering violence. Low socioeconomic status is also highlighted as an important risk factor. Circumstances that emerge from poverty, such as heightened stress in day-to-day living, create conditions for interpersonal violence or trafficking. The imperative to balance costs and benefits with limited resources contributes to excess female child mortality and child marriage. At the same time, violence also occurs in households that are not poor. Resource control is important: women's and girls' ownership of assets—either financial or land—can be protective, for instance, against child marriage for girls and intimate partner and domestic violence for women.

What Can We Learn from Interventions to Address Violence against Women and Girls in South Asia?

In much of South Asia, violence against women and girls is occurring against a backdrop of perhaps the most rapid economic and social changes the region has seen. Those changes may influence violence directly or indirectly through shifts in gender equality, described in chapter 4. For instance, women's opportunities for and participation in higher education, employment, and politics have expanded in most countries. As such opportunities arise and open the doors to greater gender equality and women's empowerment, however, women and girls may face a backlash, including an increased risk of violence as they leave their homes to work or to study. As women's greater participation in public life—including higher education and employment—eventually becomes the norm, violence may decrease.

In this shifting dynamic, the number and intensity of efforts to prevent or respond to violence is truly impressive. Rigorous evaluation is limited, however. We identified 101 interventions (figure ES.2) that were evaluated by quantitative, qualitative, or mixed methods, the largest number of which comprise broad "violence against women" interventions that also address intimate partner violence (41) or child marriage (27).

FIGURE ES.2 Evaluated Interventions by Violence Type

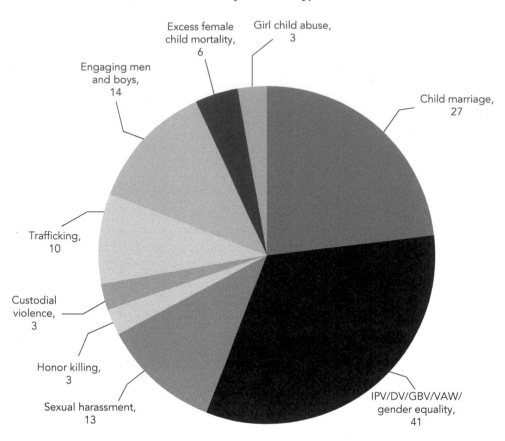

Note: DV = domestic violence; GBV = gender-based violence; IPV = intimate partner violence; VAW = violence against women.

Fourteen evaluated interventions across forms of violence explicitly engage men and boys. The smallest number of evaluated interventions address abuse specifically against girl children (3), custodial violence against women and girls (3), and honor crimes (3). Chapter 4 analyzes lessons learned and promising approaches from this set of interventions.

EVALUATIONS YIELD SOME PROMISING OR POTENTIAL PRACTICES FOR PARTICULAR FORMS OF VIOLENCE

• Conditional cash transfers, bans on practices, and media campaigns are the main evaluated interventions to address excess female child mortality. However, findings suggest the importance of multisectoral efforts with an explicit gender focus that simultaneously address risk factors at the individual, household, community, institutional, and structural levels of society.

- Most identified interventions addressing child abuse focus, appropriately, on child rights for boys and girls equally. Yet, given the particular low value of girls in South Asia, it is important to inject an explicit focus on gender into what is a human rights concern. This focus can be accomplished through existing forms of interventions—for instance, through child clubs and peer groups that can focus on girls and through training police to respond appropriately to cases of violence against girls.

- Interventions to prevent child marriage have found some success through life skills programs that empower girls. Other successful interventions include those that increase participation in secondary school as an alternative to marriage and provide livelihoods and assets to girls to counter the view of daughters as a financial liability. However, evaluations do not clarify the key essential elements of success in effective life skills, schooling, or livelihoods programs.

- Campaigns to prevent intimate partner violence show that using community networks, identifying change agents, and applying innovative media with provocative messages can at least bring intimate partner violence out of the private realm into the public eye. Interventions with boys and men demonstrate that addressing unequal gender norms early in life through approaches similar to girls' life skills programs for early marriage can influence boys' perceptions of masculinity and gender norms. There is little evidence, however, on what are the most promising services to provide to survivors of intimate partner violence, although one-stop crisis centers are drawing increasing interest.

- Campaigns and media have contributed to a growing awareness of the extent of sexual harassment in public places. Still, interventions are few and far between, and most are not evaluated in a manner that can provide promising lessons for replication or scale-up. Key gaps include the lack of evaluated interventions to address sexual harassment in the workplace, to engage bystanders to intervene effectively, and to address the sexual pressure and coercion that adolescent girls can face from partners in premarital romantic relationships.

- The increased awareness of the persistence of honor killings, particularly in Afghanistan, India, and Pakistan, provides an opportunity for more systematic intervention. Lessons can be extracted from evaluations and experiences of interventions that address other forms of violence.

- Custodial violence against women and girls needs to become more visible beyond the silo of those who work on it. This form of violence is perhaps the most hidden from the general public eye as well as from programs that address other forms of violence. Promising approaches used to prevent and respond to other forms of violence offer many lessons for addressing custodial violence.

- Trafficking presents a unique category of violence that girls and women face, one that is transnational in its nature. Some potential practices that merit further consideration include raising awareness through media and engaging trafficking survivors in prevention and response efforts. Overall, approaches to address trafficking mirror those used for preventing child marriage or for preventing or responding to intimate partner violence. As such, lessons from evaluations of child marriage and intimate partner violence interventions could be valuable to design of interventions against trafficking.

Some important challenges that need to be addressed across all forms of violence are as follows:

1. *Competent evaluation is the most imperative challenge.* The lack of competent evaluation means that a great deal of learning is lost and considerable financial and human resources are wasted. Evaluations need not only to assess whether and how interventions are effective, but also to extract the minimum critical elements necessary for success.

2. *Organizations addressing different forms of violence need to engage with each other to enable opportunities for learning.* Even when risk factors and approaches are similar across forms of violence, there is little overlap or cross-fertilization across interventions or actors, resulting in a loss of learning.

3. *Men and boys should be more systematically engaged at all levels and across all forms of violence.* The only systematic and evaluated engagement of men and boys that we were able to identify in connection with violence prevention and response for South Asia was in the domain of intimate partner violence or interventions addressing norms of masculinity.

4. *Interventions need to engage key household members and address key risks within the household that have been inadequately addressed thus far.* Interventions should systematically work with household members who may perpetrate violence or offer support, such as parents, in-laws, and siblings. There are important risk factors on which more focused attention is critical, such as alcohol abuse, parent-child interaction, and intergenerational transmission of violence.

5. *Interventions need to be sensitive to particular needs and vulnerabilities of adolescents.* We found little evidence of attention to adolescent vulnerabilities in interventions that consider adolescents together with girls and women at other stages of their lives. Such a perspective is crucial, given that young people form the bulk of the population across South Asia.

6. *Interventions should occur early in life and should engage survivors and those at risk as active participants.* A range of interventions addressing child marriage and notions of masculinity and femininity among young girls and boys attest to the importance of intervening early before biased gender norms are internalized. Efforts to prevent child abuse and trafficking need to explicitly engage survivors and those at risk. Efforts to address other forms of violence also need to more explicitly engage children, adult women at risk, and survivors as active participants in designing and implementing programs, and not as passive recipients.

7. *Strengthen legal implementation and increase institutional accountability.* Last but not least, the many laws and policies across the region's countries to prevent and address violence and gender inequality need to be rigorously implemented, and relevant institutions held accountable for enforcement. To do so, governments need to make addressing violence against women and girls more of a political priority than it has been to date.

What Do Different Stakeholders Need to Do to Advance the Agenda?

All stakeholders across society need to be involved in some capacity in order to effectively address these challenges. The recommendations in chapter 5 detail possible actions for each set of stakeholders. Governments have a critical role to play in ensuring that existing laws and policies protecting women and girls from violence are implemented effectively and that government instruments, such as health sector crisis centers, reach the intended populations. Moreover, governments need to commit adequate funding across ministries for policies and programs that address specific forms of violence. Most important, governments need to recognize and acknowledge that violence against women and girls is not the purview of a specific ministry or department but requires coordinated efforts across ministries.

Donors support the bulk of programs and research on violence against women and girls. These organizations need to better support learning across interventions and research on different forms of violence. Donors also need to send a clear message regarding the importance of monitoring and evaluation. At the same time, evaluations should be designed in ways that take into account the current and potential capacity of implementing organizations. Unless program organizations can take ownership of and successfully integrate monitoring and evaluation into their primary mandate of program implementation, evaluation research will not be institutionalized into program work. In addition to rigorous evaluations, donors need to fund longitudinal studies on the costs and consequences of violence.

NGOs are at the front line of violence prevention and response programs. First, NGOs need to improve documentation of processes to allow for comparisons of the merits of different intervention components. Second, greater dialogue, sharing of experiences, and collaboration among NGOs is necessary. Third, NGOs need to better identify potential unintended consequences of their interventions. Finally, NGOs need to improve their capacity for monitoring and evaluation. NGOs and researchers together should ensure that this evaluation is carried out in ways that not only illustrate promising approaches for the future, but also allow for NGOs to make midcourse corrections and integrate monitoring and evaluation into program design to improve the effectiveness and sustainability of an intervention.

Researchers, media, and the private sector also need to be more systematically involved in interventions. Researchers can work to improve documentation, design, and monitoring and evaluation. The media has a role to play in increasing awareness, promoting gender-transformative messaging, and influencing norms at the macro level. The private sector can engage in ongoing efforts to prevent violence by supporting school-to-work transitions, employment programs, and more effective help lines, shelters, and other response services.

Addressing the challenges to strengthen the effectiveness, reach, and sustainability of interventions for violence against women and girls will involve multiple and long-lasting coordination across all actors. Risk factors identified in the research need to be addressed more pointedly; laws and institutions need to be strengthened and held accountable; and boys, men, and other household and community members will have to be more systematically engaged. Governments and donors need to provide dedicated funding and emphasize feasible, yet rigorous, evaluation to identify and scale up promising approaches. The recognition of women and girls as equal citizens, not victims, should be central in these efforts.

Reference

Heise, L. 1998. "An Integrated, Ecological Framework." *Violence Against Women* 4 (3): 262–90.

Abbreviations

ATSEC	Action against Trafficking and Sexual Exploitation of Children
BPL	below poverty line
CCT	conditional cash transfer
CYF	Choose Your Future
DHS	Demographic and Health Surveys
ECPAT	End Child Prostitution, Child Pornography and Trafficking of Children for Sexual Purposes
GDP	gross domestic product
GEP	Gender Equality Program
HAWCA	Humanitarian Assistance for Women and Children of Afghanistan
HIV/AIDS	human immunodeficiency virus/ acquired immune deficiency syndrome
ICRW	International Center for Research on Women
ILO	International Labour Organization
IPV	intimate partner violence
LACC	Legal Aid and Consultancy Center
MARD	Men Against Rape and Discrimination
MASVAW	Men's Action to Stop Violence Against Women
MDG	Millennium Development Goals
NGO	nongovernmental organization
OCMC	One-Stop Crisis Management Centre
PLaCES	Protective Learning and Community Emergency Services

PPVHTB	Prevention and Protection for Victims of Human Trafficking in Bangladesh
RCT	randomized control trial
SAARC	South Asian Association for Regional Cooperation
STI	sexually transmitted infection
TOLI	Team Organizing Local Institution
UN	United Nations
UNDP	United Nations Development Programme
UNFPA	United Nations Population Fund
UNICEF	United Nations Children's Fund
WHO	World Health Organization
WOREC	Women's Rehabilitiation Centre (Nepal)
WRHP	Women's Rights Helpline Project

CHAPTER 1

Introduction and Overview

At the time of this writing, a year or more has passed since unprecedented protests erupted across South Asia in response to violent attacks on women and challenges to their human rights. Such challenges and events of extreme violence have included the failure of the Afghan Parliament to reaffirm a law banning violence against women and setting a minimum age of marriage—thus undermining the law's credibility—in May of 2013; the kidnapping and rape of a 15-year-old girl in Bangladesh, which ignited a human chain of protest outside the National Press Club in Dhaka in January of 2013; the brutal gang rape and murder of a young female medical student in India in December of 2012 and the nationwide protests that followed; mass demonstrations against sexual violence organized by Pakistan's powerful women's movement in January of 2013; and Nepal's months-long "Occupy Baluwatar" protest, launched in late December of 2012, in reaction to custodial violence against a female migrant worker.

These events and the ensuing public uproar have brought international attention to issues of violence against women and girls in South Asia, as well as reflection about the pervasive and intractable nature of violence against women in all parts of the world. In the South Asia region, these events also bring to light the fact that whereas violence against women may be pervasive, there is perhaps an inkling of change. In recent years, and particularly within the past 12 months, individuals, nongovernmental organizations (NGOs), media, schools, local and national politicians, and religious and community leaders are quietly building on the momentum—at least in parts of the region's countries—to change norms around various types of violence that women and girls face. They are participating in campaigns against daughter aversion and son preference, highlighting sexual harassment on the streets or in schools, and breaking the silence on sexual abuse and rape.

Why This Report and Why Now?

The violence that women and girls face throughout their lives prevents them from realizing their rights as human beings and equal citizens. Most directly, the physical, psychological and other forms of injury they sustain prevent women and girls from leading healthy, productive lives. More broadly, violence represents a critical tool to perpetuate the underlying patriarchy that persists in much of South Asia, wherein women and girls are identified strictly by their relationships to men and boys, as their mothers, daughters, sisters, and wives (Kapur 2013). Men must protect—and control—female household members in ways that ensure female conformity to these roles as defined by traditional patriarchal norms. Violence against women and girls constitutes a key manner of such control and prevents women from asserting their roles as individuals with rights. This study's underlying principle is that women and girls are first and foremost citizens, individuals who should be accorded the same rights and privileges as men and boys. We integrate throughout our discussion the ways in which violence against women and girls transgresses this principle and highlight practices that seek to empower women and girls as equal citizens.

Violence against women and girls is also a gender and development issue. It has been recognized as a matter of global concern because of its enormous human, social, and economic costs. These costs are constantly accumulating, proving significantly detrimental to the lives of women and their families, and to the poverty reduction and development efforts of governments, NGOs, multilateral institutions, and other regional partners.

Without sufficient budget dedicated to assessing which programs are effective, and to implementing programs that have proven effective in violence prevention and response, the problem will continue—and perhaps grow—in spite of legislation and other measures to combat violence in South Asian countries. Given heightened attention to the problem in the region, the time is now to impress upon those in charge of budget decisions the immense damage wrought by violence against women and girls and the urgent need to act.

VIOLENCE AGAINST WOMEN AND GIRLS HAMPERS ACHIEVEMENT OF MDGS

Several studies (for example, Ellsberg 2006; Jayaweera et al. 2007) and the evidence provided throughout this report demonstrate how violence against girls and women has a strong potentially deleterious effect on countries' achievements of at least six of the eight United Nations (UN) Millennium Development Goals (MDGs) (box 1.1). Conversely, reducing women's and girls' exposure to violence—especially repeated and severe forms of violence—is likely to improve their health and education status and increase

---

BOX 1.1 Violence against Women and Girls Hampers Achievement of the Millennium Development Goals

- *Goal 1—Eradicate Extreme Poverty and Hunger.* Violence is often preceded or accompanied by withdrawal of resources for women, exacerbating their poverty and lack of opportunities. Violence contributes directly to the poverty faced by widows; by women and girls who are trafficked into prostitution, bonded labor, or any other form of trafficking; by children in prostitution; and by women who encounter abuse in custody. Violence also can contribute to women's and households' poverty by hampering their ability to access and learn from education and to compete in the labor market.

- *Goal 2—Achieve Universal Primary Education.* When sexual harassment, child abuse, excess female child mortality, or child marriage cut short a girl's life, a girl's life chances, or parents' willingness to send girls to school, these forms of violence directly hamper the goal of universal primary education.

- *Goal 3—Promote Gender Equality and Empower Women.* Gender equality and women's empowerment cannot be achieved without addressing all the types of violence that girls and women face. In fact, male-biased gender norms and women's disempowerment trigger attitudes and behaviors that lead to persistent, repeated, and severe violence against women and girls.

- *Goal 4—Reduce Child Mortality.* Child marriage and intimate partner violence experienced by married women, particularly when they are pregnant, impede this goal's achievement because of the documented impact on fetal growth and the health and survival of newborns and infants. Excess female child mortality and child abuse directly affect efforts to achieve this MDG. Girls who are trafficked, physically or psychologically abused, or prostituted also face higher risks of child mortality than children who lead a harm-free childhood.

- *Goal 5—Improve Maternal Health.* All the forms of violence that adolescent girls and women face, whether from intimate partners or from sexual abuse and rape perpetrated by non-intimate partners, can affect their health when pregnant. Sexual and physical violence against pregnant women and the early childbearing that accompanies child marriage directly undermine maternal health.

- *Goal 6—Combat HIV/AIDS, Malaria, and Other Diseases.* A large body of research documents women's increased vulnerability to sexually transmitted infections, including human immunodeficiency virus and acquired immune deficiency syndrome (HIV/AIDS), when they are subjected to sexual violence including—but not limited to—rape. Other diseases, including malaria and tuberculosis, may not be triggered by violence as such, but women's ability to seek care may be hindered if spouses and in-laws use violence to prevent them from doing so.

Source: UN Millennium Development Goals.

---

their productivity through a number of possible pathways, such as increased stamina, better overall attentiveness, and improved capacity and knowledge (Duvvury et al. 2013). This, in turn, is bound to have a positive effect on overall economic growth and attainment of the MDGs. Although the extent of this effect is difficult to quantify, the final section of this chapter examines these costs and consequences in further detail, summarizing literature that has adopted quantitative approaches to estimate these costs at various levels of society.

MAKING THE CASE FOR ACTION: HIGHLIGHTING COSTS, MECHANISMS, AND PROMISING APPROACHES

Building on the current momentum to address violence against women and girls in South Asia, this report aims to document its prevalence and typology throughout the region, the attendant risk and protective factors, the costs and consequences of this violence, and promising approaches to prevention and response. The intended audience for the report is deliberately broad, following recent efforts in South Asia to bring together policy makers, practitioners, and research experts from a diverse range of backgrounds to share information and coordinate efforts to address violence against women and girls. Report findings and recommendations, however, are tailored to specific stakeholders: the report clarifies the constructive roles that civil society; researchers; donors; media; the private sector; and—most notably—the budgeting, policy-making, and programming arms of government can and do play to lessen the problem of violence against women and girls in the region.

This report is but one component of the World Bank's regional program, launched in January 2013, to attend to issues of gender-based violence in its operations, analytics, and collaborative work with other practitioners in South Asia. The process followed for this study illustrates a collaborative approach, facilitated by concerted efforts and collective attention on the issues. Its focus, themes, organization, and content have benefited greatly from consultation, guidance, and direct inputs from experts in the public, NGO, private, donor, and research sectors of South Asia.

Scope of the Report

Using existing literature and available data from the region, this report examines the prevalence and factors associated with various types of violence against women and girls in Afghanistan, Bangladesh, Bhutan, India, Maldives, Nepal, Pakistan, and Sri Lanka. Despite a tremendous pool of literature on intimate partner violence and a few other violence types in South Asia, no comprehensive, region-wide stocktaking of research, data, evaluations, policy analysis, and measures to address violence against women has heretofore been undertaken. This report is not an exhaustive review of this knowledge base, and efforts to attempt such a review would be beyond the scope of any one document. Rather, its aim is to analyze the broad landscape of violence against women and girls in the region—including the much-researched forms, such as intimate partner violence, as well as the less-researched forms, such as child abuse of girls or abuse of women in custody—in order to gain a common understanding of what drives this violence, where knowledge gaps lie, and what are the most effective approaches for prevention and response.

The analysis is based on a vast literature that includes peer-reviewed and published journal articles, organizational reports, and an array of unpublished working papers or other documents. Unfortunately, the eight countries in South Asia are not equally represented in the literature: we found much less research on Bhutan and the Maldives, for instance, than on India, Bangladesh, and Nepal. In fact, studies on India and Bangladesh comprise the largest proportion of the literature, followed by Nepal, and then Pakistan, Sri Lanka, and Afghanistan. Similarly, data on prevalence of particularly common forms of violence—such as intimate partner violence, excess female child mortality, and child marriage—are more easily available for India, Bangladesh, and Nepal than for other South Asian countries. Any resulting apparent focus on India or Bangladesh, particularly in chapter 2, is not intended to suggest that violence is worse in these countries than in other countries in the region. Rather, it represents where the research on prevalence and patterns of violence is currently focused and available. On the flip side, the evaluated interventions highlighted in chapter 4 are also largely from India and Bangladesh, illustrating that documentation of action to address violence is also higher in these countries than in other parts of South Asia.

The Bank's broader portfolio of work on gender-based violence in South Asia gives considerable attention to violence against men and boys as well as to violence against women and girls. Whereas this study focuses specifically on violence against women and girls, it takes into consideration the key factors (such as childhood exposure to violence, substance abuse, length and quality of the marital relationship, and—in select countries— spousal differences in age, education, and employment status) that increase the risk of men and boys becoming perpetrators of violence against women and girls. Male-centered approaches to reducing violence against women are considered alongside approaches that target women and girls in interventions.

Physical, sexual, and emotional violence perpetrated against boys and men is a widespread and pernicious problem throughout South Asia, as it is globally.[1] The patterns and drivers of this violence are, in some ways, similar to those for girls and women. In many ways, however, they are distinctive. The study of violence against men and boys requires distinct approaches that center on how masculinities are defined, perceived, and manifested in societies, communities, and households (Pawlak and Barker 2012). With an objective similar to this report's, a stocktaking of the growing body of research and programming on violence against men and boys in South Asia could help break down silos in research and programs and bring together findings to better understand the problem. Groundbreaking studies of these issues in select countries (see, for example, Barker et al. 2011; Contreras et al. 2012), research reviews of specific types of violence against men and boys in the region (for example, Frederick 2008), and numerous programmatic efforts to address violence against boys and men are highly deserving of such stocktaking and analysis. The time and resources required to do justice to such an exercise render it beyond the scope of the current report.

Organizational Framework: Life-Cycle and Ecological Approaches

The report's organizing framework and analysis draw from a combination of the life-cycle approach and the ecological model of abuse adapted by Heise (1998) from Belsky (1980), with contributions from Edleson and Tolman (1992). Because South Asian girls and women are at risk of experiencing violence throughout their lives, the analysis adopts a life-cycle perspective. The life-cycle approach is accepted and widely used to study a range of social issues concerning women (Foner 1984; Das Gupta 1995), including violence perpetrated against them (WHO 1997; Watts and Zimmerman 2002). Girls and women in South Asia typically are at or near the bottom of the social and familial hierarchy because of a multitude of economic, historical, cultural, and social reasons (for India, for example, see Das Gupta et al. 2004; Rahman and Rao 2004). Because they have low status, lack power, and face a host of other related social and economic challenges, most girls and women in South Asia are exposed to some form of violence throughout their lives. Such violence can occur across the physical spaces of a girl's or a woman's life—within the home, in public settings (for example, on the street), and in institutional settings (such as schools or workplaces). Violence can take many forms in and across these spaces and can be committed by any type of intimate or non-intimate perpetrator.

Using the life-cycle approach, this report aims to build a comprehensive narrative of the violence experienced by South Asian girls and women. To accurately reflect the nature of violence throughout their lifetimes, its interpretation of the life-cycle stages for women—infancy, girlhood, adolescence, adulthood, and old age—takes into account the critical significance of marriage in South Asia. In most parts of the region, marriage signifies the shift in life stage for girls from childhood to adulthood. Regardless of the age at which a young girl is married, she is expected from that point to take on the roles and responsibilities of adulthood, including sexual interaction with her spouse (Haberland, Chong, and Bracken 2003). As such, married girls and adolescents presumably are exposed to violence that unmarried girls and adolescents do not face—that is, marital spousal violence, violence from others in the marital home (such as in-laws), and dowry-related violence (see, for example, Purkayastha et al. 2003 for India).

DEFINITIONS AND FORMS OF VIOLENCE ACROSS LIFE STAGES

This report uses the UN General Assembly's 1993 definition of violence against women as "any act of gender-based violence that results in, or is likely to result in, physical, sexual or psychological harm or suffering to women" (United Nations 1993). This definition's reference to "gender-based" violence is an acknowledgment of its origins in gender inequality; as such, laws, institutions, and social and community norms tend to tolerate and condone violence against women, helping to enforce it (Heise, Ellsberg, and Gottemoeller 1999; Bott, Morrison, and Ellsberg 2005). The analysis of types and forms of violence experienced by girls and women is organized roughly by the life stage in which they occur. Table 1.1 lays out the definitions adopted for the various types of violence discussed in this report, and figure 1.1 displays these types as they occur by life stage.

The earliest life stages covered in this report are *infancy* and *childhood before adolescence*. Our version of the life-cycle framework does not include the period

TABLE 1.1 Definitions of Types of Violence Addressed in This Report

Types of violence experienced by unmarried girl children and adolescents	
Excess female child mortality	A mortality rate of females from birth to 5 years that exceeds that of boys in the same age range beyond what is biologically expected.
Female infanticide	The practice of killing girls from birth to 1 year.
Child abuse or maltreatment	"...all forms of physical and/or emotional ill-treatment, sexual abuse, neglect or negligent treatment or commercial or other exploitation, resulting in actual or potential harm to the child's health, survival, development, or dignity in the context of a relationship of responsibility, trust or power" (WHO 1999, 15; Hyder and Malik 2007, 168).
Child sexual abuse	"Contacts or interactions between a child and an older or more knowledgeable child or adult (a stranger, sibling or person in a position of authority, such as a parent or caretaker) when the child is being used as an object of gratification for an older child's or adult's sexual needs. These contacts or interactions are carried out against the child using force, trickery, bribes, threats or pressure" (UNICEF 2001, 9).
Nonmarital intimate partner violence: unmarried adolescents	The violence that adolescent girls (ages 12 to 18) may face while engaging in relationships outside marriage, which involve a pattern of threatened or actual acts of sexual, physical, or emotional maltreatment or abuse.[a]
Child marriage	A formal or informal union that occurs before age 18 (UNICEF 2001).
Forced marriage	Any marriage that is conducted without both parties' full consent and in which duress is a factor, thereby violating Article 1 of the United Nations Convention on Consent to Marriage, Minimum Age for Marriage and Registration of Marriages: "No marriage shall be legally entered into without the full and free consent of both parties, such consent to be expressed by them in person after due publicity and in the presence of the authority competent to solemnize the marriage and of witnesses, as prescribed by law."[b]

table continues next page

TABLE 1.1 Definitions of Types of Violence Addressed in This Report *(continued)*

Types of violence experienced by married girls and adult women

Dowry violence	Violence perpetrated on an incoming bride by her spouse or marital family in retaliation for her and her family's inability to meet the dowry demands of the groom or his family or when the intended groom wishes to remarry to obtain another dowry. Dowry violence may take the form of harassment that leads to death, known as "dowry death."
Domestic intimate partner and nonpartner violence	Acts of physical, sexual, emotional, or other forms of abuse perpetrated against a married woman in the home by a husband or other household members or against a formerly married woman (widowed or divorced) by her marital or natal household members.
Violence against elderly women	Any abuse or neglect of an older person by a caregiver or another individual in a relationship with the elderly person that involves an expectation of trust.[c]

Types of violence that are not limited to a particular life stage

Sexual harassment in public spaces	"Any unwelcome sexual advance, request for sexual favor, verbal or physical conduct or gesture of a sexual nature, or any other behavior of a sexual nature that might reasonably be expected or be perceived to cause offence or humiliation to another" and that occurs in public places (UNHCR 2005, 3).
Trafficking	"The recruitment, transportation, transfer, harboring or receipt of persons, by means of the threat or use of force or other forms of coercion, of abduction, of fraud, of deception, of the abuse of power or of a position of vulnerability or of the giving or receiving of payments or benefits to achieve the consent of a person having control over another person, for the purpose of exploitation," such as prostitution or other commercial sexual exploitation and forced labor or slavery (UNODC 2004, 42).
Custodial violence	Sexual or physical violence perpetrated by a person or persons in a custodial role (anyone providing care, protection, supervision, or guarding), typically in a state institutional setting, including judicial custody, police custody, or guardianship of a country's armed forces, particularly in conflict-affected areas (Thomas and Levi 1999).
Honor crimes, with a focus on honor killing	"A variety of manifestations of violence against women, including 'honor killings,' assault, confinement or imprisonment, and interference with choice in marriage, where the publicly articulated 'justification' is attributed to a social order claimed to require the preservation of a concept of 'honor' vested in male (family and/or conjugal) control over women and specifically women's sexual conduct: actual, suspected or potential" (Welchman and Hossain 2005, 4).

a. See "Definition of Teen Dating Violence" on the website of New Choices Inc., http://www.newchoicesinc.org /educated/abuse/TDV/def.

b. See "Convention on Consent to Marriage, Minimum Age for Marriage and Registration of Marriages" on the website of the Office of the High Commissioner for Human Rights, http://www.ohchr.org/EN /ProfessionalInterest/Pages/MinimumAgeForMarriage.aspx.

c. See "Elder Abuse: Definitions" on the website of the Centers for Disease Control and Prevention, http://www.cdc.gov/violenceprevention/elderabuse/definitions.html.

FIGURE 1.1 Types of Violence Experienced by Girls and Women in South Asia, by Life-Cycle Stage

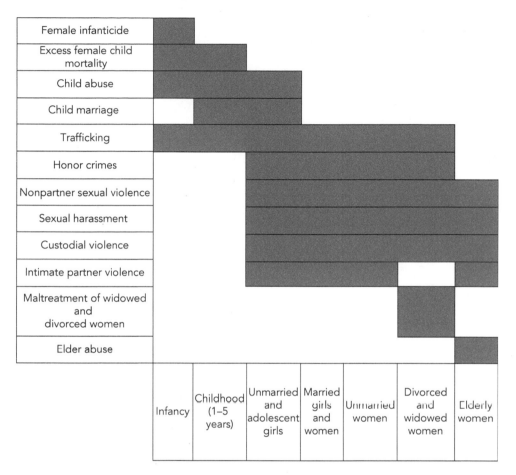

before birth, when sex-selective abortion is reported to occur on occasion in the region. Sex-selective abortion is an important manifestation of the persistence of a preference for sons and low value generally assigned to girls, particularly in some parts of India (Arnold, Kishor, and Roy 2002; Das Gupta et al. 2003). A discussion of sex-selective abortion is outside the scope of this study, however, as this report focuses on violence experienced by girls and women from birth to old age. As such, we do examine the role of son preference as manifested by excess female child mortality from birth to age 5. Child labor is another type of violence that lies beyond the scope of the report, although a strong case can be made for child labor to be classified as a form of abuse. The International Labour Organization distinguishes between child work and child labor, the latter which "deprives children of their childhood, their potential and their dignity, and that is harmful to physical and mental development."

Specifically, child labor denotes work that "is mentally, physically, socially or morally dangerous and harmful to children" and "interferes with their schooling by depriving them of the opportunity to attend school, obliging them to leave school prematurely, or requiring them to attempt to combine school attendance with excessively long and heavy work."[2] Most data on child labor, however, are not gender disaggregated, especially for countries in the South Asia region. In the rare cases where separate statistics are available for girls and boys involved in child labor, the gender differential is not sufficiently significant to argue that girls are at a greater risk of child labor than are boys in the region. For these reasons, child labor is not among the types of violence against women and girls examined in this report; however, we stress the need for research on child labor—particularly in South Asia—to use more gender-sensitive approaches in data collection and analysis.

In addition to excess female infant and child mortality, the types of violence that female infants and girls may face before adolescence in South Asia include female infanticide and child abuse. All three types fall under the United Nations definition of violence against women in their direct contributions to the psychological, physical, or sexual harm or suffering of women and girls. Decisions to rate the importance of the health and nutrition of male infants and children above that of female infants and children, for example, are interpreted here as acts of violence and neglect.

Adolescence extends over the teen years, or slightly before, and legally ends when the individual reaches the age of majority. The age of majority is almost universally recognized as 18 years, as 192 countries are state parties to the UN Convention on the Rights of the Child, which states that "a child means every human being below the age of eighteen years unless under the law applicable to the child, majority is attained earlier" (UNOHCHR 1990). Although research on violence against women and girls and on reproductive health tends to define "adolescence" as the period between ages 12 and 18, it is worth noting that the United Nations Children's Fund (UNICEF) and World Health Organization (WHO) have both used the term "adolescent" to refer to individuals ages 10 to 19 (WHO 2004; UNICEF 2011).

Once girls enter adolescence, they begin their transition from childhood to adulthood. Because girls also begin their reproductive years at this stage, societies universally associate adolescence with the beginning of female sexuality. Adolescence is one period in which biological life stage and marital life stage intersect. Given the taboo around premarital sex in much of South Asia (discussed in chapter 3), unmarried adolescent girls are at risk of sexual harassment. They are also at risk of child marriage and, in certain cases, forced marriage. Once married, given the defining role that marriage plays in South Asia, adolescent girls are at risk of the same types of violence (including physical, sexual, and emotional) as *married adult women of reproductive age* and *older married women*, which comprise the next two life stages in which South Asian women face violence. The two types of violence analyzed in depth for married women in this report are intimate partner and domestic violence, which prevails globally as a form of violence against women, and dowry violence, which is unique to South Asia.

As much as marriage exposes South Asian women to the risk of violence, the identity and status women attain through marriage can also offer certain protections. *Women who are no longer married—that is, divorcees and widows*—are no longer afforded such protections. Although relevant data are scarce, the forms of violence faced by widows and divorcees analyzed in this report include sexual, physical, and emotional violence, but also economic violence and cultural violence specific to their life stage as defined by marriage. Widowhood itself can occur in most biological life stages, given the early age of marriage across much of South Asia.

The final life stage examined is that of *elderly women*. Elderly women can cross marital stages: they may be currently married, divorced, widowed, or never married. Consequently, they may face many of the types of violence that are not limited to a particular life stage.

In addition to types of violence that are defined largely by biological and marital life stages, this study also examines some types of *violence for which the risk spans multiple life stages*. These types are sexual harassment in public spaces, honor killing, trafficking of girls and women, and custodial violence.

The continuing central position of marriage in social and cultural norms as a life stage obfuscates the increasing prevalence and concerns of *women who never marry*. With women's growing participation in labor markets, increasing rates of educational attainment, and thus expanded means of providing for themselves, remaining single—though not common—is an increasingly viable life path for women in South Asia, especially in urban areas. Almost no literature or data on violence against women for this demographic group could be found, however, and this gap is one of many key limitations on the study of violence against women in the region.

Recognizing never-married women as a discrete segment of South Asian populations is important for a number of reasons. First, ignoring women who never marry plays into the patriarchal assumption that women have a valid identity only when they are married. Second, covering this group in demographic data collection would enable interventions to be tailored to their needs for prevention and treatment of violence against them (among other issues); it would also allow greater insight into the role of never-married women in the shifting patterns of violence against women in South Asia. These women do not take part in the traditionally imperative milestone of marriage. They may be living independently; financially supporting themselves; and, to some degree, bypassing customary gender roles and familial structures in which men determine life choices for adult women. Are never-married women at greater risk of violence because they challenge these roles and structures, threatening the patriarchal system that underlies these rules? To what extent do they serve as role models for other adult women and younger generations, allowing for a different type of lifestyle to diffuse throughout communities and broader society? Would this diffusion of lifestyle put girls and women at greater risk because its increasing threat to traditional norms would mobilize widespread reaction against them? Such questions have yet to be empirically tested in South Asia, in part because of a lack of reliable data on and attention to never-married women.

RISK FACTORS FOR VIOLENCE AGAINST WOMEN AND GIRLS: FOUR LEVELS OF THE SOCIAL ECOLOGY

Research on violence considers risk factors of violence rather than causes of violence; a risk factor contributes to violence by increasing its likelihood of occurring. Similarly, protective factors decrease the likelihood of violence. The ecological approach does not attribute the cause of violence against women and girls to any single factor. Rather, the ecological model posits that violence is a function of multiple factors that interact at various levels of the social ecology, including (a) life histories and personality factors that women and men bring to their relationships; (b) situational and context factors that shape their daily lives; and (c) norms and messages that are reinforced by family members, friends, and social institutions as appropriate behavior for women and men. As Heise (2011, vi) explains: "These norms and expectations are in turn shaped by structural factors—such as religious institutions and ideology and the distribution of economic power between men and women—that work to define beliefs and norms about violence and structure women's options for escaping violent relationships." Sociocultural factors themselves can be imagined to operate at two levels: (a) through those structures that impinge directly on the individual's immediate context; and (b) through the broader social norms that influence those structures. Adapted to suit the South Asian context, our approach draws from Heise's (1998) categories to arrive at the following definitions of each social ecology level:

• *Social norms* are the sociocultural values and beliefs that overlay all other layers of the social ecology and that influence dynamics in these other layers of interaction.

• *Institutions and systems factors* are the formal and informal structures—for example, economic, legal, political, and so forth—that influence a person's immediate environment (that is, household, interpersonal relationship) and determine the dynamics in those settings. At this level, which can include local communities, factors "are often the byproducts of changes taking place in the larger social milieu" (Heise 1998, 273).

• *Household and relationship factors* pertain to the interactions in an individual's immediate environment in which a person directly engages with others, and the subjective meanings assigned to those interactions.

• *Individual factors* are those features of an individual's developmental experience or personality that shape his or her response to stressors within the household and in interpersonal relationships, as well as in the local community.

Not all risk factors fall neatly within a particular level of social ecology; there is considerable overlap—for example, a girl's relationship with her parents may be regarded as an individual factor rather than as part of her immediate environment (see figure 1.2, which summarizes risk factors that have been identified by existing research and are particularly relevant to the South Asian context). Yet, a key strength of the ecological framework is its power to identify the level or multiple levels of interaction at which

FIGURE 1.2 Risk Factors for Violence against Women and Girls at Different Levels of the Social Ecology

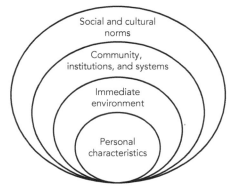

Personal characteristics
1. Witnessed marital violence as a child
2. Experienced abuse as a child
3. Relationship with parents
4. Age and other personal attributes

Immediate environment (household and interpersonal relationships)
1. Household poverty
2. Household member attributes (individuals, couples, spouses, or parents)
3. Substance abuse by partner or household member
4. Marriage characteristics
5. Male dominance in family, including male control of household wealth
6. Interaction norms within the household

Community, institutions, and systems
1. Community or neighborhood characteristics
2. Women's participation in microcredit or social groups
3. Institutional and legal development and implementation
4. Migration, conflict, natural disaster

Social and cultural norms
1. Rigid patriarchal gender roles[a]
2. Socioeconomic development influencing gender roles
3. Honor and chastity notions[b]
4. Caste and religion

a. This norm would encompass issues of the understanding of masculinity and femininity and son preference.
b. This norm would pertain to dowry, marriage, and honor.

risk factors may operate. This framework serves two purposes: (a) it is a useful and clear means of organizing a large body of literature on factors that predict violence against women and girls; and (b) because the framework identifies the level or levels of social interaction at which a risk factor operates, it allows for more precise targeting and development of interventions to address particular risks.

This book extends and modifies Heise's (1998) elaboration of the ecological model in several ways. First, the ecological model is applied to a range of perpetrators and types of violence against women in South Asia across their lifetimes—as opposed to only intimate partners as perpetrators. Second, the life-cycle approach is combined with the ecological model, and categories are composed of the risks and consequences for each type of violence at each stage of life at various levels of the social ecology. Third, each level is associated with a somewhat different set of risk factors for each type of violence at each stage of life for South Asian girls and women. This information is drawn from a broader review of available literature—particularly research from South Asia—in comparison to what was available when the model was developed. Fourth, a similar categorization of levels at which factors operate has been used to synthesize the literature on costs and consequences of violence against women (below). Specifically, consequences to the individual (such as physical injury, emotional scars, sexual harm) are examined at the level or setting in which violence occurs (such as financial costs borne by women and households because of violence); at the level of institutions and systems (such as the implications for health, education, and lost productivity nationwide); and at the broad level of social norms (such as the implications for attaining the MDGs). Finally, we conduct the analysis of interventions and other efforts to address violence against women and girls using these categories, and we examine each type of violence, looking at how the identified interventions at different levels (individual, household and community setting, institutions and systems, and social norms) respond to the different risk factors identified in the research.

Estimating the Costs and Consequences of Violence across Levels of Society

A large amount of literature investigates the costs and consequences of violence against women and girls, but available data and measurements of financial costs and nonfinancial consequences capture a tiny fraction of their totality, perpetrated as it is against such a vast proportion of the region's population. Still, even the costs and consequences that have been documented illustrate a massive drain on individuals, families, communities, and societies. Health consequences affect women and girls and their families in many ways. Economic consequences, such as productive days lost because of violence and accompanying injuries, affect women, their families, their communities, and society overall when violence is as pervasive as it is in South Asia. Health, emotional, and psychological consequences for girls who experience violence as children affect not only them and their families, but also can spiral across future generations. For governments, such violence prevents a large part of their citizenry from being healthy, attaining their full potential through education and employment, contributing to their society, and enjoying their rights as citizens with the same rights as men and boys. It also affects development outcomes, especially achievement of the MDGs, as discussed previously.

VIOLENCE PREVENTS GIRLS AND WOMEN FROM BEING EQUAL CITIZENS

By virtue of its impact on women's and girls' survival, health, education, and life opportunities, violence undermines their rights to a full and healthy life as equal citizens of societies. This fact is true of all types of violence faced across the life cycle. Sexual harassment and abuse undercut women's and girls' rights to use public spaces as freely as do men. For example, Perera, Gunawardane, and Jayasuriya (2011) report that sexual harassment on buses in Sri Lanka triggers anger and anxiety among women about using public transportation. Trafficking, bonded labor, and child prostitution by their very nature preclude girls (and boys) from leading normal lives in childhood and—in many cases because of problems with rehabilitation—as adults. Finally, abuse that leads to physical and psychological harm is bound to inhibit women's ability to seek employment and perform in a job to the extent that those who do not suffer violence are able to do; controlling actions by spouses or in-laws also prevent many women from exploring their potential in the workplace.

PHYSICAL, SEXUAL, AND MENTAL HEALTH CAN BE SEVERELY AFFECTED

The most researched effects of violence are perhaps the health consequences of intimate partner violence experienced by married women and of child marriage experienced by adolescents. Data for both men and women testify to the extent of the purely physical consequences of intimate partner violence, which range from surface cuts and bruises to deep wounds including internal bleeding, broken bones, or organ damage. About 23 percent of men in India who reported committing physical violence and 14 percent of those who reported committing sexual violence reported injury to their wives as a result of their behaviors (Duvvury, Nayak, and Allendorf 2002). Estimates based on women's reporting are even higher, as table 1.2 illustrates for India and Nepal, the two countries for which such data are available.

Gynecological and reproductive damage is also common. Campbell (2002, 1332), in a review of studies of Western countries, reports that gynecological problems are "the most consistent, longest lasting, and largest physical health difference" between battered and nonbattered women. Coker's (2007) review of studies from the developing world echoes the same theme, as do studies from across South Asia that establish links between intimate partner violence and poor physical and mental health outcomes among women and their young children (Kumar et al. 2005; Stephenson, Koenig, and Ahmed 2006; IIPS and Population Council 2009; Jeejebhoy, Santhya, and Acharya 2010; Puri, Tamang, and Shah 2011; Silverman et al. 2009). Consequences of violence can percolate through widowhood and old age, moreover: Munsur, Tareque,

TABLE 1.2 Percentage of Ever-Married Women Ages 15–49 Who Reported Injuries as a Result of Physical or Sexual Violence Experienced in the 12 Months before the Survey, India and Nepal

Type of violence	Cuts, bruises, aches (%)		Eye injuries, sprains, dislocations, burns (%)		Deep wounds, broken bones, broken teeth, other serious injury (%)		Any of these injuries (%)		Number of ever-married women who reported violence	
	Nepal 2011	India 2005–06	Nepal 2011	India 2005–06	Nepal 2011	India 2005–06	Nepal 2011	India 2005–06	Nepal 2011	India 2005–06
Physical	52.8	43.6	16.9	11.4	14.5	8.1	53.5	45.7	337	13,680
Sexual	38.6	40.8	13.9	15.5	13.6	11.4	38.9	43.5	250	4,635

Sources: Demographic and Health Surveys data, see IIPS and Macro International 2007; MOHP, New ERA, and Macro International 2012.

and Rahman (2010), in their study of women age 60 or more across seven villages in Bangladesh, find that widows are 47 percent more likely to report being unhealthy than their married counterparts.

Child marriage as a form of violence against adolescents exacerbates these health risks. A regional study of South Asia shows that women who marry at age 14 or younger have a higher risk of poor reproductive health outcomes than women who are married at age 15 or older (Godha, Hotchkiss, and Gage 2013). With limited or no knowledge about contraceptive methods or control over use of contraception, girls who marry before age 18 have a high exposure to sexually transmitted infections (STIs) and HIV/AIDS (Santhya et al. 2008; Santhya et al. 2010; Khanna et al. 2013). Child brides are less likely to deliver in a health care facility than older married women (Santhya et al. 2010; Godha, Hotchkiss, and Gage 2013), more likely to die in childbirth (Lawyer's Collective Women's Rights Initiative and ICRW 2012), more likely to experience marital violence, and more likely to deliver a premature infant with low birth weight and poor health and survival outcomes (Santhya et al. 2010; Raj et al. 2010a, 2010b; Khanna et al. 2013). In general, whether married or not, adolescents who are sexually abused face an elevated risk of unplanned pregnancy, STIs (including HIV/AIDS), emotional disorders, and self-destructive behaviors (Jejeebhoy and Bott 2003).

Violence experienced by women as mothers adversely affects not only the mother, but also her children's overall well-being. Such violence and its consequences for mother and child start from violence during pregnancy. Intimate partner violence during pregnancy is associated with physical trauma to the fetus, maternal stress, or maternal anemia, which in turn increases mortality risks for newborns or results in low birth weight and consequent child malnutrition (Ahmed, Koenig, and Stephenson 2006). Studies also report a dose–response effect, with higher mortality for newborns, infants, or young children of mothers who suffer multiple episodes of violence (Ackerson and Subramanian 2008; Koenig et al. 2010).

Women in violent partner relationships may also be less likely to—or less allowed to—seek prenatal or pediatric care, thus compromising the health of surviving infants (Koenig et al. 2010). Studies in India find that, compared to women who do not experience intimate partner violence, young children of women who experience intimate partner violence are significantly less likely to be fully immunized (Sabarwal et al. 2012) and more likely to be malnourished (Ackerson and Subramanian 2008). Further, mothers who experience violence are themselves more likely to physically abuse their children (Mohr et al. 2000).

In contrast to intimate partner violence and child marriage, the costs and consequences of abuse faced by unmarried girls are less researched, although such abuse is likely to have long-lasting consequences for girls' physical and mental health throughout their lives. Studies that do exist are not gender specific. Yet, these clearly show that sexual and physical abuse faced by children—girls and boys—leads not only to physical injuries and pain, but also to mental trauma, depression, and low self-esteem, as well as a whole range of other issues, including distrust, increased chances of being abused as an adult, and inappropriate behaviors as children, adolescents, or adults (UNICEF 2001; Conticini and Hulme 2007; Malik 2010). Children who witness or experience violence in their early years can carry the scars in their behaviors and relationships throughout their adult lives (Duvvury et al. 2013). This early exposure to violence can also trigger in children feelings of parental rejection, as demonstrated by Malik's (2010) study in Pakistan. Parental abuse and its sequelae may be even more traumatic for a child than witnessing the violence of war, as Panter-Brick et al. (2009) report from their research in Afghanistan. Still, violence through war and conflict also exact a physical and emotional toll on girls and boys according to studies from Afghanistan (Panter-Brick et al. 2011) and Sri Lanka (Catani et al. 2008). Whereas most of these studies do not use data that are gender disaggregated, one study from Pakistan does suggest that girls in South Asia may experience heightened emotional turmoil because of abuse triggered by son preference (Murtaza 2012).

Other forms of violence against girls and women, such as trafficking and sexual harassment, have similar consequences. Trafficked girls and women suffer serious psychological damage, including constant terror, guilt, embarrassment, hopelessness, denial, and self-blame; when trafficking involves sexual abuse and coercion, gynecological consequences are also triggered (Khowaja et al. 2012). The harsh living conditions to which trafficked girls and women may be subjected can also result in premature death or debilitating disease (Kumar et al. 2001). Attempts at rehabilitation may not signal an end to the consequences of being trafficked, as women and children who have been victims of trafficking are stigmatized as outcasts and may face moral isolation and legal consequences (Ghosh 2009); they also may be unable to return to their homes and may face the risk of being retrafficked.

The most extreme consequence of violence is death: in a review of studies, Ellsburg (2006) finds that worldwide 40 percent to 70 percent of women's deaths from violence are caused by intimate partners, often within the context of abusive relationships. Studies reviewed in this report also document self-immolation and suicidal thoughts among married adolescents and adults in South Asia because of the violence and abuse perpetrated by husbands and other family members. In a review of research on non-consensual sex in Asia, Jejeebhoy and Bott (2003) also note that, in parts of South Asia, disclosure of sexual harassment by a peer may result in the harassed girl becoming subject to an honor killing.

PARTICIPATION IN SCHOOLING AND THE LABOR MARKET IS DIMINISHED

The physical and emotional scars of childhood abuse are bound to have an impact on girls' participation and performance in school. Corporal physical punishment in schools has a direct effect, with research in many parts of the developing world suggesting a link with school dropout (UNICEF 2009). Yet, there is little research linking childhood abuse to schooling consequences.

Another type of violence, however, that can affect young girls' and women's schooling and productivity at work is sexual harassment in public places. Fear of sexual harassment at school is one reason that parents in South Asia may withdraw girls from school at puberty, thus constraining their lifetime opportunities for education and a career (Bott et al. 2003; Jejeebhoy and Bott 2003). Research from the garment industry in Bangladesh, a major form of employment for young women, finds that the harassment women face at work directly impairs productivity, as women fake illness or intentionally slow their work to avoid the harassment; the harassment faced by one woman affects all the others, as other young women tend to become resentful or anxious (Siddiqi 2003). Harassment faced on the street when traveling to and from school or work also generates fear among women, according to studies from Sri Lanka (Perera, Gunawardane, and Jayasuriya 2011) and Bangladesh (Siddiqi 2003; Hancock 2006), and may affect their ability to concentrate at school or work.

The relationship between intimate partner violence and employment is complex because the causality could go in both directions. Employment may be a protective factor against violence but may also trigger violence; women who experience violence may be less able to work, or violence may be used to compel women to work. There are few longitudinal studies that can disentangle these effects, and researchers have long called for such analyses (Duvvury et al. 2013). Still, a few studies from Pakistan (Ghaus and Kazi 2012; SPDC 2012), Bangladesh (ICRW and UNFPA 2009; Siddique 2011), and a large body of research across the world (Morrison and Orlando 2004; Day, McKenna, and Bowlus 2005; ICRW and UNFPA 2009; Duvvury, Minh, and Carney 2012) documents to some extent the monetary and nonmonetary costs to women's economic productivity associated with domestic violence, illustrating both how violence hinders women's ability to reach their full potential and the costs to economies and societies of this gap between their potential and their reality.

ACCURATELY MONETIZING FINANCIAL AND ECONOMIC COSTS OF VIOLENCE IS DIFFICULT

Estimating financial costs of violence may be even more methodologically challenging as well as fraught with data problems, compared with estimating nonfinancial consequences of violence. In addition to the underreporting of violence itself, discussed in chapters 2 and 3, the key challenge to estimate a monetary value for the financial and economic costs of violence is that much of South Asia still operates as an informal economy, making wage information difficult to obtain. In particular, women engage in a large amount of informal or unpaid labor in the household that is not counted in the formal economy and not monetized. Thus, in calculating the total costs of violence for women and households, accounting is tricky for this unpaid but critical work, such as child care, household work, and unpaid farm or subsistence work. Finally, it is impossible to monetize the economic costs that arise over a lifetime for children who face abuse early in their lives.

The range of definitions and methods used to estimate such costs adds to the complexity (appendix L). The resulting estimations cover a wide range. Although estimating macro costs is still more tenuous, there are a few examples that attempt to do so. Based on a household survey carried out in Bangladesh in 2010, Siddique (2011) reports that violence against women results in substantial direct and indirect costs to society. Monetary costs are also borne because of days lost to work, either because of direct injuries or because of the time spent in health care for injuries or in police and judicial arrangements. Regardless of how financial estimates are calculated, there is little doubt that they represent a tiny drop in the ocean of costs accruing from violence against women and girls in the region. Still, such estimates add to the mounting evidence that it is critical to address violence against women and girls in South Asia.

Summary of Data and Methods

This study comprises three types of analysis. The first is a review of existing research (published and unpublished) on violence against women in South Asian countries. The literature review includes impact evaluations and other assessments of programs that address violence against women and girls in South Asia and other regions. Second, existing data—mostly quantitative but some qualitative—are analyzed to describe risk factors for selected types of violence against women and girls (see appendix A for a summary of quantitative sources). Third, an extensive mapping of interventions implemented in all eight countries involves (a) an extensive—though not exhaustive— search and enumeration of organizations addressing violence against women and girls in the region, by country, listed in appendix S; (b) findings from identified evaluated programs in each country, summarized in appendixes C to K; and (c) several in-depth case studies of noteworthy programs addressing violence against women and girls in the region. A list of World Bank projects addressing gender-based violence since 2008 can be found in appendix B. Detailed descriptions of the methodologies used for the literature review and mapping exercise can be found in appendixes M and N, respectively.

DATA SOURCES USED FOR QUANTITATIVE ANALYSIS

The report's quantitative analysis has employed data from a range of sources, listed in appendix A. These include data from UNICEF'S Multiple Indicator Cluster Survey database (UNICEF 2009–2011) and *The State of the World's Children 2013* (UNICEF 2013); United Nations Office on Drugs and Crime (UNODC) 2006, 2009; UN World Population Prospects 2012 (United Nations, Department of Economics and Social Affairs, Population Division 2013); WHO/LSHTM/MRC 2013; and a range of Demographic and Health Surveys (DHS) from South Asian and other countries. Chapter 2 presents descriptive results using data from these sources, as well as data from reports and other information in published journal articles, also listed in appendix A.

Outline of Chapters

The remainder of this book is organized into four chapters. Chapter 2 describes the extent of violence against women and girls in South Asia. It compares attitudes toward violence and prevalence of violence types—organized by life stage—by region, as well as between countries in South Asia. Chapter 3 discusses social, economic, and demographic changes in South Asian countries that have had implications for girls' and women's empowerment as individuals; it also delves into the broader mechanisms by which violence occurs, as well as attempts by state, legal, and other systems to address this violence. It then summarizes existing research findings that, for each type of violence that may occur throughout the life cycle, identify specific risk and protective factors at each level of the social ecology—ranging from individual factors to the macro level of social norms. Types of violence are organized by three major groupings of life stages: (a) violence that is of particular risk to girl children and unmarried adolescent girls, (b) violence to which married adolescent girls and women tend to be exposed, and (c) types of violence that are a threat across multiple life-cycle stages. Chapter 4 tackles the complex issue of addressing violence against women and girls, summarizing efforts across South Asia to prevent and to respond to various aspects of violence in the region. Chapter 4 also presents lessons learned from these efforts and from select interventions in other regions. Chapter 5 offers recommendations for action that stakeholders can adopt in the region.

Notes

1. According to the World Health Organization, approximately 73 million boys and 150 million girls under age 18 worldwide have encountered sexual violence that involves physical contact (UNICEF Tanzania 2011). In Nepal, a 2005 study of 3,960 girls and boys found that 10.5 percent of girls and nearly 8.0 percent of boys reported contact forms of sexual abuse in 2005 (CWIN and UNICEF 2005). In Sri Lanka, an estimated 10 percent of girls and 20 percent of boys are abused at school or at home (Frederick 2008).

2. Quotations from this paragraph are from the International Labour Organization's "What Is Child Labour," http://www.ilo.org/ipec/facts/lang--en/.

References

Ackerson, Leland K., and S. V. Subramanian. 2008. "Domestic Violence and Chronic Malnutrition among Women and Children in India." *American Journal of Epidemiology* 167 (10): 1188–96.

Ahmed, Saifuddin, Michael A. Koenig, and Rob Stephenson. 2006. "Effects of Domestic Violence on Perinatal and Early-Childhood Mortality: Evidence from North India." *American Journal of Public Health* 96 (8): 1423–8.

Arnold, Fred, Sunita Kishor, and T. K. Roy. 2002. "Sex-Selective Abortions in India." *Population and Development Review* 28 (4): 759–85.

Barker, Gary, Manuel Contreras, Brian Heilman, Ajay Singh, Ravi Verma, and Marcos Nascimento. 2011. *Evolving Men: Initial Results from the International Men and Gender Equality Surveys (IMAGES).* Washington, DC: International Center for Research on Women (ICRS); Rio de Janeiro: Instituto Promundo.

Belsky, Jay. 1980. "Child Maltreatment: An Ecological Integration." *American Psychologist* 35 (4): 320–35.

Bott, Sarah, Shireen Jejeebhoy, Iqbal Shah, and Chander Puri. 2003. *Towards Adulthood: Exploring the Sexual and Reproductive Health of Adolescents in South Asia.* Geneva: World Health Organization.

Bott, Sarah, Andrew Morrison, and Mary Ellsberg. 2005. "Preventing and Responding to Gender-Based Violence in Middle- and Low-Income Countries: A Global Review and Analysis." Policy Research Working Paper 3618, World Bank, Washington, DC.

Campbell, Jacquelyn C. 2002. "Health Consequences of Intimate Partner Violence." *The Lancet* 359: 1331–36.

Catani, Claudia, Nadja Jacob, Elisabeth Schauer, Mahendran Kohila, and Frank Neuner. 2008. "Family Violence, War, and Natural Disasters: A Study of the Effect of Extreme Stress on Children's Mental Health in Sri Lanka." *BMC Psychiatry* 8 (January): 33. doi:10.1186/1471-244X-8-33.

Coker, Ann L. 2007. "Does Physical Intimate Partner Violence Affect Sexual Health? A Systematic Review." *Trauma, Violence, and Abuse* 8 (2): 149–77.

Conticini, Alessandro, and David Hulme. 2007. "Escaping Violence, Seeking Freedom: Why Children in Bangladesh Migrate to the Street." *Development and Change* 38 (2): 201–27.

Contreras, Manuel, Brian Heilman, Gary Barker, Ajay Singh, Ravi Verma, and Joanna Bloomfield. 2012. "Bridges to Adulthood: Understanding the Lifelong Influence of Men's Childhood Experience of Violence Analyzing Data from the International Men and Gender Equality Survey." International Center for Research on Women, Washington, DC, and Instituto Promundo, Rio de Janeiro.

CWIN and UNICEF (Child Workers in Nepal and United Nations Children's Fund). 2005. *Violence against Children in Nepal: Child Sexual Abuse in Nepal: Children's Perspectives.* Kathmandu: UNICEF Nepal.

Das Gupta, Monica. 1995. "Life Course Perspectives on Women's Autonomy and Health Outcomes." *American Anthropologist* 97 (3): 481–91.

Das Gupta, Monica, Jiang Zhenghua, Li Bohua, Xie Zhenming, Woojin Chung, and Bae Hwa-ok. 2003. "Why Is Son Preference so Persistent in East and South Asia? A Cross-Country Study of China, India, and the Republic of Korea." *The Journal of Development Studies* 40 (2): 153–87.

Das Gupta, Monica, Sunhwa Lee, Patricia Uberoi, Danning Wang, Lihong Wang, and Xiaodan Zhang. 2004. "State Policies and Women's Agency in China, the Republic of Korea, and India 1950–2000: Lessons from Contrasting Experiences." In *Cultural and Public Action: A Cross-Disciplinary Dialogue on Development Policy,* edited by V. Rao and M. Walton, 234–59. Stanford, CA: Stanford University Press.

Day, Tanis, Katherine McKenna, and Audra Bowlus. 2005. "The Economic Costs of Violence Against Women: An Evaluation of the Literature." Expert brief prepared for the UN Secretary-General's in-depth study on all forms of violence against women, University of Western Ontario, London, Ontario, Canada.

Duvvury, Nata, Madhabika Nayak, and Keera Allendorf. 2002. "Links between Masculinity and Violence: Aggregate Analysis." Domestic Violence in India: Exploring Strategies, Promoting Dialogue. Men, Masculinity and Domestic Violence in India. Summary Report of Four Studies. Emeryville, CA: Alcohol Research Group at the Public Health Institute.

Duvvury, Nata, Nguyen Huu Minh, and Patricia Carney. 2012. "Estimating the Costs of Domestic Violence against Women in Viet Nam." Hanoi: UN Women Viet Nam.

Duvvury, Nata, Aoife Callan, Patricia Carney, and Srinivas Raghavendra. 2013. *Intimate Partner Violence: Economic Costs and Implications for Growth and Development.* In Women's Voice, Agency, and Participation Research Series 2013 No. 3. Washington DC: World Bank.

Edleson, Jeffrey L., and Richard M. Tolman. 1992. *Intervention for Men Who Batter: An Ecological Approach.* Newbury Park, CA: Sage.

Ellsberg, Mary. 2006. "Violence against Women and the Millennium Development Goals: Facilitating Women's Access to Support." *International Journal of Gynecology and Obstetrics* 94 (3): 325–32.

Foner, Nancy. 1984. *Ages in Conflict: A Cross-Cultural Perspective on Inequality between Old and Young.* New York: Columbia University Press.

Frederick, John. 2008. "Sexual Abuse and Exploitation of Boys in South Asia: A Review of Research Findings, Legislation, Policy and Programme Reponses." Innocenti Working Paper No. 2010–02, UNICEF Innocenti Research Centre, Florence.

Ghaus, Khalida, and Aasiya Kazi. 2012. *The Socio-Economic Cost of Violence Against Women: A Case Study of Karachi.* Karachi, Pakistan: Social Policy and Development Center (SPDC).

Ghosh, Biswajit. 2009. "Trafficking in Women and Children in India: Nature, Dimensions, and Strategies for Prevention." *The International Journal of Human Rights* 13 (5): 716–38.

Godha, Deepali, David R. Hotchkiss, and Anastasia J. Gage. 2013. "Association between Child Marriage and Reproductive Health Outcomes and Service Utilization: A Multi-Country Study from South Asia." *The Journal of Adolescent Health* 52 (5): 552–58.

Haberland, Nicole, Erica Chong, and Hillary Bracken. 2003. "Married Adolescents: An Overview." Paper prepared for the WHO/UNFPA/Population Council Technical Consultation on Married Adolescents, World Health Organization, Geneva.

Hancock, Peter. 2006. "Violence, Women, Work, and Empowerment: Narratives from Factory Women in Sri Lanka's Export Processing Zones." *Gender, Technology, and Development* 10 (2): 211–28.

Heise, Lori. 1998. "Violence against Women: An Integrated, Ecological Framework." *Violence Against Women* 4 (3): 262–90.

———. 2011. *What Works to Prevent Partner Violence: An Evidence Overview.* London: STRIVE.

Heise, Lori, Mary Ellsberg, and Megan Gottemoeller. 1999. "Ending Violence against Women." Population Reports, Series L No. 11, Johns Hopkins University, Baltimore, MD.

Hyder, Adnan A., and Fauzia A. Malik. 2007. "Violence against Children: A Challenge for Public Health in Pakistan." *Journal of Health Population and Nutrition* 25 (2): 168–78.

ICRW (International Center for Research on Women) and UNFPA (United Nations Population Fund). 2009. *Intimate Partner Violence: High Costs to Households and Communities.* Washington, DC: ICRW.

IIPS (International Institute for Population Sciences) and Macro International. 2007. *National Family Health Survey (NFHS–3), 2005–06. India: Volume I.* Mumbai, India: IIPS.

IIPS (International Institute for Population Sciences) and Population Council. 2009. "Violence within Marriage among Young People in Tamil Nadu." Youth in India: Situation and Needs, Policy Brief No. 12, IIPS, Mumbai, India. http://www.popcouncil.org/pdfs/2009PGY _YouthInIndiaBriefViolenceTN.pdf.

Jayaweera, Swarna, Hiranthi Wijemanne, Leelangi Wanasundera, and Kamini Meedeniya Vitarana. 2007. *Gender Dimensions of the Millennium Development Goals in Sri Lanka.* Colombo: Centre for Women's Research.

Jejeebhoy, Shireen J., and Sarah Bott. 2003. "Non-consensual Sexual Experiences of Young People: A Review of Evidence from Developing Countries," South and East Asia Regional Working Paper, No. 16, Population Council, New Delhi.

Jejeebhoy, Shireen, K. G. Santhya, and Rajib Acharya. 2010. *Health and Social Consequences of Marital Violence: A Synthesis of Evidence from India.* New Delhi: Population Council and United Nations Population Council.

Koenig, Michael A., Rob Stephenson, Rajib Acharya, Lindsay Barrick, Saifuddin Ahmed, and Michelle Hindin. 2010. "Domestic Violence and Early Childhood Mortality in Rural India: Evidence from Prospective Data." *International Journal of Epidemiology* 39 (3): 825–33.

Khanna Tina, Ravi Verma, and Ellen Weiss. 2013. "Child Marriage in South Asia: Realities, Responses and the Way Forward." International Center for Research on Women (ICRW).

Khowaja, Shaneela S., Ambreen J. Tharani, Ajmal Agha, and Rozina S. Karamaliani. 2012. "Women in Trafficking: Causes, Concerns, Care!" *Journal of Pakistan Medical Association* 62 (8): 836–38.

Kumar K. C., Bal, Govind S. Y. Gureng, and Keshab P. Adhikar. 2001. *Nepal: Trafficking of Girls with Special Reference to Prostitution: A Rapid Assessment.* Geneva: International Labour Organization/International Programme on the Elimination of Child Labour.

Kumar, Shuba, Lakshmanan Jeyaseelan, Saradha Suresh, and Ramesh Chandra Ahuja. 2005. "Domestic Violence and Its Mental Health Correlates in Indian Women." *The British Journal of Psychiatry: The Journal of Mental Science* 187: 62–67.

Lawyer's Collective Women's Rights Initiative and ICRW (International Center for Rights of Women). 2012. *Staying Alive: Fifth Monitoring and Evaluation Report 2012 on the Protection of Women from Domestic Violence Act 2005.* New Delhi: Lawyer's Collective Women's Rights Initiative.

Malik, Farah. 2010. "Determinants of Child Abuse in Pakistani Families: Parental Acceptance-Rejection and Demographic Variables." *International Journal of Business and Social Science* 1 (1): 67–80.

MOHP (Ministry of Health and Population, Nepal), New ERA, and Macro International Inc. 2012. *Nepal Demographic and Health Survey 2011.* Kathmandu and Calverton, MD: MOHP, New ERA, and Macro International.

Mohr, Wanda K., Megan J. Noone Lutz, John W. Fantuzzo, and Marlo A. Perry. 2000. "Children Exposed to Family Violence: A Review of Empirical Research from a Developmental-Ecological Perspective." *Trauma, Violence, and Abuse* 1 (3): 264–83.

Morrison, Andrew R., and Maria Beatriz Orlando. 2004. *The Costs and Impacts of Gender-Based Violence in Developing Countries: Methodological Considerations and New Evidence.* Washington, DC: World Bank.

Munsur, Ahmed Mohammad, Ismail Tareque, and K. M. Rahman. 2010. "Determinants of Living Arrangements, Health Status, and Abuse among Elderly Women: A Study of Rural Naogaon District, Bangladesh." *Journal of International Women's Studies* 11 (4): 162–76.

Murtaza, Amir. 2012. "Pakistan: Emotional Abuse of Girl Child Is Not an Exception." Asian Human Rights Commission, May 8. http://www.humanrights.asia/news/ahrc-news/AHRC-ART-039-2012.

Panter-Brick, Catherine, Mark Eggerman, Viani Gonzalez, and Sarah Safdar. 2009. "Violence, Suffering, and Mental Health in Afghanistan: A School-Based Survey." *Lancet* 374 (9692): 807–16.

Panter-Brick et al. 2011. "Mental Health and Childhood Adversities: A Longitudinal Study in Kabul, Afghanistan." *Journal of the American Academy of Child & Adolescent Psychiatry* 50(4): 349–63.

Pawlak, Piotr, and Gary Barker. 2012. "Hidden Violence: Preventing and Responding to Sexual Exploitation and Sexual Abuse of Adolescent Boys: Case Studies and Directions for Action." Briefing paper by MenCare, Washington, DC.

Perera, Jennifer, Nalika Gunawardane, and Vathsala Jayasuriya, eds. 2011. *Review of Research Evidence on Gender Based Violence (GBV) in Sri Lanka.* Colombo: Sri Lanka Medical Association.

Puri, Mahesh, Jyotsna Tamang, and Iqbal Shah. 2011. "Suffering in Silence: Consequences of Sexual Violence within Marriage among Young Women in Nepal." *BMC Public Health* 11 (1): 1–10.

Purkayastha, Bandana, Mangala Subramaniam, Manisha Desai, and Sunita Bose. 2003. "The Study of Gender in India: A Partial Review." *Gender and Society* 17 (4): 503–24.

Rahman, Lupin, and Vijayendra Rao. 2004. "The Determinants of Gender Equity in India: Examining Dyson and Moore's Thesis with New Data." *Population and Development Review* 30 (2): 239–68.

Raj, Anita, Niranjan Saggurti, Danielle Lawrence, Donta Balaiah, and Jay G. Silverman. 2010a. "Association between Adolescent Marriage and Marital Violence among Young Adult Women in India." *International Journal of Gynecology and Obstetrics* 110 (1): 35–39.

Raj, Anita, Niranjan Saggurti, Michael Winter, Alan Labonte, Michele R. Decker, Donta Balaiah, and Jay G. Silverman. 2010b. "The Effect of Maternal Child Marriage on Morbidity and Mortality of Children under 5 in India: Cross-Sectional Study of a Nationally Representative Sample." *BMJ* 340: 1–9.

Sabarwal, Shagun, Marie C. McCormick, Jay G. Silverman, and S. V. Subramanian. 2012. "Association Between Maternal Intimate Partner Violence Victimization and Childhood Immunization in India." *Journal of Tropical Pediatrics* 58 (2): 107–13.

Santhya, K. G., Nicole Haberland, Arup Das, Aruna Lakhani, Faujdar Ram, R. K. Sinha, Usha Ram, and S. K. Mohanty. 2008. *Empowering Married Young Women and Improving Their Sexual and Reproductive Health: Effects of the First-Time Parents Project.* New Delhi: Population Council.

Santhya, K. G., Usha Ram, Rajib Acharya, Shireen J. Jejeebhoy, Faujdar Ram, and Abhishek Singh. 2010. "Associations Between Early Marriage and Young Women's Marital and Reproductive Health Outcomes: Evidence from India." *International Perspectives on Sexual and Reproductive Health* 36 (3): 132–39.

Siddiqi, Dina M. 2003. "New Trends in Violence: Sexual Harassment and Obstacles to Mobility in Bangladesh." Position paper prepared for NGO Coalition on Beijing Plus Five, Bangladesh.

Siddique, Kaniz. 2011. "Domestic Violence Against Women: Cost to the Nation." CARE, Bangladesh.

Silverman, Jay G., Michele R. Decker, Jhumka Gupta, Nitin Kapur, Anita Raj, and Ruchira T. Naved. 2009. "Maternal Experiences of Intimate Partner Violence and Child Morbidity in Bangladesh." *American Medical Association* 163 (8): 700–5.

Slugget, C. 2003. "Mapping of Psychosocial Support for Girls and Boys Affected by Child Sexual Abuse in Four Countries in South and Central Asia: Afghanistan, Bangladesh, Nepal, and Pakistan." Save the Children Sweden-Denmark, Regional Office for South and Central Asia, Dhaka.

SPDC. 2012. "The Socio-Economic Cost of Violence against Women: A Case Study of Karachi." SPDC Gender Research Programme, Research Report No. 5. Karachi, Pakistan: SPDC.

Stephenson, Rob, Michael A. Koenig, and Saifuddin Ahmed. 2006. "Domestic Violence and Symtoms of Gynecologic Morbidity Among Women in North India." *International Family Planning Perspectives* 32 (4): 201–8.

Thomas, D. Q., and R. S. Levi. 1999. "Common Abuses against Women." In vol. 1 of *Women and International Human Rights Law*, edited by K. D. Askin and D. M. Koenig. New York: Transnational Publishers.

UNHCR (United Nations High Commissioner for Refugees). 2005. "UNHCR's Policy on Harassment, Sexual Harassment, and Abuse of Authority." UNHCR, Geneva. http://www.un .org/womenwatch/osagi/UN_system_policies/(UNHCR)policy_on_harassment.pdf.

UNICEF Tanzania. 2011. *Violence against Children in Tanzania: Findings from a National Survey, 2009.* Dar es Salaam, Tanzania: UNICEF.

UNICEF (United Nations Children's Fund). 2001. *Commercial Sexual Exploitation and Sexual Abuse of Children in South Asia.* Kathmandu: UNICEF Regional Office for South Asia. http:// www.unicef.org/rosa/commercial.pdf.

———. 2009. *Progress for Children: A Report Card on Child Protection (No. 8).* New York: UNICEF.

———. 2009–2011. Multiple Indicator Cluster Survey (MICS)—Round 4. UNICEF, New York. http://www.unicef.org/statistics/index_24302.html.

————. 2011. "The State of the World's Children 2011: Adolescence, An Age of Opportunity. Executive Summary." UNICEF, New York. http://www.unicef.org/sowc2011/pdfs/SOWC-2011-Executive-Summary-LoRes_EN_12132010.pdf.

————. 2013. *The State of the World's Children 2013: Children with Disabilities.* New York: UNICEF. http://www.unicef.org/sowc2013/.

United Nations. 1993. *Declaration on the Elimination of Violence against Women.* United Nations General Assembly A/RES/48/104, 85th plenary meeting, December 20, 1993. http://www.un.org/documents/ga/res/48/a48r104.htm.

United Nations, Department of Economics and Social Affairs, Population Division. 2013. "World Population Prospects: The 2012 Revision, Key Findings and Advance Tables." Working Paper No. ESA/P/WP.227, United Nations, New York.

UNODC (United Nations Office on Drugs and Crime). 2004. "United Nations Convention against Transnational Organized Crime and the Protocols Thereto." UNODC, Vienna. http://www.unodc.org/documents/treaties/UNTOC/Publications/TOC%20Convention/TOCebook-e.pdf.

————. 2006. "Trafficking in Persons: Global Patterns." United Nations.

————. 2009. *Global Report on Trafficking in Persons.* Vienna: UNODC.

UNOHCHR (United Nations Office of the High Commissioner for Human Rights). 1990. "Convention on the Rights of the Child." http://www.ohchr.org/en/professionalinterest/pages/crc.aspx.

Verma, Ravi, Tara Sinha, and Tina Khanna. 2013. "Asia Child Marriage Initiative: Summary of Research in Bangladesh, India, and Nepal." Plan Asia, Bangkok. http://plan-international.org/where-we-work/asia/publications/asia-child-marriage-initiative-summary-of-research-in-bangladesh-india-and-nepal/.

Watts, Charlotte, and Cathy Zimmerman. 2002. "Violence against Women: Global Scope and Magnitude." *Lancet* 359 (9313): 1232–27.

Welchman, Lynn, and Sara Hossain. 2005. "Introduction: 'Honour,' Rights and Wrongs." In *"Honour": Crimes, Paradigms and Violence against Women,* edited by L. Welchman and S. Hossain, 1–21. London: Zed Press.

WHO (World Health Organization). 1997. "Violence against Women: Definition and Scope of the Problem." WHO, Geneva. http://www.google.com/url?sa=t&rct=j&q=&esrc=s&source=web&cd=1&sqi=2&ved=0CCcQFjAA&url=http%3A%2F%2Fwww.who.int%2Fgender%2Fviolence%2Fv4.pdf&ei=DhIWU_CeIYXP2AWOsYGADQ&usg=AFQjCNGu9ShRuqIqYU38ZLeA_t5HC_kwFw&sig2=NxTibSO0TXyBx6RelK8C4A&bvm=bv.62286460,d.b2I.

————. 1999. "Report of the Consultation on Child Abuse Prevention." WHO, Geneva.

————. 2004. "Adolescent Health." WHO, Geneva. http://www.who.int/topics/adolescent_health/en/.

WHO/LSHTM/MRC (WHO, London School of Hygiene and Tropical Medicine, South African Medical Research Council). 2013. *Global and Regional Estimates of Violence against Women: Prevalence and Health Effects of Intimate Partner Violence and Non-Partner Sexual Violence.* WHO, Geneva. http://www.who.int/reproductivehealth/publications/violence/9789241564625/en/.

CHAPTER 2

Patterns of Violence against Women and Girls in South Asia

Violence against women and girls in South Asia is particular by virtue of its unrelenting pervasiveness throughout a woman's life—from childhood through adolescence, adulthood, and eventually to old age. It is a persistent part of their lives, throughout their lives. Such violence is not just domestic violence—although that is perhaps the best known and most widely researched. Rather, women and girls in South Asia face a staggering array of forms of violence perpetrated by a range of men, other women, family, community, and the state, from birth to old age. Some of these forms of violence occur in many parts of the world (such as intimate partner violence, child abuse, sexual harassment, child marriage, and trafficking); others are particularly persistent in South Asia (such as excess female child mortality, child marriage, and honor crimes); and still others are unique to the region (such as dowry-related violence).

The efficiency with which violence is perpetrated systemwide is also startling, such that women are constantly and daily vulnerable, not just to the threat of violence by individual intimate partners or family members, but also by strangers (such as in the case of sexual harassment or trafficking), whole communities (such as occurs with honor killings), and the state (in cases of custodial violence).

Despite the pervasiveness of violence that women and girls face, research continues to be limited on most of its forms. Most widespread quantitative and qualitative analysis is in the realms of intimate partner violence, child marriage, and excess female child mortality. Statistics are patchy, at best, for all other forms of violence, but in particular for honor crimes. For custodial violence and child abuse, the data and analyses that exist rarely differentiate by gender. Reliable quantitative statistics that would enable programmers and policy makers to track progress in addressing violence are lacking for almost all forms of violence. Partly for this reason, intercountry and international comparisons are fraught with problems.

Despite large gaps in available information, the data that do exist still present a compelling picture of the extent of violence that South Asian women and girls face, hampering their full potential as equal citizens. In this chapter we explore these patterns, starting with those forms of violence for which most data are available, and then moving to those about which information is limited. Chapter 3 analyzes the causes and underlying risk and protective factors.

Excess Female Child Mortality

Some degree of son preference is evident in most societies. But son preference so strong as to cause daughter aversion and consequent sex differences in child mortality in excess of what is biologically expected occurs only in a few parts of the world, of which South Asia is a prominent example.

We analyzed the prevalence of this form of violence in South Asia by comparing the ratios of mortality rates for girls and boys from birth through age 5 years (termed the "under-5 mortality rate ratio"). These ratios are presented here as the number of female deaths for every hundred male deaths among children aged zero to five. We compared these ratios to biological standards developed by Hill and Upchurch (1995), based on populations from countries in which discrimination against girls is negligible.[1] Positive deviance of female to male under-five mortality rate ratios from expected standards can be interpreted as evidence of excess female child mortality due to some form of discrimination.

Compared to other regions of the world, South Asia has the greatest difference between actual and expected under-five mortality rate ratios, as evident from figure 2.1. Four of the eight South Asian countries are among the 10 countries with the highest excess female child mortality (figure 2.2). India has the largest deviation, thus the largest excess female child mortality, of all countries for which data are available; Bangladesh, Nepal, and Pakistan also show high levels.

The most direct postnatal driver of excess female child mortality is female infanticide. Historically, female infanticide is not unique to South Asia and has deep roots across the world (Milner 1998). In 1789, the British brought attention to female infanticide in the regions of South Asia they controlled—that is, throughout present-day northwest of India going into Pakistan (Miller 1987; Bedi and Srinivasan 2012). Despite being illegal across the region, infanticide continues to exist, though data on infanticide is extremely difficult to obtain. Existing data are likely unreliable because early infanticides may be reported as stillbirths or not reported at all if birth registration systems are incomplete (Das Gupta 2005; Sahni et al. 2008). Still, small-scale studies and newspaper reports give some indication of the continued prevalence of this practice and suggest that it is now concentrated in southern India, with a smattering of incidents elsewhere in the region (Vella 2004; Chohan 2011).

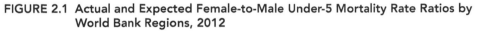

FIGURE 2.1 Actual and Expected Female-to-Male Under-5 Mortality Rate Ratios by World Bank Regions, 2012

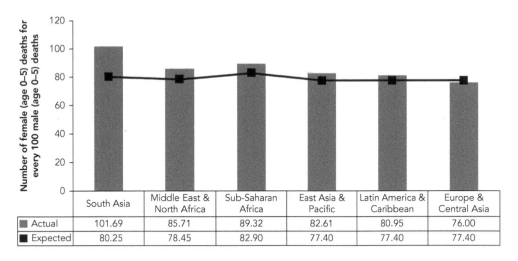

	South Asia	Middle East & North Africa	Sub-Saharan Africa	East Asia & Pacific	Latin America & Caribbean	Europe & Central Asia
■ Actual	101.69	85.71	89.32	82.61	80.95	76.00
■ Expected	80.25	78.45	82.90	77.40	77.40	77.40

Source: WDI, World Bank.
Note: Under-5 mortality rates for both girls and boys are based on at least 50 deaths between ages 0–5 years per 1,000 live births for South Asia and Sub-Saharan Africa, and less than 30 deaths per 1,000 live births for each of the other regions.

FIGURE 2.2 10 Countries with Biggest Difference in Actual and Expected Under-5 Mortality Rate Ratios

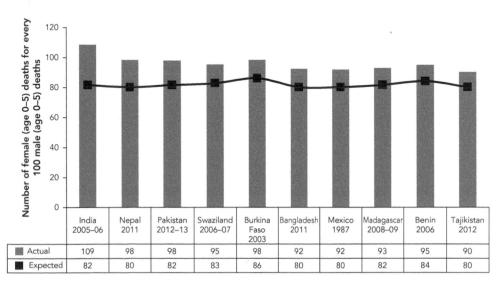

	India 2005–06	Nepal 2011	Pakistan 2012–13	Swaziland 2006–07	Burkina Faso 2003	Bangladesh 2011	Mexico 1987	Madagascar 2008–09	Benin 2006	Tajikistan 2012
■ Actual	109	98	98	95	98	92	92	93	95	90
■ Expected	82	80	82	83	86	80	80	82	84	80

Source: DHS, multiple years.
Note: Under-5 mortality rates for both girls and boys in each country are based on at least 50 deaths between ages 0–5 years per 1,000 live births.

Research suggests, however, that much of the observed excess female child mortality is achieved not by outright infanticide or other physical abuse leading to death, but by more indirect forms of violence in the shape of neglect and discrimination resulting in death. Several studies show that boys are significantly more likely to be immunized than girls in Pakistan and India (Hazarika 2000; Pande 2003; Pande and Yazbeck 2003; Corsi et al. 2009; Singh 2012), and that in India, this discrimination has intensified over time (Singh 2012). When sick, daughters are less likely to be taken to a health facility than are sons in Bangladesh, India, Nepal, and Pakistan (Koenig and D'Souza 1986; Das Gupta 1987; Basu 1989; Hazarika 2000; Pokhrel and Sauerborn 2004; Najnin et al. 2011).

Although the analysis above paints a dismal picture, since the early 1990s large reductions in excess female child mortality have occurred in Bangladesh, Nepal, and Sri Lanka (Klasen and Wink 2002). Excess mortality in early childhood among girls has dropped particularly dramatically in Bangladesh (Alam, van Ginneken, and Bosch 2007; Adams et al. 2013; Kabeer, Huq, and Mahmud 2013), and also in Sri Lanka and Pakistan (Klasen and Wink 2002).

Excess female child mortality in India has remained largely unchanged, however, particularly in the northwestern states, as evidenced by the 2011 census (John 2011; Navaneetham and Dharmalingam 2011). In fact, girls in India have higher mortality than do boys from *all* causes of death, starting as early as 1 month through 5 years of age (Million Death Study Collaborators 2010).

Child Marriage

Girls who survive through infancy and early childhood face the threat of another form of violence that is highly prevalent in South Asia: child marriage. Heiberg and Thukral (2013) estimate that South Asia has the highest rate of child marriage globally with 46 percent of girls married before 18 years of age. India is estimated to have the highest number of child brides in the world with more than one-third of child brides globally (Heiberg and Thukral 2013). However, India does not have the highest national prevalence of child marriage in South Asia. Analysis of Demographic and Health Surveys (DHS) data presented in figures 2.3 and 2.4 shows that Bangladesh has the highest prevalence of child marriage in the region, and the second-highest in the world, with 77 percent of married women aged 25–49 reporting being married before the age of 18. Bangladesh is followed by India and Nepal where prevalence of child marriage for the same age group is 57 percent and 55 percent, respectively. Note that Bangladesh has the highest prevalence of particularly early marriage—that is, by age 15 (figure 2.4).

Afghanistan and Pakistan have forms of child and forced marriage that are particular to those countries (box 2.1). One study estimates that about a third of marriages in rural Pakistan involve the exchange of brides between two households (Jacoby and Mansuri 2010). We found no reliable prevalence data for the other particular forms of forced or

FIGURE 2.3 Child Marriage Prevalence: Countries with Highest Proportion Married by Age 18

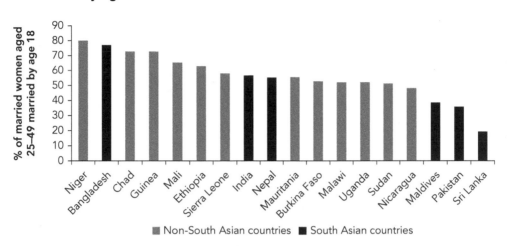

Source: DHS, multiple years.
Note: Sample size = more than 1,000 in each country. DHS data is not available for Afghanistan and Bhutan.

FIGURE 2.4 Child Marriage Prevalence: Countries with Highest Proportion Married by Age 15

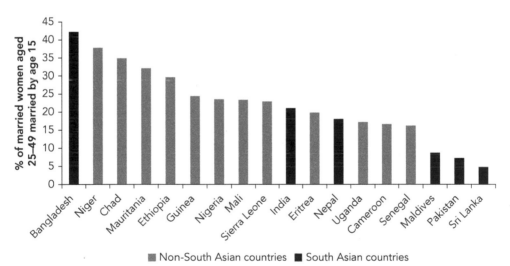

Source: DHS, multiple years.
Note: Sample size = more than 1,000 in each country. DHS data is not available for Afghanistan and Bhutan.

child marriage. Pakistan on the whole is estimated to have a moderate level of child marriage with about 35 percent of married women having married by age 18 (figure 2.3); however, this varies tremendously by district. A large-scale survey of six districts found that almost two-thirds (61 percent) of girls were married before age 18 (Qayyum, n.d.). Although child marriage is rare in Sri Lanka, qualitative research suggests a pattern of

---

BOX 2.1 Forms of Child Marriage and Forced Marriage in Afghanistan and Pakistan

Particular forms of child marriage that are typically forced marriage persist in certain areas of Afghanistan and Pakistan. Research points to a heightened risk of violence for girls married under these customs. The key such customs are the following:

- *Baadal (or Badal).* A form of marriage in Afghanistan where families exchange daughters in marriage, often to avoid paying bride-price. This form of marriage, while not peculiar to child marriage, often may involve minors, particularly daughters. Moreover, this practice can trigger very early marriage, as fathers may exchange their daughter for a bride for themselves. Such exchange marriages can place young girls at increased risk because the young girl becomes the means to take revenge on her natal family for any abuse of her husband's sister; however, a girl may also be less at risk since her in-laws have sent a daughter to the exchanging family, who would be treated in a reciprocal manner (Smith 2009).

- *Baad (or Bad).* A practice in Afghanistan in which a girl is given to an opposing family as a means to settle a conflict. This situation places a young girl in a household that has been feuding with hers, clearly thus increasing her vulnerability (Smith 2009).

- *Swara.* A practice in Pakistan whereby a minor girl is given to a family in compensation for a crime committed by her family against that family. As with *baad*, this places her into a household that is in opposition to her own. A girl undergoing a *swara* marriage loses all rights to any dowry or maintenance and cannot have the marriage dissolved (Perveen 2012).

- *Watta satta.* A practice in rural Pakistan whereby two households exchange daughters to marry a son in the other household. As in Afghanistan, bride exchange in Pakistan may put daughters at increased risk of violence or it may be viewed as a means of insurance against "mistreatment" of daughters (Jacoby and Mansuri 2010).

---

cohabitation without marriage for underage girls with similar consequences as might exist for child marriage (Goonesekere and Amarasuriya 2013).

As with excess female child mortality, analysis of DHS data suggests that rates of child marriage too are slowing in the region, with successive cohorts of women less likely to have married as children than older cohorts (figure 2.5). Maldives shows the largest such change over cohorts: 63 percent of surveyed married women ages 45 to 49 at the time of the survey reported having been married before age 18, compared to less than 4 percent of married women ages 20 to 24. Although the shift is not so dramatic in other countries, it still exists, even in Bangladesh, which had and continues to have the highest rates of child marriage in the region.[2]

Qualitative data provide cautious optimism that attitudes toward child marriage may also be changing. In Bangladesh, Rashid (2010) found that sample girls voiced reservation about early marriage, wanted to study, and were starting to be assertive in arguing with their parents against early marriage. In India, a majority of fathers, mothers, and girls interviewed by the International Center for Research on Women (ICRW 2011) prioritized education over marriage for their daughters. Similarly, Smith (2009) finds

FIGURE 2.5 Changes in Child Marriage by Age Cohort: South Asia

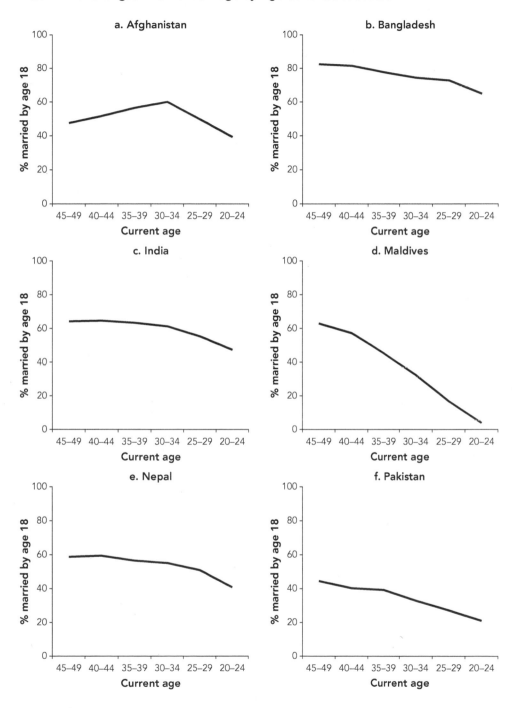

Source: DHS, multiple years.
Note: Sample size = more than 700 ever-married women, in any age group, in any country.

examples of individuals across the eight Afghan sites of her study who do not want to marry their daughters early. The shift is likely to be partly related to education or socioeconomic status and partly generational: in a World Bank qualitative study in Afghanistan cited by Smith (2009), while older participants did not see traditional marriage practices changing, young men and women voiced their preference for later marriage. Still, as Smith (2009) points out, a divide persists between individual desires and perceived cultural norms and compulsions for early marriage, thus contributing to the persistence of child marriage in the region.

Intimate Partner Violence within Marriage

Intimate partner violence is perhaps the most widely known and well researched type of violence against women and girls. It is difficult to say where South Asia ranks globally in the prevalence of this type of violence as regional estimates can often be misleading. For example, map 2.1 suggests that South Asia has the highest regional prevalence of intimate partner violence. However, the estimates presented here for South Asia include only three of eight South Asian countries (Bangladesh, India, and Sri Lanka) and thus cannot be considered representative of the whole South Asia region (WHO et al. 2013, 44). The very macro-level regional groupings in this map hide important subregional variations (WHO et al. 2013, 47).

MAP 2.1 Share of Women Who Have Experienced Physical/Sexual Intimate Partner Violence

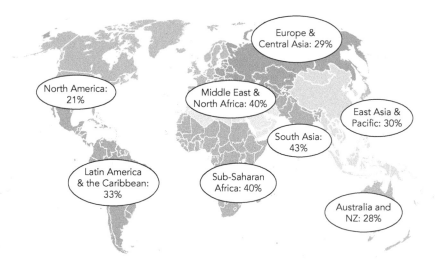

Source: World Bank, using World Bank regional definitions, with data from WHO et al. 2013.
Note: Regional prevalence figures are calculated by regression models using population survey estimates for each region. Prevalence for South Asia and East Asia and Pacific combined is based on 34 estimates. Countries included for South Asia are Bangladesh, India, and Sri Lanka (only three of eight South Asian countries).

By examining intimate partner violence by country and separating physical and sexual violence, we see that, while the three South Asian countries for which DHS data are available are among those with high levels of physical and sexual spousal violence, several other countries report higher rates (figures 2.6 and 2.7). Still, levels are unacceptably high, particularly in India and Bangladesh. In fact, Bangladesh has the highest prevalence of intimate partner sexual and physical violence among South Asian countries for which a DHS violence module is available. Among the 15 countries with the highest global prevalence of physical intimate partner violence, Bangladesh ranks second only to the Republic of Congo (figure 2.7). India is seventh on this list, with Pakistan and Nepal 11th and 14th, respectively.

It is important to note that large surveys such as the DHS are unlikely to capture the true extent of such abuse (Jejeebhoy and Bott 2003). Comparing survey estimates of partner sexual violence across countries is particularly problematic because, although the same questions are asked in all DHS violence modules, the understanding of what constitutes sexual abuse and the willingness to discuss it in the format of a survey vary tremendously across cultures (Santhya et al. 2007; Coast, Leone, and Malviya 2012). In general, because of variations in definitions, survey area and measurement across studies, the range of estimates for all forms of violence varies tremendously by study even within the same country, as illustrated in appendix O.

Data from women's reports in studies across the region show that the violence that married women face at the hands of their husbands does not just occur once; rather, it is severe, of multiple forms, and frequent (box 2.2). Reports from male respondents

FIGURE 2.6 15 Countries with Highest Prevalence of Intimate Partner Sexual Violence

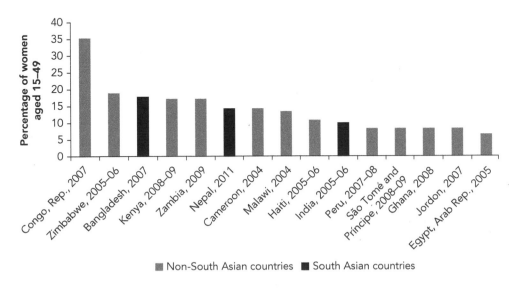

Source: DHS, multiple years.
Note: Sample size = more than 1,000 ever-married women in each country.

FIGURE 2.7 15 Countries with Highest Prevalence of Intimate Partner Physical Violence

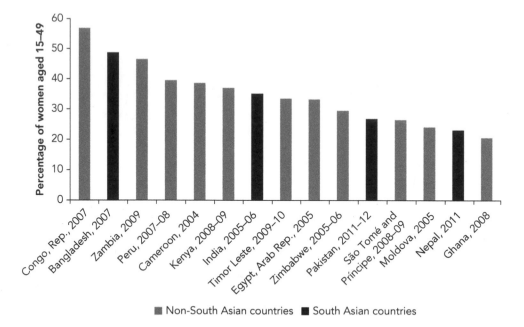

■ Non-South Asian countries ■ South Asian countries

Source: DHS, multiple years.
Note: Sample size = more than 1,000 ever-married women in each country.

BOX 2.2 Illustrations of Intensity and Frequency of Spousal Abuse Reported by Women

- 45 percent of Nepali women reported suffering two or more types of sexual coercion in their lifetime (Adhikari and Tamang 2010).

- More than 60 percent of Indian women reported three or more episodes of physical or psychological violence in their lifetime (ICRW 2000a).

- 61 percent of women in Maldives said they had experienced severe violence, which included being punched, kicked, choked, or having a weapon used against them (Fulu 2007).

- In Sri Lanka, Jayasuriya, Wijewardena, and Axemo (2011) note that 57 percent of surveyed women reported instances of abuse that were severe, including being choked, burned, or hit with a weapon.

---

on perpetration of severe violence concur, although estimates vary, ranging from 8 percent of men reporting perpetrating more than one form of violence on their wife in Bangladesh (Silverman et al. 2013) to 39 percent of men in India (Koenig et al. 2006). In ICRW's (2000b) India study, 80 percent of men reported engaging in at least two of four forms of violence—sexual, physical, emotional, and controlling; 22 percent reported all four; and only 15.3 percent reported none. In the same study, the majority of Indian

TABLE 2.1 Percentage of Ever-Married Women Who Think a Husband Is Justified to Beat His Wife

Reasons	Bangladesh 2011	India 2005–06	Maldives 2009	Nepal 2006	Pakistan 2012–13
Burns the food/does not cook properly	4.2	17.8	7.1	2.9	18.4
Argues with him	22.6	27.6	18.7	7.6	33.7
Goes out without telling him	16.9	27.4	15.0	9.4	29.6
Neglects the children	18.4	35.4	20.5	21.0	31.1
Refuses to have sexual intercourse with him	8.3	12.5	22.1	2.6	30.6
She shows disrespect to/ neglects in-laws	—	—	—	—	27.6
At least one specified reason	32.3	46.7	35.5	24.3	42.5
Number of ever-married women	17,796	121,853	6,845	10,767	13,558

Source: DHS, multiple years.
Note: — = Not available. Nepal's 2011 DHS does not have questions on attitudes towards spousal violence.

men reported being emotionally, physically, or sexually violent three or more times in the previous year (ICRW 2000b).

As important as analyzing the prevalence of violence is assessing the attitudes that support it. Some studies suggest that attitudes condoning violence are associated with greater experience of violence (Santhya et al. 2007; Hindin, Kishor, and Ansara 2008; Abramsky et al. 2011; Johnson and Das 2008), but this may reflect that women who experience violence tend to internalize it, and convince themselves that it was justified, as a coping mechanism (Santhya et al. 2007).

Table 2.1 shows the acceptance of intimate partner physical violence by a husband among ever married women in South Asia. While Bangladesh has the highest prevalence of intimate partner physical violence among married women in South Asia (figure 2.7), it is most accepted among married women in India and Pakistan. The importance of specific reasons for which married women justify intimate partner violence varies by country. For instance, arguing with the husband is the reason for which most women seem to think a husband is justified to beat his wife in Bangladesh and Pakistan. For India and Nepal, this reason is neglect of children, whereas for the Maldives, it is refusal to have sexual intercourse with the husband.

Other studies, in Bangladesh (Schuler et al. 1996; Schuler and Islam 2008; Yount et al. 2013), Bhutan (NSB 2011), India (Jejeebhoy 1998), Sri Lanka (Jayasuriya, Wijewardena, and Axemo 2011), Nepal (Paudel 2007), and Pakistan (Hyder et al. 2007) also find that significant proportions of men and women accept or condone spousal violence against women for many behaviors or believe that such violence is condoned by religion (Rabbani, Qureshi, and Rizvi 2008; Schuler et al. 1996). Studies from India (ICRW 2000b), Pakistan (Qayyum, n.d.) and Nepal (Nanda, Gautam, and Verma 2012) find that most men agree that women "deserve" to be beaten for certain "transgressions" and "so that there is a sense of fear in them and they can be controlled" (Jejeebhoy et al. 2013, 16). Men also agree that women do not have a right to refuse sex unless they are unwell, pregnant, or menstruating (Jejeebhoy et al. 2013).

At the same time, an increasing body of research suggests that attitudes toward marital intimate partner violence are not unequivocally supportive of violence, but vary by the reason and extent of violence. In studies in Bangladesh, southern India and Vietnam, women reported that spousal violence was acceptable for what they considered "intended transgressions," such as disobedience, but rarely for reasons that women did not consider to "go against the rules" (Schuler et al. 1996; Rao 1997; Yount et al. 2013). Moreover, women who have had opportunities allowing them greater exposure to the outside world were less inclined to continue to accept violence (Yount et al. 2013). Women also do not condone very severe violence that immobilizes or seriously hurts the woman, regardless of the reason (Schuler et al. 1996; Rao 1997; Jejeebhoy et al. 2013).

Attitudes and prevalence both vary by age, suggesting that adolescents are most vulnerable. For instance, a notably higher percent of married adolescents report recent physical spousal violence than do married adults in Bangladesh and India (figure 2.8). Interestingly, this is not the case in the other two South Asian countries for which these data are available, but reasons are unclear. In India and Nepal, the two countries for which data on sexual intimate partner violence are available, adolescents also show a higher prevalence: 11 percent of married adolescents report having experienced sexual violence from their husbands compared to 6 percent of adults in India. Similarly, in

FIGURE 2.8 Reported Physical Spousal Violence in Past 12 Months: Select South Asian Countries

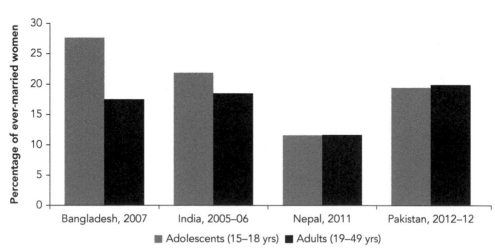

Source: DHS, multiple years.
Note: Sample size = more than 1,000 for adults, for each country. Sample sizes for adolescents are 72 (Pakistan), 138 (Nepal), 333 (Bangladesh), and 1,902 (India).

Nepal, 12 percent of married adolescents report having suffered sexual violence from their husbands compared to 9 percent of adult women.

Data from other studies also show that much of the marital intimate partner abuse that women suffer likely occurs in the first few years of marriage, which, given the early average age at marriage in much of South Asia, implies highest prevalence among adolescent married women. In India, for instance, 62 percent of married women who had ever experienced marital intimate partner violence had first experienced it in the first two years of their marriage (Jejeebhoy et al. 2013). Others in India (Raj et al. 2010a, 2010b; ICRW et al. 2012) and in Bangladesh (Hindin, Kishor, and Ansara 2008) also find that women married as adolescents had statistically significantly higher risks of marital physical and sexual intimate partner violence than women who were not adolescent brides. For instance, young married women in Nepal enter marriage with no information about sexuality or skills to negotiate sex and are thus highly vulnerable to sexual abuse within their marriage (Pradhan et al. 2011). Significant proportions of young women may try to refuse sex, but in many cases husbands force sex (Santhya et al. 2007). Moreover, because of their subservient place in the home and their stage of life as newlyweds or first-time mothers, married adolescents may also face harassment from mothers-in-law (Hamid, Johansson, and Rubenson 2009).

Married adolescents themselves appear to condone this violence more than adult women. Recent data from the DHS show that acceptance of at least one reason to condone spousal violence among adolescent girls in South Asia ranges from about

FIGURE 2.9 Percentage of Ever-Married Women Who Give at Least One Reason to Justify Spousal Physical Abuse: Select South Asian Countries

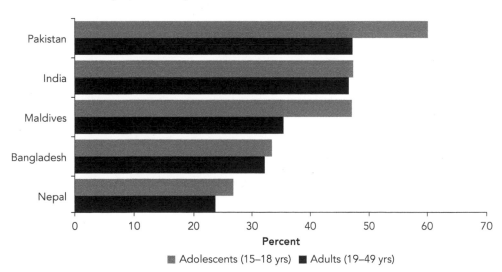

Source: DHS, multiple years.
Note: Sample size = more than 3,000 for adults, for each country. Sample size = more than 300 for adolescents, for each country, except Maldives (sample size = 34 adolescents).

one-quarter of married adolescents in Nepal to almost two-thirds of married adolescents in Pakistan (figure 2.9). Dalal et al. (2011) find that such attitudes among men start early as well—large proportions of their study's unmarried boys and young men between ages 15 and 19 in Bangladesh, India, and Nepal justified wife beating.

ASPECTS OF INTIMATE PARTNER VIOLENCE THAT NEED MORE RESEARCH

Despite being the most widely researched type of violence suffered by women and girls, there are several aspects of intimate partner violence in the South Asian context that need further study. These include but are not limited to forms of violence other than physical and sexual, such as economic violence or controlling behavior, and intimate partner violence faced by never-married women.

Controlling Behavior and Economic Violence within Marriage

The limited data on controlling behavior and economic violence suggest that these are important forms of marital intimate partner violence that merit more attention. For instance, in the baseline report of the Population Council's SAFE study in Bangladesh, almost all women (92 percent) reported experiencing spousal controlling behavior (Parvin, Sultana, and Naved 2012). In the study by Jayasuriya, Wijewardena, and Axemo (2011), 30 percent of Sri Lankan women reported controlling behavior by husbands; more than half the men interviewed by de Mel, Peiris, and Gomez (2013) in Sri Lanka said they controlled who their partners could spend time with. Similarly, studies in Bangladesh (Parvin, Sultana, and Naved 2012) and Pakistan (Rabbani, Qureshi, and Rizvi 2008) report notable levels (55 percent and 39 percent, respectively) of women respondents facing some form of economic violence, including not being allowed to work or control any financial resources. In Sri Lanka, 16 percent of women reported that their partners did not allow them to work (Fulu et al. 2013).

Violence during pregnancy

Also difficult to establish with confidence for countries or regions is the prevalence of intimate partner violence during pregnancy. As with overall measurement of domestic and intimate partner violence, estimating violence during pregnancy is fraught with methodological issues related to the nature of the questions asked, the type of quantitative method used, and sample size and characteristics (Taillieu et al. 2009). These issues contribute, at least in part, to the extremely wide range of prevailing estimates for intimate partner or domestic violence during pregnancy, ranging from 3 percent to 30 percent globally (Van Parys et al. 2014). Studies from South Asia on domestic or intimate partner violence during pregnancy reviewed for this book (appendix O) illustrate a range from 6.3 percent of sampled women in Maldives (Fulu 2007) to 28 percent in India (Khosla et al. 2005).

Some research suggests that pregnancy may not exacerbate women's vulnerability to intimate partner or domestic violence. For instance, a global review of evidence by

Taillieu et al. (2009) finds no studies that show an increase in intimate partner physical violence during pregnancy. Similarly, in South Asia, less than 3 percent of respondents in a study by Bates et al. (2013) in Bangladesh reported that violence increased during pregnancy. Other studies in India (Varma et al. 2007) and Bangladesh (Naved et al. 2006) found violence unchanged during pregnancy, while Fikree et al. (2006) found in their Pakistan study that violence decreased during pregnancy. There are still too few studies specifically examining the change in violence during pregnancy, however, to come to a firm conclusion. Persistent methodological problems add to the lack of certainty about whether and under what circumstances pregnancy may increase a woman's risks of intimate partner or domestic violence.

Violence against Never-Married Women

The majority of adult women in South Asia marry; nonetheless, as norms continue to change toward acceptability of non-marital roles for women, this situation is expected to change (Jones 2010). Data from the DHS show that 16 and 9 percent of never-married women ages 35–39 report having experienced physical violence in their lifetime in India and Nepal, respectively. In India and Nepal, 4.8 percent and 6.8 percent of never-married women of the same age group report having experienced sexual violence in their lifetime, respectively.

Forms of Violence That Need More Research to Establish Prevalence

Research to establish prevalence and trends is limited for all forms of violence other than excess female child mortality, child marriage, and marital intimate partner physical and sexual violence. Data thus are limited on physical and sexual abuse in childhood suffered by girls. Within the domain of marriage, while there are several studies that examine intimate partner violence, fewer collect data on or describe patterns of domestic violence perpetrated by others. Within domestic violence itself, data are scarce on such violence suffered by elderly and divorced or widowed women. Another form of violence faced by married women is dowry-related violence, for which data are also scarce. Finally, data are rare on all forms of violence that cut across life stages, namely, trafficking, non-partner sexual harassment[3] outside the home (on the street or in the workplace, for example), custodial violence, and honor crimes. This section covers the limited information we could find on the prevalence of these types of violence in South Asia.

CHILD ABUSE[4]

South Asian girls who survive through birth and early childhood, and who are not married early, still suffer other types of violence in the home, at school, and in society at large.

Such abuse includes emotional, physical, and sexual abuse at home and in school for those girls who live at home and get an education; violence on the streets for homeless girls; sexual and physical abuse in juvenile facilities; and commercial sexual exploitation. During times of conflict or natural disasters, the vulnerability of girls to some of these forms of violence may increase as household structures and protection are disrupted.

Much of the large body of regional work on child abuse is, unfortunately, not disaggregated by the sex of the child. One exception is a national survey conducted by the government of India (GOI 2007)[5] on child abuse. Fifty percent or more of all surveyed girls experienced one or more forms of physical or sexual violence and emotional violence (figures 2.10 and 2.11). Physical violence is particularly prevalent for girls living on the streets or in correctional institutions (figure 2.10).

A range of other studies in many different countries suggests that reported sexual abuse is typically higher among girls than boys across regions, including South Asia

FIGURE 2.10 Child Physical Abuse in India

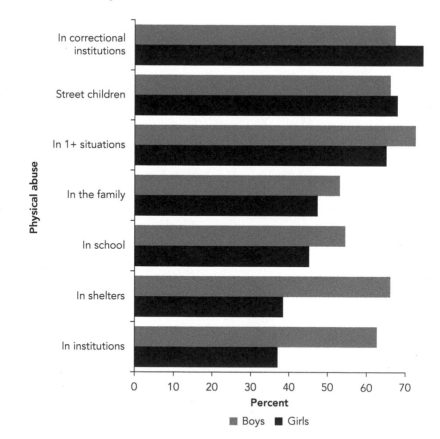

Source: GOI 2007.
Note: Sample size = 12,447 children ages 5–18 years, of which 51.9 percent (6,460 children) are boys and the remainder (5,987 children) are girls.

FIGURE 2.11 Child Sexual and Emotional Abuse in India

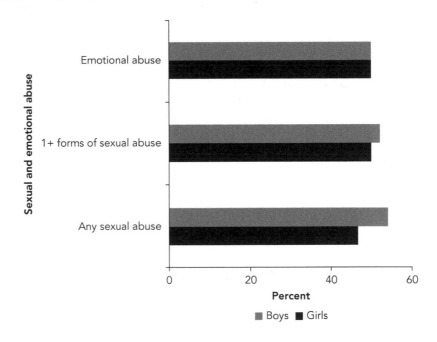

Source: GOI 2007.
Note: Sample size = 12,447 children ages 5–18 years, of which 51.9 percent (6,460 children) are boys, and the remainder (5,987 children) are girls.

(Pinheiro 2006; Stoltenborgh et al. 2011), while reported physical violence, corporal punishment in schools, and homicide of children is more prevalent among boys (Pinheiro 2006). While these studies, reviewed below, provide a picture of such abuse faced by girls, these numbers can rarely be used to generate prevalence or trend estimates as studies vary by area, date, sample, and methodology.

Girl Child Sexual and Physical Abuse in the Home and School

Multiple national-level and small-scale studies illustrate that sexual and physical abuse faced by girls is a critical yet inadequately documented issue, both in the home and at school. While the GOI (2007) data in figures 2.10 and 2.11 show higher reported sexual violence for boys than girls, other studies find that girls may be more vulnerable to sexual abuse than boys, although it is important to note that these variations may exist partly because of differential rates of reporting for girls and boys. Iravani (2011) found that in India, 30 percent of men and 40 percent of women in her study remembered being sexually molested during childhood. In Bhutan (Heiberg and Thukral 2013) and Nepal (Slugget 2003) also, more girls than boys reported sexual abuse. A report by the Pakistani nongovernmental organization (NGO) Sahil (2012) estimated that of all cases of child sexual abuse in Pakistan reported by news media in 2012, 71 percent of suffering children were girls. Research also shows that in most cases the perpetrator is someone known to the girl (Iravani 2011; Sahil 2012; Goonesekere and Amarasuriya 2013; Qayyum, n.d.).

Girl children and adolescents also report sexual violence and abuse in schools. For adolescent girls, nonconsensual sexual experiences at school are one of the most common types of sexual harassment (Jejeebhoy and Bott 2003). An unpublished 2009 study, "National Study on Violence against Children in Maldives," cited in Heiberg and Thukral (2013), found that one in seven children in secondary school had been sexually abused, with twice as many girls as boys sexually abused. Studies in Nepal and Pakistan also report sexual abuse of girls by schoolteachers (UNICEF 2005). The persistence of sexual abuse of girls in schools may reflect current trends, such as an increasing number of young girls continuing education beyond primary school or increased mingling of girls and boys in schools. Alternatively, it could also reflect that adults in positions of authority over young children and adolescents are taking advantage of it (Jejeebhoy and Bott 2003).

Boys seem to be more at risk than girls for harsh physical punishment and abuse (Krug et al. 2002; UNICEF 2005) at home and at school. Nonetheless, the risks of physical punishment that girls face are unacceptable. In India, half of girls ages 5 to 18 have experienced at least one form of physical punishment or violence (GOI 2007). Data from UNICEF's Multiple Indicator Cluster Surveys in Afghanistan (CSO and UNICEF 2012) and Nepal (Central Bureau of Statistics 2012) show that a majority of girls have experienced some violent discipline or psychological aggression (figure 2.12).

Other reports document emotional or psychological violence of other types. In India, reportedly almost every second child, whether girl or boy, perceives herself or himself as emotionally abused. This abuse can range from being shouted at (20.1 percent of children reporting emotional abuse) to being threatened or locked up (just under 2 percent of those reporting emotional abuse) (GOI 2007). In Afghanistan, girls have been found to have double the risk of predicted psychopathology and symptoms of depression related to emotional abuse as compared to boys (Panter-Brick et al. 2009).

Violence against Girl Children on the Street

Very little gender-disaggregated data were found on violence faced by the large percentage of girls across the world that comprise so-called "street children."[6] Children who have run away from home and then face violence on the streets are likely to be doubly abused: research from Bangladesh (Conticini and Hulme 2007), India (GOI 2007), and Pakistan (Malik 2010) shows that most children end up on the streets escaping violence in the home. A study in Bangladesh (Conticini and Hulme 2007) found that once on the street, girls were twice as likely as boys on the streets to experience all forms of violence, especially sexual violence. At least part of girls' greater vulnerability to sexual violence may relate to the composition of street children at different ages. For instance, in India the largest proportion of girls among street children were between ages 10 and 14 (GOI 2007), when they are vulnerable to sexual exploitation but perhaps less able to protect themselves than are older adolescents.

FIGURE 2.12 Girls' Experience of Physical and Psychological Discipline in Nepal and Afghanistan

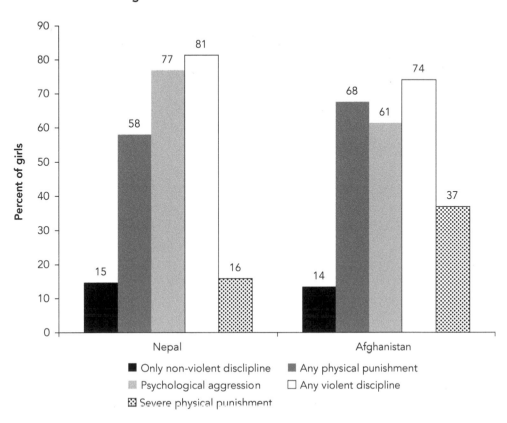

Sources: Central Bureau of Statistics 2012; CSO and UNICEF 2012.
Note: Sample size = 5,480 girls ages 2–14 years for Nepal and 22,040 girls ages 2–14 years for Afghanistan.

Violence against Girl Children in Institutions and in Conflict Settings

By one estimate (GOI 2007), in 2006–07, 70 percent of Indian children in correctional (juvenile detention) facilities reported some abuse, of which three-quarters were girls, and about 52 percent of children in shelters reported abuse, of which one-third were girls. Evidence from Bangladesh, Bhutan, Nepal, Pakistan, and Sri Lanka cited by UNICEF (2005) shows that girls face sexual and physical abuse in police custody, juvenile detention, and residential facilities in those countries as well. Girls within the juvenile justice system in Afghanistan are more likely than are boys to be detained with adults (albeit women, not men) and to be denied some of the rights within the system (such as education) to which boys in juvenile detention have access (UNICEF 2008). Girls may be particularly vulnerable to sexual and physical abuse because of chaos created by war and unrest. In Nepal, for instance, the deaths and disappearances of thousands of boys and men during the decade of civil unrest between 1996 and 2006 forced women and girls to support their families whereby, in desperation, many turned to the sex trade (ECPAT 2011c). Girls in Nepal were also vulnerable to forced recruitment by the Maoists, who were then the rebel group in the country's civil unrest (Mazurana and Carlson 2006). In Afghanistan, girl child orphans in refugee camps eke out a living as best they can and are subject to all types of physical and sexual abuse (UNICEF 2005). In Sri Lanka, Catani et al. (2007) reported that as a result of the abuse experienced during war, girls were slightly more likely to report suffering posttraumatic stress disorder than were boys (32.5 percent and 28 percent, respectively).

Commercial Sexual Exploitation of Girls

Child prostitution is possibly one of the most frequent forms of violence faced by girls and adolescents in South Asia (UNICEF 2001; Goonesekere 2006; Hyder and Malik 2007). As elsewhere in the world, it is largely underground (ECPAT 2011d), however, making it almost impossible to acquire reliable data on prevalence. UNICEF (cited in ECPAT 2011b) estimates that 40 percent of the roughly 3 million women prostitutes in India are minor girls. Studies in Nepal suggest that between 16 percent and 33 percent of female prostitutes are girls under the age of 18 (ECPAT 2011c). Many of these girls in India and Nepal are from Dalit, minority and poor households (ECPAT 2011b, 2011c).

Some forms of prostitution of children in South Asia have persisted through cultural traditions, such as the *Deuki* tradition in Nepal (Singh and Kapur 2001; UNICEF 2001) and the *devadasi* system in India (Jaising 1995). Both are practices whereby girls, at puberty or even younger, are offered to a god, after which they are expected to devote their lives to that god. Both practices, however, often result in girls thus dedicated to a god becoming a prostitute, often for temple officials (ECPAT 2011b, 2011c). Though Deuki and devadasi are now both illegal, still these practices continue (ECPAT 2011b). In Pakistan, reports show that the tradition of dancing girls has morphed into inclusion of child prostitution (ECPAT 2011d; SCF 2005). More modern forms of abuse through prostitution include forcing girl child prostitutes to take hormonal steroids to enhance body development, as reported by ActionAid in Bangladesh (cited in ECPAT 2011a). In India, the belief that sex with a virgin can cure a man of human immunodeficiency virus (HIV) feeds girl prostitution (ECPAT 2011b).

Sexual Violence Faced by Unmarried Adolescent Girls

Most of the children who were sexually exploited in South Asia in 2001 were girls between ages 13 and 18 (UNICEF 2001). In addition to sexual abuse and rape experienced by adolescent girls, for example as documented in India (GOI 2007; Sodhi and Verma 2003; NCRB 2012) and Pakistan (Qazi 2003), the social denial of premarital sex across South Asia increases the vulnerability of unmarried adolescent girls even in intimate relationships. Several studies note that boys use girls' fear of the taboo on premarital sex to threaten disclosure of a relationship if girls do not acquiesce to demands for sex made by their "boyfriends" (Jejeebhoy and Bott 2003; Sodhi and Verma 2003; Rashid 2010). In Bhutan, such pressure takes a unique form through a perversion of a traditional form of courtship known as "night hunting." A dynamic that is in decline, night hunting, whereby a young man secretly visits a young woman to have sex with her, is intended to be consensual. But there is evidence that urban men abuse this form of courtship to force sex on adolescent and young women (Black and Stalker 2006). There is also increasing evidence of cyber bullying and cyber sexual harassment among South Asian adolescents. The Aurat Foundation (2012) estimates that in Pakistan, 10 percent of sexual harassment incidents reported by their survey respondents included sexually explicit emails and text messages.

NON-INTIMATE PARTNER DOMESTIC VIOLENCE AMONG MARRIED WOMEN

Studies examining domestic violence largely focus on violence by an intimate partner, which, in the case of domestic violence within cohabitation in South Asia primarily is the spouse. This is not surprising: partner violence is the most prevalent form of physical and sexual violence against women in the world (Heise 2011). Yet, in the South Asian family structure and hierarchy, where mothers-in-law and other elders in the marital family exercise great and often unchallenged authority and power over daughters-in-law, violence by these other domestic relatives needs further study. In studies that do compare marital domestic violence by different family members, women respondents named mothers-in-law as the second-most frequent source of domestic violence after husbands in India (Krishnan et al. 2012; Jejeebhoy et al. 2013) and Pakistan (Rabbani, Qureshi, and Rizvi 2008). Mothers-in-law were also named as the most frequent instigators of violence among self-immolation victims in Afghanistan (Raj et al. 2008). Mothers-in-law in India were cited as the main perpetrators of dowry-related violence (ICRW 2000a); they were also reportedly likely to be violent if a daughter-in-law was not obedient (particularly in the case of a young or adolescent daughter-in-law), if she threatened the mother-in-law's relationship with her son, or if she did not conceive soon after marriage (Krishnan et al. 2012; Jejeebhoy et al. 2013). At the same time, Schuler et al. (2008) report from their qualitative study in Bangladesh that several women noted their mothers-in-law could diffuse spousal violence. Other studies in Bangladesh (Koenig et al. 2003) and Pakistan (Naeem et al. 2008) report a lower risk of physical abuse among women living in an extended family with in-laws than women living with only their husband and minor children.

DOWRY-RELATED DOMESTIC VIOLENCE

Dowry is one important reason for the high levels of violence within marriage in South Asia. The system of dowry is not unique to South Asia, but the transformations in the meaning and forms of dowry in South Asia over the past several decades have triggered a form of violence that is unique to the region—namely, dowry-related violence that often results in a young married woman's death. Specifically, dowry has morphed from a traditional parental bequest or voluntary gift to a daughter upon marriage to an obligatory, increasingly onerous "groom-price" that the groom and his family own and over which the bride has no control (Anderson 2000, 2004; Suran et al. 2004; Srinivasan 2005; Arunachalam and Logan 2008; Naripokkho and Bangladesh Mahila Parishad, n.d.).

The resulting violence takes many forms, the predominant form being physical. In India, Pakistan, and Nepal, dowry violence can take the form of harassment (Rao 1997) that often propels young brides to commit suicide in sheer desperation (Jaising 1995) or can manifest as outright murder claimed as a kitchen accident (Jaising 1995; Purkayastha et al. 2003; Perveen 2010a).

In Afghanistan it is the practice of bride-price paid by a groom's family to a bride's family that can encourage violence. Bride prices can be extremely high (Smith 2009), and impoverished households may be forced to marry off daughters to settle debts incurred in their sons' marriages. Bride price also precipitates forced marriage because this money often forms an important source of income for impoverished households (Landinfo 2011); paying for a bride also contributes to the belief that a woman is her husband's property to do with as he likes, which may be further fuelled by anger if he and his family paid a high bride-price (Smith 2009). For instance, there is a saying in Dai Kundi Province, Afghanistan: *"Da zar kharidim da sang mekoshim"* [We bought you with money and will kill you with a stone] (UNAMA 2010, 5).

Data on the prevalence of dowry-related violence are even harder to find than are data on dowry itself. As evident in table 2.2, estimates range widely.

Nonetheless, that dowry deaths have been persistent for a while, at least in India, is illustrated well by data from India's National Crime Records Bureau, which show a steady increase since 2001. At the same time, the percentage of cases investigated has also increased, suggesting growing attention to this form of violence (figure 2.13).

DOMESTIC VIOLENCE AMONG ELDERLY WOMEN

Global statistics of domestic abuse faced by elderly women suggest that 4 percent to 6 percent are abused in some manner in their homes (Krug et al. 2002). However, research on abuse in the home specifically faced by elderly women is seriously lacking in South Asia, possibly because the existence of such abuse has only recently started to be recognized (Munsur et al. 2010). Still, in Bangladesh, Munsur et al. (2010) found that one-third of their respondents (age 60 and over) had suffered some abuse because of their old age, with mental abuse being the most prevalent. Poverty and dependency on others were the main reasons for this abuse. In Sri Lanka, among the elderly, women were more likely than men to be victims of abuse; the most common forms of such abuse were assault and denial of health care (Perera, Gunawardane, and Jayasuriya 2011).

TABLE 2.2 Estimates of Dowry Violence in Select South Asian Countries

Estimates of dowry violence	Year and source
Bangladesh	
25%–30% of violence against women reported to police was dowry-related	Farouk 2005
330 women in 2011 killed because of dowry, vs. 137 in 2010	Islam 2012
255 women faced dowry-related violence in first 6 mo. of 2013	Islam 2013
India	
5,000 dowry deaths annually	1995; Indira Jaising 1995
12,000–20,000 dowry deaths annually	Early 1990s; Purkayastha et al. 2003
25,000 dowry deaths annually	Late 1990s; Menski (1998) cited in Anderson (2007)
8,000 dowry deaths annually	2007–11; NCRB 2012
Pakistan	
50 cases of stove burning reported by news media in 2009	Perveen 2010a
As of 2003, 4 women burned to death by relatives every day	Bukhari 2003
More than 6,500 women in Islamabad-Rawalpindi area burned by family members; less than 1% survived	1994–2003; Bukhari 2003
4,000 women burned by relatives in Islamabad	1994–2002; Terzieff 2002

FIGURE 2.13 Cases of Dowry-Related Violence Reported to and Investigated by Authorities, India 2001–12

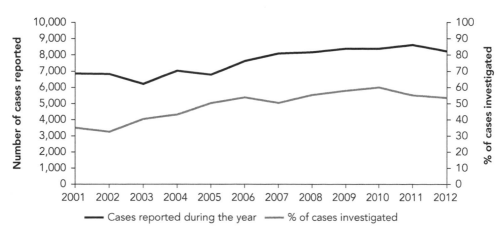

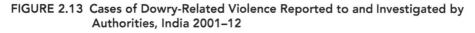

Source: NCRB, India.

DOMESTIC VIOLENCE AMONG WIDOWED OR DIVORCED

The very limited data on domestic violence among widows suggests that forms of physical violence unique to widowhood exist in South Asia and include some that are fatal. One example is widow burning or *Sati* in India, where a Hindu widow sacrifices herself on her husband's funeral pyre (United Nations 2001; Martin et al. 2002; Cramer 2007). Although the practice is illegal, it continues, albeit rarely, and women who commit Sati are regarded with reverence by their community (Martin et al. 2002). In Pakistan, familial belief that a young widow brings dishonor to the family can result in these young women being imprisoned or killed by the family (United Nations 2001).

Widows also face increased vulnerability to sexual violence by other men in their marital household if they are regarded as unprotected after their husband dies (Chen and Dreze 1995). Studies from Afghanistan (WPD 2011), Bangladesh (United Nations 2001), India (Mohindra et al. 2012) and Pakistan (Perveen 2010b) also provide evidence of economic violence tied to the fact that a family may withdraw economic support for a woman once her husband dies. In Afghanistan, widows may be forced to remarry within the family, often motivated by the resultant opportunity to seize any inherited property (UNAMA 2010). Those who try to escape face severe punishment, including having their children taken away (Landinfo 2011), or incarceration (WPD 2011). Across the region, unmarried widows may be physically and socially isolated (United Nations 2001; Mohindra et al. 2012). Finally, particularly in India and Nepal, widows face certain unique forms of cultural and psychological violence—such as markers of diminished status or prohibitions on diet and social communication—because they are considered unlucky or impure to have had their husbands die before they did. They are also called insulting names (United Nations 2001; WPD 2011).

There is some emerging evidence that the situation of widows may be improving. The baseline from an ongoing program by the United Nations for and with widows in India, Sri Lanka and Nepal found that a majority of participating widows had the freedom to choose what they wear, access to religious places, and freedom to work (Thakur 2012). It is possible that participating widows are more empowered than non-participants, however. Fear of violence is nonetheless substantial even among this group of participants: almost 30 percent reported fearing sexual or physical abuse (Thakur 2012).

No literature on violence against divorced women could be found for this study, except for a study from Afghanistan (Nijhowne and Oates 2008). This is a serious gap, as divorce is undergoing a transition in the region. While divorce rates are on the rise, divorced women continue to face social stigma, thus creating a space for increased risks of violence for divorced women. The data from Afghanistan show just such a pattern. Though divorce rates are low (1.2 percent of the sample for figure 2.14), still the study found divorced women reporting much higher rates of physical, sexual, and psychological violence than either married or widowed women (figure 2.14).

FIGURE 2.14 Reported Violence by Marital Status, Afghanistan

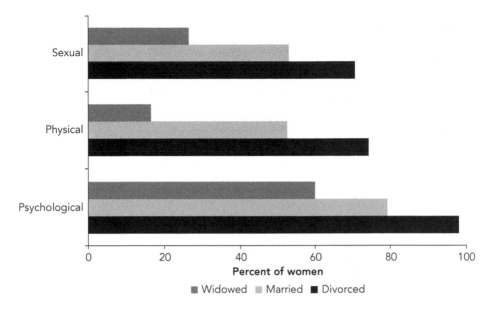

Source: Nijhowne and Oates, 2008.
Note: Sample size = one woman from each of 4,700 households in 16 districts, selected to represent geographic, ethnic, linguistic, and cultural diversity. Of these, 96 percent (4,512 women) were married, 2.9 percent (136 women) were widowed, and 1.2 percent (56 women) were divorced.

TRAFFICKING

More than three-quarters of trafficked persons globally are girls and women (United Nations 2012), with an increase over time in the proportion of female victims who are girls, according to a United Nations (2012) study. Nepal is the only South Asian country for which this United Nations study provides gender-disaggregated data. It stands out as having a much larger proportion of girls among reported trafficking victims than any other country or region included in this report (figure 2.15).

According to UNODC, 150,000 girls and women are trafficked within South Asia every year; in addition, an estimated 225,000 women, men, and children annually are trafficked elsewhere from South Asia (Huda 2006). In 2010, India was the only South Asian country to be ranked among the world's top seven countries of origin for adults trafficked into the United States.[7] However, on the whole and despite the enormity of this issue in the region, reliable country-specific statistics within the region are scant, presumably because of the illegal nature of human trafficking.

Most South Asian countries are both destination and source countries for trafficking of women and girls (Ali 2005; Huda 2006; Cheema 2011), though Bhutan and Maldives are primarily destination countries. Internal trafficking is also widespread. For instance, in Pakistan, although data on internal trafficking are minimal, qualitative reports by a

FIGURE 2.15 Trafficked Persons by Age and Gender: Global and Select Regions/Countries, 2009–10

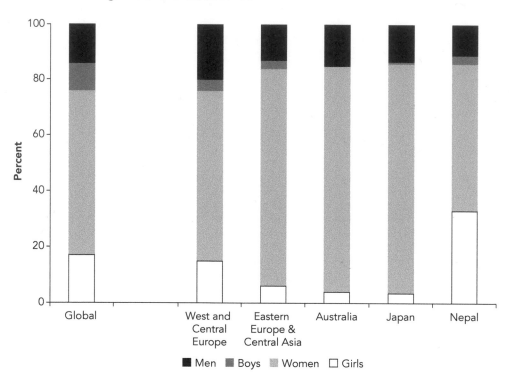

Source: United Nations 2012.
Note: Sample size = 43,000 global reported victims of trafficking. For regions, the sample sizes are 22,000 (West and Central Europe), 4,000 (Eastern Europe and Central Asia), and 38,000 (Australia, Japan, and Nepal combined).

number of civil society organizations find that girls and women are internally trafficked all over the country. For example, researchers from SCF (2005) find that poor laws and extreme poverty in the Swat region make young girls particularly vulnerable to being sought out by traffickers from other parts of the country under the guise of marriage. Others note that trafficked girls are not solely from poor households and are trafficked also for bonded labor (Perveen 2012). Trafficking occurs for sex work, undocumented domestic help (for instance, in Bhutan), and forced labor (for instance, in the Maldives) (U.S. Department of State 2012, 2013).

SEXUAL HARASSMENT

A global survey by Gallup in 143 countries in 2011 found that more than 60 percent of women reported sexual harassment on the street or in public transport in multiple cities in China, the Arab Republic of Egypt, India, Israel, Japan, Pakistan, the Republic of Korea, and the United States, among others.[8] Small-scale studies from within South Asia find that women in the region face frequent harassment in public places, for instance, in Pakistan (Aurat Foundation 2012). Several studies from Sri Lanka, reviewed by Perera, Gunawardane, and Jayasuriya (2011), found that more than 80 percent of women and girls faced sexual harassment while taking public transport. Jagori and UN Women (2011) in India conducted a first-of-its-kind large survey of women and men on street safety for women in Delhi. More than 85 percent of male and female respondents reported that women's sexual harassment on city streets was pervasive.

Sexual Harassment In the Workplace

Sexual harassment in the workplace is also likely pervasive in South Asia, but data are confined to a few small-scale studies (box 2.3). Working women across the region may well face double risks of harassment—both at work and on the way to and from work (Siddiqi 2003; Hancock 2006; Perera, Gunawardane, and Jayasuriya 2011). Types of harassment range from explicitly sexual to offensive language, intimidation, and other forms of exploitation (Naved 2003; Chaudhuri 2007; Perera, Gunawardane, and Jayasuriya 2011; Aurat Foundation 2012).

Women who engage in sex work face different circumstances that perhaps make them more vulnerable to workplace harassment, though again data are sporadic and available only from small-scale studies (box 2.4). Data from a particularly detailed study from Rawalpindi, Pakistan, illustrate the range of sexual abuse that female sex workers have to deal with, including assault from their customers, their husbands, and the police (figure 2.16). Because of the stigma associated with sex work, sex workers may also feel they have little recourse to justice in cases of violence or rape, and perpetrators of violence against female sex workers rarely are punished (Rekart 2005;

BOX 2.3 Sexual Harassment in the Workplace Faced by Women in South Asia

- International Labour Organization data from Nepal suggest that slightly more than half (53.8 percent) of women employees have faced workplace sexual harassment (ILO 2004).

- Studies in Pakistan of women in different professions report that 58 percent of women nurses faced sexual harassment by patients and their relatives, colleagues, and doctors, whereas almost all women (93 percent) working in private and public sectors were sexually harassed by supervisors or senior colleagues (Naved 2003).

- In Bangladesh, at least one-quarter of women in electronics and garments industries have experienced sexual, physical, or verbal abuse (Siddiqi 2003).

- Across studies in Sri Lanka, more than two-thirds of women reported physical and sexual harassment in the workplace or on the way to work (Hancock 2006; Perera, Gunawardane, and Jayasuriya 2011).

- In India, 17 percent of women respondents in a survey by Oxfam in eight cities reported some sexual harassment at work; the most unsafe jobs for women were as laborers, domestic help, and in small-scale manufacturing (Biswas 2012).

> **BOX 2.4 Illustrative Rates of Sexual Abuse Faced by Female Sex Workers in India, Nepal, and Pakistan**
>
> - Karnataka, India: 11 percent to 26 percent of female sex workers report rape or physical abuse, depending on their age (Beattie et al. 2010)
> - Andhra Pradesh, India: 77 percent of contract sex workers report sexual violence at place of work (George, Sabarwal, and Martin 2011)
> - Andhra Pradesh, India: 12 percent of sex workers report sexual assault in past 12 months (Reed et al. 2010)
> - Pakistan: 66 percent of sex workers report being sexually assaulted by husbands, 38 percent by clients (Hawkes et al. 2009)
> - Nepal: young girls and women working in massage parlors, "cabin restaurants," and "dance bars" are often forced by employers to endure sexual abuse by customers (Maiti-Nepal 2010)

FIGURE 2.16 Sexual Harassment Faced by Sex Workers, Past 12 Months, Rawalpindi, Pakistan

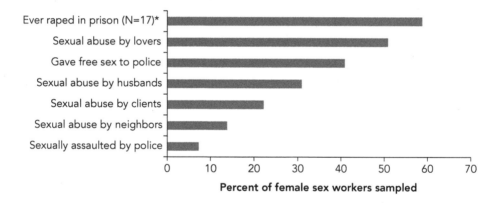

Source: Mayhew et al. 2009.
Note: Sample size = 427 female sex workers, except where noted with an asterisk; the sample was recruited through peer identification.

Beattie et al. 2010). Child sex workers may be even more vulnerable to all forms of abuse than adult sex workers (Silverman et al. 2011).

HONOR CRIMES

Despite popular perception, honor crimes are not a purely South Asian phenomenon, nor does its concept originate in Islam. Rather, it dates back to pre-Islam Arabia and has been traced also to ancient Roman times (Lari 2011). In modern times, honor killings have been recorded in several countries in the Middle East and North Africa, such as

Jordan, Lebanon, Morocco, Syria, and Yemen. Although statistics are rare, research also shows that honor crimes do not occur solely against young, poor women in South Asia. Moreover, honor crimes occur not just in Islamic countries but also among Hindus in India and across the world among people of multiple religions or faiths (Terman 2010); cover the entire age spectrum from "pre-pubescent girls to grandmothers" (Amnesty International 1999, 3); and are reported from urban and rural areas and across wealth and education categories (Amnesty International 1999). Available estimates do suggest that such crimes are more prevalent in South Asia than in the Middle East, but the wide range and unreliability of these figures make any definitive conclusions difficult to reach.

Estimates of honor crimes range widely. For instance, a report by the United Nations Population Fund (UNFPA) in 2000[9] and other estimates by Amnesty International put the number of girls and women murdered in honor killings globally by family members at 5,000 per year (Amnesty International 2012).[10] Civil society organizations estimate that as many as 20,000 honor killings occur globally per year, according to newspaper reports (Kiener 2011; Basu 2013). In a rare survey in Pakistan that asked about honor killings, 26 percent of women were able to identify at least one honor killing in the last decade (Qayyum, n.d.)

Within South Asia, honor crimes have been reported in the news media in India and Pakistan, and more recently in Afghanistan, Bangladesh, and Nepal.[11] Worryingly, the rationales offered for honor crimes in Pakistan appear to have widened from punishment for perceived immoral or illegal sexual interactions to encompass also perceived disobedience to the family (Palo 2009) or actions that challenge male control (Welchman and Hossain 2005). In Afghanistan, Bangladesh, India, and Pakistan, quasi-judicial or extrajudicial community-based forums issue verdicts on the lack of "honor" of a "crime" and dictate the "punishment" (AFPPD and UNFPA 2003; Lari 2011). Both women and men in question may be declared guilty by such "courts," such as *jirgas* in Pakistan and *khap panchayats* in India, and both may be killed or maimed in punishment. However, although men sometimes get a reprieve, women never do (Lari 2011).

Honor crimes as a whole follow the same trajectory of verdict in the same forums, but do not necessarily culminate in murder. One particularly pernicious form that originated in South Asia is that of acid attacks, a form of violence that straddles honor-related violence and sexual harassment (box 2.5).

RAPE

Though prevalence data are lacking, still several studies from the region highlight the pervasiveness of this form of sexual violence against women across their lives. Annual qualitative assessments of reported rape in Pakistan, conducted by the Aurat Foundation, show that in the period 2008–12 rape consistently comprised 10 percent to 11 percent of total reported violent crimes against women and has been among one of the top three to five categories of violence against women thus estimated (Azhar 2011; Perveen 2012). A quarter (25 percent) of married girls and women surveyed in six districts in Pakistan reported having been forced to perform a sexual act by men other than their husband

BOX 2.5 Acid Attacks on Women and Girls in South Asia

Acid violence is a particularly damaging and shocking form of violence: acid is hurled at the victim, often targeting the head and face, with the intention to maim, disfigure, and blind. The great majority of victims are women and girls, many of them below 18 years of age, but men and boys are also targeted. Acid violence reflects deeply ingrained gender inequality and discrimination in a society, whereby women are attacked for transgressing the traditional gender roles that place them in subordinate positions.

Prevalence of acid attacks. The increase in acid violence throughout South Asia is a human rights issue of growing concern. In Bangladesh, 3,000 victims have been reported since 1999. In India, news media and other research increasingly report acid attacks as well. Attacks on schoolgirls by the Taliban in Afghanistan have been well publicized. It has been estimated that 150 acid attacks occur per year in Pakistan, though, as with many countries in the region, incidents regularly go unreported. Attacks have also been reported in Nepal and Sri Lanka. Generally, however, there is a frustrating lack of data and information on the true scale and nature of the problem, making evidence-based action difficult.

Reasons for acid attacks. Acid attacks, especially on women and girls, have taken place for a number of reasons, including family or land disputes, dowry demands, rejection of a man's advances, daring to snub a boy, turning down an offer of marriage, and even going to school. Most acid attacks are carried out by someone known to the victims, including family members. In some cases, men have thrown acid in women's faces to assert their masculinity and superiority within a strongly patriarchal society. Combating acid violence is rendered more difficult by a cultural setting in which legislation against such action is weak, contradictory, or often lacking; conviction rates of perpetrators are low; and the sale of acid is often unregulated.

Consequences of acid violence. For victims, the consequences of acid attacks are devastating and lifelong and include severe disfigurement, loss of sight, and maiming, rendering everyday tasks difficult if not impossible. Acid violence rarely kills but causes severe psychological and social (as well as physical) scarring, and victims are often left with no legal recourse, limited access to medical or psychological assistance, and without the means to support themselves. The trauma of an attack often results in depression, insomnia, fear of facing the outside world, and, in some cases, psychosis and suicides. In addition, considerable stigma is attached to the victims, and they face a lifetime of shame, discrimination, and exclusion from society, whereby they are unable to earn a livelihood and remain continually dependent on their families.

Combating acid violence. There have been few programmatic efforts across the South Asia region to address acid attacks. Several organizations and networks, however, have been active and vocal in raising awareness (for example, Naripokkho and the Acid Survivors Foundation in Bangladesh and in Pakistan) through a five-pronged approach including public awareness, case reporting, short-term treatment, long-term treatment, and legal justice. Burn units at national hospitals and other dedicated care facilities have been established, and the response network is expanding. While these efforts are significant, a huge amount of work remains to change traditional mindsets that still tolerate and sanction acid violence.

Sources: Acid Survivors Trust International; Acid Survivors Foundation (Bangladesh and Pakistan); Project SAAVE (Stand Against Acid Violence); Sridharan 2013; The Virtue Foundation 2011. See also Ahmad 2011; Kalantry and Kestenbaum 2011; Massage 2011; Sharma 2013.

(Qayyum, n.d.). In Afghanistan, 11.2 percent of women sampled by Nijhowne and Oates (2008) reported having been raped. Studies from Sri Lanka (Perera, Gunawardane, and Jayasuriya 2011) and Bangladesh (Naripokkho and Bangladesh Mahila Parishad, n.d.) suggest that rape is one of the most prevalent forms of violence against women in these countries. Official government data on reported rapes in India (NCRB 2012 and other years) show a steady increase in the numbers of reported rapes since 2008. Moreover, one-third (about 36 percent) of reported rape cases in 2012 were of minors, and 12.5 percent of the victims were under age 14.

Data from men who perpetrate rape show that rape can start very early in life. Jewkes et al. (2013) reported that 38.9 percent of men who reported perpetrating rape in Sri Lanka had done so the first time before they turned age 19; in Bangladesh, this percentage was the majority (61.7 percent). Further, about half of all those who acknowledged having perpetrated rape in either country also said they had done so more than once.

CUSTODIAL VIOLENCE AGAINST WOMEN

In South Asian countries, abuse or violence against women by police and other custodial authorities is rampant, though exact estimates are difficult to obtain (Ali and Shah 2011; Garg and Singla 2012). Scholars argue that custodial violence in South Asia takes on different dimensions when women are targeted, because of the addition of "gender" to the elements of power that custodians have over prisoners. Thus, for example, Khair (2003) documents multiple instances of police officers "capturing" a young woman on pretense of helping her or on fictional charges, only to rape or otherwise abuse her instead of going through proper legal channels of indictment.

Women "rescued" from honor crimes also suffer abuse when remanded to safe houses where conditions are abysmal and akin to a prison. Moreover, reintegration into family and society of women who have been in custody is made even harder if women are sexually abused, as they are then regarded as "dishonored" or "spoiled," bringing shame to their families (Khair 2004).

Various human rights and other organizations document cases of custodial torture and sexual abuse of women in custody in Afghanistan (United Nations 2007), Bangladesh (SAARC 2006), India (ACHR 2011), Pakistan (SAARC 2006), and Sri Lanka (ACHR 2005). According to Amnesty International (1999) and the Human Rights Commission of Pakistan (2012), women are frequently raped by police officers, including in police stations, and many incidents go unreported. Several studies across the region also cite examples of women in police custody who were victimized and raped for political reasons (Human Rights Watch 2013). Officially, women prisoners have access to general police stations to file complaints. Yet, in reality they may not have the information or the resources to take recourse to complaint mechanisms (United Nations 2007).

Although in popular perception custodial violence is considered limited to police custody, it refers also to violence perpetrated by military and related personnel in times of armed conflict. In testimonies and other findings described in a recent report by

Sri Lanka's Commission of Inquiry on Lessons Learned and Reconciliation (2011), women reported facing physical and sexual violence during the country's civil conflict and noted that, even after the conflict, they continued to "...feel unsafe in the presence of the armed forces... Many women were killed even after the conflict came to an end" (Government of Sri Lanka 2011, 182). Further, the report notes that many women survivors of such violence had not, at the time of the report, received any justice.

In Afghanistan, a large oral history project involving over 700 women reports many instances over the decades of opportunistic rape by armed groups or by individual militia men. Women also frequently reported armed groups stealing girls and young women as "brides" (UN Women 2013). Often courts have been unable or reluctant to bring abusers to justice, and women are shamed or threatened into silence (United Nations 2007).

Disclosure and Care-Seeking across Forms of Violence Faced by Women and Girls

The high rates of violence across the life cycle notwithstanding, most women and girls—and, often, their families—are reluctant to disclose experiences of violence or to seek care for consequences of violence. Disclosure is particularly problematic in the case of abuse and other forms of violence against girl children and adolescents since most such forms of violence are illegal across the region. Thus, families and individuals focus on trying to hide such abuse rather than disclose it. For instance, in Indian states with high levels of child marriage, when parents marry multiple daughters at once, the wedding card bears only the name of the daughter who is above 18 so as to not attract attention to child marriage (ICRW 2011). In Nepal, adolescent female employees of dance bars in Kathmandu (who are often coerced into commercial sex work) are instructed to say if asked that they are 18 years old (Maiti-Nepal 2010). Studies from India (GOI 2007; Human Rights Watch 2013), Pakistan (Hyder and Malik 2007), and Afghanistan (Slugget 2003) also find that disclosure of child sexual abuse for girls and boys is practically non-existent, at least partially because of the shame and stigma attached to such abuse.

Azami (2013) suggests that reporting of child sexual abuse has increased over the last few years in Pakistan, possibly because awareness campaigns, media efforts, and government punitive actions are helping render this topic less taboo. In India, the Protection of Children from Sexual Offences (POSCO) Act 2012 mandates reporting and legal adjudication of cases of child sexual abuse; however, it is unclear how effective this act has been to-date in significantly increasing reporting and adjudication of such cases.

Disclosure is also rare for sexual harassment of adolescent girls. Several studies of young people in India and Pakistan show that most adolescent girls do not admit or disclose sexual harassment to anyone, including parents (Jejeeboy and Bott 2003; Saeed et al. 2003), often because girls who disclose such abuse may themselves be victimized and blamed for it (Chaudhuri 2007; Aurat Foundation 2012; Jaising 1995; Siddiqi 2003). Girls may also fear that talking about such harassment can focus "negative attention"

(Verma and Sodhi in Bott and Jejeebhoy 2003, 53) on them as sexual beings who transgress the silence about sexuality that norms demand of them (Siddiqi 2003).

Disclosure of marital spousal abuse is also infrequent. Studies from Nepal (Naved et al. 2006; Ali et al. 2011), Bangladesh (Parvin, Sultana, and Naved 2012), Maldives (Fulu 2007), Sri Lanka (Jayasuriya, Wijewardena, and Axemo 2011), India (Jejeebhoy et al. 2013), and Pakistan (Shaikh 2003; Rabbani, Qureshi, and Rizvi 2008) find that most women do not disclose intimate partner violence within marriage to anyone. When women do disclose, they appear to do so under duress—either when violence becomes unbearably severe or if children are threatened (Naved et al. 2006; Jejeebhoy et al. 2013; Jayasuriya, Wijewardena, and Axemo 2011). Studies in Bangladesh find that highly educated women are more likely to disclose than uneducated or less educated women and that women are also more likely to disclose when there is family support (Naved et al. 2006; Parvin, Sultana, and Naved 2012).

Most disclosure is to either natal or marital family (Naved et al. 2006; Parvin, Sultana, and Naved 2012; Jayasuriya, Wijewardena, and Axemo 2011; Rabbani, Qureshi, and Rizvi 2008; Shaikh 2003; Jejeebhoy et al. 2013) or neighbors (Naved et al. 2006). Women typically do not disclose to institutions or authority figures (Naved et al. 2006; Parvin, Sultana, and Naved 2012), nor do women reach out for help or care to medical or other institutions, as evidence shows from India (ICRW 2000a), Pakistan (Ali et al. 2011; Fikree et al. 2006), Sri Lanka (Jayasuriya, Wijewardena, and Axemo 2011; Subramanian and Sivayogan 2001), and among Afghan refugees in Pakistan (Hyder et al. 2007).

Why do women not disclose or seek care, even when formal and informal mechanisms to do so exist? Women may not disclose because they consider violence a "normal" or inevitable aspect of marriage (Schuler et al. 2008). On the other hand, women also do not disclose because of fear of reprisal and additional violence if their spouse finds out, or because of stigma and shame at being in a violent relationship, or fear of bringing shame upon their families upon disclosure (Schuler et al. 2008; Naved et al. 2006; Parvin, Sultana, and Naved 2012; Jayasuriya et al. 2011; Jejeebhoy et al. 2013; ICRW 2000a). Women may not disclose because they are not allowed to seek care for disclosed injuries. For instance, in a survey of women in six districts in Pakistan, a little over one-third (35 percent) said they were not allowed to seek medical care for injuries from intimate partner violence (Qayyum, n.d.). Finally, women may not bother to disclose because of apathy and the belief that disclosure would resolve nothing (Naved et al. 2006; Parvin, Sultana, and Naved 2012; Jayasuriya, Wijewardena, and Axemo 2011). As one respondent in the Schuler et al. (2008) study noted: "There is nowhere to go" (331).

Ultimately, the reasons for women's reluctance to disclose or seek care for the violence they experience lie at the intersection of poverty and gender inequality (Schuler et al. 2008). In the case of spousal violence, for instance, women's own poverty means they have no other source of maintenance than their marriage and thus nowhere to go if they leave an abusive husband; poverty also means that their natal families cannot often afford to give them shelter. Gender-unequal social norms increase the risk that women—and not their husbands—will face shame if violence is disclosed, but attempts to seek recourse fail. Perhaps women also do not disclose because they are aware of men's impunity, as reported by recent studies in Sri Lanka and Bangladesh (de Mel, Peires, and Gomez 2013; Naved et al. 2011; Fulu et al. 2013). This research finds that only a small minority of perpetrators in their studies had experienced any legal consequences of being violent or had expressed any concern about any consequences at all.

Understanding the Violence That South Asian Women and Girls Face

This chapter illustrates that women and girls in South Asia face a battery of violent behaviors, by intimate partners, parents, brothers, mothers-in-law, employers, strangers, and the state. Despite limitations in availability of data, it is evident that the violence they face is relentless, threatening to occur at every age and stage of their lives. Supporting this violence is the persistence of certain forms of patriarchy that insist on regarding women as lesser beings to be protected, rather than equal citizens of a country. These forms of patriarchy and accompanying institutions and rules lie at the heart of the nature of violence against South Asian women and girls. The next chapter addresses some of the underlying social norms; socio-economic context; institutional, historical, and legal reasons; and risk factors for this violence.

Notes

1. Hill and Upchurch (1995) note that a simple comparison of female to male mortality as a measure of the 'excess' mortality suffered by girls does not take into account the fact that in most populations females have lower rates of mortality than males at all ages, and that at least some part of this female mortality advantage is genetic. They argue, therefore, that "... requiring that girl mortality rates should exceed those of boys to demonstrate a female disadvantage...[is] too stringent a condition" (129). Instead, Hill and Upchurch (1995) measure girls' excess mortality as the difference between the actual ratio of female to male mortality (at infancy, between 1–5 years, and for children 0–5 years of age), and a 'standard' for an expected ratio of female to male mortality at these ages. Hill and Upchurch developed the standards using the historical experience of countries in northwestern Europe (or populations of that origin) in the 19th and 20th centuries covering the period 1820 to 1964 for England and Wales, France, the Netherlands, New Zealand, and Sweden. They obtained a standard of female advantage for a given value of the male under-5 mortality rate by fitting a smooth curve to observations of under-5 mortality rates for males and female to male mortality rate ratios, using a locally weighted least squares (LOWESS) procedure (Hill and Upchurch 1995).
2. Note that older women may suffer from larger recall bias, or be less likely to know the exact age at which they were married, than younger women. Still, the trend is compelling.
3. Men also face sexual harassment, typically in the form of younger boys being harassed by older boys or men (Jeejeebhoy and Bott 2003; Aurat Foundation 2012). They are also vulnerable to trafficking (for example, as forced labor) or custodial violence. Whereas violence

faced by men and boys falls outside the scope of this report, more research is needed also on these experiences.

4. Rates of physical, sexual, and emotional violence among children in South Asia are likely high for both girls and boys. Discussing child abuse suffered by boys in great detail is beyond the scope of this report, but it is worth pointing out that children, both boys and girls, are vulnerable to a wide array of abuse in South Asia.

5. The authors of the GOI (2007) report and others (Human Rights Watch 2013, 14–15) have noted that the children interviewed for the GOI study were not randomly sampled. Thus estimates should be taken as illustrative rather than generalizable to the population of children in India at large.

6. The exact definition of what constitutes "street children" remains hotly debated, with the only agreement being that street children constitute a very varied group, are difficult to count statistically, and live in a huge range of conditions (de Benítez 2007; Ray et al. 2011).

7. Human Trafficking Statistics, http://www.handsacrosstheworldmn.org/resources/Human +Trafficking+Statistics.pdf.

8. See "Statistics: Academic and Community Studies," Stop Street Harassment website, http://www.stopstreetharassment.org/resources/statistics/statistics-academic-studies/.

9. See United Nations 2006, at para. 78.

10. See also Honour Based Violence Awareness Network website, http://hbv-awareness.com/.

11. Though honor killings are relatively rare in Nepal, the news media have started reporting honor killings in Nepal since about 2010 as a new form of violence. See, for example, articles in the *Times of India* (http://articles.timesofindia.indiatimes.com/2010-10-25 /south-asia/28258045_1_honour-killings-kathmandu-nepal), the *Himalayan Voice*, October 25 (http://thehimalayanvoice.blogspot.com/2010/10/honour-killings-on-rise-in-both-nepal .html), and the *Huffington Post* (http://www.huffingtonpost.com/vday/nepal-rising-in-the -himal_b_1943008.html).

References

Abramsky, T., C. H. Watts, C. Garcia-Moreno, K. Devries, L. Kiss, M. Ellsberg, H. AFM Jansen, and L. Heise. 2011. "What Factors Are Associated with Recent Intimate Partner Violence? Findings from the WHO Multi-Country Study on Women's Health and Domestic Violence." *BMC Public Health* 11: 109.

ACHR (Asian Centre for Human Rights). 2005. "Torture and Lawless Law Enforcement in Sri Lanka." A Shadow Report to the UN Committee against Torture, 35th session, November 7–25, 2005, Palais des Nations.

———. 2011. *Torture in India 2011*. New Delhi: ACHR.

Acid Survivors Foundation. 2014. http://www.acidsurvivors.org.

Acid Survivors Trust International. 2007. "Acid Violence." http://www.acidviolence.org/index .php/acid-violence/.

Adams, A. M., A. Rabbani, S. Ahmed, S. S. Mahmood, A. Al-Sabir, S. F. Rashid, and T. G. Evans. 2013. "Explaining Equity Gains in Child Survival in Bangladesh: Scale, Speed, and Selectivity in Health and Development." *Lancet* 382 (9909): 2027–37.

Adhikari, R., and J. Tamang. 2010. "Sexual Coercion of Married Women in Nepal." *BMC Women's Health* 10 (1): 31.

AFPPD (Asian Forum of Parliamentarians on Population and Development) and UNFPA (United Nations Population Fund). 2003. *Violence against Women in South Asia: A Regional Analysis.* Kathmandu: UNFPA.

Ahmad, N. 2011. "Acid Attacks on Women: An Appraisal of the Indian Legal Response." *Asia-Pacific Journal on Human Rights and the Law* 12 (2): 55–72.

Alam, N., J. van Ginneken, and A. Bosch. 2007. "Decreases in Male and Female Mortality and Missing Women in Bangladesh." In *Watering the Neighbour's Garden: The Growing Demographic Female Deficit in Asia,* ed. Isabelle Attané and Christophe Z. Guilmoto, 161–82. Paris: Committee for International Cooperation in National Research in Demography.

Ali, A. K. M. Masud. 2005. "Treading along a Treacherous Trail: Research on Trafficking in Persons in South Asia." *International Migration* 43 (1/2): 140–64.

Ali, A., and N. A. Shah. 2011. "Women Prisoners in Pakistan: Changing Practices to Enforce Laws and Rights." *Kuwait Chapter of Arabian Journal of Business and Management Review* 1 (4): 57–63.

Ali, T. S., N. Asad, I. Mogren, and G. Krantz. 2011. "Intimate Partner Violence in Urban Pakistan: Prevalence, Frequency, and Risk Factors." *International Journal of Women's Health* 3: 105–15.

Amnesty International. 1999. *Pakistan: Honour Killings of Girls and Women.* http://www.amnesty.org/en/library/info/ASA33/018/1999.

———. 2012. *Culture of Discrimination: A Fact Sheet on "Honor" Killings.* http://www.amnestyusa.org/sites/default/files/pdfs/honor_killings_fact_sheet_final_2012.doc.

Anderson, S. 2000. "The Economics of Dowry Payments in Pakistan." Center for Economic Research No. 2000-82, Center and Department of Economics, Tilburg University, Tilburg, Netherlands.

———. 2004. "Dowry and Property Rights." Working Paper, Department of Economics, University of British Columbia, Vancouver.

———. 2007. "The Economics of Dowry and Brideprice." *Journal of Economic Perspectives* 21 (4): 151–74.

Arunachalam, R., and T. Logan. 2008. "Is There Dowry Inflation in India?" Working Paper No. 13905, National Bureau of Economic Research, Cambridge, MA.

Aurat Foundation. 2012. *Sexual Harassment: A Primary Data Research Study.* Islamabad: Aurat Foundation and Information Service Foundation.

Azami, A. S. 2013. "Child Sex Abuse Steps Out of the Shadows in Pakistan." Radio Free Europe Radio Liberty, November 17. http://www.rferl.org/content/pakistan-child-sex-abuse/25170821.html.

Azhar, N. 2011. *Violence against Women in Pakistan: A Qualitative Review of Statistics 2011.* Islamabad: Aurat Foundation.

Basu, A. M. 1989. "Is Discrimination in Food Really Necessary for Explaining Sex Differentials in Childhood Mortality?" *Population Studies: A Journal of Demography* 43 (2): 193–210.

Basu, N. 2013. "Honour Killings: India's Crying Shame." *Aljazeera,* November 28. http://www.aljazeera.com/indepth/opinion/2013/11/honour-killings-india-crying-shame-20131127105910392176.html.

Bates, L. M., S. R. Schuler, F. Islam, and M. K. Islam. 2013. "Socioeconomic Factors and Processes Associated with Domestic Violence in Rural Bangladesh." *International Family Planning Perspectives* 30 (4): 190–99.

Beattie, T. S. H., P. Bhattacharjee, B. M. Ramesh, V. Gurnani, J. Anthony, S. Isac, H. L. Mohan, A. Ramakrishnan, T. Wheeler, J. Bradley, J. F. Blanchard, and S. Moses. 2010. "Violence against Female Sex Workers in Karnataka State, South India: Impact on Health, and Reductions in Violence Following an Intervention Program." *BMC Public Health* 10: 476.

Bedi, A. S., and S. Srinivasan. 2012. "Bare Branches and Drifting Kites: Tackling Female Infanticide and Foeticide in Tamil Nadu, India." In *Development, Freedom and Welfare: Essays Presented to Amartya Sen by Young Scholars*. Oxford: Oxford University Press.

Biswas, S. 2012. "17% of Working Women Report to Have Faced Acts of Sexual Harassment at Work Place: Oxfam Poll." *Economic Times*, November 27. http://articles.economictimes .indiatimes.com/2012-11-27/news/35385887_1_sexual-harassment-women-report-complaint -mechanism.

Black, M., and P. Stalker. 2006. *A Situation Analysis of Children and Women in Bhutan*. Thimpu: UNICEF Bhutan.

Bukhari, S. 2003. "Human Rights for Women in Pakistan Needed." *The Progressive*, December 4. http://progressive.org/media_975.

Catani, C., N. Jacob, E. Schauer, M. Kohila, and F. Neuner. 2007. "Family Violence, War, and Natural Disasters: A Study of the Effect of Extreme Stress on Children's Mental Health in Sri Lanka." *BMC Psychiatry* 8: 33.

Central Bureau of Statistics. 2012. *Nepal Multiple Indicator Cluster Survey 2010, Mid- and Far Western Regions, Final Report*. Kathmandu: Central Bureau of Statistics and UNICEF Nepal.

Chaudhuri, P. 2007. "Experiences of Sexual Harassment of Women Health Workers in Four Hospitals in Kolkata, India." *Reproductive Health Matters* 15 (30): 221–29.

Cheema, I. K. 2011. "Trafficking of Women in South Asia." http://www.academia.edu/2939588 /Dr_Iqtidar_Karamat_Cheema_Trafficking_of_Women_in_South_Asia.

Chen, M., and J. Dreze. 1995. "Recent Research on Widows in India: Workshop and Conference Report." *Economic & Political Weekly* 30 (39): 2435–39.

Chohan, A. 2011. "A Female Baby, a Waste of Space." *Express Tribune* (blogs), December 7. http://blogs.tribune.com.pk/story/9404/a-female-baby-a-waste-of-space.

Coast, E., T. Leone, and A. Malviya. 2012. "Gender-Based Violence and Reproductive Health in Five Indian States." In *Gender-Based Violence and Public Health: International Perspectives on Budgets and Policies*, ed. Keerty Nakray. New York: Routledge.

Commission of Inquiry on Lessons Learned and Reconciliation Commission. 2011. Final Report. Sri Lanka.

Conticini, A., and D. Hulme. 2007. "Escaping Violence, Seeking Freedom: Why Children in Bangladesh Migrate to the Street." *Development and Change* 38 (2): 201–27.

Corsi, D. J., D. G. Bassani, R. Kumar, S. Awasthi, R. Jotkar, N. Kaur, and P. Jha. 2009. "Gender Inequity and Age-Appropriate Immunization Coverage in India from 1992 to 2006." *BMC International Health and Human Rights* 9 (suppl. 1): S3.

Cramer, S. 2007. "Gaaro: Nepali Women Tell Their Stories." Independent Study Project Collection Paper 134, SIT Study Abroad, Brattleboro, VT. http://digitalcollections.sit.edu /isp_collection/134.

CSO (Central Statistics Organisation) and UNICEF. 2012. *Afghanistan Multiple Indicator Cluster Survey 2010–2011: Final Report*. Kabul: CSO and UNICEF.

Dalal, K., S. L. Ming, and M. Gifford. 2012. "Male Adolescents' Attitudes Toward Wife Beating: A Multi-Country Study in South Asia." *Journal of Adolescent Health* 50 (5): 437–42.

Das Gupta, M. 1987. "Selective Discrimination against Female Children in Rural Punjab, India." *Population and Development Review* 13 (1): 77–100.

———. 2005. "Explaining Asia's 'Missing Women': A New Look at the Data." *Population and Development Review* 31 (3): 529–35.

de Benítez, S. T. 2007. *State of the World's Street Children: Violence*. London: Consortium for Street Children.

de Mel, N., P. Peiris, and S. Gomez. 2013. *Broadening Gender: Why Masculinities Matter: Attitudes, Practices, and Gender-Based Violence in Four Districts in Sri Lanka*. Colombo: Care International Sri Lanka.

ECPAT. 2011a. *Status of Action against Commercial Sexual Exploitation of Children—Bangladesh*. 2nd Edition. Bangkok: ECPAT.

———. 2011b. *Status of Action against Commercial Sexual Exploitation of Children—India*. 2nd Edition. Bangkok: ECPAT.

———. 2011c. *Status of Action against Commercial Sexual Exploitation of Children—Nepal*. 2nd Edition. Bangkok: ECPAT.

———. 2011d. *Status of Action against Commercial Sexual Exploitation of Children—Pakistan*. 2nd Edition. Bangkok: ECPAT.

Farouk, S. A. 2005. *Violence against Women: A Statistical Overview, Challenges and Gaps in Data Collection and Methodology and Approaches for Overcoming Them*. New York: UN Wonen, Division for the Advancement of Women.

Fikree, F. F., S. N. Jafarey, R. Korejo, A. Afshan, and J. M. Durocher. 2006. "Intimate Partner Violence Before and During Pregnancy: Experiences of Postpartum Women in Karachi, Pakistan." *Journal of Pakistan Medical Association* 56 (6): 252–57.

Fulu, E. 2007. "Domestic Violence and Women's Health in Maldives." *Regional Health Forum* 11 (2): 25–32.

Fulu, E., X. Warner, S. Miedema, R. Jewkes, T. Roselli, and J. Lang. 2013. *Why Do Some Men Use Violence Against Women and How Can We Prevent It? Quantitative Findings from the United Nations Multi-country Study on Men and Violence in Asia and the Pacific*. Bangkok: UNDP, UNFPA, UN Women, and UN Volunteers.

Garg, M., and N. Singla. 2012. "Rights of Women Prisoners in India: An Evaluation." *International Journal of Advanced Research in Management and Social Sciences* 1 (2): 134–52.

George, A., S. Sabarwal, and P. Martin. 2011. "Violence in Contract Work among Female Sex Workers in Andhra Pradesh, India." *The Journal of Infectious Diseases* 204 (suppl. 5): S1235–40.

GOI (Government of India). 2007. *Study on Child Abuse: India 2007*. India: Ministry of Women and Child Development.

Goonesekere, S. 2006. "The Elimination of all Forms of Discrimination and Violence against the Girl Child." Background paper prepared for United Nations Division for the Advancement of Women in collaboration with the United Nations Children's Fund Expert Group Meeting, Elimination of all Forms of Discrimination and Violence against the Girl Child, Florence, Italy, September 25–28.

Goonesekere, S., and H. Amarasuriya. 2013. *Emerging Concerns and Case Studies on Child Marriage in Sri Lanka*. Sri Lanka: UNICEF.

Government of Sri Lanka. 2011. "Report of the Commission of Inquiry on Lessons Learnt and Reconciliation." Colombo. http://www.priu.gov.lk/news_update/Current_Affairs/ca201112 /FINAL%20LLRC%20REPORT.pdf.

Hamid, S., E. Johansson, and B. Rubenson. 2009. "'Who Am I? Where Am I?' Experiences of Married Young Women in a Slum in Islamabad, Pakistan." *BMC Public Health* 9: 265.

Hancock, P. 2006. "Violence, Women, Work, and Empowerment: Narratives from Factory Women in Sri Lanka's Export Processing Zones." *Gender, Technology and Development* 10 (2): 211–28.

Hawkes, S., M. Collumbien, L. Platt, N. Lalji, N. Rizvi, A. Andreasen, J. Chow, R. Muzaffar, N. Siddiqui, and S. Hasan. 2009. "HIV and Other Sexually Transmitted Infections among Men, Transgenders, and Women Selling Sex in Two Cities in Pakistan: A Cross-Sectional Prevalence Survey." *Sexually Transmitted Infections* 85 (suppl. II): S34–S44.

Hazarika, G. 2000. "Gender Differences in Children's Nutrition and Access to Health Care in Pakistan." *The Journal of Development Studies* 37 (1):73–92.

Heiberg, T., and E. G. Thukral, ed. 2013. *The South Asian Report: On the Child-Friendliness of Governments.* Save the Children, HAQ: Centre for Child Rights, Plan International, Child Rights and You, Terre des Hommes Germany.

Heise, L. L. 2011. *What Works to Prevent Partner Violence? An Evidence Overview.* London: STRIVE.

Hill, K., and D. M. Upchurch. 1995. "Gender Differences in Child Health: Evidence from the Demographic and Health Surveys." *Population and Development Review* 21 (1): 127–51.

Hindin, M. J., S. Kishor, and D. L. Ansara. 2008. *Intimate Partner Violence Among Couples in 10 DHS Countries: Predictors and Health Outcomes.* DHS Analytical Studies 18. Calverton, MD: Macro International.

Huda, S. 2006. "Sex Trafficking in South Asia." *International Journal of Gynaecology and Obstetrics* 94 (3): 374–81.

Human Rights Commission of Pakistan. 2012. *State of Human Rights in 2011.* Lahore: Human Rights Commission of Pakistan.

Human Rights Watch. 2013. *Breaking the Silence: Child Sexual Abuse in India.* Washington, DC: Human Rights Watch.

Hyder, A. A., and F. A. Malik. 2007. "Violence against Children: A Challenge for Public Health in Pakistan." *Journal of Health, Population, and Nutrition* 25 (2): 168–78.

Hyder, A. A., Z. Noor, and E. Tsui. 2007. "Intimate Partner Violence among Afghan Women Living in Refugee Camps in Pakistan." *Social Science & Medicine* 64 (7): 1536–47.

ICRW (International Center for Research on Women). 2000a. *Domestic Violence in India: A Summary Report of a Multi-Site Household Survey.* Washington, DC: ICRW and Center for Development and Population Activities.

———. 2000b. *Domestic Violence in India: Men, Masculinity, and Domestic Violence in India.* Washington, DC: ICRW and Center for Development and Population Activities.

ICRW, UNFPA (United Nations Population Fund), AusAID (Australian Agency for International Development), and AFPPD (Asian Forum of Parliamentarians on Population and Development). 2012. *Child Marriage in Southern Asia: Policy Options for Action.* Washington, DC: ICRW.

ICRW and UNICEF (United Nations Children's Fund). 2011. *Delaying Marriage for Girls in India: A Formative Research to Design Interventions for Changing Norms.* New Delhi: UNICEF.

ILO (International Labour Office). 2004. *Sexual Harassment at the Workplace in Nepal—Series 2.* Kathmandu: ILO.

Iravani, M. R. 2011. "Child Abuse in India." *Asian Social Science* 7 (3): 150–53.

Islam, N. 2012. "Dowry Deaths Plague Rural Bangladesh." *Khabar South Asia*, February 5. http://khabarsouthasia.com/en_GB/articles/apwi/articles/features/2012/02/15/feature-02.

Islam, U. 2013. "Dowry Related Violence: Victims Opting for Out of Court Solutions." *Dhaka Tribune*, September 29. http://www.dhakatribune.com/law-amp-rights/2013/sep/29/dowry -related-violence-victims-opting-out-court-solutions.

Jacoby, H. G., and G. Mansuri. 2010. "Watta Satta: Bride Exchange and Women's Welfare in Rural Pakistan." *American Economic Review* 100 (4): 1804–25.

Jagori and UN Women. 2011. *Safe Cities Free of Violence against Women and Girls Initiative: Report of the Baseline Survey Delhi 2010.* New Delhi: Jagori and UN Women.

Jaising, I. 1995. "Violence against Women: The Indian Perspective," in *Women's Rights, Human Rights: International Feminist Perspectives*, ed. J. S. Peters and A. Wolper, 51–56. New York: Routledge.

Jayasuriya, V., K. Wijewardena, and P. Axemo. 2011. "Intimate Partner Violence against Women in the Capital Province of Sri Lanka: Prevalence, Risk Factors, and Help Seeking." *Violence against Women* 17 (8): 1086–102.

Jejeebhoy, S. J. 1998. "Adolescent Sexual and Reproductive Behavior: A Review of the Evidence from India." *Social Science & Medicine* 46 (10): 1275–90.

Jejeebhoy, S. J., and S. Bott. 2003. "Non-Consensual Sexual Experiences of Young People: A Review of the Evidence from Developing Countries." Working Paper No. 16, Population Council, New Delhi.

Jejeebhoy, S. J., K. G. Santhya, and S. Sabarwal. 2013. *Gender-Based Violence: A Qualitative Exploration of Norms, Experiences, and Positive Deviance.* New Delhi: Population Council.

Jewkes, R., E. Fulu, T. Roselli, and C. Garcia-Moreno. 2013. "Prevalence of and Factors Associated with Non-Partner Rape Perpetration: Findings from the UN Multi-Country Cross-Sectional Study on Men and Violence in Asia and the Pacific." *Lancet Global Health* 1 (4): e208–18.

John, M. E. 2011. "Census 2011: Governing Populations and the Girl Child." *Economic and Political Weekly* 46 (16): 10–12.

Johnson, K. B., and M. Bordia Das. 2008. "Spousal Violence in Bangladesh as Reported by Men: Prevalence and Risk Factors." *Journal of Interpersonal Violence* 24 (6): 977–95.

Jones, G. W. 2010. *Changing Marriage Patterns in Asia.* Singapore: Asia Research Institute, National University of Singapore.

Joshi, S., and J. Kharel. 2008. "Violence against Women in Nepal—An Overview." *The Free Library.* http://www.academia.edu/183952/Violence_against_Women_in_Nepal—An_Overview.

Kabeer, N., S. Huq, and S. Mahmud. 2013. "Diverging Stories of 'Missing Women' in South Asia: Is Son Preference Weakening in Bangladesh?" *Feminist Economics.* doi: 10.1080/13545701.2013.857423.

Kalantry, S., and J. G. Kestenbaum. 2011. "Combatting Acid Violence in Bangladesh, India, and Cambodia." Paper 1, Avon Global Center for Women and Justice and Dorothea S. Clarke Program in Feminist Jurisprudence, Ithaca, NY.

Khosla, A. H., D. Dua, L. Devi and S. S. Sud. 2005. "Domestic Violence in Pregnancy in North Indian Women." *Indian Journal of Medical Sciences* 59 (5): 195–99.

Kiener, R. 2011. "Honor Killings: Can Murders of Women and Girls Be Stopped?" *CQ Global Researcher* 5 (8): 183–208.

Khair, S. 2003. "Institutional Violence against Women: The Saga of Women in Safe Custody." *Asia-Pacific Journal on Human Rights and the Law* 4 (2): 28–51.

Klasen, S., and Wink, C. 2002. "A Turning Point in Gender Bias in Mortality? An Update on the Number of Missing Women." *Population and Development Review* 28 (2): 285–312.

Koenig, M., R. Stephenson, S. Ahmed, S. J. Jejeebhoy, and J. Campbell. 2006. "Individual and Contextual Determinants of Domestic Violence in North India." *American Journal of Public Health* 96 (1): 132–38.

Koenig, M. A., S. Ahmed, M. B. Hossain, and A. B. M. K. A. Mozumder. 2003. "Women's Status and Domestic Violence in Rural Bangladesh: Individual- and Community-Level Effects." *Demography* 40 (2): 269–88.

Koenig, M. A., and S. D'Souza. 1986. "Sex Differences in Childhood Mortality in Rural Bangladesh." *Social Science & Medicine* 22 (1): 15–22.

Krishnan, S., K. Subbiah, S. Khanum, P. S. Chandra, and N. S. Padian. 2012. "An Intergenerational Women's Empowerment Intervention to Mitigate Domestic Violence: Results of a Pilot Study in Bengaluru, India." *Violence against Women* 18 (3): 346–70.

Krug, E. G., L. L. Dahlberg, J. A. Mercy, A. B. Zwi, and R. Lozano, eds. 2002. *World Report on Violence and Health*. Geneva: World Health Organization.

Landinfo. 2011. *Afghanistan: Marriage*. Norway: Landinfo. http://www.landinfo.no/asset/1852 /1/1852_1.pdf.

Lari, M. Z. 2011. *"Honour Killings" in Pakistan and Compliance of Law*. Islamabad: Aurat Foundation.

Maiti-Nepal. 2010. *Youth-Led Study on the Vulnerability of Young Girls Working in Restaurants, Bars and Massage Parlours in Kathmandu*. Kathmandu: Maiti-Nepal, supported by ECPAT International.

Malik, F. 2010. "Determinants of Child Abuse in Pakistani Families: Parental Acceptance-Rejection and Demographic Variables." *International Journal of Business and Social Science* 1 (1): 67–80.

Martin, S. L., K. E. Moracco, J. Garro, A. O. Tsui, L. L. Kupper, J. L. Chase, and J. C. Campbell. 2002. "Domestic Violence across Generations: Findings from Northern India." *International Journal of Epidemiology* 31 (3): 560–72.

Massage, I. 2011. "Acid and Burns Violence in Nepal. A Situational Analysis." Kathmandu: Burns Violence Survivors-Nepal, and London: Acid Survivors Trust International.

Mazurana, D., and K. Carlson. 2006. "The Girl Child and Armed Conflict: Recognizing and Addressing Grave Violations of Girls' Human Rights." Paper prepared for United Nations Division for the Advancement of Women in collaboration with the United Nations Children's Fund Expert Group Meeting, Elimination of all Forms of Discrimination and Violence against the Girl Child, Florence, Italy, September 25–28.

Menski, Werner. 1998. *South Asians and the Dowry Problem*. New Delhi: Vistaar Publications.

Miller, B. D. 1987. "Female Infanticide and Child Neglect in Rural North India." In *Child Survival*, ed. M. Lock and A. Young, 95–112. Dordrecht, Netherlands: D. Reidel Publishing Company.

Million Death Study Collaborators. 2010. "Causes of Neonatal and Child Mortality in India: Nationally Representative Mortality Survey." *Lancet* 376 (9755): 1853–60.

Milner, L. S. 1998. *A Brief History of Infanticide*. Society for the Prevention of Infanticide. http://www.infanticide.org/history.htm.

Mohindra, K. S., S. Haddad, and D. Narayana. 2012. "Debt, Shame, and Survival: Becoming and Living as Widows in Rural Kerala, India." *BMC International Health and Human Rights* 12: 28.

Munsur, A. M., I. Tareque, and K. M. Rahman. 2010. "Determinants of Living Arrangements, Health Status, and Abuse among Elderly Women: A Study of Rural Naogaon District, Bangladesh." *Journal of International Women's Studies* 11 (4): 162–76.

Naeem, F., M. Irfan, Q. A. Zaidi, D. Kingdon, and M. Ayub. 2008. "Angry Wives, Abusive Husbands: Relationship between Domestic Violence and Psychosocial Variables." *Women's Health Issues* 18 (6): 453–62.

Najnin, N., C. M. Bennett, and S. P. Luby. 2011. "Inequalities in Care-Seeking for Febrile Illness of Under-Five Children in Urban Dhaka, Bangladesh." *Journal of Health, Population, and Nutrition* 29 (5): 523–31.

Nanda P., A. Gautam, R. Verma, K. T. Hong, M. Puri, T. G. Linh, J. Tamang, and P. Lamichhane. 2012. *Study on Gender, Masculinity and Son Preference in Nepal and Vietnam*. New Delhi: International Center for Research on Women.

Naripokkho and Bangladesh Mahila Parishad. n.d. "Baseline Report Violence against Women in Bangladesh Naripokkho and Bangladesh Mahila Parishad." Part of a South Asia regional compilation coordinated by International Women's Rights Action Watch Asia Pacific, Kuala Lumpur, Malaysia.

Navaneetham, K., and A. Dharmalingam. 2011. "Demography and Development: Preliminary Interpretations of the 2011 Census." *Economic & Political Weekly* 46 (16): 13.

Naved, R. T. 2003. "A Situational Analysis of Violence against Women in South Asia." *Violence against Women in South Asia - A Regional Analysis*, ed. Asian Forum of Parliamentarians on Population and Development and United Nations Population Fund (UNFPA). Kathmandu: UNFPA.

Naved, R. T., S. Azim, A. Bhuiya, and L. A. Persson. 2006. "Physical Violence by Husbands: Magnitude, Disclosure, and Help-Seeking Behavior of Women in Bangladesh." *Social Science & Medicine* 62 (12): 2917–29.

Naved, R. T, H. Hamidul, S. Farah, and M. Shuvra. 2011. *Men's Attitudes and Practices Regarding Gender and Violence against Women in Bangladesh: Preliminary Findings*. Dhaka: ICDDR,B.

NCRB (National Crime Records Bureau). 2012. *Crime in India 2012: Statistics*. India: National Crime Records Bureau, Ministry of Home Affairs.

Nijhowne, D., and L. Oates. 2008. *Living with Violence: A National Report on Domestic Abuse in Afghanistan*. Washington, DC: Global Rights: Partners for Justice.

NSB (National Statistics Bureau). 2011. *Bhutan Multiple Indicator Survey, 2010*. Thimpu: NSB.

Palo, S. 2009. "Charade of Change: Qisas and Diyat Ordinance Allows Honor Killings to Go Unpunished in Pakistan." *UC Davis Journal of International Law & Policy* 15: 93.

Pande, R. 2003. "Selective Gender Differences in Childhood Nutrition and Immunization in Rural India: The Role of Siblings." *Demography* 40 (3): 395–418.

Pande, R. P., and A. S. Yazbeck. 2003. "What's in a Country Average? Income, Gender, and Regional Inequalities in Immunization in India." *Social Science & Medicine* 57 (11): 2075–88.

Panter-Brick, C., M. Eggerman, V. Gonzalez, and S. Safdar. 2009. "Violence, Suffering, and Mental Health in Afghanistan: A School-Based Survey." *Lancet* 374 (9692): 807–16.

Parvin, K., N. Sultana, and R. T. Naved. 2012. "Spousal Violence against Women and Help Seeking Behaviour." In *Growing Up Safe and Healthy (SAFE): Baseline Report on Sexual and Reproductive Health and Rights and Violence against Women and Girls in Dhaka Slums*, ed. R. T. Naved and S. Amin. Dhaka: ICDDR,B.

Paudel, G. S. 2007. "Domestic Violence against Women in Nepal." *Gender, Technology and Development* 11 (2): 199–233.

Perera, J., N. Gunawardane, and V. Jayasuriya, eds. 2011. *Review of Research Evidence on Gender Based Violence (GBV) in Sri Lanka*. Colombo: Sri Lanka Medical Association.

Perveen, R. 2010a. *Violence against Women in Pakistan A Qualitative Review of Statistics for 2009*. Islamabad: Aurat Foundation.

———. 2010b. *A Tax Break for Economic Freedom? The Case of Divorced Mothers, Divorced, Disabled and Never Married (above 40 years) Pakistani Women: A Civic Entrepreneur's Perspectives*. Islamabad: Economic Freedom Network, Pakistan.

———. 2012. *Beyond Denial: Violence against Women in Pakistan—A Qualitative Review of Reported Incidents January–December 2012*. Islamabad: Aurat Foundation.

Pinheiro, P. S. 2006. *World Report on Violence against Children*. Geneva: United Nations.

Poudel, P., and J. Carryer. 2010. "Girl-Trafficking, HIV/AIDS, and the Position of Women in Nepal." *Gender & Development* 8 (2): 74–79.

Pokhrel, S., and R. Sauerborn. 2004. "Household Decision-Making on Child Health Care in Developing Countries: The Case of Nepal." *Health Policy and Planning* 19 (4): 218–33.

Pradhan, A., P. Poudel, D. Thomas, and S. Barnett. 2011. *A Review of the Evidence: Suicide among Women in Nepal*. London: Options Consultancy Services Ltd., for U.K. Department of International Development and United Nations Population Fund.

Purkayastha, B., M. Subramaniam, M. Desai, and S. Bose. 2003. "The Study of Gender in India A Partial Review." *Gender & Society* 17 (4): 503–24.

Qayyum, K. n.d. Domestic Violence Against Women: Prevalence and Men's Perception in PGRN Districts of Pakistan. Rutgers WPF-Pakistan.

Qazi, Y. S. 2003. "Adolescent Reproductive Health in Pakistan." In *Towards Adulthood: Exploring the Sexual and Reproductive Health of Adolescents in South Asia*, ed. S. Bott, 78–80. Geneva: World Health Organization.

Rabbani, F., F. Qureshi, and N. Rizvi. 2008. "Perspectives on Domestic Violence: Case Study from Karachi, Pakistan." *Eastern Mediterranean Health Journal* 14 (2): 415–26.

Raj, A., C. Gomez, and J. G. Silverman. 2008. "Driven to a Fiery Death: The Tragedy of Self-Immolation in Afghanistan." *New England Journal of Medicine* 358 (21): 2201–03.

Raj, A., N. Saggurti, M. Winter, A. Labonte, M. R. Decker, D. Balaiah, and J. G. Silverman. 2010a. "The Effect of Maternal Child Marriage on Morbidity and Mortality of Children Under 5 in India: Cross Sectional Study of a Nationally Representative Sample." *BMJ* 340:b4258.

Raj, A., N. Saggurti, D. Lawrence, D. Balaiah, and J. G. Silverman. 2010b. "Association between Adolescent Marriage and Marital Violence among Young Adult Women in India." *International Journal of Gynaecology and Obstetrics* 110 (1): 35–39.

Rao, V. 1997. "Wife-Beating in Rural South India: A Qualitative and Econometric Analysis." *Social Science & Medicine* 44 (8): 1169–80.

Rashid, S. F. 2010. "Providing Sex Education to Adolescents in Rural Bangladesh: Experiences from BRAC." *Gender and Development* 8 (2): 28–37.

Ray, P., C. Davey, and P. Nolan. 2011. "Still on the Street—Still Short of Rights: Analysis of Policy and Programmes Related to Street Involved Children." London: Plan and Consortium for Street Children.

Reed, E., J. Gupta, M. Biradavolu, V. Devireddy, and K. M. Blankenship. 2010. "The Context of Economic Insecurity and Its Relation to Violence and Risk Factors for HIV among Female Sex Workers in Andhra Pradesh, India." *Public Health Reports* 125 (suppl. 4): 81–89.

Rekart, M. L. 2005. "Sex-Work Harm Reduction." *Lancet* 366 (9503): 2123–34.

Saeed, S., I. Naseem, D. Moosa, and A. Afaal. 2003. *Reproductive and Sexual Health of Adolescents in the Maldives.* Maldives: Commerce, Development, and Environment Private Limited.

Sahil. 2012. *Cruel Numbers 2011: A Compilation of Statistics on Child Sexual Abuse of Reported Cases in Pakistan.* Islamabad: Sahil.

Sahni, M., N. Verma, D. Narula, R. M. Varghese, V. Sreenivas, and J. M. Puliyel. 2008. "Missing Girls in India: Infanticide, Feticide, and Made-to-Order Pregnancies? Insights from Hospital-based Sex-Ratio-at-Birth Over the Last Century." *PloS One* 3 (5): e2224.

Santhya, K. G., N. Haberland, F. Ram, R. K. Sinha, S. K. Mohanty, and K. G. Santhya. 2007. "Consent and Coercion: Examining Unwanted Sex among Married Young Women in India." *International Family Planning Perspectives* 33 (3): 124–32.

SCF (Save the Children Fund). 2005. *Commercial Sexual Exloitation of Children: A Situation Analysis of Pakistan.* Peshawar: Save the Children Sweden Pakistan Programme.

Schuler, S. R., S. M. Hashemi, A. P. Riley, and S. Akhter. 1996. "Credit Programs, Patriarchy and Men's Violence against Women in Rural Bangladesh." *Social Science & Medicine* 43 (12): 729–42.

Schuler, S. R., and F. Islam. 2008. "Women's Acceptance of Intimate Partner Violence within Marriage in Rural Bangladesh." *Studies in Family Planning* 39 (1): 49–58.

Schuler, S. R., L. M. Bates, and F. Islam. 2008. "Women's Rights, Domestic Violence, and Recourse Seeking in Rural Bangladesh." *Violence against Women* 14 (3): 326–45.

Shaikh, M. 2003. "Is Domestic Violence Endemic in Pakistan: Perspective from Pakistani Wives." *Pakistan Journal of Medical Sciences* 19 (1): 23–28.

Sharma, D. C. 2013. "India Promises to Curb Acid Attacks." *Lancet* 382 (9897): 1013.

Siddiqi, D. M. 2003. "The Sexual Harassment of Industrial Workers: Strategies for Intervention in the Workplace and Beyond." Centre for Policy Dialogue–United Nations Population Fund Paper 26, Centre for Policy Dialogue, Dhaka.

Silverman, J. G., M. R. Decker, D. M. Cheng, K. Wirth, N. Saggurti, H. L. Mccauley, and A. Raj. 2011. "Gender-Based Disparities in Infant and Child Mortality Based on Maternal Exposure to Spousal Violence." *American Medical Association* 165 (1): 22–27.

Silverman, J. G., M. R. Decker, N. A. Kapur, J. Gupta, and A. Raj. 2013. "Violence against Wives, Sexual Risk, and Sexually Transmitted Infection among Bangladeshi Men." *Sexually Transmitted Infections* 83 (3): 211–15.

Singh, A. 2012. "Gender Based within-Household Inequality in Childhood Immunization in India: Changes over Time and across Regions." *PloS One* 7 (4): e35045.

Singh, K., and D. Kapur. 2001. "Law, Violence, and the Girl Child." *Health and Human Rights* 5 (2): 8–29.

Singh, P. K. 2013. "Trends in Child Immunization across Geographical Regions in India: Focus on Urban-Rural and Gender Differentials." *PloS One* 8 (9): e73102.

Slugget, C. 2003. *Mapping of Psychosocial Support for Girls and Boys Affected by Child Sexual Abuse in Four Countries in South and Central Asia*. Dhaka: Save the Children Sweden Denmark, Regional Office for South and Central Asia.

Smith, D. J. 2009. *Decisions, Desires, and Diversity: Marriage Practices in Afghanistan*. Kabul: Afghanistan Research and Evaluation Unit.

Sodhi, G., and M. Verma. 2003. "Sexual Coercion among Unmarried Adolescents of an Urban Slum in India." In *Towards Adulthood: Exploring the Sexual and Reproductive Health of Adolescents in South Asia*, ed. S. Bott, 91–94. Geneva: World Health Organization.

South Asian Association for Regional Cooperation (SAARC). 2006. SAARC Human Rights Report 2006. New Delhi: Asian Centre for Human Rights.

Sridharan, V. 2013. "India to Restrict Sale of Acids to Curb Increasing Attacks on Women." *International Business Times*, July 19. http://au.ibtimes.com/articles/492355/20130719/india -acid-attacks-delhi-compensation-court-rule.htm#.U4tBopRdW2k.

Srinivasan, A. 2011. "Gender Violence as Insecurity: Research Trends in South Asia." New Voices Series No. 9, Global Consortium on Security Transformation, Sri Lanka.

Srinivasan, S. 2005. "Daughters or Dowries? The Changing Nature of Dowry Practices in South India." *World Development* 33 (4): 593–615.

Stoltenborgh, M., M. H. van Ijzendoorn, E. M. Euser, and M. J. Bakermans-Kranenburg. 2011. "A Global Perspective on Child Sexual Abuse: Meta-Analysis of Prevalence Around the World." *Child Maltreatment* 16 (2): 79–101.

Subramanian, P., and S. Sivayogan. 2001. "The Prevalence and Pattern of Wife Beating in the Trincomalee District in Eastern Sri Lanka." *Southeast Asian Journal of Tropical Medicine and Public Health* 32 (1): 186–95.

Suran, L., S. Amin, L. Huq, and K. Chowdury. 2004. "Does Dowry Improve Life for Brides? A Test of the Bequest Theory of Dowry in Rural Bangladesh." Policy Research Division Working Papers No. 195, Population Council, New York.

Taillieu, T. L., and D. A. Brownridge. 2009. "Violence against Pregnant Women: Prevalence, Patterns, Risk Factors, Theories, and Directions for Future Research." *Aggression and Violent Behavior* 15: 14–35.

Terman, R. L. 2010. "To Specify or Single Out: Should We Use the Term 'Honor Killing'?" *Muslim World Journal of Human Rights* 7 (1): Article 2.

Terzieff, J. 2002. "Pakistan's Fiery Shame: Women Die in Stove Deaths." *WeNews: Womensenews. org*, October 24. http://womensenews.org/story/domestic-violence/021027/pakistans-fiery -shame-women-die-stove-deaths#.Ur2EgmRDuQl.

Thakur, M. 2012. *From Exclusion to Empowerment: A Baseline Assessment of the UN Women's Programme for Empowerment of Widows and Their Coalitions*. New Delhi: UN Women.

UNAMA (United Nations Assistance Mission in Afghanistan). 2010. "Harmful Traditional Practices and Implementation of the Law on Elimination of Violence against Women in Afghanistan." Human Rights, UNAMA Kabul, and Office of the United Nations High Commissioner for Human Rights, Geneva.

UNICEF (United Nations Children's Emergency Fund). 2001. *Commercial Sexual Exploitation and Sexual Abuse of Children in South Asia*. Kathmandu: UNICEF Regional Office for South Asia.

———. 2005. "Regional Study on Violence against Children in South Asia." Report of the Regional Consultation on Violence against Children in South Asia, Islamabad, Pakistan, May 19–21.

————. 2008. "Double Victims: The Treatment of Child Abuse and Exploitation in the Justice System." Justice for Children in Afghanistan Series, Issue 2, UNICEF Afghanistan, Kabul.

United Nations. 2001. "Widowhood: Invisible Women, Secluded or Excluded." *Women 2000*: 2–19.

————. 2006. "United Nations In-Depth Study on All Forms of Violence against Women." Report of the Secretary-General, A/61/122/Add.1, para. 78.

————. 2007. *Afghanistan: Female Prisoners and Their Social Reintegration*. Vienna: United Nations Office on Drugs and Crime.

————. 2012. *Global Report on Trafficking in Persons 2012*. Vienna: United Nations Office on Drugs and Crime.

UN Women. 2013. "Like A Bird With Broken Wings": Afghan Women Oral History, 1978–2008. Kabul: UN Women Afghanistan Country Office.

United States Department of State. 2012. *Trafficking in Persons Report 2012*. Washington, DC: Department of State.

————. 2013. *Trafficking in Persons Report 2013*. Washington, DC: Department of State.

Van Parys, A., A. Verhamme, M. Temmerman, and H. Verstraelen. 2014. "Intimate Partner Violence and Pregnancy: A Systematic Review of Interventions." *PLoS ONE* 9(1): e85084. doi:10.1371/journal.pone.0085084.

Varma, D., P. S. Chandra, and T. Thomas. 2007. "Intimate Partner Violence and Sexual Coercion among Pregnant Women in India: Relationship with Depression and Post-Traumatic Stress Disorder." *Journal of Affective Disorders* 102(1–3): 227–235.

Vella, S. 2004. "Sexual Discrimination in South India." *International Institute for Asian Studies Newsletter* (33): 16.

Virtue Foundation. 2011. *Combating Acid Violence in Bangladesh, Cambodia and India*. A report by Avon Global Center for Women and Justice at Cornell Law School, the Committee on International Human Rights of the New York City Bar Association, the Cornell Law School International Human Rights Clinic, and the Virtue Foundation. http://www.acidviolence.org/uploads/files/Virtue_Foundation_Combating-Acid-Violence-Report-2011.pdf.

Welchman, L., and S. Hossain. 2005. "Introduction: 'Honour,' Rights and Wrongs." In *Honour: Crimes, Paradigms, and Violence against Women*, ed. S. Hossain and L. Welchman. New York: Palgrave Macmillan.

WHO (World Health Organization), Department of Reproductive Health and Research, London School of Hygiene and Tropical Medicine, South African Medical Research Council. 2013. *Global and Regional Estimates of Violence against Women: Prevalence and Health Effects of Intimate Partner Violence and Non-Partner Sexual Violence*. Geneva: World Health Organization.

WPD (Widows for Peace through Democracy). 2011. *Dossier on Widowhood: Issues of Discrimination for the Attention of CEDAW*. London: Widows for Peace through Democracy.

Yardley, J. 2010. "In India, Castes, Honor and Killings Intertwine." *New York Times*, July 9. http://www.nytimes.com/2010/07/10/world/asia/10honor.html?pagewanted=all.

Yount, K. 2014. "Worldwide Prevalence of Non-Partner Sexual Violence." *Lancet* 6736 (13): 12–13.

Yount, K. M., K. Vanderende, S. Zureick-Brown, T. H. Minh, S. R. Schuler, and H. T. Anh. 2013. "Measuring Attitudes about Women's Recourse after Exposure to Intimate Partner Violence: The ATT-RECOURSE Scale." *Journal of Interpersonal Violence* 28 (18): 3369–417.

CHAPTER 3

What Underlies Violence against Women and Girls in South Asia?

I n seeking to address the phenomenon of violence against women and girls in South
Asia, we explore not only the more quantifiable factors that contribute to the incidence and prevalence of such acts, but also the features of the spaces women inhabit.
Accordingly, this chapter is organized in two parts. The first part summarizes the macro
economic and demographic changes, social norms, and legal and institutional structures that provide the context within which the risk and protective factors that influence
violence are situated. The second part of this chapter then analyzes research findings on
specific risk and protective factors at the four levels of the social ecology—individual,
household, systems, and norms—for each type of violence against women and girls.
Types of violence are organized in the order of their occurrence at successive stages of
the life cycle.

Socioeconomic and Demographic Changes

South Asian countries have seen marked developmental and demographic shifts over
the past two decades. Economic reforms of the 1990s brought impressive growth to the
region, with most countries averaging more than 5 percent GDP growth for consecutive
years before and after the turn of the century (Devarajan and Nabi 2006). Although this
growth arguably has exacerbated income inequalities in the region, it also has substan-
tially reduced poverty in most countries, with poverty rates between 1990 and 2000
falling by as much as 9, 10, and 11 percentage points in Bangladesh, India and Nepal,
respectively (Deverajan and Nabi 2006). Although growth has slowed in the past two
years, between 2002 and 2012, GDP per capita rose by at least 28 percent for all eight
South Asian countries and as much as 84 percent for Bhutan and India (figure 3.1).

Economic growth has coincided with a number of changes in human development outcomes (country gender profiles in appendix P present these and several gender indicators for each of the South Asian countries). Among them is fertility. Total fertility rates have declined across South Asia in the last 20 years. They have dropped sharply— by at least half—in all countries except India and Sri Lanka, which in 1990 already had relatively low rates of 3.8 and 2.5 births per woman, respectively (figure 3.2). Fertility rates have decreased for adolescent girls in South Asia as well, from 77 births per 1,000 women age 15–19 in 2001 to 42 births per 1,000 women in 2011.[1]

With fewer children, women spend fewer of their reproductive and productive years on child-rearing and thus theoretically should have more time to explore opportunities outside the domestic sphere, such as in education and employment (Pande et al. 2012). Indeed, girls' enrollment in secondary education has increased in all countries across the region since the 1990s (table 3.1).

Girls' educational attainment at the secondary level has improved not only in absolute terms, but in relation to boys' secondary educational attainment as well. Bangladesh in particular has shown dramatic increases in the ratio of female-to-male enrollment, and the gender gap also has reversed in Nepal and Bhutan (table 3.2).

FIGURE 3.1 GDP per Capita, 2002 and 2012: South Asian Countries

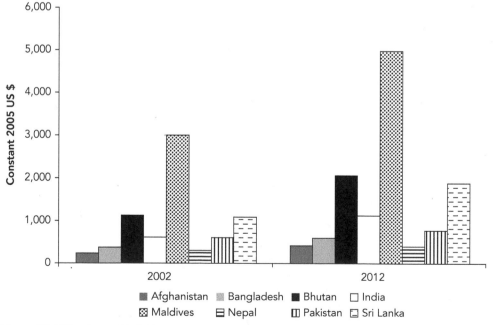

Source: World Development Indicators.

FIGURE 3.2 Total Fertility Rate in South Asian Countries, 1990–2010

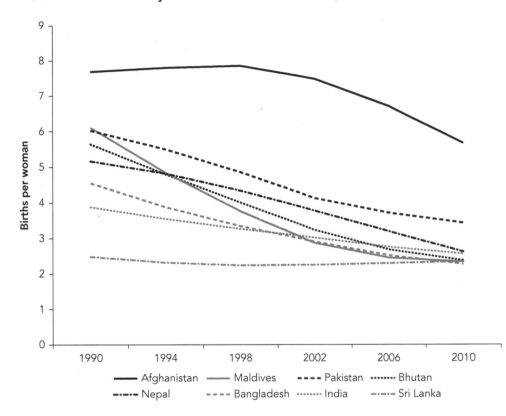

Source: World Development Indicators.

TABLE 3.1 Female Secondary School Enrollment, 1990–2012

Country	% Gross (Year)	
Afghanistan	10.9 (1991)	36.5 (2011)
Bangladesh	13.6 (1990)	54.5 (2011)
Bhutan	20.7 (1998)	76.1 (2012)
India	34.6 (1993)	66.3 (2011)
Maldives	54.7 (1994)	76.7 (2004)
Nepal	20.5 (1990)	67.1 (2012)
Pakistan	12.3 (1990)	30.9 (2012)
Sri Lanka	74.8 (1990)	100.7 (2011)

Source: World Development Indicators.

TABLE 3.2 Ratio of Female-to-Male Secondary Enrollment, 1990–2013

Country	% (Year)	
Bangladesh	51 (1990)	115.4 (2011)
Maldives	103.5 (1994)	112.8 (2004)
Sri Lanka	108.1 (1990)	106.1 (2012)
Bhutan	75.6 (1998)	105.8 (2012)
Nepal	42.6 (1990)	105.2 (2013)
India	62.5 (1993)	94 (2011)
Pakistan	41.6 (1990)	73.5 (2012)
Afghanistan	51.4 (1991)	55.3 (2012)

Source: World Development Indicators.

Despite low rates compared to most other regions, female labor force participation rates have increased overall in South Asia, although patterns vary by country (figure 3.3). Women are working outside the home at higher rates, possibly due to jobs in the garment industry, information technology, and other sectors that are nourished by globalization.

Women have become more empowered in the public sphere through increased political participation as well, although the level of political participation varies by country. A common measure of this participation is the share of female members in higher-level government bodies. Although gender gaps remain large, there is at least some presence of women in parliament in all South Asian countries (table 3.3).

Research suggests, however, that significant gains in life chances, empowerment, and opportunities for women and girls occur with women's increased involvement in local governance structures, rather than at higher levels of government (ICRW and UN Women 2012). There is considerable variation across countries in women's access to participation in lower levels of government. Their participation is low in Sri Lanka, possibly because of women's time constraints and the gendered nature of male leadership (ADB 2008). In contrast, both Pakistan and India have made significant strides in women's political representation by instituting reservation quotas for their participation at lower levels of government. In Pakistan, in addition to women's direct election, the Local Government Ordinance of 2001 reserves 33 percent of seats for women at the local government level, while the 2002 Legal Framework Order also reserves 17 percent of seats in national and provincial assemblies for women (ADB 2000). In India, amendments to the Constitution established a third tier of governance: Panchayati Raj Institutions (PRIs)—or Village Councils—and urban local bodies of governance that are authorized to address local economic development and social justice. Since 2009, 50 percent of seats in these PRIs have been reserved for women.

FIGURE 3.3 Female Labor Force Participation in South Asian Countries, 1990–2010

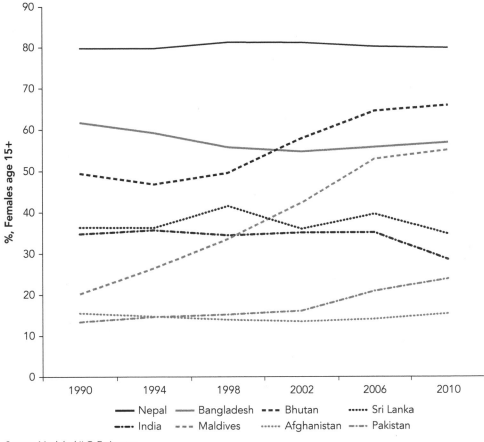

Source: Modeled ILO Estimates.

TABLE 3.3 Percentage of Women in Parliament, South Asia, 2012

Country and higher government body	% women
Afghanistan: *Wolesi Jirga*, lower house of parliament	27.6
Bangladesh	19.7
Bhutan	13.9
India	10.9
Maldives	6.5
Nepal	33.2
Pakistan	12.3
Sri Lanka	5.8

Source: UNDP 2013.

Government, Religious Institutions, and Legal Systems

Governments in South Asia can be instrumental in how violence against women is addressed. Governments influence the context underlying violence against women in that they can implement policies that improve women's access to general health care and law enforcement, and strengthen support services for those who experience violence. According to some research from the region, however, many government services provided to women may reflect a patriarchal gender bias (e.g., Amnesty International 1999; Faizal and Rajagopalan 2005; Choudhury 2007). Regardless, the vast effects of state intervention require further assessment.

Religious institutions play a significant and complex role in the lives of women. They interact dynamically with political, judicial, and other institutions, often reinforcing or upholding unequal gender relations (Kapur 2013). Religious institutions inherently affect day-to-day understanding of gender relations, and religious leaders are integral in shaping beliefs, preferences, and ideologies of community members. The role of religion in shaping women's lives is pronounced in South Asia because of its influence on legal systems and political movements.

All eight countries in the region possess state-sanctioned laws that have codified preexisting frameworks of religious legalism or morality to a greater or lesser degree. Legal reforms that must be compatible with preexisting religious frameworks have the potential to serve as barriers to enhancing the rights of women and girls and impede development of sufficient legal protections against violence (Choudhury 2007). The rise of religious fundamentalism in South Asian politics and society also can influence the rights and protections granted to women by transforming the understanding of rape and violence against women, as well as of gender and sexuality (Kapur 2013).

UNDERPINNINGS OF LEGAL FRAMEWORKS IN SOUTH ASIAN COUNTRIES

Law and the bodies that enforce it—including courts and police departments—are critical to the context underlying violence against women and girls in South Asia. Laws can challenge gender-biased social norms, particularly those rooted in informal and formal institutions. When improperly designed, however, they may uphold or reinforce inequalities. Likewise, the extent to which such laws are enforced at all levels—community, municipal, provincial, and state—may challenge biased gender norms or allow deplorable acts of violence against women to go unpunished. The legal mechanisms of the eight countries in South Asia certainly reflect the region's diversity. Each country has a unique history, shaped by both internal and external sources. Nevertheless, there are many commonalities. The legal systems in many of the countries use structures developed during the colonial period. They contend with significant barriers to reform as well as structural deficiencies that inhibit women's access to justice.

Collectively, the British, Dutch, French, and Portuguese engaged in colonial activity throughout South Asia from the 15th century onward. During this era, colonial governance held jurisdiction over legal matters. A tension existed between the colonizers and the colonized regarding the control and legal regulation of public and private spaces. Colonial legislation largely governed public spaces, whereas indigenous laws that were maintained or codified by colonial institutions governed private spaces. For instance, the British attempt to raise the age of marriage through the Age of Consent Act (1891) in India met with significant opposition from local populations and was viewed as an incursion on the private space of the household (Sarkar 1993). Today, this theme continues to resonate throughout the region and may limit the enactment of more progressive measures to ensure women's rights (Kapur 2013).

As a result of colonial intervention, Bangladesh, India, Pakistan, and Sri Lanka directly inherited codified systems of personal law, which afford varying rights to women based on religious or ethnic identity (Panditaratne 2008). In Bangladesh, a person is afforded different rights and privileges under law depending on religious affiliation (Hindu, Christian, or Muslim); for instance, Hindus and Buddhists have no legal provision for divorce by mutual consent or contest (BLAST 2009). Although the initial implementation of personal laws may correspond with the theme of the public-private divide in South Asia, the continued presence of such legal systems is problematic in that there is a visible imbalance with regard to the number of reforms implemented to personal law for majority groups (that is, Muslim personal law in Bangladesh and Pakistan; Hindu personal law in India) and personal law for minority communities (that is, Hindu and Christian personal law in Bangladesh and Pakistan; Muslim personal law in India). History has witnessed distinct resistance to abolition of personal law in South Asia, as exemplified by opposition to the adoption of a uniform civil code in India (Guha 2007).

BARRIERS TO REFORM: WOMEN AND GIRLS AS VICTIMS, NOT EQUAL CITIZENS

The principle that women and girls are first and foremost citizens—individuals who should be accorded the same rights and privileges as men and boys—stands in direct contrast to the traditional understanding, still pervasive across South Asian societies, of women and girls identified strictly by their relationships to men and boys. Women are the mothers, daughters, sisters, and wives of male family members, who are supposed to monitor and maintain control over female sexuality and ensure female conformity to rigid gender roles that have been determined by traditional norms (Kapur 2013). This perception of women as victims or subjects—rather than as individuals with rights to their own identities, sexualities, and other forms of self-expression—has circumscribed the social and legal provisions for women's safety. Only girls and women who fulfill their roles and duties in the private space of the household have the right to protection from violence in the public space (box 3.1). As the rest of this report illustrates, however, efforts to prevent or respond to violence are most effective when they overcome the perception of women and girls as victims and engage them as active participants with equal rights.

BOX 3.1 Equal Rights versus Protection of Victims: Women and the Private and Public Divide

Throughout the 20th century in South Asia, laws that guarantee equality between the sexes have been passed in the public spheres of politics, education, employment, and select aspects of family law, but discourse on equality has had little impact on the domestic or private sphere, where personal laws as well as the belief in a man's unconditional access to his wife continue to be justified and reinforced.

> The private space is thus both a space of cultural production as well as reinscription of sexual norms that are consistent with women's sexual purity and honour. For example, in the contemporary period, the legal regulation of rape is concerned only with sex within the public realm, that is, with rape that occurs outside of the realm of the family, quite specifically the marital relationship. And even when the rape has occurred in the public sphere, the legal regulation is shaped by whether women's sexuality is of a public or private nature. Where woman's sexuality is considered private, guarded within the confines of the family … as a virgin daughter or a loyal wife, the criminal law may protect her. So long as she adheres to dominant sexual ideology and cultural norms, she receives protection. But when she deviates from these sexual norms and cultural values, by having consensual sex outside of marriage, same sex relations, or commercial sex, the law considers her sexuality to have become public, to have transgressed cultural norms, and thus, not within the purview of the protection of the criminal law. Public sexuality is conflated with being western, contaminating, and corrupting.[a]

Source: Kapur 2013.
a. This quote is from Kapur 2013, 10.

DEVELOPMENT AND CURRENT STATUS OF LAWS RELATED TO GENDER AND VIOLENCE

In recent years, all of the countries in South Asia have made notable progress toward developing laws against violence faced by women and girls. All eight countries also have specific constitutional provisions addressing gender equality. Similarly, all have signed the Convention on the Elimination of All Forms of Discrimination Against Women (CEDAW), although several maintain reservations and declarations regarding certain provisions of the convention.[2]

There are a number of common elements and some variation in laws related to violence across South Asian countries (table 3.4). For example, female infanticide is prohibited in all the countries because penal codes and other legislation typically criminalize such acts as murder. Each country also contains protections against child abuse in its penal, civil, or criminal codes against acts of sexual violence, and human trafficking laws often include provisions to specifically address the needs of children. Likewise, all countries possess anti-trafficking laws that protect women (see appendix Q for specific names and dates of the laws related to particular types of violence against women for each country in South Asia).

In the past decade, South Asia has witnessed a plethora of important legislation that is focused on the private sphere and aimed at mitigating intimate partner violence.

TABLE 3.4 Availability of State-Sanctioned Legal Protections across South Asian Countries, by Type of Violence

	Afghanistan	Bangladesh	Bhutan	India	Maldives	Nepal	Pakistan	Sri Lanka
Female infanticide	✓	✓	✓	✓	✓	✓	✓	✓
Excess female child mortality	–	–	–	–	–	–	–	–
Child abuse	✓	✓	✓	✓	✓	✓	✓	✓
Child marriage	✓	✓	✓	✓	✓	✓	✓	✓
Trafficking	✓	✓	✓	✓	✓	✓	✓	✓
Honor crimes	–	–	–	–	–	–	✓	–
Non-partner sexual violence	✓	✓	✓	✓	✓	✓	✓	✓
Sexual harassment	–	✓	✓	–	–	✓	✓	✓
Custodial violence	–	✓	–	✓	–	–	–	✓
Intimate partner violence	✓	✓	✓	✓	✓	✓	✓	✓
Maltreatment of widows/divorced	✓	✓	✓	✓	✓	✓	✓	✓
Elderly abuse	–	–	–	✓	–	✓	–	✓

Aside from Pakistan, which has ratified domestic violence legislation only for the Sindh and Balochistan provinces, each country has specific measures that define and address such violence. Such legislation signals a gradual shift toward a broader understanding of intimate partner violence that is wholly inclusive of physical, emotional, and even economic violence.

Most countries also include specific legislation intended to protect divorced and widowed women against maltreatment. These laws exist primarily in the area of family law, where a number of specific acts (often falling under the purview of personal laws) regulate matters of separation and child custody. Recent reforms to family and inheritance laws include the Divorce Amendment Act (2001) in India, which removes some discriminatory provisions that made it difficult for Christian women to obtain a divorce. On the other hand, only India, Nepal, and Sri Lanka maintain specific provisions against elderly abuse. A notable example is India's Maintenance and Welfare of Parents and Senior Citizens Act (2007), which enables individuals to reclaim gifted property and request maintenance from children or other relatives who are able to inherit property from them.

These are all significant strides in the right direction. Still, several problems remain. First, important pieces of legislation are on the horizon but face various obstacles to ratification. For instance, as a result of the 18th amendment to the Constitution of Pakistan, legislation in a number of areas, including those regarding issues faced by women, has been delegated to provinces. In some areas, there has been opposition to provincial-level domestic violence bills, such as in Khyber Pakhtunkhwa, where such legislation is considered by some to be an intrusion upon the privacy of the home.[3] In Maldives, a bill that aims to at least partially criminalize marital rape has been returned to parliament because it was deemed incompatible with Islamic teachings.[4]

Second, although each country has constitutional clauses that prescribe gender equality for all citizens, legal provisions that explicitly discriminate against women remain prevalent across the region. The Shiite Personal Status Law (2009) in Afghanistan enables husbands to end financial support to wives who do not fulfill "sexual duties" (ICG 2013). Such legislation contradicts national constitutions and requires immediate and comprehensive reform. Moreover, contemporary legislation on rape is often centered on public acts of sexual violence and ignores acts occurring in the privacy of the home (Kapur 2013). Currently, marital rape is not criminalized in Afghanistan, Bangladesh, India, Maldives, Pakistan, or Sri Lanka.

The design of many laws in South Asia pertaining to violence against women and girls remains inextricably linked to the regulation of sexuality (Kapur 2013). Such regulation extends itself to another category of laws that are harmful to women—namely, those regarding *zina*, or extramarital sexual relations. Legal punishments for *zina* exist in Afghanistan, Maldives and Pakistan (Alder and Polk 2004; UNODC 2007; Cheema and Mustafa 2009). Although recent reforms in Pakistan have removed many harmful legal provisions pertaining to zina, conviction may carry a prison term in Afghanistan and result in public lashings in Maldives (Alder and Polk 2004; UNODC 2007; Butt and Zia 2012).

Further reform of gender-based restrictions on women's legal capacity and property rights is needed. Inheritance laws in Maldives and Pakistan still prevent women from

FIGURE 3.4 Evolution of Restrictions over Time in 100 Economies, 1960–2010

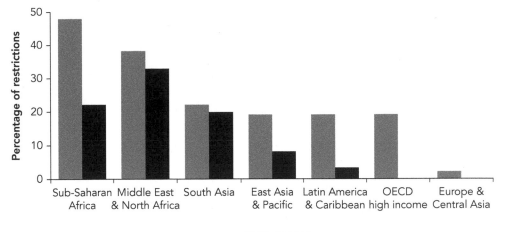

Source: Replicated from World Bank 2013. Original data from 50 Years of Women's Legal Rights database, Hallward-Driemeier, Hasan and Rusu forthcoming.
Note: OECD = Organisation for Economic Co-operation and Development.

acquiring shares equal to those of male heirs. As shown in figure 3.4, between 1960 and 2010, the percentage of restrictions on women's legal capacity and property rights has declined the least in South Asia. Such restrictions have adverse impacts on women's potential to attain economic and other forms of empowerment, including freedom from gender-based violence (see appendix R for more detailed summaries of country legal frameworks as they pertain to gender equality).

IMPLEMENTATION OF LAWS AND POLICIES

As illustrated in the last section, laws exist for most forms of violence described in this report. However, a number of structural deficiencies in these laws and related policies weaken South Asian women's access to state justice mechanisms. Across the region, courts contend with a severe backlog of cases, and the time required to bring a case to court and produce a resolution or outcome is often extremely long, thereby discouraging women from seeking justice through formal mechanisms. In Pakistan, lack of personnel, facilities, and access to necessary legal materials are contributing factors (Khan 2001). Generally low rates of female participation in justice mechanisms and processes—ranging from women's inability to stand before courts to their minimal presence as lawyers, judges, and other judiciary personnel—also contribute to poor outcomes for women in the courtroom.

Further exacerbating these issues is a general lack of legal awareness. A recent World Bank report, conducted across 20 countries (including Afghanistan, Bhutan, and India), did not find either men or women to be "really well-informed of their rights, entitlements, or obligations with respect to key laws intended to promote gender equality" (World Bank 2013, 151). To some extent, a lack of awareness may be attributed to illiteracy, particularly among women, as well as poor public outreach and dissemination of laws. A deficit of familiarity with laws is even more problematic when it exists among those officials who are tasked with upholding them. For instance, in Afghanistan, officials who were not familiar with the protections provided for women under the Elimination of Violence Against Women law were observed to not prosecute individuals who committed actions that the law qualified as offenses (UNAMA 2012).

POOR INSTITUTIONAL DEVELOPMENT IN OTHER REALMS

Often in South Asia, government institutions are stronger and more established in urban areas. In rural areas, where federal governments often have a minimal footprint because of geography, limited infrastructure, or other reasons, a vacuum exists that encourages the development of parallel systems of law and governance. Such systems are found in parts of Pakistan and in Afghanistan, where tribal and customary systems of law and governance predominate, and in rural areas of northern India, where *khap* and *jati panchayats*[5] control many facets of community life. Parallel legal mechanisms—as found in Afghanistan, Bangladesh, India, Nepal (for details on Nepal, see appendix R), and Pakistan—may cost less and be more accessible, but they may not ensure justice for women. For instance, the *shalish*[6] in Bangladesh are often composed of male elders and lack codified standards, hence providing little assurance of gender equality (HRW 2012).

Where formal police departments and other support services for survivors of violence are available, women must often work with professionals and institutions that lack proper training to provide appropriate levels of care and support. Police officials, who are the initial enforcers of law, often lack gender sensitivity. In Sri Lanka, officials commonly record incidents of intimate partner violence improperly as "accidents," rather than categorizing them as punishable offenses (Wijayatilake and Guneratne 2002). In Pakistan, police often do not treat honor killings with appropriate seriousness and may improperly record them (Lari 2011). Part of the reason for this poor institutional development is that police departments and other support services in South Asia typically face a dearth of material resources needed to adequately serve those facing violence (ADB 2008; Asia Foundation et al. 2010).

SPECIAL CONCERNS IN SITUATIONS OF CONFLICT OR OTHER INSTABILITY

Necessary resources tend to become even more scarce—and risks of violence more pronounced—when institutions and systems are in flux or upheaval. Whether caused by full-blown armed conflict or political fragility, deteriorating security and rule of law create conditions that are conducive to abuse of girls and women. Within the context of war and conflict, a woman's role as bearer of family and community honor is increasingly magnified and complex, adding incentive for combatants to commit acts of violence against women from the opposing community or nation. Widespread sexual and physical violence against women reportedly has occurred during recent conflicts in Afghanistan and Pakistan, the 1971 War of Independence in Bangladesh, and the Sri Lankan Civil War (1983–2009). According to literature from the region, the increasing fragility of Afghanistan and Pakistan enables circumvention of laws against trafficking, honor killing, and sexual harassment, including rape by armed groups (UNODC 2007; Khowaja et al. 2012). Trafficking of women and children remains elevated in both countries, where non-state militant groups kidnap children or trick parents into giving them away under false pretenses and subject them to physical, sexual, and psychological abuse, even forcing them to fight, spy, or die as suicide bombers. Afghan refugees are especially vulnerable (Huda 2006).

Custodial violence against women also thrives when laws and security are undermined by war or other destabilizing circumstances. Most women in custody in conflict areas are detained for ordinary crimes; very few female combatants are held as prisoners of war because women are still in the minority in armed forces and are less likely to be captured in frontline areas (Ashdown and James 2010). Nonetheless, by simply living in occupied areas (particularly conflict zones), women can be regarded as under custody by the armed forces and are at higher risk of abuse (ACHR 2007). The Report of the Commission of Inquiry on Lessons Learnt and Reconciliation and other sources cite numerous alleged cases of armed personnel raping and torturing women and girls in the 1990s and later years of the conflict in Sri Lanka, and on occasion even abducting them (SAARC 2006; Government of Sri Lanka 2011).

Social Norms and Gender Relations

Scholars, development specialists, and other regional experts commonly note that gender relations in South Asia are typified by patriarchy. Here we refer to Deniz Kandiyoti's (1998, 278) definition of *classic patriarchy*, under which "girls are given away in marriage at a very young age into households headed by their husband's father. There, they are subordinate not only to all the men but also to the more senior women, especially their mother-in-law. The extent to which this represents a total break with their own kin group varies in relation to the degree of endogamy in marriage practices and different conceptions of honor." Classic patriarchy gives rise to a system in which men not only possess superiority to women in most aspects of life, but also maintain control over women across the life cycle: women are first subordinate to men as daughters and later, after marrying, as wives or daughters-in-law. Some scholars argue that this subordination enables the perception that women and girls are commodities that can be sold, bought, or exchanged by men—and are thus completely deprived of the dignity and rights enjoyed by men (see, for example, Kirti et al. 2011). Patriarchal systems provide men and boys with incentives to devalue women and girls. In South Asia, family systems and societies that designate men as providers for women and enforcers of women's obedience also tend to reward women for compliance (Kandiyoti 1998). Hence, women may condone and perpetuate violence against younger women in some countries (Yount et al. 2011).

Patriarchy shapes gender relations in myriad ways, ranging from defining acceptable roles and duties for women to prescribing the protections afforded them by law. Despite the vast levels of ethnic, cultural, linguistic, religious, and other forms of diversity in the region, rigid patriarchy tends to manifest across most countries in the region through a range of prominent social norms—albeit with some variation, such as Bhutan's matrilineal inheritance system and the loosening of some of these norms in southern India. We describe these norms in general terms that apply to the region as a whole. Variations at the country or sub-country level are captured—to the extent possible—in discussions of risk and protective factors for specific types of violence against women and girls by life cycle stage.

SON PREFERENCE, MALE PREFERENCE, AND FEMALE ROLES

Benazir Bhutto, the 11th prime minister of Pakistan, once stated, "My mother says nobody came to see her for three days in the hospital when I was born because they were all in mourning, because a girl had been born. I remember once she had mentioned to me that even the dogs were giving birth to boys and even the cats were giving birth to boys" (Baughman and O'Hara 2010).

This quote highlights the long-standing preference in South Asia for sons. The effects of this preference include the phenomena of sex-selective abortions (leading to skewed gender ratios); higher rates of malnutrition, illness, and death among girls described in chapter 2; and lower rates of girls' education (Self and Grabowski 2012).

Son preference is shaped primarily by the existence of a "clan" as the basis of social organization, with strict exogamy in marriage such that the men of a clan can only marry women from outside the clan. Thus, lineage and "belonging" to a clan is essential for the social order. Lineage passes only through males; females shift from their father's to their husband's lineage when they move from their parents' home into their husband's home. Women also may not be allowed to inherit land, a key clan asset. As Das Gupta et al. (2003) describe, "[m]en are the fixed points in this social order, and women are the moving points..." and are valued primarily as "...the means whereby men reproduce themselves" (161; see also Srinivas 1984). Adult women also have value in their marital households for their productive potential as sources of labor. However, because of the rigidity of the marital norms defining exogamy in this social system, girl children do not have value to the household into which they are born—their natal household has to bring them up, spend money getting them married (especially through the common practice of dowry, whereby parental property is transferred to the new family of the bride), and thereafter has practically no contact with them. Das Gupta et al. (2003) point to this complete lack of any perceived value to a household of a daughter as the key motivation for a strong preference for sons, aversion to daughters, and resultant systematic and pervasive discrimination against daughters unto death.

UNDERSTANDINGS OF MASCULINITY, FEMININITY, HONOR, AND SEXUALITY

Linked to son preference, female and male roles, social dynamics, and the comprehensive regulation of sexuality and honor contribute to constructions of what is considered masculine and feminine in South Asia. Both women and men are prescribed numerous attributes that are tied directly to feminine and masculine social identities. Accepted differences between men and women are enforced not only by men (in both public and private spaces) but also by women, who as mothers and mothers-in-law "update the norms of acceptable and unacceptable behavior towards women" (Faizal and Rajagopalan 2005, 44). Purportedly, a cycle of gender-based violence results.

Throughout much of the region, women have historically served as caretakers of progeny and household, thus fulfilling the roles of daughter, wife, and mother. They are often expected not to actively express their sexuality and to be sexually passive. These roles assist in controlling and disciplining women's sexuality; additionally, throughout all communities and classes in the region, women are expected to observe certain modesty norms (Jayawardena and De Alwis 1996). A range of expectations is imposed on young women in particular, such as immediately following marriage. Young women must bear children and are discouraged from expressing independent desires or goals or making decisions (Stark 1993; Schuler et al. 1996).

Similarly, men encounter a construction of what is masculine in South Asia. Studies draw connections between violence against women and the fulfillment of masculinities, such as providing for the family, appearing strong, and maintaining control (Moore 1994; Nanda et al. 2013). A connection has also been established between the expression of masculinity and the control of women within the family—namely, with regard to ensuring fulfillment of expected roles (ICRW 2002).

Norms of femininity and masculinity may be reinforced through various venues, including popular media, the state, and religious institutions (Banerjee 2005). In particular, the media are thought to reinforce ideas of acceptable social behaviors by men and women. For instance, in the widely distributed Hindi and Tamil films from India, male protagonists often court women through harassment, subsequently followed by more aggressive acts, such as grabbing and kissing them (Faizal and Rajagopalan 2005).

In both public and private spaces, men are charged with regulating women's sexuality to uphold familial or community honor, which is deeply interconnected with understandings of masculinity and femininity. Known as *izzat* in India and Pakistan, honor is maintained by adhering to certain accepted sociocultural norms. Transgressing these norms not only is detrimental to the reputation of an individual in most South Asian societies but, particularly with regard to the behavior of women, tarnishes the reputation of the individual's family and possibly her community.

Although honor is typically associated with women in South Asia, there is also a pervasive understanding of a man's personal honor, which is closely tied to a woman's sexual behavior and even public presence (Mandelbaum 1988). Hence, men regulate the mobility of women through various means, including *purdah* (seclusion or conservative dress), sex segregation, and violence (ADB 2000). The phenomenon of honor crime is a means of upholding male honor. For such crimes, "the publicly articulated 'justification' is attributed to a social order claimed to require the preservation of a concept of 'honour' vested in male (family and/or conjugal) control over women and specifically women's sexual conduct, actual, suspected or potential" (Welchman and Hossain 2005, 4).

The pervasive desire for families to preserve their daughters' honor has adverse implications for girls' and women's access to education and employment. For example, in rural Nepal, parents may prevent their daughters from attending distant schools for fear of harassment and other threats to their sexual purity (Mathur et al. 2001). We turn now to a discussion of how, according to literature from the region, these social norms manifest as risk factors for violence against girls and women across the life cycle and at different levels of the social ecology: individual, household, systems, and norms.

Risk Factors for Violence against Girls and Adolescents in the Ecological Framework

Heise (1998, 265) notes in her elaboration of the ecological model for violence against women that the framework includes "only those factors shown empirically to be related to differential rates of violence against women and girls." However, the literature analyzing potential risk factors or causes of violence against girls and adolescents in South Asia is limited and shows mixed findings. Furthermore, determining which factors are unequivocally related to violence and which appear related because of problems in methodology or sampling is difficult. A key methodological concern is that most studies are cross-sectional, even if multivariate, and thus show association but not causation. We summarize in table 3.5 the research findings for all potential risk factors across levels of the social ecology for girls' and female adolescents' vulnerability to violence in South Asian countries, whether or not their relationship with violence against girls and adolescents is unequivocally established.

INDIVIDUAL RISK FACTORS FOR FEMALE CHILDREN AND ADOLESCENTS

The overriding individual-level risk factor for excess female child mortality is a child's gender: being a girl increases that risk, subject to characteristics of the girl's family, immediate environment, and social norms of that environment. For child marriage, it is education. Several studies have established an association between education and delay of

TABLE 3.5 Risk and Protective Factors for Violence against Girls and Adolescents at Different Levels of the Social Ecology and for Different Forms of Violence

Risk or protective factor	Excess female child mortality	Child abuse	Adolescent sexual harassment	Child marriage
Individual (girl, adolescent)				
Education				✓
Employment				✓
Relationship with parents		✓	✓	
Negotiation skills			✓	✓
Household, parents				
Poverty		✓		✓
Parental substance abuse		✓		
Intimate partner violence at home	✓	✓		
Mother's education	✓	✓		✓
Sex composition of the family	✓			
Childhood exposure to son preference	✓			
Institutions and systems				
Birth registration	✓	✓		✓
Disregard for laws	✓	✓	✓	✓
Conflict and war	✓	✓		✓
Social norms				
Place of girls in family hierarchy	✓	✓	✓	✓
Taboo on discussing sex		✓	✓	✓
Fear of premarital relationships				✓
Caste and religion	✓		✓	✓
Dowry	✓			✓

marriage (Bajracharya and Amin 2010). In particular, studies in India (Verma et al. 2013), Bangladesh (Amin and Huq 2008; Field and Ambrus 2008), and Nepal (Verma et al. 2013) find that girls with secondary schooling or higher are significantly less likely to be married as children than girls with less schooling. Another study in India suggests a different relationship: the expectation that a more educated girl would require a larger dowry because she is likely to marry a more educated boy discourages parents from educating their daughter and encourages them to marry her early (ICRW 2011).

These studies do not prove causality, however. Girls' schooling may be endogenous: girls who delay marriage may end up continuing school; girls who leave school may marry earlier (Bajracharya and Amin 2010). Moreover, delaying marriage will not necessarily lead to improved schooling outcomes for girls (Field and Ambrus 2008).

Some studies do attempt to measure causality, for both girls' schooling and maternal education. For instance, Bates et al. (2007) analyze panel data for Bangladesh to find that five or more years of schooling among mothers is, indeed, associated with a higher age at marriage for their daughters. Using an instrumental variable approach, Field and Ambrus (2008) find that higher schooling among Bangladeshi girls is a consequence of delaying marriage. They estimate that, at an aggregate level, legally restricting marriage to age 17 increases average female schooling by half a year.

Bajracharya and Amin (2010) find also that adolescent girls who are employed may marry later. Although the association is likely endogenous, the weight of the evidence suggests a strong association across most South Asian countries. This relationship could arise for several reasons. First, the possibility of increased household income from such employment may motivate parents to delay marriage. Second, adolescent girls who earn an income may have a higher status within their family and community and thus greater autonomy to decide on marriage. Finally, having the skills to be employed may contribute to greater autonomy and financial power within the home and community and thus to increased self-efficacy in deciding when to marry (Bajracharya and Amin 2010).

Self-efficacy, negotiation skills, and overall relationship with parents are also factors in their own right that are associated with child abuse, adolescent sexual harassment, and child marriage. Malik (2010) administered a Parental Acceptance-Reject Questionnaire and indigenously developed a Child Abuse Scale to identify children exposed to varying degrees and forms of abuse and neglect. Using a randomly selected sample of 200 children aged 8–12 years in Pakistan (half boys, half girls), Malik (2010) finds parental rejection to be the strongest predictor of child abuse in the home. The effect is stronger and more significant than mother's education and small family size (which are both significant and inversely associated with child abuse) and socio-economic status and father's education (which are not significant).[7] For adolescents, Jejeebhoy and Bott (2003) find that a lack of communication and negotiation skills among *both* adolescent boys and girls can exacerbate the chances that young men will use force. Conversely, being able to discuss sexual and other concerns with one's parents—and having a relationship with one's parents that allows such discussion—can protect adolescent girls from sexual harassment (Jejeebhoy and Bott 2003). Girls' lack of self-efficacy and lack of ability to make independent decisions also is significantly and positively associated with early marriage (Santhya et al. 2006, 2010).

HOUSEHOLD RISK FACTORS FOR FEMALE CHILDREN AND ADOLESCENTS

Findings on the association between poverty and violence against children and adolescents are mixed. The strongest evidence comes from research on child marriage. In Bangladesh, poverty is considered one of the most powerful drivers of child marriage (ICRW and Plan 2013). Key reasons include the apprehension and inability to pay higher dowries if a girl is married later or if she is educated longer before marriage. Studies in India (Santhya et al. 2006; Das Gupta et al. 2008; ICRW 2011), Nepal (Bajracharya and Amin 2010), and Bangladesh (ICRW and Plan 2013) find that girls from poor households are significantly more likely to marry early. Poor parents in a qualitative study in Bangladesh (Schuler et al. 2006) also opined that they could not ensure their daughters' sexual safety and thus preferred to get them married soon after puberty. Details vary by country, of course. In Nepal, for instance, analysis of longitudinal data from the Nepal Living Standards Survey finds the association between poverty and early marriage to be greater for the second-poorest quintile than for the poorest quintile (Bajracharya and Amin 2010).

One might expect poverty to be associated with excess female child mortality since fewer resources would have to be allocated between preferred sons and unwanted daughters. Studies in Pakistan (Hazarika 2000) and India (John et al. 2009; Gaudin 2011), however, find no evidence that poorer households perpetrate neglect or trigger greater mortality for girls. Studies in India (Murthi et al. 1995; Pal 1999) and Bangladesh (Bairagi 1986) find, in fact, that wealthier households manifest higher levels of neglect or mortality. Basu (1989) suggests that the relationship between household poverty and discrimination against girls may be mediated by context, with a stronger detrimental relationship in contexts of greater gender inequality than in more gender egalitarian contexts. Unfortunately, we found no gender-disaggregated studies on the association of poverty with sexual harassment or sexual or physical abuse of girls (though evidence suggests that poverty is associated with child abuse overall).

A household factor unique to excess female child mortality is the sex composition of children in the household. Increasingly, studies across the region are finding that even in very patriarchal settings at least one daughter is wanted. However, second or higher birth-order daughters face excess neglect or mortality (Pal 1999; Pande 2003; Mishra et al. 2004; Corsi et al. 2009). Conversely, analysis of National Family Health Survey data from India (1992–93) suggests that daughters are more likely to be nurtured if parents already have sons (Pande and Malhotra 2006).

Research also shows that maternal education can protect against child abuse and child marriage but not necessarily excess female child mortality. Children of poorly educated mothers face greater risk of child abuse in India (Hunter et al. 2000) and Pakistan (Malik 2010). Unfortunately, these studies do not disaggregate their findings by the child's gender. Maternal education could influence the age at marriage for girls because educated mothers may be more aware of the costs of early marriage for their daughters, more exposed to media messages about early marriage, and better able to support and encourage alternate roles for daughters. Some studies find, however, that this effect is statistically significant only for maternal post-primary schooling (Bates et al. 2007). Verma et al. (2013) find in India that girls with less educated parents—mother or father—are more likely to marry early.

The link between maternal education and excess neglect and mortality for girls is far from clear. Some studies in Bangladesh (Muhuri and Preston 1991) and Pakistan (Hazarika 2000) find no significant association. Other studies across the region find that maternal education does decrease the risk of excess neglect or mortality for daughters

(Murthi et al. 1995; Pokhrel and Sauerborn 2004; Monden and Smits 2013). Still others, however, find that educated mothers are more likely to perpetrate neglect that could lead to death of their daughters in Bangladesh (Bhuiya and Streatfield 1991) and India (Das Gupta 1987; Basu 1989; Pal 1999; Pande 1999). Researchers suggest that in a strong patriarchal system, a little education may not be enough to overcome strong gender-biased social norms and may, in fact, provide women with the means to better implement existing gender biases. However, even higher levels of female education may only make women increasingly adept at discriminating against daughters if underlying gender preferences are retained (Mukherjee 2013).

We find some—albeit limited—research on the effects of other parental characteristics for child abuse, specifically, intimate partner violence and parental substance abuse. Studies in Sri Lanka (Catani et al. 2008) and India (Hunter et al. 2000) find parental abuse of alcohol or drugs (in Sri Lanka, specifically father's substance abuse) to be a significant risk factor for physical child abuse.

Hunter et al. (2000) suggest that violence is intergenerational: women who have suffered spousal abuse are more likely to abuse their children. Similar findings are emerging that link intimate partner violence to excess female child mortality in India (Silverman et al. 2011) and Bangladesh (Asling-Monemi et al. 2009). However, while Ackerson and Subramanian (2009) find in India that maternal intimate partner violence significantly raises the risk of excess child mortality, there is no evidence of greater mortality implications for female children than for male children. More recent research does show evidence in India (Nanda et al. 2013) and Nepal (Nanda et al. 2012) that men who experienced or witnessed gender inequities in their home as children are likely to prefer sons and that son preference is the direct motivation for excess female child mortality. Nanda et al. (2013), who conducted a study of seven geographically representative states in India, find from a sample of 1,500 men age 18–49 that those who experienced in their childhood rigid gender roles between their father and mother are significantly more likely to be rigidly masculine as adults and to prefer sons.

SYSTEMS AND INSTITUTIONAL RISK FACTORS FOR CHILDREN AND ADOLESCENTS

A key systemic factor that works against mitigating child abuse, excess female child mortality, and child marriage is the abysmal state of birth registration. South Asia has the second-lowest regional rate of birth registration at 39 percent of children under the age of five (UNICEF 2013). Birth registration exceeds 90 percent only in Bhutan, Maldives, and Sri Lanka. Lack of birth registration makes falsification of identity documents easier in cases of child marriages and prostitution (ECPAT 2011), thus exacerbating the problem of tracing and prosecuting child marriages (ICRW et al. 2012).

Blatant disregard of existing laws or mechanisms to enforce them—such as laws addressing female infanticide, female child abuse, and child marriage, as well as sexual harassment of adolescents—also is a key systemic risk factor. For instance, although all countries in the region have some form of legal protections for children, none has created any systematic mechanism to monitor the implementation of such laws (Heiberg and Thukral 2013). Poor legal protection is a specific risk factor for child physical and sexual abuse in India (Iravani 2011; HRW 2013) and in Pakistan (Hyder and Malik 2007).

Lack of proper police training, particularly in dealing with abuse of girls, fuels the problem, although relevant research in South Asia is limited to case studies. In India, police officers are not trained to understand or adequately address sexual assault of girls and may refuse to register cases of familial abuse (Singh and Kapur 2001). Child sexual abuse continues in unregistered juvenile detention homes and other unregistered child-care institutions because separate facilities and authorities for different genders are lacking, and other legal provisions, such as child welfare committees and inspection committees, are not implemented (ACHR 2013; HRW 2013). Registration of child marriages is not enforced, and because birth registration is also poor, cases of child marriages are difficult to identify. Moreover, government officials themselves acknowledge that laws against child marriage are not enforced (ICRW 2011).

Instability because of conflict, war, or natural disasters can exacerbate physical and sexual abuse of girls, as well as precipitate early marriage. In Bangladesh, child marriages spiked following cyclone Sidr in 2007 (Verma et al. 2013). In India and Sri Lanka, girls were rushed into child marriages to "tsunami widowers" who sought government subsidies for marrying and starting a family (UNFPA 2012). One-third (31 percent) of women and girls in conflict zones in Sri Lanka interviewed in 2009 said they had been married between 15 and 16 years of age—vastly more than the national average (ICRW et al. 2012). Older studies also have established increased neglect and mortality among girls in Bangladesh in times of famine compared to other times (D'Souza and Chen 1980; Bairagi 1986).

RISK FACTORS FOR VIOLENCE AGAINST FEMALE CHILDREN AT THE LEVEL OF SOCIAL NORMS

Clearly the place and value of girls in the family hierarchy is a key factor that underlies violence that girls and adolescents face in their natal homes. The rigidity of the marital norms defining exogamy in much of South Asia contributes to girls' lack of value to their natal household, as noted earlier in this chapter. Because we could find no quantitative research linking social norms to violence against girls and adolescents in South Asia, we briefly summarize the assertions of other literature reviews here.

Commercial sexual exploitation and abuse of children often reflects underlying gender discrimination. Although boys are at risk, girls are at greater risk: sexual abuse and exploitation are the most frequent form of violence experienced by girls and adolescents (UNICEF 2001; Goonesekere 2006; Hyder and Malik 2007).[8] The fact that girls' sexual "innocence" is a mark of family honor contributes to the silence around sexual abuse of girls and feeds into the reluctance to acknowledge and discuss the presence of sexual abuse across the region (Singh and Kapur 2001; Slugget 2003; GOI 2007; Iravani 2011).

These norms also pose a hurdle for reintegrating girls who have suffered commercial sexual exploitation. Families may refuse to take them back (UNICEF 2001) or girls may think the abuse is their fault (Slugget 2003). Similar norms are at play for sexual harassment of adolescent girls, with the added factor that, in adolescence, a double standard exists: boys' sexuality is accepted, but girls are expected to not understand or be interested in sexual activity (Jejeebhoy and Bott 2003). Chastity and fear of premarital relationships are an emblem of family honor for girls, but not for boys—a key underlying norm precipitating child marriage (Santhya et al. 2006; Schuler et al. 2006; Amin and Huq 2008; Mathur et al. 2003; Das Gupta et al. 2008; ICRW 2011; Verma et al. 2013).

The norm of dowry plays a similar role. Necessary to gain an acceptable marriage for a girl, dowry creates a strong disincentive for parents to have daughters and contributes to excess female child mortality, especially if there is already a girl in the household (Srinivasan 2005). Families fear they will have to pay a higher dowry to find a suitable spouse if a daughter's marriage is delayed, creating an incentive for her early marriage (Amin and Huq 2008; Field and Ambrus 2008; ICRW 2011).

Researchers suggest that the relationship of religion and caste to excess female child mortality in India reflects differing levels of son preference across caste and religion. Even after controlling for socioeconomic status, several studies find that high-caste Hindus in India, who tend to manifest the highest son preference of all caste and tribal groups, have higher levels of excess female childhood mortality than other Hindu castes and groups (Murthi et al. 1995; John et al. 2009) and Muslims (Rahman and Rao 2004; Bhalotra et al. 2009). In contrast, child marriage is more prevalent among more disadvantaged lower-caste groups (specifically the Dalit community in Nepal) and Muslims than among so-called higher-caste groups, as is the case in Nepal (Bajracharya and Amin 2010; ICRW et al. 2012; Verma et al. 2013). Sexual abuse faced by lower-caste girls and perpetrated by higher-caste boys is not infrequent in certain parts of India (ICRW 2011).

Risk Factors in Marriage: Dowry Violence and Intimate Partner Violence

Newlywed adolescents and young widows or divorced women may face some additional or different risks of violence within marriage, compared to adult married women, because of their lower position in the familial social hierarchy. However, most research on violence within marriage does not separate out risk factors for married adolescents relative to adults (other than age at marriage), for married women of reproductive age relative to older married women, or for currently married women relative to widowed or divorced women. In this section, we discuss risk factors for married women as a whole, pointing out differences by biological life stage where singled out by existing research.

Although married adolescent girls and married adult women are at risk of violence perpetrated by non-intimate partners within the marital household, it is intimate partner violence and dowry violence that pose the greatest threat to them. We find

TABLE 3.6 Risk and Protective Factors for Intimate Partner Violence at Different Levels of the Social Ecology

Individual level	Household and partner	Systems and institutions	Social norms
• Age, education, and employment • Ownership of assets, especially land • Witnessing or suffering of abuse as a child	• Partner's age, education, and employment • Partner's substance abuse • Spousal differences in age, education, and employment • Partner or perpetrator's witnessing or suffering of abuse as a child • Marriage characteristics • Role of children (especially sons) • Household poverty • Household structure • Household members' attitudes toward sexual abuse	• Legal definition and implementation gaps • Participation in microcredit and social groups • Community and neighborhood characteristics	• Understandings of masculinity and femininity and gender roles • Notions of "honor" • Caste and religion • Marriage squeeze • Shifts in marriage norms and practices • Dowry practices and norms

no research examining the role of individual, household, or institutional risk factors on dowry violence, however. In terms of social norms, risk factors for dowry violence are similar to those for intimate partner violence. Table 3.6 thus provides an overview of the risk factors for intimate partner violence only.

The lack of consistency across studies in the determination of risk and protective factors at the individual, household or community level for intimate partner violence may, at least in part, be due to methodological issues in this research. There is no single accepted definition of physical or sexual intimate partner violence, nor are definitions for key risk factors standardized, such as for education, employment, or poverty measures. Studies of physical and sexual intimate partner violence may thus use a range of definitions for these outcomes as well as for key risk or protective factors. Different studies also use a wide variety of statistical methods or models, with a different combination of variables included in multivariate studies. All such research decisions are likely to influence the conclusions of these studies.

INDIVIDUAL-LEVEL FACTORS: EXPOSURE TO VIOLENCE, LEVEL OF EDUCATION, EMPLOYMENT STATUS, AND AGE

Multiple studies point to childhood exposure to violence as a strong determinant of the risk of marital violence in adulthood. Studies across Bangladesh and India find that women who witnessed their mother being abused are at increased risk of spousal violence (Jeyaseelan et al. 2007; ICRW 2000a). Similarly, women who were harshly abused as children are more likely to be abused as adults (ICRW 2000a; Abramsky et al. 2011; Heise 2011; Nanda et al. 2012).

It is not entirely clear whether the higher reported prevalence reflected in such increased risk is a reporting effect; that is, women who grew up seeing violence in their households may consider it a normal occurrence and be less hesitant to report it as adults. It is also unclear why early exposure to violence should increase risks of violence in adulthood, though research from developed countries, reviewed by Heise (2011), suggests that girls who witness or experience abuse in childhood may internalize violence as an acceptable part of life and thus be more prone to experiencing and reporting violence against them in the home.

Although women's education is considered an important protective factor, the strength of this effect may depend on the level of schooling. Jewkes (2002) notes that often there is a non-linear relationship between women's education and risk of violence in the home that changes over time and spread of education. This relationship is especially observed in conservative societies, where a little education initially may be perceived to threaten male authority and thus could increase a woman's risk of violence (Srinivasan and Bedi 2007). As more women are educated, risks of violence may decrease. Overall, the role of education changes as the spread of education and its meaning for women undergoes the transition from revolutionary (where education may exacerbate violence) to critical mass (where education can make women less vulnerable to violence).

Consistent with this hypothesis, studies in Bangladesh (Bates et al. 2004; Naved et al. 2006), Bhutan (NSB 2011), and India (Koenig et al. 2006; Ackerson et al. 2008; Population Council 2009) also show that post-primary schooling is significantly associated with lower risks and greater disclosure of intimate partner violence. Naved et al. (2006) find that in rural areas of Bangladesh, women with education beyond grade 10 are three times more likely than women with no education to disclose their experience of spousal violence. Other studies document a dose-response effect: the more years of schooling, the lower the risk of violence (Koenig et al. 2006; Santhya et al. 2007; Ackerson et al. 2008). Respondents in Kabeer's (1998, 63) qualitative study believe that girls with more education are likely to marry better-educated and "better-behaved" husbands who respect them more. Some studies from India and Nepal, however, find no significant effect of schooling when controlling for other factors (Rao 1997; Rocca et al. 2009; Lamichhane et al. 2011). Research suggests that with post-primary education women may be less abused because they have the skills to be financially independent, speak for themselves, gain higher respect from other household members, and better manage or bring more resources to the household (Bates et al. 2004; Ackerson et al. 2008).

The role of women's employment status in intimate partner violence is unclear. Bates et al. (2004) find that women's employment increases violence risks in Bangladesh, whereas Rocca et al. (2009) find no significant association in India. The relationship likely depends on the context. For instance, women's employment may carry higher risks where other factors—such as poverty and gender inequality—create a situation conducive to violence (Krishnan et al. 2010). Also, women who start out with low bargaining power—such as less educated adolescent brides—may face increased risks of violence if they work (Heath 2013). Women who work outside the home may also face higher risks of violence than women who do not, as they could pose an actual or perceived challenge to a man's role as breadwinner and thus to his power and masculinity (Bates et al. 2004; Krishnan et al. 2010). However, the direction of causality in these studies is unclear. For instance, are women more at risk because they work, or do they work as "insurance" because they are more at risk?

It is also unclear whether any significant effect of a woman's age, observed in multivariate analyses that control for age, reflects something particular about the stage of marriage or life associated with that age or merely reflects increased exposure over time to the risk of intimate partner violence. Findings are contradictory. For instance, studies in Bangladesh show that women ages 20–29 are at a higher risk of violence than are younger and older women (Schuler et al. 1996; Koenig et al. 2003). In contrast, Abramsky et al.'s (2011) multicountry study finds older women to be at higher risk than young women.

SPOUSAL RISK AND PROTECTIVE FACTORS: ALCOHOL ABUSE AND EXPOSURE TO VIOLENCE; POST-PRIMARY EDUCATION

Studies across the region find that men who witnessed violence as a child are significantly more likely to be sexually and physically violent against their wives (Jewkes 2002; Martin et al. 2002; Koenig et al. 2006; Heise 2011; Nanda et al. 2012, 2013; de Mel et al. 2013; Fulu et al. 2013) and to be "rigidly masculine" (Nanda et al. 2013). According to Nanda et al.'s (2013) study in India, in most states covered by the study, rigidly masculine men are three times more likely to perpetrate violence against a partner.

Similarly, a two-stage sampling study that interviewed 1,000 men age 18–49 from urban and rural Nepal finds that among men who report more gender-equitable beliefs, 55 percent are likely to perpetrate intimate partner violence—significantly less than the 84 percent of men who report having less gender-equitable beliefs (Nanda et al. 2012). Men who were harshly abused as children are significantly more likely to be abusers as adults, according to research in Bangladesh (Abramsky et al. 2011), India (ICRW 2000a), Nepal (Nanda et al. 2012), and several South Asian countries cited in a multi-regional review (Heise 2011). In one of the few empirical studies we find that test specifically for this relationship, Martin et al. (2002) surveyed 6,902 married men in northern India. Using descriptive statistics (table 3.7) and multivariate modeling, they find non-violence in one generation to be strongly predictive of non-violence in the next generation, and one-third of wife abuse in the second generation to be attributable to parent-to-parent violence in the earlier generation.

Why early exposure to violence should lead to violent behavior in adulthood is unclear. Research from developed countries, reviewed by Heise (2011), suggests that emotional scars from early abuse may contribute to bullying or other antisocial behavior in adolescence, which may morph into violent behavior in adulthood. Boys who witness or experience childhood abuse may internalize violence as an acceptable way to

TABLE 3.7 Percentages of Men Who Abused Their Wives, Stratified by Men's Experiences of Witnessing Parent-to-Parent Violence (or No Violence) in Their Families of Origin, Northern India

	Father and mother beat or physically mistreated one another (%)	Father beat or physically mistreated mother (%)	No violence in family of origin (%)
No wife abuse	23	29	65
Physical wife abuse only	26	26	14
Sexual wife abuse without physical force	34	36	16
Sexual wife abuse with physical force	17	9	5

N = 6,902
Source: Martin et al. 2002, p. 568, table 6.

exert dominance and control. Finally, early trauma may biologically or chemically affect the brain in ways that create or exacerbate a propensity for violence.

Studies worldwide report a husband's alcohol use as a significant risk factor for spousal violence (Jewkes 2002; Hindin et al. 2008; Heise 2011). Multivariate analyses across sites in India (ICRW 2000a; Jeyaseelan et al. 2004, 2007) and Nepal (Adhikari and Tamang 2010; Nanda et al. 2012) find alcohol's association with various types of spousal violence to be statistically significant. Smaller descriptive studies in India (Varma et al. 2007) and Sri Lanka (Subramanian and Sivayogan 2001) also find the relationship to be signficant. Researchers posit that alcohol use may decrease inhibition and diminish self-control, thereby increasing the risk that any interaction might trigger violence.

Several studies in Bangladesh and India suggest that post-primary education of the husband offers women some protection against physical violence (Martin et al. 1999; Koenig et al. 2003, 2006; Ackerson et al. 2008; Johnson and Das 2008; Population Council 2009; Nanda et al. 2013). Nanda et al. (2013) also find secondary and higher education to be significantly associated with reportedly less rigid understandings of masculinity among Indian men. Lower levels of education may not have the same effect: according to Martin et al. (2002), men with fewer than six years of education are significantly more likely to believe in controlling their wives than are more educated men.

Other studies, however, either find no significant association (e.g., Nanda et al. 2012 in Nepal) or find that a husband's higher education is associated with a greater risk of violence against his wife, perhaps because men with more education may command a higher dowry, which is associated with higher violence risks (see Rao's 1997 study of rural South India). Still other research from India suggests that even where men's education is associated with lower risks for perpetration of physical violence, this relationship may not hold for sexual violence (Koenig et al. 2006; Population Council 2009). The reasons for this differential are uncertain.

The role of age is also uncertain. Johnson and Das (2008) find from their multivariate analysis of Demographic and Health Survey data that younger men in Bangladesh are more likely to perpetrate violence than are older men and that men age 25–29 are the most likely to perpetrate violence. Nanda et al.'s (2013) multivariate analysis of data from seven states suggests that Indian men age 18–24 are most likely to have rigidly traditional masculine behavior, perhaps because at this marriageable age they are under the highest pressure to conform. According to one study in Nepal, older men are significantly more likely to have ever perpetrated intimate partner violence, but the survey, which was administered in three districts of Nepal, is representative only at the district level, rather than at the national level. The fieldwork also encountered sampling issues as it coincided with peak monsoon season, and high migration of men for work required replacements in the sample (Nanda et al. 2012).

The reasons we might expect a husband's employment to be associated with lower risks of violence are the inverse of the reasons suggested for women's employment to be associated with higher risks of violence: the symbolic meaning of male employment for the perceived breadwinner gender role (Krishnan et al. 2010). If men are unable to perform this role or to be confident in and control public aspects of their lives as denoted by stable employment, they may be more likely to exert control through violence in their private lives (ICRW 2000b). The research does not entirely support this hypothesis, however. Krishnan et al. (2010) find that a husband's job stability is associated with lower risks of violence, but if after an initial period of stability the job becomes less stable, risk of violence increases. Hindin et al. (2008) find that agricultural employment is associated with lower risks of perpetrating violence, though the reason for this result is unclear. Finally, Schuler et al. (1996) and Rocca et al. (2009), in Bangladesh and India, respectively, find no association between men's employment and the propensity to abuse wives.

Also ambiguous is whether and how spousal differences in age, education, or employment status might be associated with intimate partner violence against women. The expected direction of effects is itself uncertain. If a husband is younger, less educated or less employed than his wife, he may be more likely to use violence to assert his authority over his older, better educated or better employed wife. On the other hand, husbands who are significantly older, more educated, or better employed than their wives may exert more power and control over the wives by virtue of these characteristics, resulting in greater violence. Multicountry reviews of spousal employment differentials yield inconsistent evidence of its role in intimate partner violence against women, and effects vary by context (Jewkes 2002; Abramsky et al. 2011).

In Nepal, Adhikari and Tamang (2010) find that an age difference of at least five years in either direction is associated with higher risks of violence for a wife. In contrast, studies in Bangladesh (Hindin et al. 2008; Abramsky et al. 2011) and India (Santhya et al. 2007) suggest that a spousal age gap is not significant. Results are also mixed for spousal differences in education, with some studies reporting lower risks for women with less education than their husbands compared to those with more education (ICRW 2000a; Ackerson et al. 2008; Nanda et al. 2012). Others, in Bangladesh (Hindin et al. 2008) and India (ICRW 2000a; Santhya et al. 2007), find no significant association between spousal education gap and risk of violence.

RISK FACTORS FOR THE COUPLE: QUALITY OF RELATIONSHIP MATTERS

Several small-scale, qualitative studies suggest that the nature of the marital relationship is significantly associated with a woman's risks of marital intimate partner violence. Risks of violence are found to be higher in marriages where the wife is unhappy (Schuler et al. 1996). In Bangladesh (Schuler et al. 1996) and India (ICRW 2000a), if wives are unhappy because of their husbands' extramarital relationships and voice suspicion, violence frequently results. Husbands who have had extramarital relationships are generally more likely to physically and sexually abuse wives in India (Koenig et al. 2006) and Bangladesh (Johnson and Das 2008). According to Santhya et al. (2007), adolescent wives in India who have a good relationship with their husbands (measured as support in family conflicts), or who knew their husband fairly well before marriage, are at lower risk of unwanted sex than others.

Yet, research in Bengaluru, India finds that married young women who have "love" marriages are at a greater risk of spousal violence than those who have arranged marriages (Rocca et al. 2009; Krishnan et al. 2010). This result, it is suggested, likely reflects underlying gender norms: young women who transgress social marital norms by choosing their spouse risk losing future support from their natal family if violence arises. After marrying, husbands may also regret the social stigma attached to love marriage and consequently perpetrate more violence. In a study among Afghan refugees in Pakistan, Hyder et al. (2007) find love marriage to be associated with greater violence from mothers-in-law and suggest that mothers-in-law may resent their son's closeness to the wife in a love marriage. These results convey the importance of considering how characteristics of marital life and relationships relate to violence in different contexts.

The effect of years of marriage seems to vary by type of violence and research location, though studies are few. Research of men in India suggests either minimal association between years of marriage and violence risks for the wife (Martin 1999) or that longer marriages are associated with lower risks of sexual violence but higher risks of physical violence (Koenig et al. 2006). In contrast, women respondents in another study (Jejeebhoy et al. 2013) almost uniformly asserted that violence increases with years of marriage. The authors posit that this may reflect either that men's impunity increases as the couple have children and women are less likely to leave, or that women become more "disobedient" as they get comfortable in their marriage. However, sexual and physical violence may well decrease as a marriage goes on, such that adolescent and younger wives—as measured by their age at marriage or how long they have been married—may face higher risks of violence than women further on in their marital lives (Kabeer 1998; Santhya et al. 2006).

Similarly, the presence of children could exacerbate or ameliorate intimate partner violence. Because women are expected to bear children, childlessness could increase risks of violence. Conversely, the presence of many children may exert financial and emotional stress on a couple, thus exacerbating violence. In their multivariate analysis of a sample of 4,520 married Indian men, Koenig et al. (2006) find a significant association between childlessness and greater likelihood of physical and sexual violence.

In contrast, 150 patients interviewed at a women's health clinic in Karachi, Pakistan (Fikree and Bhatti 1999) reported the presence of children to be the most common reason for violence by spouses. Where son preference is strong, women who do not bear sons may be at higher risk of violence from husbands or marital household members (Rao 1997; Schuler et al. 2006).

HOUSEHOLD RISK FACTORS FOR MARITAL VIOLENCE: POVERTY AND FAMILY STRUCTURE

Household poverty is a strong risk factor, primarily because the stress of poverty may exacerbate a husband's frustration at not being able to provide for the family—thus increasing the hazard of violence against a wife. Studies in Bangladesh (Koenig et al. 2003; Bates et al. 2004), India (Santhya et al. 2007; Population Council 2009; Koenig et al. 2010), and Pakistan (Fikree and Bhatti 1999) indicate a significant association between household poverty and risks of intimate partner violence. Koenig et al. (2003) and Panda and Agarwal (2005) find in particular that a household's landholding size is significantly and inversely associated with risks of intimate partner violence for women in that household. In contrast, results from Srinivasan and Bedi's (2007) study in southern India show that landholding is not significantly associated with spousal abuse. In Bangladesh, Schuler et al. (2008) find that poverty may prevent women (who have nowhere to go) from leaving an abusive husband and natal families from sheltering an abused daughter. Conversely, violence against women may decrease with women's earning and resultant household economic prosperity because husbands realize that their wives have more options for survival outside of marriage (Schuler et al. 2013). Women's ownership of assets also can serve as a protective factor. From their survey of 500 households in Kerala, India, Panda and Agarwal (2005) find that women who own immovable property—that is, land or a house—have a significantly lower risk of marital intimate partner violence than women who do not own property.

Poverty may be a risk factor for attitudes toward intimate partner violence as well, though findings are mixed. In Bhutan, there is a 7 percentage point difference in acceptance of spousal violence between women from the poorest quintile of households (40 percent) and those from the wealthiest (33 percent) (NSB 2011). Martin et al. (2002) find that men from poorer households in north India are more likely to believe in controlling their wives than men from wealthier households.

Other studies in Bangladesh and India find no statistically significant association between household poverty and spousal physical violence (Schuler et al. 1996; Johnson and Das 2008) or sexual violence (Koenig et al. 2006). Martin et al.'s (1999) study in five districts in India finds that the association between poverty and men's likelihood of physical abuse toward wives varies by district.

Findings on the role of household structure are also contradictory. Tensions between a couple may be exacerbated by the presence of extended household members and the consequent lack of privacy or couple's inability to control their own lives. Results from studies in Pakistan show that the presence of in-laws is associated with greater marital conflict (Fikree and Bhatti 1999) and higher risk of sexual coercion (Kapadia et al. 2009). Conversely, the presence of other family members may dampen spousal violence, as found in Bangladesh and Pakistan (Koenig et al. 2003; Naeem et al. 2008) and among Afghan refugees in Pakistan (Hyder et al. 2007), or increase the opportunities for disclosure, as found in Bangladesh (Naved et al. 2006). Multi-country reviews also find natal family support to be protective (Jewkes 2002). Finally, research in India by Rocca et al. (2009) and Martin et al. (1999) shows no significant association between household structure and intimate partner violence risks.

INSTITUTIONAL RISK AND PROTECTIVE FACTORS

Aside from the role of legal provisions and implementation in both dowry-related violence and intimate partner violence, discussed earlier in this chapter, we found no other research on the role of particular institutional risk factors in dowry-related violence, even at the community level. We thus highlight institutional and systemic factors found to be important specifically for intimate partner violence risks.

Active debate rages about the role of women's participation in microcredit groups in exacerbating or diminishing their risks of intimate partner abuse. Much of this research originates from Bangladesh, which has had the most vibrant increase in women's participation in microcredit groups in the region. Such participation could be protective because it exposes a woman to the outside world and allows her to be part of a group of women who could offer support if her husband were violent. When women join microcredit groups and bring in money, respect in their marital homes may increase, according to ethnographic research in Bangladesh (Schuler et al. 1996) and summaries of research from multiple countries (Jewkes 2002). The added income may also reduce the stresses of poverty, thereby decreasing the likelihood of poverty-related violence (Kabeer 1998). Bajracharya and Amin (2013) note that the relationship could depend on the program and the services it offers. For example, they find that a microcredit program in South Africa that offered human immunodeficiency virus (HIV) prevention and care also mitigated the risks of violence to women at home. There may be a community effect as well: Koenig et al. (2003) find no effect of individual membership, but at the village or community level, the higher the participation of women in microcredit programs, the lower an individual woman's risk of physical abuse.

Microcredit group participation, like higher education or employment, however, also could exacerbate risks of intimate partner violence for women if public participation of women in spheres outside of the customary roles that are socially mandated for them is seen to threaten patriarchal norms and a husband's power. Rocca et al. (2009) find this to be true in their study in Bengaluru slums in India, where women who join community vocational training groups are at increased risk of violence. Schuler et al. (1996)

suggest a nonlinear relationship: initially, women participating in microcredit programs may face higher risks of intimate partner violence because such participation is seen as threatening the status quo, but eventually risks may decrease as benefits are appreciated and participation becomes the norm. Increased participation may also change women's perceptions of themselves and their rights, further contributing to a decline in risks of violence. One study in Bangladesh finds just such a trajectory (Ahmed 2005).

More recent research argues that many studies suffer from a selection bias, however. For instance, a lower risk of violence within a microcredit group may not reflect an effect of the membership per se but rather that women whose husbands allow them to join are less patriarchal in their outlook. In contrast, women who are pressured by their husbands to join may be at higher risk of violence in any case (Bates et al. 2004; Bajracharya and Amin 2013).

Several studies find that community characteristics may influence individual women's risks of violence. Some discern a beneficial effect of community-level education of men (Hindin et al. 2008) or of both men and women (Ackerson et al. 2008) on dampening risks of intimate partner violence for women. However, Koenig et al. (2006) find no significant association between community gender norms or community socioeconomic development and men's perpetration of sexual or physical violence. Research does show a higher prevalence of intimate partner violence for women in areas where violence is condoned (Koenig et al. 2006; Hindin et al. 2008), where violence is commonly used in conflict situations or political struggles (Jewkes 2002), and where murder rates are higher than average (Koenig et al. 2006).

A few studies note that community norms may mediate the effect of other risk or protective factors on violence. Schuler et al. (1996) find that residing in areas with Grameen Bank and BRAC groups decreases the risk of violence for Bangladeshi women regardless of group membership. Koenig et al. (2003) find that participation in community groups in Bangladesh may increase violence risks in communities with very patriarchal cultural norms, but not in communities with less rigid norms. Similarly, Jejeebhoy (1998) suggests that her observed relationship between wife beating and infant and fetal loss is stronger in Uttar Pradesh in northern India than in Tamil Nadu in southern India because gender norms are more rigid and natal family support less accessible or acceptable in the former than in the latter area. However, women may also face more violence in areas where gender-related transformations have gone the furthest and thus challenge male supremacy the most (Kabeer 1998).

THE ROLE OF SOCIAL NORMS IN EXACERBATING OR MITIGATING RISKS

As discussed earlier, the most significant risk factor at the "macro" level of social norms is the understanding of masculinity and femininity and notions of honor related to gender roles arising from patriarchal systems. Dowry-related violence is associated with the combination of these social and normative factors with demographic or economic factors that increase the demand for grooms with higher education and employability.

This association is found in Bangladesh (Suran et al. 2004; Amin and Suran 2005), India (Purkayastha et al. 2003; Srinivasan 2005), and Pakistan (Anderson 2000, 2004).

Dowry itself has the potential to increase or decrease the likelihood of spousal sexual and physical violence. Women in Bangladesh whose marriages involve dowry are at significantly higher risk of spousal abuse than other married women; moreover, the risk of abuse increases with the level of dowry payment (Suran et al. 2004; Amin 2008). Other studies show similar findings in Bangladesh (Schuler et al. 1996; Bates et al. 2004), India (Rao 1997; ICRW 2000a; Jeyaseelan et al. 2007), and Nepal (several studies cited in Pradhan et al. 2011) and among Afghan refugees in Pakistan (Hyder et al. 2007).

In contrast, Srinivasan and Bedi (2007) find dowry to be protective in Tamil Nadu, even after taking into account that dowry and violence risks are endogenous: the same types of families may have a propensity for both dowry and intimate partner violence. They reason that larger dowries reduce marital violence by increasing the household's economic resources, thereby enhancing the social status of the groom and his family and providing a source of wealth over which a woman enjoys relatively more control. Yet, it is unclear whether this argument holds for other parts of India or other countries in South Asia. Evidence is mixed for Bangladesh: Volart (2004) finds that dowry is protective against divorce among Muslims in the Matlab area, but Suran et al. (2004) find that women who pay no dowry are at lowest risk of violence. Using multivariate analysis, however, Rocca et al. (2009) discern no association between dowry and violence in Bengaluru, India.

Caste and religion present other potential socio-cultural risks for violence, though directionality is far from clear. Although many studies control for caste or religion, few examine the specific role of these factors. Some research results suggest that women from Muslim families are at a higher risk of intimate partner violence than those from non-Muslim families in Bangladesh (Koenig et al. 2003; Silverman et al. 2013), India (Santhya et al. 2007), and Nepal (Lamichhane et al. 2011). Other studies from Bangladesh (Schuler et al. 1996; Johnson and Das 2008), India (Rocca et al. 2009), and Sri Lanka (Jayasuriya et al. 2011) find no significant association.

The caste system is a peculiarity of India and Nepal. Recent research in Nepal suggests that women from the Dalit community experience higher levels of intimate partner violence that is associated with caste gender norms (Pradhan et al. 2011). The Newārs—who allow women to be involved with men in business and trade and to have some household decision-making power over managing money—have lower rates of intimate partner violence than do the relatively poorer Tharu and Dalit castes, in which men dominate women in all aspects of household decision-making, according to Paudel (2007).

As a whole, however, it is difficult to tease out whether an observed effect of caste or religion represents the effect on intimate partner violence of being of a particular caste or religion, or whether these characteristics are standing in as markers for other factors that exacerbate violence, such as gender norms or poverty. For instance, being of a particular religion likely has different social meanings depending on whether it is a minority or majority religion. Both Hindu and Muslim religious texts contain male-biased teachings; thus, any significant relationship of one over the other with violence is likely to reflect local social, cultural, or political adaptations of religious doctrine. Caste-based differentials in intimate partner violence are based on variations in gender and patriarchal norms and may reflect the existence of those norms rather than the effect of belonging to a particular caste. Furthermore, increased violence reported among the lowest castes may reflect, at least in part, the effect of poverty.

Risk and Protective Factors for Violence That Is Not Limited to a Particular Life Stage or Marital Status

The remainder of this chapter explores risk and protective factors for types of violence that can occur during different periods of the female life cycle in South Asia: trafficking, custodial violence, sexual harassment outside of the home, and honor killing. According to our review of published and unpublished research, databases, and online news and other media sources, most of these forms of violence can first be encountered in girlhood and continue as a threat throughout adolescence, adulthood, and old age. For trafficking, however, even infants are at risk.

CHALLENGES IN IDENTIFYING RISK FACTORS FOR MULTIPLE-STAGE[9] TYPES OF VIOLENCE

Few studies of trafficking, honor violence, custodial violence, and even sexual harassment are conducted with sufficient rigor to definitively identify risk factors. One major constraint is lack of data: as with intimate partner violence, a substantial gap exists between the experience and reporting of these types of abuse. In addition, however—and unlike for intimate partner violence—survey efforts to ascertain the prevalence for multiple-life-stage forms of violence are practically nonexistent. These measurement problems are compounded by the fact that many survivors of, for example, trafficking or honor killing may no longer be capable of reporting such violence or seeking treatment, while children trafficked at an early age are likely to forget their real identities (Ali 2005). Those who are supposed to protect individuals may be the primary perpetrators (as with custodial violence and cases where parents have sold their children into trafficking), and those to whom survivors are supposed to report experiences of violence may collude with and enable perpetrators (as with honor killing, sexual harassment, custodial violence, and even, on occasion, trafficking) (Jejeebhoy and Bott 2003; Maher 2003; Khair 2003; AIHRC 2013).

For these less studied forms of violence, a review of existing material must allow for alternative information sources to supplement peer-reviewed research, such as discussion pieces or qualitative studies of specific populations. We cite the relevant findings of quantitative analysis where possible. However, the discussion of risk and protective factors that follows relies also on other sources—including media coverage—to convey current storylines regarding factors on which there is no quantitative research and, where relevant, to enable triangulation with meager data and existing studies. Original case studies conducted by report team members and presented in boxes are used to complement summaries of existing research. Table 3.8 summarizes key risk and protective factors for the four multi-life-stage violence types we examine in this report.

TABLE 3.8 Risk and Protective Factors for Violence against Girls and Women at Different Levels of the Social Ecology for Multiple-Life-Stage Types of Violence

Risk or protective factor	Trafficking	Custodial violence	Sexual harassment outside home	Honor killing
Individual (girl, adolescent, adult)				
Education	✓	✓		
Employment	✓	✓	✓	
Relationship with parents			✓	
Negotiation skills			✓	
Youth	✓		✓	✓
Marital status				✓
Household, partner				
Poverty	✓	✓	✓	
Debt	✓			✓
Partner's substance abuse	✓			
Systems and Institutions				
Lack of birth or employment registration	✓	✓		
Extrajudicial decision-making bodies	✓		✓	✓
Poor enforcement and awareness of laws	✓	✓	✓	✓
Conflict and war	✓	✓	✓	
Enabling infrastructure		✓	✓	✓
Social Norms				
Place of girls or women in family hierarchy	✓			✓
Fear of premarital relationships			✓	✓
Migration and globalization	✓		✓	
Caste and religion	✓	✓	✓	✓
Honor			✓	✓

RISK AND PROTECTIVE FACTORS AT THE INDIVIDUAL AND HOUSEHOLD LEVEL

Youth

Multiple life-stage forms of violence can occur anytime between childhood and adulthood, but adolescence and early adulthood appear to be high-risk periods for sexual harassment, trafficking, and honor killing in South Asia. In most cases, the onset of puberty brings a girl the new identity of a potentially sexually active person and a potential bride. Both put her at risk of these forms of violence.

Perveen's (2012) qualitative review of reported cases of violence against women in Pakistan suggests that women who are sexually harassed are typically in their teens and early twenties. Although women can experience sexual coercion at any point in their lives, young women may not have developed the negotiating skills and tools to confront and resist such coercion. Girls may also acquiesce because they fear a perpetrator's threats to reveal their "relationship," in which case the girl is most likely to be blamed and stigmatized, according to Jejeebhoy and Bott (2003) in their review of research on non-consensual sexual experiences among youth in developing countries. In India, being aware, possessing negotiating skills, and having a "good" relationship with one's parents that allows the girl to talk about sex or other sensitive matters are found to protect against such sexual abuse (Jejeebhoy and Bott 2003).

As intimate relationships before marriage become more common in some South Asian countries, adolescent girls increasingly face pressure from young men to engage in sexual relations, as Sodhi and Verma (2003) find through in-depth interviews of 71 adolescents living in a Delhi slum. Rape of young and adolescent girls reportedly also has been rising in India, Pakistan, and Sri Lanka, though reasons for the increase (including possible increased reporting of rape) are not specified (Naved 2003; Perera et al. 2011; HRCP 2012). Studies in India and Nepal suggest also that adolescent female sex workers are at a significantly higher risk of violence and HIV infection than are older female sex workers (Panchanadeswaran et al. 2008; Sarkar et al. 2008; Beattie et al. 2010; Silverman et al. 2011).

Adolescence and early adulthood appear to be high-risk phases for honor violence, trafficking, and custodial violence as well. There is little statistical information on such violence—not to mention analysis of risk factors—and even efforts to track prevalence are sporadic and estimates unreliable.

According to the India Human Rights Commission, half of trafficked children in India are 11–14 years old, and most trafficked brides are between the ages of 13 and 23.[10] National-level estimates suggest that 11–18 percent of honor killing victims are under 18 (Nasrullah et al. 2009; HRCP 2012). Articles that attempt to summarize existing literature and data or describe the problem of custodial violence and trafficking of adolescent girls in specific countries hint at risk factors—such as child marriage, low education, and lack of job opportunities (e.g., Khair 2003; Ali 2005; Ghosh 2009)—but admit serious limitations to their data and sources.

Working Outside the Home

As with intimate partner violence, working outside the home for pay can be either a risk or a protective factor for multiple-life-stage forms of violence. Some studies find that women who work outside the home are at significantly greater risk of sexual harassment than women who work from the house or are unemployed (Naved 2003; Hancock 2006; Perveen 2012). In Bangladesh and Sri Lanka, low-income women—such as those who do factory or other blue-collar work—are regarded as "bad women" who have lost virtue and thus deserve harassment (Siddiqi 2003; Hancock 2006). Poor women may be at a particularly high risk of sexual harassment that is related to travel for work as they are more likely to walk or use public transportation than professional women, who can afford private transport.

In addition to the threats that employed women face outside of work, there are, of course, the risks of harassment that emanate from the workplace. Such harassment may manifest as emotional or mental abuse (offensive language, swearing, prejudice, blaming, exploitation, deprivation, defaming, or intimidation) or may be sexual in nature (touching, stroking, fondling, rape, pornography, blackmailing, or exhibition of body parts) (Naved 2003; Perera at al. 2011; Perveen 2012). Working women also may feel pressured to succumb to sexual advances of supervisors who have decision-making power over their jobs (Siddiqi 2003). Women involved in sex work, which tends to be illegal in South Asia, may believe they have little recourse to justice in cases of rape or other violence; indeed, perpetrators of violence against female sex workers are rarely punished (Beattie et al. 2010).

Paradoxically, working outside the home may protect women from some types of multiple-life-stage violence—for example, from being trafficked and becoming subject to custodial violence—given that poor women who lack job opportunities are at high risk of experiencing both (Ali 2005; Ghosh 2009). Women who lack income are at double risk of custodial violence. Short on finances, they cannot seek legal counsel and other resources when they are accused of a crime; once in custody, they are more likely than male prisoners to be subjected to violence, according to one study of women prisoners in India (Garg and Singla 2012).

Poverty, Debt, and Alcohol Abuse

As with other forms of violence discussed in this chapter, household poverty appears to make women and girls more susceptible to trafficking, sexual harassment, and custodial violence. Studies from India and Nepal suggest that statistically significant risk factors for violence among sex workers include debt, young age at entering sex work (under 20), having entered sex work through trafficking rather than voluntarily, and alcohol use by sex partners (Sarkar 2008; Panchanadeswaran et al. 2008; Beattie et al. 2010; George et al. 2011; Silverman et al. 2011). In the case of trafficking, research from the region is limited to descriptive literature, some of which—in addition to other factors—suggests that prolonged poverty, short-term poverty punctuated with severe contingencies, seasonal poverty, and family debt are among the factors associated with a higher risk of being trafficked (Bal Kumar 2001; UNICEF 2001; Cheema 2005; Ali 2005; Huda 2006;

Sarkar et al. 2008; Ghosh 2009; UNODC 2012). In Nepal, an especially pernicious form of trafficking by parents is that of children being sold into bonded servitude (box 3.2).

Opinions and evidence on whether household poverty is a risk factor for honor killing are mixed. According to the Afghanistan Independent Human Rights Commission, which studied 243 registered cases of honor killings between 2011 and 2013, household poverty puts women and girls at greater risk (AIHRC 2013). Perhaps economic pressures increase the chances that family conflict is expressed through psychological and physical violence. However, studies from India and Pakistan point out that honor killings also occur in urban, educated, and even wealthy families (Amnesty International 1999; Shaikh et al. 2010; BBC News India 2013). Still, it is worth noting that in Afghanistan, India, and Pakistan, honor killing tends to be perceived as the payment of a debt—though, rather than being material in nature, the cost incurred is more specifically the besmirched honor of a man, family, or community—and the vast

---

BOX 3.2 The Curse of Being a Tharu Girl: Kamlari System in Nepal

Kamaiyas are bonded laborers from landless families, traditionally in southern Nepal, who live and work in their landlords' homes to pay off loans taken for subsistence reasons. The traditional Kamaiya system has been compared to modern-day slavery (Haviland 2007). Kamlaris are female Kamaiyas. They are the young daughters of indigenous families with little or no land who are compelled to hand over their children to landlords—and increasingly to wealthy families in Kathmandu—in exchange for food or a small sum of money, or as repayment of a debt. At the master's house, Kamlaris undertake various manual tasks instead of going to school. Those in the city toil within the four walls, working in the kitchen, washing clothes, and cleaning floors, while those in the villages go to the forest to gather firewood or work in the fields; in all cases, they face a high risk of sexual, physical, and emotional abuse (Poudel 2013).

The Kamlari practice originated, and is usually associated with, the landless Tharu people in western Nepal, who had to send their sons and daughters to their masters' houses in exchange for the privilege of cultivating their land. Many of the Tharus residing in Nepal's southern plains, once infested with malaria, were rendered destitute when the disease was eradicated and new settlers appropriated their land (Pradhan 2006). The practice is tied inextricably to the land ownership regime in Nepal, and the Tharus believe that only an equitable redistribution of land can eradicate the practice.

Nepal's Supreme Court declared the Kamlari system illegal in 2006, along with other forms of child exploitation (UN News Centre 2009). The practice continues, however, and the exact number of Kamlaris in Nepal is not known, partly because the girls are often confined to their masters' houses. Many have been freed from captivity, thanks to the initiatives of individuals and NGOs such as the Free Kamlari Development Forum, but those still indentured face a high probability of being sexually and physically abused (Ekantipur 2013). In June 2013, the suspected killing of a Kamlari girl in Kathmandu (the police and her master claim it was suicide) led to protests across Nepal. After cracking down on the Kamlari protesters and Tharu activists, the government agreed to abolish the practice and provide compensation to those injured (Poudel 2013; Pun 2013).

majority occur over marital or extra-marital matters (Irfan 2008; Nasrullah et al. 2009; Shaikh et al. 2010; Chesler and Bloom 2012; HRCP 2012; AIHRC 2013).

RISK FACTORS IN LAWS, SYSTEMS, AND COMMUNITY INSTITUTIONS

Few of the individual- and household-level factors previously mentioned would increase risks of violence without enabling risk factors that are embedded within institutions and systems. These factors operate through legislative, judicial, and other organized systems that have the potential to support the perverse incentives of abusers—a potential that is easily realized in a society that enforces male power. According to literature from the region, these risk factors range from laws themselves to police, justice, and other state-sanctioned law enforcement systems; to schools and health systems; to the dynamic and rapidly shifting circumstances brought on by migration, globalization, natural disaster, conflict, and deteriorating rule of law; to extrajudicial bodies that make decisions on behalf of communities, even when those decisions fall outside of the law. The empirical research concerning these factors is scant, and case studies conducted by members of this report team are included to help enrich understanding of the issues.

Lack of Enforcement and Awareness of Laws

Earlier in this chapter, we enumerate the laws enacted in South Asia to combat violence against women and girls and identify gaps in country or local legal frameworks. Even where such laws exist, ignorance, disregard, and deliberate flouting of legal requirements are widespread. Numerous authors decry the inability of national governments and the international community to enforce laws and respond effectively to custodial violence, honor killing, and increased trafficking of women and children (Goonesekere 2000; Huda 2006; Haile 2007; Kirti et al. 2011; Chesler and Bloom 2012; Khowaja et al. 2012). According to several quantitative studies of sexual harassment in Sri Lanka, police officers are unresponsive because they fail to take complaints seriously due to gender bias (Jayaweera et al. 2007; Perera et al. 2011).

Law enforcement and the general public simply may be insufficiently aware of such laws to either recognize or report violence, or to hold perpetrators accountable— moreover, vagueness and inconsistencies in laws and law enforcement exacerbate the problem (as in Nepal, for example, where prostitution has been ruled a legal occupation, but prostitutes are arrested under the General Code's "public obscenity" clause and subsequently are at risk of custodial violence)—according to research in Afghanistan (AIHRC 2013), Bangladesh (Naripokkho and Bangladesh Mahila Parishad 2002), Bhutan (Druk Associates 2011), India (ACHR 2007), Nepal (Asia Foundation et al. 2010), Pakistan (Lari 2011; Khowaja et al. 2012; Blue Veins 2013), and Sri Lanka (Perera, et al. 2011). For instance, focus group discussions in Bhutan reveal urban respondents to be more aware than rural respondents of various laws and institutions that provide for or protect the rights of women (Druk Associates 2011). A recent survey in Khyber

Pakhtunkhwa, Pakistan, reveals that out of the 300 respondents—all from civil society organizations, who presumably are better informed than the general public—a minority are aware of any women-related laws in Pakistan or of institutional mechanisms nationally and in the province to deal with complaints registering various forms of abuse (Blue Veins 2013).

Enabling Infrastructure and Lack of Accountability

Even women who are aware of laws designed to protect them and punish perpetrators may decide not to report violent experiences because they occur within a system that tends to protect perpetrators and punish those who come forward. Research suggests this to be the case for all four multi-stage types of violence. At the most basic level of such institutional negligence are the low rates of birth registration in several countries in the region. As noted in chapter 2, birth registration rates are extremely low in countries such as Afghanistan and Pakistan. Children who lack birth registration often do not have an official identity, which can increase their vulnerability to sexual exploitation, sex trafficking, and prostitution (UNICEF 2001). Similarly, the failure of employers to register the names of (often female) domestic servants deprives those employees of both a source of protection against sexual harassment and other forms of abuse and a way to be located if they were trafficked (Ghosh 2009).

More broadly, ineffective or corrupt judicial and law enforcement systems are at least partly to blame for continuing violence against women. In some cases, law enforcement officials protect and collude with perpetrators or even become perpetrators themselves. The Afghanistan Independent Human Rights Commission (AIHRC 2013) reports, for instance, that 14.6 percent of the sexual assaults and honor killings in the period considered by the study were perpetrated by police. Further, judicial proceedings in more than one-third of registered sexual assault and honor killing cases were not conducted according to the law.

Custodial violence also reflects such institutional failures and is a frequent occurrence for women prisoners in India (Garg and Singla 2012) and Pakistan (Ali and Shah 2011). The poor conditions in which women and girls are detained encourage sexual assault by male prisoners, as well as abuse by male police, guards, or army personnel. Prison overcrowding exacerbates these conditions, especially in institutions where women occupy the same quarters as hardened male criminals, as documented in parts of India (Garg and Singla 2012). Lack of female custodians is another problem: female prisoners are at greater risk of violence when overseen by male custodians, according to research in Kabul, Afghanistan (UNODC 2007); Bangladesh (Shafique 2008); Nepal (Dolan and Larney 2009); and Pakistan (Khair 2003). Although Pakistan established its first women's police station in Islamabad in 1994, all criminal cases registered in the decade between its inception and a 2004 study were handled by male police officers because female officers were not allowed to handle criminal cases (SAARC 2006). As a result of these and other failures of accountability, public trust in judicial and recourse mechanisms has eroded. According to a Gallup poll of 300 Pakistani professionals,

85 percent place the greatest level of trust in teachers and the least (only 18 percent) in police officers (*Daily Times* 2011).

Organized Illicit Systems, Collusion with Law Enforcement, and Extrajudicial "Courts"

Along with systemic failures, active collusion by law enforcement may have enabled many cross-cutting forms of violence to become organized systems in themselves. In some cases, local authorities allegedly have been able to use their positions to enable and even profit from honor killings and trafficking, according to select reports from the region (Amnesty International 1999; Shah et al. 2002; Ghosh 2009). Several news reports implicate law enforcement in collaborating with family members to complete honor killings in Pakistan (HRCP 2012).

In part because of problems in official systems, feudal extra-judicial structures are thriving across many parts of the region. Several studies of the social aspects of honor crimes, for example, suggest that heightened risk of such violence can be attributed less to class, ethnicity, or religion per se than to persistent feudal structures that have incentives to maintain political and social control over local communities (Srivastava 2009; Kirti et al. 2011; Chesler and Bloom 2012). According to numerous sources, wherever ad hoc and standing local councils (i.e., *Shuras* and *Jirgas*) in Afghanistan and Pakistan, and the *khap panchayats* in India, remain strong, they have been known at times to condone or encourage honor killings, rapes, and other forms of sexual harassment and, in the case of India and Pakistan, even trafficking (Human Rights Watch 2010; Kachhwaha 2011; Kirti et al. 2011; Ribin 2012; Basu 2013; Gandhara 2013). Given that many cases of such violence tried by these "courts" come to light only because local media report them, actual numbers are certainly much higher.

In Afghanistan, *jirgas'* rulings sometimes do not even follow sharia law, which requires trials before calling for honor killings, adhering instead to tribal customs that are especially severe for females (Ribin 2012). In India, *khap panchayats* are known to mete out honor killing sentences. Despite their unconstitutionality, *khap panchayats* are trusted by local sections of castes to protect family honor and to take "quick, unilateral and incontestable decisions on multiple issues like social transgressions, marriage, offences, property rights, inheritance, or regarding situations threatening tranquility in the village. It is through them that 'the most regressive social views' are sought to be implemented" (Kachhwaha 2011, 297–98).

In some instances, the formal legal system has tried to hold local leaders and extrajudicial courts accountable. In Pakistan, the only country in the region with a law against honor killing, the Criminal Law (Amendment) Act was passed in 2004 and became law in January 2005. This amendment to Pakistan's Penal Code of 1860 defines honor violence and imposes a minimum 10 years' imprisonment for perpetrators; it also outlaws and imposes a punishment for forced marriage (Lari 2011). In India, alarmed by the rise in honor killings being reported across the country, the Indian Supreme Court issued notices to the central government and seven states in 2010, instructing them to take measures to protect potential victims (Chesler and Bloom 2012; Vasudevan 2010). In 2011, the court declared all honor killings ordered by *khap panchayats* to be illegal, remarking that honor killing was a barbaric practice that must be eradicated (Chesler and Bloom 2012). Other actions have originated at the highest levels of the government of India. In 2010, Prime Minister Manmohan Singh ordered a cabinet-level commission to draft national legislation to eradicate honor killings. Key proposals included a penal code amendment that allows *khap panchayat* leaders who sanction honor killings to be charged with murder and revokes the 30-day notice period of the Special Marriage Act, which enables families to track down and preemptively kill couples (Chesler and Bloom 2012). In 2011, the Law Commission of India, under the Ministry of Law and Justice, drafted the Endangerment of Life and Liberty (Protection, Prosecution, and Other Measures) Act. The bill was designed to prevent *khap panchayats* from denouncing couples that transgress caste restrictions (Venkatesan 2011). These legal efforts have met with considerable resistance from political groups, some state governments, and local leadership—particularly the powerful *khap panchayats*, which claim that such legislation violates traditional and customary rights (Human Rights Watch 2010; Sharma 2013). Partly as a consequence, India still has no explicit active legislation against honor killing.

Conflict and Natural Disasters

As noted earlier in this chapter, women and girls are particularly vulnerable to violence in circumstances of armed conflict or political instability (box 3.3). Like conflict, natural disasters also tend to heighten the threat of violence against women and girls. First, restrictive migration policies exclude unskilled workers—especially women—and poor families who are displaced by disasters, forcing them to seek livelihoods in devastated areas through illicit channels that can expose women to additional risks of violence (Skeldon 2000; Ali 2005). For instance, floods, drought, and other natural disasters in Bangladesh, India, and Pakistan are documented as putting women and girls at greater

---

BOX 3.3 Custodial Violence in Conflict-Affected Areas: Sri Lanka

Estimating prevalence of violence against women in conflict areas is difficult given the very low likelihood of women ever reporting these crimes, especially for women in captivity, as occurred during Sri Lanka's civil war (Government of Sri Lanka 2011). Violence against women in numerous forms can continue in these same areas, even after the official end of the conflict. One presentation made in 2010 to Sri Lanka's Commission of Inquiry on Lessons Learned and Reconciliation Commission reported that such violence, as well as structural discrimination against women, had escalated in former conflict areas. "It was stated that discriminatory policies and practices, heavy military presence, lack of authority to control their environment, limited access to basic needs combined with weak institutional protection mechanisms and breakdown of traditional support networks, norms and prejudices against women in the society and attitudes and behavior of power players have led to a culture of violence and impunity. As such, it was claimed that such a situation exposes women to various forms of sexual and gender based violence that compromise their dignity, security, well being and rights..." (Government of Sri Lanka 2011, 185).

risk of trafficking (Gazi et al. 2001; Ali 2005; Ghosh 2009). Female refugees displaced by conflict or disasters face an extremely high threat of violence, sometimes with little recourse to justice (box 3.4).

SOCIAL NORMS AS RISK FACTORS

Conceptions of honor, femininity, and regulated sexuality that form the parameters of socially acceptable notions of a "good" woman underlie many of the risks of violence that South Asian women and girls face throughout their lives. Most directly, these notions influence perpetrators' decisions to sexually harass women and girls, who may be perceived as transgressing these social "rules" by choosing a marital or sexual partner deemed inappropriate, by venturing into public spaces at night or without socially acceptable escorts, or by leading lives that are not considered sufficiently traditional or protected. Having transgressed—and thereby undermining the honor of their bodies, families, or communities—these women and girls are at heightened risk of custodial violence, trafficking, rape, and other forms of sexual harassment (Jejeebhoy and Bott 2003; Naved 2003; AIHRC 2013). A case in point is the ongoing discrimination and violence experienced by women in Nepal's Badi community, who are stigmatized by their identification with prostitution (box 3.5).

BOX 3.4 Gender-Based Violence in Refugee Camps in Bhutan

In the early 1990s, around 100,000 Lhotsampa, people of Nepali origin living in southern Bhutan, were evicted from their homes when the government introduced a new law revoking their citizenship and civil rights due to ancestry. This resulted in the flight of individuals to Nepal. Most of these refugees have been resettled in Western countries, including Australia, Canada, and the United States: of the more than 108,000 refugees in camps in eastern Nepal, 86,000 had been resettled by December 2013 to eight different countries (IRIN 2013).

Prior to their resettlement, the issue of gender-based violence in the refugee camps of eastern Nepal attracted widespread attention after Human Rights Watch published a report detailing sexual exploitation and violence among these refugees (Human Rights Watch 2003). In 2002, investigations carried out by the United Nations High Commissioner for Refugees had also revealed 18 cases of gender-based violence, including some perpetrated by employees of the United Nations agency or its implementing partners. Such abuses sometimes occurred in schools, which, according to the 2003 report, may have resulted in the community becoming afraid to send girls to school (Human Rights Watch 2003).

Given the stigma surrounding rape and sexual abuse, many cases reported to the camp authorities were settled by the camp committees encouraging the survivors to marry the perpetrators. Cases of intimate partner violence were also settled without any recourse to judicial action because the camp management committees preferred reconciliation. In the absence of legal recourse, these reconciliations, which are widespread in Nepali society as well as inside the camps, allowed the continuation of sexual violence and exploitation and further inhibited the survivors from speaking out. A report by Oxfam in 2000 corroborated earlier reports of widespread intimate partner violence that was exacerbated by social pressures to keep such abuse hidden (Poudel 2000).

BOX 3.5 Stigma of Tradition: Badi Women of Nepal

They supposedly came to Nepal in the 14th century to work as entertainers, singers, and dancers in the courts of petty kings in the mid- and far-western parts of Nepal, but over centuries the fortunes of the Badi community have declined significantly (Cox 2000). When subsequent rulers imposed a rigid caste system on society, as exemplified by the Muluki Ain (General Code) of 1857, the Badi were categorized as "untouchables," meaning that members of so-called higher castes could forbid them to enter their houses, marry their children, or even drink from a cup they had touched. A further blow came in the 1960s, when the rulers of Nepal abolished the semiautonomous feudatory principalities in the western hills (Regmi 1977), depriving the Badi of patrons. Although the Muluki Ain of 1963 banned all forms of caste-based discrimination, it continues to exist. Today, due to the shackles of the caste system and destitution, the community is known all over Nepal for prostitution. Many Badi elders, men who once earned a livelihood making musical instruments or fishing, live off their daughters, who turn to selling their bodies when they reach puberty. The daughters' earnings remain in the maternal family.

In 1999–2000, the Tole Sudhaar Samiti (Community Improvement Committee) of Rajpura village in Dang decided to end the tradition of prostitution, in a collective effort by both Badi and non-Badi people. A watch group was formed to keep surveillance over the Badi community. When they found customers going into the community, they either talked to them or, after repeated interceptions, fined them. Through this grassroots effort and raising awareness, they were able to significantly reduce the prevalence of this traditional profession of prostitution.

Today, Badi women claim that the tradition of prostitution has ended; however, this cannot be verified because of the sensitivities involved in asking women if they are engaged in the sex trade. Badi girls born into this small community of 38,000 continue to face violence from an early age (CBS 2011). Because of the nature of the profession, children born to Badi women are often denied citizenship in the absence of a recognized father, despite laws that allow citizenship based on maternal lineage. In addition, stereotypes from the past still haunt them. They are discriminated against and treated as inferior beings due to the popular perception of them, rooted in their traditional role as sex workers. Nirmal Gupta, president of Dalit Mahila Ekta Kendra, said that she once heard a Dalit man say to a Badi woman, "Yesterday you would have been sold for 50 rupees."[11]

The government of Nepal has formed a Badi Upliftment and Development Committee within the Ministry of Federal Affairs and Local Development. The Dalit Welfare Organization and Backward Society Education have been working with Badi women since the 1990s, with supporting funds from UNICEF, the Danish International Development Agency, and Save the Children Norway, to prevent the spread of HIV/AIDS and to provide nonformal education to Badi women and children. NGOs that target marginalized populations, such as the Social Development Centre, also provide skills training to Badi women.

In the case of honor killings, these norms can twist the very definition of violence. This is because notions of "honor" and its preservation are intertwined with notions of the "good" and "chaste" woman, as well as belief in the supremacy of the male-headed family unit in making decisions about a woman's sexuality and choice of partner. Thus, for instance, Baxi et al. (2006) and Siddiqi (2012) find in India and Bangladesh that when a woman chooses a marriage or a non-marital sexual relationship that may go against the will of her family, such a consensual relationship is treated as a "crime" against "honor" and judged as such; a woman is denied her rights in the domestic sphere. This is not to say that the honor killings meted out to young women and men who dare to choose their own partner are not a serious violation of rights for both. Rather, feminist scholars caution that until political and social norms move away from regarding women as needing protection and toward recognizing women as citizens with equal rights in public and domestic spheres, legal and social systems seeking to address or prevent honor killings, rape, and similar forms of "honor-related" violence may inadvertently or deliberately override women's rights (see discussions, for example, in Siddiqi 2003; Welchman and Hossain 2005).

The very existence of these norms triggers violence: research suggests that simply by having rigid proscriptions on female behavior (such as taboos against the intermingling of boys and girls and female sexuality), societies put women at greater risk of sexual harassment (Jejeebhoy and Bott 2003; Perera et al. 2011; Perveen 2012). These notions interact with various other situations at the macro social level to increase risks of multi-life-stage forms of violence for particular groups of women and girls or in particular living situations. Potential circumstances include the additional risks triggered by migration and globalization and by caste, religion, tribe, ethnicity, or other group identity.

Migration and Globalization

A growing pool of literature from South Asia attributes rising rates of honor killing, trafficking, and sexual harassment of women in the region to the clash between contemporary values brought in by globalization and modernization, on the one hand, and the deeply entrenched and gendered beliefs and systems that have ordered South Asian societies for centuries and even millennia, on the other (Siddiqi 2003; Choudhury 2007; Ghosh 2009; Chowdhry 2010; Chesler and Bloom 2012; Ribin 2012; Kapur 2013). Globalization and related socioeconomic shifts can bring empowering benefits to women, such as increased employment opportunities, greater involvement in public life, and enhanced access to information and services. They also may place women and girls in unfamiliar and dangerous environments, such as when women migrate across long distances for work opportunities (Bal Kumar 2001; Gazi et al. 2001; Huda 2006; Ghosh 2009; UNODC 2012). Unfortunately, we could find no data or research that tests these proposed relationships between such violence and these particular macro-level factors.

Caste, Tribe, Ethnicity, and Religion

Membership in excluded communities interacts not only with social norms but also with poverty to place women from such groups at particularly high risk of various forms of violence. Women from groups that are traditionally excluded and discriminated against in South Asian countries—whether because of ethnicity, religion, caste, or tribe—tend to be poorer than the majority. Doubly disadvantaged by poverty and their particular social group status, they are especially vulnerable to trafficking, sexual harassment, and custodial violence (box 3.6). For example, police investigations across

BOX 3.6 Double Marginalization and Violence

Women within an economically, historically, and socially marginalized community are at double risk of violence because of their gender and disadvantaged status as members of a minority or other marginalized group. In South Asia, this violence is institutionalized at all life stages of women in such groups and hence becomes normalized. Some of these groups include lower-caste Dalit women in India, Nepal, and Pakistan (PDSN and IDSN 2013); women from scheduled tribes or indigenous communities in Bangladesh, India, and Nepal; and women from ethnic, religious, and sexual minority groups throughout South Asia.

In India, Dalit and Adivasi schoolgirls are more vulnerable than other schoolgirls to bullying, violence, and verbal abuse, negatively affecting their learning (Balagopalan and Subramanian 2003). In Nepal, ethnic minority and Dalit girls are more at risk of being trafficked due to lack of education and severe poverty (Hennink and Simkhada 2004). Women and girls from these communities might underreport violence for fear of stigma (Dutta et al. 2010), apathy and prejudice from the justice system (Irudayam et al. 2006), repercussions of reporting violence—or because of an undue burden to represent the men in their community positively. Risks to women increase in times of conflict, when women's bodies can become spaces for men to reassert dominance and seek revenge (Nussbaum 2009). Across countries in the region, women from socially disadvantaged groups and religious minorities are particularly vulnerable to rape and other sexual violence in times of sectarian conflict (GOI 2002; Kapadia 2002; National Human Rights Commission of India 2002; SAARC 2006; Sen 2007; Government of Sri Lanka 2011).

A 2006 study in Andhra Pradesh, Bihar, Tamil Nadu, and Uttar Pradesh, India, finds a wide range of forms of violence perpetrated against Dalit women, within and outside of the home, and including verbal abuse, sexual harassment and assault, sexual exploitation, forced prostitution, kidnapping and abduction, and forced incarceration. The majority of women surveyed had experienced several of these kinds of violence (Irudayam et al. 2006, 4), with over 20 percent reporting gang rape. Women from minority and other disadvantaged groups in particular are targeted for violence when they transgress norms to demand their constitutional rights, such as access to public services (for example, transportation), temples, or food rations; or attempt to access their political rights or aspire to political life (Irudayam et al. 2006). Women of the scheduled tribes in the northeastern states of India, where conflict is rife, are highly vulnerable to violence, including rape and sexual harassment (McDuie-Ra 2012).

A study examining violence experienced by women sex workers, lesbian women, and disabled women in Bangladesh, India, and Nepal finds that the violence they face because of their marginalized status is exacerbated by social stigma and large gaps in their awareness of and access to services (CREA 2012). In its 2013 report, Minority Rights Group International also notes that a great disparity in access to health services is one of the key areas of structural violence against indigenous, lower caste communities and religious minorities across most of South Asia. In Nepal, for instance "untouchability" affects Dalit women's access to education, health care and employment (Bhattachan et al. 2009; OHCHR 2011).

When attempting to achieve the Millennium Development Goals, many governments neglect to measure the progress of minority groups, instead targeting populations that are easiest to reach and whose level of inequality is least costly to address (Minority Rights Group International 2013, 12). Failure to recognize or discuss the issues of these distinct

box continues next page

> **BOX 3.6 Double Marginalization and Violence** *(continued)*
>
> social groups means that there is little systematic research or intervention that tracks or addresses the risks and prevalence of violence they face or their access to services. As the discussion of their increased vulnerability illustrates, however, such analysis of double marginalization and its effect on risks of violence is imperative to help policy makers and women's and minority movements better strategize and implement policies and programs that protect the rights of minority women (Irudayam et al. 2006).

northern India document how minor girls from disadvantaged groups can be kidnapped to be raised and sent away to practice prostitution (UNODC 2012). Recruitment agencies in India also tend to target children from distant tribal villages, who are falsely promised gainful employment and then sold to employers who neither pay them nor give them time off. Often the children are physically and sexually abused, and no money is remitted to their families (UNODC 2012).

In Nepal, the Dalit community and hill ethnic groups are most at risk of trafficking (Bal Kumar 2001) and have experienced higher-than-average rates of custodial violence while in detention. In a study of torture of female Nepalis who were detained in 2010, analysis of caste and ethnic data reveals that women from Terai ethnic groups (representing 9.4 percent of detainees) had higher levels of reported torture than the Brahmin and Chhetri caste majority (40.7 percent) (Advocacy Forum 2011). Other research does not estimate violence prevalence among women from disadvantaged groups, but it does offer case studies to illustrate how minority and indigenous women in Bangladesh, low-caste and tribal women in India, ethnic minority women in Nepal, and women in conflict zones of Sri Lanka have been at particular risk of sexual violence and other abuse by security forces while in custody (SAARC 2006; Government of Sri Lanka 2011).

The role of religion and caste in marriage is a key way in which these social identities interact with underlying gender norms to increase the risks for violence. Communities based on religion and caste are deeply invested in the marital and sexual aspects of community dynamics, in large part in order to maintain the gendered aspects of the patriarchal system prevalent in much of the region, including male bias, son preference, feminine and masculine roles, honor and regulation of sexuality, and dowry. Most honor killings in South Asia are punitive responses to marriage or sexual relations outside of the acceptable religion or caste or within the same sub-caste or *gotra*.[12] In another example of the interaction between caste and gender norms, because trafficked brides in India tend to be of lower caste than the families into which they marry, they often are judged to have brought dishonor to these families. Hence, they are at extremely high risk of psychological and physical abuse and rape in their new families and communities. Because of their low status, trafficked brides also are vulnerable to being trafficked again (Gazi et al. 2001; Ali 2005).

Most disturbingly, societies at large—including women—continue to defend these social, normative, and caste- and religion-based rules, across urban as well as rural populations. For instance, despite the 1955 Hindu Marriage Act's legalization of inter-caste and intra-gotra marriages in India, two-thirds of Indian people surveyed in 2006 opposed inter-caste marriage (Chesler and Bloom 2012). The same is true of religion. Of 601 sampled individuals in Islamabad, Pakistan, 49 percent of whom were women, more than half (57.1 percent) approved of honor killings under adulterous circumstances described to them in a vignette (Shaikh et al. 2010). More men than women approved, however, of death as an appropriate punishment for an honor crime, for accused women as well as men. A considerably greater share of women (28.1 percent) than men (15.2 percent)—but still the minority of individuals sampled—opined that the man should have forgiven his wife (Shaikh et al. 2010).

Summary and Conclusion

Our review illustrates the extent to which women's own characteristics; those of their partners, households, and communities; the failure of institutions; and rigidly patriarchal social norms all create a dynamic landscape of risks and potential protection for women's vulnerability to myriad forms of violence in South Asia. Certain risk and protective factors stand out. At the individual level, the research unequivocally notes that childhood exposure to violence is a key risk factor for women's future vulnerability to violence as adults, and for men's greater risk of being perpetrators. Life stage itself would appear to be important as well, such that young girls and adolescents are at heightened risk of many forms of violence, such as excess female child mortality, child marriage, intimate partner violence, trafficking, and sexual harassment. The ability of women and girls to negotiate—with peers, parents, spouses, family members, and society at large—is likely to be protective, but rigorous research unfortunately is scarce, especially regarding what kinds of negotiation skills are most useful. Secondary education is considered protective as well, possibly by providing women the opportunity to gain more skills and confidence; however, education may not be protective for all types of violence, as research on excess female child mortality illustrates. At the level of the immediate environment, a small but unequivocal body of research posits that alcohol abuse is a key risk factor for triggering violence. Low socio-economic status is also highlighted as an important risk factor because of the circumstances that emerge from poverty, such as heightened stress in day-to-day living that creates conditions for interpersonal violence or trafficking; and the imperative to balance costs and benefits with limited resources, which contributes to excess female child mortality and child marriage. Yet, women from higher-income groups or households may continue to be vulnerable to some forms of violence.

While there is limited econometric analysis on the role of institutional, community, and social normative factors in perpetuating violence against women and girls, a vast body of qualitative research makes clear their seminal role in enabling violence to occur in the home, in schools, in workplaces, and elsewhere. For the most part, governments in South Asia have instituted at least a minimum basket of laws that ostensibly should not allow violence to be as pervasive as it is. However, it is in the implementation of these laws that the system breaks down. Many studies repeatedly and consistently point to system failures, such as lack of monitoring and follow-up in law enforcement, gender biases among those tasked with implementing laws, corruption in systems, and the impunity enjoyed by perpetrators. In part because of the failure of formal systems across much of the region, informal judicial and governance systems that further entrench gender inequality flourish, with implications for forms of violence such as honor killings and consequences for the type of recourse women can expect. These systems also maintain entrenched traditional patriarchal norms that perpetuate a low value of women and, hence, violence against them.

The ongoing collision of age-old gendered traditions and the countervailing forces of modernity and globalization may also partially explain the intense involvement of the *shalish*, *khap panchayats*, and *loya jirgas* in cases of violence against women and girls. Women's and girls' enhanced sense of independence from greater exposure to public life and from earning their own incomes has enabled the emergence of a "new" citizen in South Asian countries, where freedom of expression has embarked on a struggle with "...subversive expressions of gender or sexuality" (Kapur 2013, 31). This emerging identity of equal citizen—in direct contrast to potential victim under male protection—can have unsettling implications for the rigid gender norms that men and male-controlled institutions are expected to protect. Given the inevitability of continuing economic growth and modernization in the region, mitigating violence will depend in part on loosening these traditions and norms. In particular, it will require efforts to shift citizens' and leaders' conceptions of women and girls, not as bearers of honor to be protected and essentially owned within the male-dominated power structures, but as individual citizens with their own powers of self-determination and rights, including the right to sexual expression (Kapur 2013). Chapter 4 summarizes such efforts in the region, among other interventions, to prevent and respond to violence against women and girls.

Notes

1. World Bank Gender Statistics. http://datatopics.worldbank.org/gender/region/south-asia.

2. Bangladesh, India, Maldives, and Pakistan have signed the convention with reservations; India and Pakistan have signed with declarations.

3. Qasim Shah, Sadia. "Women Activists, Religious Parties Differ on Domestic Violence." *Dawn*. 29 March 2014. http://www.dawn.com/news/1096299/women-activists-religious-parties -differ-on-domestic-violence.

4. Rolfes, Ellen. "Maldivian president rejects 'un-Islamic' ban on some forms of marital rape." PBS Newshour. 16 January 2014. http://www.pbs.org/newshour/rundown/maldivian -president-rejects-un-islamic-ban-on-some-forms-of-marital-rape/.

5. *Khap* and *jati* panchayats are councils based on clan (*khap*) or caste (*jati*) that were organized in ancient societies to serve as community-level representative bodies. Despite being
   outlawed and not recognized as part of India's official third-tier Panchayati Raj system
   of government, these councils maintain great power over communities in select parts of
   India—typically rural areas in the North—and often act as local courts.

6. An outgrowth of traditional rural power structures in Bangladesh, the shalish system is a
   process of mediation. The mediators, or "Shalishkars," tend to be wealthy, powerful, and
   socially accepted male members of communities. Although they fall outside the legal court
   system, shalish councils are often used to resolve local disputes or conflicts.

7. The correlation of the child abuse scale with the parental acceptance-rejection scale for
   fathers and mothers was highly significant (= .60, .57, p < .0001).

8. Sexual abuse suffered by boys cannot be minimized, but it is beyond the scope of this report,
   as noted in chapter 1.

9. We use the term "multiple-stage" or "cross-cutting" to refer to forms of violence that can
   occur at multiple points in the life cycle.

10. For more information, see http://justiceforwomenindia.wordpress.com/tag/trafficking
    -statistics-in-india/.

11. Interview with Nirmal Gupta, January 2014.

12. Hindu religious law and tradition prohibit relationships between members of the same caste-
    based clan or sub-caste (gotra) to prevent descendants of common ancestry from marrying
    (Panniyankara 2013).

References

Abramsky, Tanya, Charlotte H Watts, Claudia Garcia-Moreno, Karen Devries, Ligia Kiss, Mary
   Ellsberg, Henrica AFM Jansen, and Lori Heise. 2011. "What Factors Are Associated with
   Recent Intimate Partner Violence? Findings from the WHO Multi-Country Study on Women's
   Health and Domestic Violence." *BMC Public Health* (1): 11–109.

ACHR (Asian Centre for Human Rights). 2007. "Addressing Custodial Violence: Recommendations
   to the NHRC." ACHR, New Delhi.

———. 2013. "India's Hell Holes: Child Sexual Assault in Juvenile Justice Homes." ACHR,
   New Delhi.

Ackerson, Leland K, Ichiro Kawachi, Elizabeth M Barbeau, and S V Subramanian. 2008.
   "Effects of Individual and Proximate Educational Context on Intimate Partner Violence:
   A Population-Based Study of Women in India." *American Journal of Public Health* 98 (3):
   507–14.

Ackerson, Leland K, and S V Subramanian. 2009. "Intimate Partner Violence and Death among
   Infants and Children in India." *Pediatrics* 124 (5): e878–89.

ADB (Asian Development Bank). 2000. "Country Briefing Paper: Women in Pakistan." ADB,
   Washington, DC.

———. 2001. "Country Briefing Paper: Women in the Republic of Maldives." ADB,
   Washington, DC.

———. 2008. "Country Gender Assessment: Sri Lanka." ADB, Mandaluyong City, Philippines.

Adhikari, Ramesh, and Jyotsna Tamang. 2010. "Sexual Coercion of Married Women in Nepal." *BMC Women's Health* (1): 10–31.

Advocacy Forum. 2011. *Torture of Women in Detention: Nepal's Failure to Prevent and Protect.* Kathmandu: Advocacy Forum of Nepal.

Ahmed, Syed Masud. 2005. "Intimate Partner Violence against Women: Experiences from a Woman-Focused Development Programme in Matlab, Bangladesh." *Journal of Health, Population, and Nutrition* 23 (1): 95–101.

AIHRC (Afghanistan Independent Human Rights Commission). 2013. "National Inquiry on Rape and Honor Killing in Afghanistan Report Summary." http://www.aihrc.org.af/home /research_report/1571.

Alder, C., and K. Polk. 2004. "Gender Issues in the Criminal Justice System of the Maldives." University of Melbourne, Department of Criminology, 2 September 2004. http://www.unicef .org/maldives/Gender_Issues_in_the_Criminal_Justice_System.pdf.

Ali, A. K. M. Masud. 2005. "Treading along a Treacherous Trail: Research on Trafficking in Persons in South Asia." *International Migration* 43 (1–2): 142–64.

Ali, Aliyah, and Nasreen Aslam Shah. 2011. "Women Prisoners in Pakistan: Changing Practices to Enforce Laws & Rights." *Kuwait Chapter of Arabian Journal of Business and Management Review* 1 (4): 57–63.

Amin, Sajeda. 2008. "Reforming Marriage Practices in Bangladesh" Brief No. 31, Population Council, Washington, DC.

Amin, Sajeda, and Lopita Huq. 2008. "Marriage Considerations in Sending Girls to School in Bangladesh: Some Qualitative Evidence." Working Paper No. 12, Population Council, Washington, DC.

Amin, S., and L Suran. 2005. "The Impact of Marriage Payments on Leisure Housework and Abuse of Young Wives: Evidence from Rural Bangladesh." [Unpublished]. Presented at the 2005 Annual Meeting of the Population Association of America, Philadelphia, Pennsylvania. March 31–April 2 2005.

Amnesty International. 1999. "Pakistan: Honour Killings of Girls and Women." http://www .amnesty.org/en/library/asset/ASA33/018/1999/en/9fe83c27-e0f1-11dd-be39-2d4003be4450 /asa330181999en.pdf.

———. 2002. "Sri Lanka: Rape in Custody." http://www.amnesty.org/en/library/info/ASA37 /001/2002.

Anderson, Siwan. 2000. "The Economics of Dowry Payments in Pakistan." Center for Economic Research, Tilburg University.

———. 2004. "Dowry and Property Rights." Department of Economics, University of British Columbia.

Ashdown, Julie, and Mel James. 2010. "Women in Detention." *International Review of the Red Cross* 92 (877): 123–141.

Asia Foundation, DFID, and SAATHI. 2010. "Preliminary Mapping of Gender Based Violence: Nepal." The Asia Foundation, Kathmandu.

Asling-Monemi, K., R. T. Naved. 2009. "Violence against Women and Increases in the Risk of Diarrheal Disease and Respiratory Tract Infections in Infancy." *Journal of the American Medical Association* 163 (10): 931–36.

Azhar, Nasreen. 2011. "Violence Against Women in Pakistan: A Qualitative Review of Statistics for 2011." Islamabad: Aurat Publication and Information Service Foundation.

Bairagi, Rasheshywam. 1986. "Food Crisis, Nutrition, and Female Children in Rural Bangladesh" *Population and Development Review* 12 (2): 307–15.

Bajracharya, Ashish, and Sajeda Amin. 2010. "Poverty, Gender, and Youth: Poverty, Marriage Timing, and Transitions to Adulthood in Nepal: A Longitudinal Analysis Using the Nepal Living Standards Survey." Population Council, New York.

Bajracharya, Ashish, and Sajeda Amin. 2013. "Microcredit and Domestic Violence in Bangladesh: An Exploration of Selection Bias Influences." *Demography* 50 (5): 1819–43.

Bal Kumar, K. 2001. "Trafficking of Girls in Nepal with Special Reference to Prostitution—A Rapid Assessment." Kathmandu: International Labour Organisation/International Programme on Elimination of Child Labour.

Balagopalan, S. and R. Subramanian. 2003. "*Dalit* and *Adivasi* Children in Schools: Some Preliminar Research Themes and Findings." *IDS Bulletin* 34 (1): 43–54.

Banerjee, Sikata. 2005. *Make Me a Man! Masculinity, Hinduism, and Nationalism in India*. Albany: SUNY Press.

Basu, Alaka M. 1989, "Is Discrimination in Food Really Necessary for Explaining Sex Differentials in Childhood Mortality?" *Population Studies: A Journal of Demography* 43 (2): 193–210.

Basu, Nupur. 2013. "Honour Killings: Crying Shame." *Aljazeera*. http://www.aljazeera.com /indepth/opinion/2013/11/honour-killings-india-crying-shame-20131127105910392176 .html.

Bates, L. M., S. R. Schuler, F. Islam, and Md. K. Islam. 2004. "Socioeconomic Factors and Processes Associated with Domestic Violence in Rural Bangadesh." *International Family Planning Perspectives* 30 (4): 190–99.

Bates, Lisa M, Joanna Maselko, and Sidney Ruth Schuler. 2007. "Women's Education and the Timing of Marriage and Childbearing in the Next Generation: Evidence from Rural Bangladesh." *Studies in Family Planning* 38 (2): 101–12.

Baughman, D. and J. O'Hara. 2010. "Bhuto" *Yellow Pad Productions in Association with ICON TMI*.

Baxi, Pratiksha, Shirin M. Rai and Shaheen Sardar Ali. 2006. "Legacies of Common Law: 'Crimes of Honour' in India and Pakistan." *Third World Quarterly* 27(7): 1239–53.

BBC (British Broadcasting Corporation) News India. 2013. "India Honour Killings: Paying the Price for Falling in Love." BBC (http://www.bbc.co.uk/news/world-asia-india-24170866).

Beattie, Tara S H, Parinita Bhattacharjee, B M Ramesh, Vandana Gurnani, John Anthony, Shajy Isac, H L Mohan, et al. 2010. "Violence against Female Sex Workers in Karnataka State, South India: Impact on Health, and Reductions in Violence Following an Intervention Program." *BMC Public Health* 10: 476–87.

Bedi, Arjun Singh, and Sharada Srinivasan. 2012. "Bare Branches and Drifting Kites: Tackling Female Infanticide and Foeticide in Tamil Nadu." In *Development, Freedom and Welfare: Essays Presented to Amartya Sen by Young Scholars*. Cambridge, UK: Oxford University Press.

Bhalotra, Sonia, Christine Valente, and Arthur van Soest. 2009. "The Puzzle of Muslim Advantage in Child Survival in India." *Journal of Health Economics* 29 (2): 191–204.

Bhattachan, Krishna B., Tej B. Sunar, and Yasso K. Bhattachan (Gauchan). 2009. "Caste-based Discrimination in Nepal." Working Paper Series, Volume III Number 08. Indian Institute of Dalit Studies, New Delhi.

Bhuiya, Abbas, and Kim Streatfield. 1991. "Mothers' Education and Survival of Female Children in a Rural Area of Bangladesh." *Population Studies* 45 (2): 253–64.

BLAST (Bangladesh Legal Aid and Services Trust). 2009. "Report on Legislative Initiatives and Reforms in the Family Laws." http://www.blast.org.bd/content/publications/Legislative _Inititiatives_Family_Law.pdf.

Blue Veins. 2013. "Breaking the Barriers: Going the Distance to Make Swara History." n.p.

Bott, Sarah, Shireen Jejeebhoy, Iqbal Shah, and Chander Puri. 2003. *Towards Adulthood: Exploring the Sexual and Reproductive Health of Adolescents in South Asia*. Geneva: World Health Organization.

Butt, R., and M. Zia. 2012. "Pakistan NGO Alternative Report on CEDAW—2005–2009 (with Updated Notes 2009–2012)." Aurat Publication and Information Service Foundation, Islamabad.

Catani, Claudia, Nadja Jacob, Elisabeth Schauer, Mahendran Kohila, and Frank Neuner. 2008. "Family Violence, War, and Natural Disasters: A Study of the Effect of Extreme Stress on Children's Mental Health in Sri Lanka." *BMC Psychiatry* 8 (1): 33.

CBS (Central Bureau of Statistics). 2011. *National Population and Housing Census 2011*.

Cheema, Iqtidar K. 2005. "Trafficking of Women in South Asia." *Humanities* 41 (1): 83–97.

Cheema, M. H., and A. R. Mustafa. 2009. "From the Hudood Ordinances to the Protection of Women Act: Islamic Critiques of the Hudood Laws of Pakistan." *UCLA Journal of Islamic and Near Eastern Law* 8 (2008–2009): 1–48.

Chesler, Phyllis, and Nathan Bloom. 2012. "Hindu vs. Muslim Honor Killings." *Middle East Quarterly* 19 (3): 43–52.

Choudhury, Nusrat. 2007. "Constrained Spaces for Islamic Feminism: Women's Rights and the 2004 Constitution of Afghanistan." *Yale Journal of Law and Feminism* 19: 155–99.

Chowdhry, Prem. 2010. "Redeeming 'Honour' through Violence: Unraveling the Concept and Its Application." http://cequinindia.org/images/ResourcesItem/Pdf/Honour%20killings%20by %20Prem%20Choudhury.pdf.

Corsi, Daniel J, Diego G Bassani, Rajesh Kumar, Shally Awasthi, Raju Jotkar, Navkiran Kaur, and Prabhat Jha. 2009. "Gender Inequity and Age-Appropriate Immunization Coverage in India from 1992 to 2006." *BMC International Health and Human Rights* 9 (Suppl 1), S3.

Cox, Thomas E. 2000. "The Intended and Unintended Consequences of AIDS Prevention among Badi in Tulispur." *Himalaya, the Journal of the Association for Nepal and Himalayan Studies.* 20 (1): Article 8.

CREA (Creating Resources for Empowerment in Action). 2012. "Count Me IN! Research Report on Violence against Disabled, Lesbian, and Sex-Working Women in Bangladesh, India, and Nepal." CREA, New Delhi, India.

Daily Times. 2011. "Police Least Trusted among Professions in Pakistan: Gallup Poll." http://tribune .com.pk/story/178778/police-least-trusted-among-professions-in-pakistan-gallup-poll.

Das Gupta, Monica. 1987. "Selective Discrimination against Female Children in Rural Punjab, India." *Population and Development Review* 13 (1): 77–100.

Das Gupta, Monica, Jiang Zhenghua, Li Bohua, Xie Zhenming, Woojin Chung, and Bae Hwa-ok. 2003. "Why Is Son Preference so Persistent in East and South Asia? A Cross-Country Study of China, India and the Republic of Korea." *The Journal of Development Studies* 40 (2): 153–87.

De Mel, N., P. Peiris, and S. Gomez. 2013. "Broadening Gender: Why Masculinities Matter: Attitudes, Practices, and Gender-Based Violence in Four Districts in Sri Lanka." Care International, Sri Lanka.

Devarajan, S., and I. Nabi. 2006. "Economic Growth in South Asia: Promising, Un-equalizing, ... Sustainable?" South Asia Region, World Bank, Washington, DC.

Dolan, K., and S. Larney. 2009. "A Review of HIV in Prisons in Nepal." *Kathmandu University Medical Journal* 7 (4, 28): 351–54.

Druk Associates. 2011. "Country Synthesis Report: Bhutan." Background paper for Muñoz Boudet et al. 2013.

D'Souza, Stan, and Lincoln C Chen. 1980. "Sex Differentials in Mortality in Rural Bangladesh." *Population and Development Review* 6 (2): 257–70.

Dutta, Mondira, Bupinder Zutshi, and Alok Vajpeyi. 2010. "UNIFEM Regional Anti-Trafficking Programme in South Asia (2000–2009)." *Evaluation Report. India: UNIFEM.*

ECPAT International (End Child Prostitution, Child Pornography and Trafficking of Children for Sexual Purposes). 2011. "Global Monitoring: Status of Action against Commercial Sexual Exploitation of Children (Bangladesh)." *ECPAT International*, 2nd Edition.

Ekantipur Report. 2013. "Kamlaris Call Strike in 22 Tarai Districts." *Kantipur*, Dang, June 4, 2013. http://www.ekantipur.com/2013/06/04/top-story/kamlaris-call-strike-in-22-tarai-districts/372732.html.

Faizal, Farah, and Swarna Rajagopalan. 2005. *Women, Security, South Asia: A Clearing in the Thicket.* New Delhi: SAGE Publications.

Field, Erica, and Attila Ambrus. 2008. "Early Marriage, Age of Menarche, and Female Schooling Attainment in Bangladesh." *Journal of Political Economy* 116 (5): 881–930.

Fikree, F F, and L I Bhatti. 1999. "Domestic Violence and Health of Pakistani Women." *International Journal of Gynaecology and Obstetrics* 65 (2): 195–201.

Fulu, Emma, Xian Warner, Stephanie Miedema, Rachel Jewkes, Tim Roselli, and James Lang. 2013. *Why Do Some Men Use Violence Against Women and How Can We Prevent It? Quantitative Findings from the UN Multi-country Study on Men and Violence in Asia and the Pacific.* Bangkok: UNDP, UNFPA, UN Women and UNV.

Gandhara. 2013. "Honor-Killing Case Raises Fears for Women's Rights In Afghanistan." *Radio Free Europe Radio Liberty.* http://www.rferl.org/content/gandhara-afghanistan-honor-killing-womens-rights/25062565.html.

Garg, Mukesh, and Nareshlta Singla. 2012. "Rights of Women Prisoners in India: An Evaluation." *International Journal of Advanced Research in Management and Social Sciences* 1 (2): 134–52.

Gaudin, Sylvestre. 2011. "Son Preference in Indian Families: Absolute versus Relative Wealth Effects." *Demography* 48 (1) (February): 343–70.

Gazi, Rukhsana, Faiz Ahmed, Suraiya Begum, Faiz Ahmend, and Elma Chowdhury. 2001. "Trafficking of Women and Children in Bangladesh." ICDDR,B (International Centre for Diarrhoel Disease Research, Bangladesh), Dhaka.

George, Annie, Shagun Sabarwal, and P. Martin. 2011. "Violence in Contract Work among Female Sex Workers in Andhra Pradesh, India." *The Journal of Infectious Diseases* 204 (Suppl 5) (December 1): S1235–40.

Ghosh, Biswajit. 2009. "Trafficking in Women and Children in India: Nature, Dimensions and Strategies for Prevention." *The International Journal of Human Rights* 13 (5) (December): 716–38.

GOI (Government of India). 2002. "Committee on Empowerment of Women (2002–2003) Ninth Report (Thirteenth Lok Sabha): Violence Against Women During Riots." Ministry of Human Resource Development (Department of Women and Child Development) and Ministry of Home Affairs, New Delhi. http://164.100.24.208/ls/committeeR/Empowerment/9th/9th.html#CONTENTS.

———. 2007. "Study on Child Abuse: INDIA 2007." Ministry of Women and Child Development, GOI, New Delhi.

Goonesekere, Savitri. 2006. "The Elimination of All Forms of Discrimination and Violence against the Girl Child." UNICEF (United Nations Children's Fund) Innocenti Research Center, Florence. http://www.un.org/womenwatch/daw/egm/elim-disc-viol-girlchild/Backgroundpaper /Goonesekere.pdf.

Government of Sri Lanka. 2011. "Report of the Commission of Inquiry on Lessons Learnt and Reconciliation." Colombo. http://www.priu.gov.lk/news_update/Current_Affairs/ca201112 /FINAL%20LLRC%20REPORT.pdf.

Guha, Ramachandra. 2007. *India after Gandhi: The History of the World's Largest Democracy*. London: Macmillian Publishers Limited.

Haile, Jane. 2007. "Policy Department External Policies Honour Killing: Its Causes & Consequences: Suggested Strategies for the European Parliament." European Parliament, Brussels.

Hancock, P. 2006. "Violence, Women, Work and Empowerment: Narratives from Factory Women in Sri Lanka's Export Processing Zones." *Gender, Technology and Development* 10 (2) (July 1): 211–28.

Haviland, Charles. 2007. "Desperate Plight of Nepal 'Slave Girls.'" *BBC News* online, Dang, western Nepal, March 2, 2007. http://news.bbc.co.uk/2/hi/south_asia/6405373.stm.

Hazarika, G. 2000. "Gender Differences in Children's Nutrition and Access to Health Care in Pakistan." *The Journal of Development Studies* 37 (1): 73–92.

Heath, Rachel. 2013. "Women's Access to Labor Market Opportunities, Control of Household Resources, and Domestic Violence: Evidence from Bangladesh." Policy Research Working Paper 6149, World Bank, Washington DC.

Heiberg, Turid, and Enakshi Ganguly Thukral, eds. 2013. *The South Asian Report: On the Child-Friendliness of Governments*. Save the Children, HAQ: Centre for Child Rights, Plan International, CRY: Child Rights and You, Terre des Hommes Germany.

Heise, L. L. 1998. "Violence Against Women: An Integrated, Ecological Framework." *Violence Against Women* 4 (3) (June 1): 262–90.

———. 2011. "What Works to Prevent Partner Violence? An Evidence Overview Working Paper." STRIVE, London.

Hennink, Monique, and Padam Simkhada. 2004. "Sex Trafficking in Nepal: Context and Process." Opportunities and Choices Working Paper No. 11 April 2004.

Hindin, Michelle J., Sunita Kishor, and Donna L. Ansara. 2008. "Intimate Partner Violence Among Couples in 10 DHS Countries: Predictors and Health Outcomes." DHS Analytical Studies 18, Macro International Inc, Claverton, MD.

HRCP (Human Rights Commission of Pakistan). 2012. "State of Human Rights in 2012." HRCP, Lahore.

HRW (Human Rights Watch). 2003. "Trapped by Inequality: Bhutanese Refugee Women in Nepal." http://www.hrw.org/sites/default/files/reports/nepal0903full.pdf.

———. 2010. "India: Prosecute Rampant 'Honor' Killings." http://www.hrw.org/news/2010/07/16 /india-prosecute-rampant-honor-killings.

———. 2012. "Will I Get My Dues ... Before I Die?: Harm to Women from Bangladesh's Discriminatory Laws on Marriage, Separation, and Divorce." Human Rights Watch.

———. 2013. "Breaking the Silence: Child Sexual Abuse in India." Human Rights Watch.

Huda, S. 2006. "Sex Trafficking in South Asia." *International Journal of Gynaecology and Obstetrics* 94 (3) (September): 374–81.

Hunter, W M, D Jain, L S Sadowski, and a I Sanhueza. 2000. "Risk Factors for Severe Child Discipline Practices in Rural India." *Journal of Pediatric Psychology* 25 (6) (September): 435–47.

Hyder, Adnan Ali, and Fauzia Aman Malik. 2007. "Violence against Children: A Challenge for Public Health in Pakistan." *Journal of Health, Population, and Nutrition* 25 (2) (June): 168–78.

Hyder, Adnan Ali, Zarin Noor, and Emma Tsui. 2007. "Intimate Partner Violence among Afghan Women Living in Refugee Camps in Pakistan." *Social Science & Medicine (1982)* 64 (7) (April): 1536–47.

ICG (International Crisis Group). 2013. "Women and Conflict in Afghanistan." ICG, Brussels. http://www.crisisgroup.org//media/Files/asia/south-asia/afghanistan/252-women-and -conflict-in-afghanistan.pdf.

ICRW (International Center for Research on Women). 2000a. "Domestic Violence in India: A Summary Report of a Multi-Site Household Survey." ICRW.

———. 2000b. "Domestic Violence in India: Exploring Strategies, Promoting Dialogue." ICRW.

———. 2002. "Men, Masculinity and Domestic Violence in India: Summary Report of 4 Studies." ICRW.

———. 2011. "Delaying Marriage for Girls in India: A Formative Research to Design Interventions for Changing Norms." ICRW Report to UNICEF (United Nations Children's Fund).

ICRW, AFPPD (Asian Forum of Parliamentarians on Population and Development), AusAID (Australian Government Overseas Aid Program) and UNFPA (United Nations Population Fund). 2012. "Child Marriage in Southern Asia." ICRW. http://www.icrw.org/publications /child-marriage-southern-asia.

ICRW (International Center for Research on Women), and Plan International. 2013. "Asia Child Marriage Initiative: Summary of Research in Bangladesh, India and Nepal." ICRW and Plan Asia Regional Office.

ICRW (International Center for Research on Women) and UN Women (United Nations Entity for Gender Equality and the Empowerment of Women). 2012. "Opportunities and Challenges of Women's Political Participation in India." ICRW and UN Women.

Iravani, Mohammad Reza. 2011. "Child Abuse in India." *Asian Social Science* 7 (3): 150–53.

IRIN (Integrated Regional Information Networks). 2008. "Afghanistan: Self-Immolation on the Rise among Women." IRIN Humanitarian News and Analysis.

———. 2013. "Analysis: Nepal's Successful Refugee Resettlement Operation." *IRIN News*, December 30, 2013. United Nations Office for the Coordination of Humanitarian Affairs. http://www.irinnews.org/report/99405/analysis-nepal-s-successful-refugee-resettlement -operation.

Irudayam, A., S. J. Jayshree, P. Mangubhai, and J. G. Lee. 2006. *Dalit Women Speak Out: Violence against Dalit Women in India*. Overview report of study in Andhra Pradesh, Bihar, Tamil Nadu/Pondicherry, and Uttar Pradesh. New Delhi: National Campaign on Dalit Human Rights. http://idsn.org/uploads/media/Violence_against_Dalit_Woment.pdf.

Jayasuriya, Vathsala, Kumudu Wijewardena, and Pia Axemo. 2011. "Intimate Partner Violence against Women in the Capital Province of Sri Lanka: Prevalence, Risk Factors, and Help Seeking." *Violence against Women* 17 (8): 1086–102.

Jayawardena, Kumari, and Malathi De Alwis. 1996. *Embodied Violence: Communalising Women's Sexuality in South Asia*. New Jersey: Zed Books Ltd.

Jayaweera, S., H. Wijemanne, L. Wanasundera, and K. M. Vitarana. 2007. "Gender Dimensions of the Millennium Development Goals in Sri Lanka." Centre for Women's Research, Colombo.

Jejeebhoy, S. J. 1998. "Adolescent Sexual and Reproductive Behavior: A Review of the Evidence from India." *Social Science & Medicine (1982)* 46 (10) (May): 1275–90.

Jejeebhoy, S. J., and S. Bott. 2003. "Non-Consensual Sexual Experiences of Young People: A Review of the Evidence from Developing Countries." Population Council Regional Working Papers (16).

Jejeebhoy, Shireen J., K. G. Santhya, and Shagun Sabarwal. 2013. "Women's Autonomy and Experience of Physical Violence Within Marriage in Rural India: Gender-Based Violence." *Journal of Interpersonal Violence* 29 (2): 332–47.

Jewkes, Rachel. 2002. "Intimate Partner Violence: Causes and Prevention." *Lancet* 359: 1423–29.

Jeyaseelan, L., S. Kumar, N. Neelakantan, A. Peedicayil, R. Pillar, and N. Duvvury. 2007. "Physical Spousal Violence against Women in India: Some Risk Factors." *Journal of Biosocial Science* 39 (5): 657–70.

Jeyaseelan, L, Laura S Sadowski, Shuba Kumar, Fatma Hassan, Laurie Ramiro, and Beatriz Vizcarra. 2004. "World Studies of Abuse in the Family Environment—Risk Factors for Physical Intimate Partner Violence." *Injury Control and Safety Promotion* 11 (2) (June): 117–24.

John, Mary E, Ravinder Kaur, Rajni Palriwala, Saraswati Raju, and Fatehgarh Saheb. 2009. "Dispensing with Daughters: Technology, Society, Economy in North India" *Economic and Political Weekly* xliv (15): 16–19.

Johnson, Kiersten Blair, and Maitreyi Bordia Das. 2008. "Spousal Violence in Bangladesh as Reported by Men: Prevalence and Risk Factors." *Journal of Interpersonal Violence* 24 (6) (June): 977–95.

Kabeer, Naila. 1998. "'Can Buy Me Love'? Re-Evaluating the Empowerment Potential of Loans to Loans to Women in Rural Bangladesh." Institute of Development Studies, Sussex, UK.

Kachhwaha, Kavita. 2011. "Khap Adjudication in India : Honouring the Culture with Crimes." *International Journal of Criminal Justice Sciences* 6 (1): 297–308.

Kandiyoti, Deniz. 1998. "Bargaining With Patriarchy." *Gender and Society* 2 (3): 274–90.

Kapadia, Karin, ed. 2002. *The Violence of Development: The Political Economy of Gender and Social Inequalities in India.* New Delhi and London: Kali for Women and Zed Books.

Kapadia, Mufiza Zia, Sarah Saleem, and Mehtab S Karim. 2009. "The Hidden Figure: Sexual Intimate Partner Violence among Pakistani Women." *European Journal of Public Health* 20 (2) (April): 164–68.

Kapur, Ratna. 2013. *Violence against Women in South Asia and the Limits of Law.* Background paper for current report.

Khair, Sumaiya. 2003. "Institutional Violence Against Women: The Saga of Women in Safe Custody." *Asia-Pacific Journal on Human Rights and the Law* 4 (2): 28–51.

Khan, Irshad Hasan. 2001. "The Judicial System of Pakistan: Measures for Maintaining Independence and Enforcing Accountability." In *Comprehensive Legal and Judicial Development: Towards an Agenda for a Just and Equitable Society in the 21st Century*, ed. Van Puymbroeck, Rudolf V: 241–73. Washington, DC: World Bank.

Khowaja, Shaneela Sadaruddin, Ambreen Jawed Tharani, Ajmal Agha, and Rozina Sherali Karamaliani. 2012. "Women Trafficking: Causes, Concerns, Care!" *Journal of Pakistan Medical Association* 62 (8): 835–38.

Kirti, Anand, Prateek Kumar, and Rachana Yadav. 2011. "The Face of Honour Based Crimes: Global Concerns and Solutions." *International Journal of Criminal Justice Sciences* 6 (1 & 2): 343–357.

Koenig, Michael, Saiduddin Ahmed, Mian Bazle Hossain, and A.B.M. Khorshed Alam Mozumder. 2003. "Women's Status and Domestic Violence in Rural Bangladesh: Individual- and Community Level Effects." *Demography* 40 (2): 269–88.

Koenig, Michael, Rob Stephenson, Rajib Acharya, Lindsay Barrick, Saifuddin Ahmed, and Michelle Hindin. 2010. "Domestic Violence and Early Childhood Mortality in Rural India: Evidence from Prospective Data." *International Journal of Epidemiology* 39 (3): 825–33.

Koenig, Michael A., Rob Stephenson, Saifuddin Ahmed, Shireen J. Jejeebhoy, and Jacquelyn Campbell. 2006. "Individual and Contextual Determinants of Domestic Violence in North India." *American Journal of Public Health* 96 (1) (January): 132–38.

Krishnan, Suneeta, Corinne H. Rocca, Alan E. Hubbard, K. Subbiah, Jeffrey Edmeades, and Nancy S. Padian. 2010. "Do Changes in Spousal Employment Status Lead to Domestic Violence? Insights from a Prospective Study in Bangalore, India." *Social Science and Medicine* 70 (1): 136–43.

Lamichhane, Prabhat, Mahesh Puri, Jyotsna Tamang, and Bishnu Dulal. 2011. "Women's Status and Violence against Young Married Women in Rural Nepal." *BMC Women's Health* 11: 19–27.

Lawyers Collective Women's Rights Initiative, ICRW, and UN Trust Fund to End Violence against Women. "Staying Alive: Fifth Monitoring and Evaluation 2012 on the Protection of Women from Domestic Violence Act, 2005." Lawyers Collective http://www.unwomensouthasia.org /assets/Final_Staying_Alive_-_Lawyers_collective_1.pdf.

Lari, Maliha Zia. 2011. "'Honour Killings' in Pakistan and Compliance of Law." Aurat Publication and Information Service Foundation.

Maher, T. M. 2003. "Police Sexual Misconduct: Officers' Perceptions of Its Extent and Causality." *Criminal Justice Review* 28 (2): 355–81.

Malik, F. 2010. "Determinants of Child Abuse in Pakistani Families: Parental-Acceptance-Rejection and Demographic Variables." *International Journal of Business and Social Science* 1 (1): 67–80.

Mandelbaum, David G. 1988. *Women's Seclusion and Men's Honor: Sex Roles in North India, Bangladesh, and Pakistan.* Tucson, AZ: University of Arizona Press.

Martin, S. L., A. O. Tsui, K. Maitra, and R. Marinshaw. 1999. "Domestic Violence in Northern India." *American Journal of Epidemiology* 150 (4): 417–26.

Martin, S. L., K. E. Moracco, J. Garro, A. O. Tsui, L. L. Kupper, J. L. Chase, and J. C. Campbell. 2002. "Domestic Violence across Generations: Findings from Northern India." *International Journal of Epidemiology* 31 (3): 560–72.

Mathur, S., A. Malhotra, and M. Mehta. 2001. "Adolescent Girls' Life Aspirations and Reproductive Health in Nepal." *Reproductive Health Matters* 9 (17): 91–100.

Mathur, S., M. Greene, and A. Malhotra. 2003. "Too Young to Wed: The Lives, Rights, and Health of Young Married Girls." International Center for Research on Women (ICRW).

McDuie-Ra, D. 2012. "Violence Against Women in the Militarized Indian Frontier Beyond "Indian Culture" in the Experiences of Ethnic Minority Women." *Violence against Women* 18, no. 3 (2012): 322–45.

Minority Rights Group International. 2013. "State of the World's Minorities and Indigenous Peoples 2013." http://www.minorityrights.org/12071/state-of-the-worlds-minorities/state-of -the-worlds-minorities-and-indigenous-peoples-2013.html.

Mishra, Udaya S., T. R. Dilip, Annie George, and Anil Kumar V. K. 2004. *Declining Child Sex Ratio (0–6 Years) in India: A Review of Literature and Annotated Bibliography.* Thiruvananthapuram, India: Centre for Development Studies.

Monden, C., and J. Smits. 2013. "Maternal Education Is Associated with Reduced Female Disadvantages in Under-Five Mortality in Sub-Saharan Africa and Southern Asia." *International Journal of Epidemiology* 42: 2011–18.

Moore, Henrietta. 1994. "The Problem of Explaining Violence in the Social Sciences." In *Sex and Violence: Issues in Representation and Experience,* ed. Penelope Harvey and Peter Gow, 139–55. London: Routledge.

Muhuri, P., and S. Preston. 1991. "Effects of Family Composition on Mortality Differentials by Sex Among Children in Matlab Bangladesh." *Population and Development Review* 17 (3): 415–34.

Mukherjee, Sucharita Sinha. 2013. "Women's Empowerment and Gender Bias in the Birth and Survival of Girls in Urban India" *Feminist Economics* 19 (1): 37–41.

Muñoz Boudet, A. M., P. Petesch, and C. Turk with A. Thumala. 2013. *On Norms and Agency: Conversations about Gender Equality with Women and Men in 20 Countries.* Directions in Development. World Bank: Washington, DC.

Murthi, Mamta, Anne Guio, and Jean Dreze. 1995. "Mortality, Fertility, and Gender Bias in India: A District-Level Analysis." *Population and Development Review* 21 (4): 745–82.

Naeem, Farooq, Muhammad Irfan, Qaiser a Zaidi, David Kingdon, and Muhammad Ayub. 2008. "Angry Wives, Abusive Husbands: Relationship between Domestic Violence and Psychosocial Variables." *Women's Health Issues* 18 (6): 453–62.

Nanda, P., A. Gautam, R. Verma, S. Kumar, and D. Brahme. 2013. "Masculinity, Son Preference and Intimate Partner Violence." A Study Conducted by ICRW in Partnership with UNFPA. http://www.icrw.org/files/publications/Masculinity%20Study_WEB%20Version.pdf.

Nanda, P., G. Abhishek, R. Verma, H. K. Thu, P. Mahesh, L. T. Giang, T. Jyotsna, and L. Prabhat. 2012. "Study on Gender, Masculinity and Son Preference in Nepal and Vietnam." New Delhi: ICRW (International Center for Research on Women).

Naripokkho and Bangladesh Mahila Parishad. "Baseline Report: Violence Against Women in Bangladesh." International Women's Rights Action Watch Asia Pacific, Kuala Lumpur, Malaysia.

Nasrullah, M. S. Haqqi, and K. J. Cummings. 2009. "The Epidemiological Patterns of Honour Killing of Women in Pakistan." *European Journal of Public Health* 19 (2): 193–97.

Naved, R., H. Huque, S. Farah, and M. M. R. Shuvra. 2011. *Men's Attitudes and Practices Regarding Gender and Violence against Women in Bangladesh.* Dhaka: ICDDR,B (International Centre for Diarrhoeal Disease Research, Bangladesh).

Naved, R. T. 2003. "A Situational Analysis of Violence against Women in South Asia," in *Violence Against Women in South Asia—A Regional Analysis,* AFPPD (Asian Forum of Parliamentarians on Population and Development) and UNFPA (United Nations Population Fund) Bangladesh and Country Technical Services Team for South and West Asia, Bangkok and Kathmandu, pp. 1–27.

Naved, Ruchira Tabassum, Safia Azim, Abbas Bhuiya, and Lars Ake Persson. 2006. "Physical Violence by Husbands: Magnitude, Disclosure and Help-Seeking Behavior of Women in Bangladesh." *Social Science & Medicine* (1982) 62 (12): 2917–29.

National Human Rights Commission of India. 2002. "National Human Rights Commission Report, March–May Gujarat 2002," New Delhi. http://nhrc.nic.in/guj_finalorder.htm.

NSB (National Statistics Bureau). 2011. *Bhutan Multiple Indicator Survey, May 2011.* Thimphu, Bhutan: National Statistics Bureau.

Nussbaum, M. 2009. *The Clash Within: Democracy, Religious Violence, and India's Future.* Cambridge, MA: Harvard University Press.

OHCHR (Office of the High Commissioner for Human Rights). 2011. *Opening the Door to Equality: Access to Justice for Dalits in Nepal.* Kathmandu: OHCHR.

Pal, Sarmistha. 1999. "An Analysis of Childhood Malnutrition in Rural India: Role of Gender, Income and Other Household Characteristics." *World Development* 27 (7): 1151–71.

Panchanadeswaran, Subadra, Sethulakshmi C. Johnson, Sudha Sivaram, A. K. Srikrishnan, Carl Latkin, Margaret E. Bentley, Suniti Solomon, Vivian F. Go, and David Celentano. 2008. "Intimate Partner Violence Is as Important as Client Violence in Increasing Street-Based Female Sex Workers' Vulnerability to HIV in India." *The International Journal on Drug Policy* 19 (2): 106–12.

Panda, P., and B. Agarwal. 2005. "Marital Violence, Human Development and Women's Property Status in India." *World Development* 33 (5): 823–50.

Pande, R. P. 1999. "Grant a Girl Elsewhere, Here Grant a Boy: Gender and Health Outcomes among Rural Indian Children." Johns Hopkins University, Baltimore, MD.

———. 2003. "Selective Gender Differences in Childhood Nutrition and Immunization in Rural India: The Role of Siblings." *Demography* 40 (3): 395–418.

Pande, R. P., and A. Malhotra. 2006. "Son Preference and Daughter Neglect in India: What Happens to Living Girls?" ICRW, Washington, DC.

Pande, R. P., A. Malhotra, and S. Namy. 2012. "Fertility Decline and Changes in Women's Lives and Gender Equality in Tamily Nadu, India." International Center for Research on Women Fertility & Empowerment Working Paper Series. 007-20120ICRW-FE.

Panditaratne, Dinusha. 2008. "Towards Gender Equality in Developing Asia: Reforming Personal Laws within a Pluralist Framework." *New York University Review of Law and Social Change* 32 (83): 83–129.

Panniyankara, Abdullah. 2013. "Honor Killing in India." Civil Service India. http://www .civilserviceindia.com/subject/Essay/honor-killing-in-india2.html.

Paudel, G. S. 2007. "Domestic Violence against Women in Nepal." *Gender, Technology and Development* 11 (2): 199–233.

PDSN and IDSN (Pakistan Dalit Solidarity Network and International Dalit Solidarity Network). 2013. "Scheduled Caste Women in Pakistan: Denied a Life in Dignity and Respect." http:// idsn.org/fileadmin/user_folder/pdf/New_files/Pakistan/SCHEDULED_CASTE_WOMEN _IN_PAKISTAN_-_Alternative_report_to_CEDAW_-_PDSN_and_IDSN_-_Jan_2013.pdf.

Perera, J., N. Gunawardane, and V. Jayasuriya. 2011. *Review of Research Evidence on Gender Based Violence (GBV) in Sri Lanka.* Colombo: Sri Lanka Medical Association.

Perveen, Rakhshinda. 2012. "Beyond Denial: Violence against Women in Pakistan: A Qualitative Review of Reported Incidents." Islamabad: Aurat Publication and Information Service Foundation.

Pokhrel, S., and Rainer Sauerborn. 2004. "Household Decision-Making on Child Health Care in Developing Countries: The Case of Nepal." *Health Policy and Planning* 19 (4): 218–33.

Poudel, Arjun. 2013. "For Kamalaris, the Battle for Justice Is Far from Over." *Republica/ Nagarik News*, December 30, 2013. http://www.myrepublica.com/portal/index.php?action =news_details&news_id=67077.

Poudel, Meena. 2000. "Oxfam Bhutan Violence Report." Oxfam-GB in Nepal.

Population Council. 2009. "Violence within Marriage among Young People in Tamil Nadu." Youth in India: Situation and Needs, Policy Brief Number 12. International Institute for Population Sciences (IIPS) and Population Council.

Pradhan, A., P. Poudel, D. Thomas, and S. Barnett. 2011. "A Review of the Evidence: Suicide among Women in Nepal." Options Consultancy Services Ltd., London.

Pradhan, Suman. 2006. *Nepal: Land Reforms, Key to Social Harmony.* Galdu Resource Centre for the Rights of Indigenous Peoples. http://www.galdu.org/web/index.php?odas=1475&giella1=eng.

Pun, Weena. 2013. "Govt, Kamlaris Ink Deal; Protests End." *Kathmandu Post*, June 07, 2013. http://www.ekantipur.com/the-kathmandu-post/2013/06/07/related_articles/govt-kamlaris -ink-deal-protests-end/249673.html.

Purkayastha, B., M. Subramaniam, M. Desai, and S. Bose. 2003. "The Study of Gender in India: A Partial Review." *Gender & Society* 17 (4) (August 1): 503–24.

Qasim Shah, Sadia. 2014. "Women Activists, Religious Parties Differ on Domestic Violence." *Dawn*. 29 March 2014. http://www.dawn.com/news/1096299/women-activists-religious -parties-differ-on-domestic-violence.

Rahman, L., and V. Rao. 2004. "The Determinants of Gender Equity in India: Examining Dyson and Moore's Thesis with New Data Infant." *Population and Development Review* 30 (2): 239–68.

Rao, V. 1997. "Wife-Beating in Rural South India: A Qualitative and Econometric Analysis." *Social Science & Medicine (1982)* 44 (8): 1169–80.

Regmi, Mahesh C. 1997. *Landownership in Nepal.* Delhi: Adroit Publishers.

Ribin, A. 2012. "With Help, Afghan Survivor of 'Honor Killing' Inches Back." Dec. 1 2012. New York Times (http://www.nytimes.com/2012/12/02/world/asia/doctors-and-others-buck -tradition-in-afghan-honor-attack.html?_r=0).

Rocca, Corinne H., Sujit Rathod, Tina Falle, Rohini P. Pande, Suneeta Krishnan. 2009. "Challenging Assumptions about Women'S Empowerment: Social and Economic Resources and Domestic Violence among Young Married Women in Urban South India." *International Journal of Epidemiology* 38: 577–85.

Rolfes, Ellen. "Maldivian President Rejects 'Un-Islamic' Ban on Some Forms of Marital Rape." PBS Newshour. 16 January 2014. http://www.pbs.org/newshour/rundown/maldivian -president-rejects-un-islamic-ban-on-some-forms-of-marital-rape/.

SAARC (South Asian Association for Regional Cooperation). 2006. "Human Rights Report 2006." Population Council, New Delhi.

Santhya, K. G., N. Haberland, F. Ram, R. K. Sinha, S. K. Mohanty, and K. G. Santhya. 2007. "Consent and Coercion: Examining Unwanted Sex among Married Young Women in India." *International Family Planning Perspectives* 33 (3): 124–32.

Santhya, K. G., N. Haberland, and A. Singh. 2006. "'She Knew Only When the Garland Was Put around Her Neck': Findings from an Exploratory Study on Early Marriage in Rajasthan." Population Council, New Delhi.

Santhya, K. G., U. Ram, R. Acharya, S. J. Jejeebhoy, F. Ram, and A. Singh. 2010. "Associations Between Early Marriage and Young Women's Marital and Reproductive Health Outcomes: Evidence from India." *International Perspectives on Sexual and Reproductive Health* 36 (3): 132–39.

Sarkar, Tanika. 1993. "Rhetoric Against Age of Consent: Resisting Colonial Reason and Death of a Child-Wife." *Economic and Political Weekly* (4 September, 1993): 1869–78.

Sarkar, Kamalesh, Baishali Bal, Rita Mukherjee, Sekhar Chakraborty, Suman Saha, Arundhuti Ghosh, and Scott Parsons. 2008. "Sex-Trafficking, Violence, Negotiating Skill, and HIV

Infection in Brothel-Based Sex Workers of Eastern." *Journal of Health, Population, and Nutrition* 26 (2): 223–31.

Schuler, S. R., S. M. Hashemi, A. P. Riley, and S. Akhter. 1996. "Credit Programs, Patriarchy and Men's Violence Against Women in Rural Bangladesh." *Social Science & Medicine* 43 (12): 1729–42.

Schuler, Sidney Ruth, Lisa M. Bates, and Farzana Islam. 2008. "Women's Rights, Domestic Violence, and Recourse Seeking in Rural Bangladesh." *Violence against Women* 14 (3): 326–45.

Schuler, Sidney Ruth, Lisa M Bates, Farzana Islam, and Md. Khairul Islam. 2006. "The Timing of Marriage and Childbearing among Rural Families in Bangladesh: Choosing between Competing Risks." *Social Science & Medicine* 62 (11): 2826–37.

Schuler, Sidney Ruth, Rachel Lenzi, Sohela Nazneen, and Lisa M. Bates. 2013. "Perceived Decline in Intimate Partner Violence against Women in Bangladesh: Qualitative Evidence." *Studies in Family Planning* 44 (3): 243–57.

Self, Sharmistha, and Richard Grabowski. 2012. "Son Preference, Autonomy and Maternal Health in Rural India." *Oxford Development Studies* 40 (3): 305–23.

Sen, Amartya. 2007. *Identity and Violence: The Illusion of Destiny*. New York: Norton.

Shafique, T. 2008. http://tahminashafique.electrikblues.net/?p=86, accessed on 9 January 2014.

Shah, V., B. Brar, and S. Y. Rana. 2002. "Layers of Silence: Links between Women's Vulnerability, Trafficking and HIV/AIDS in Bangladesh, India and Nepal." Draft paper prepared for the UNRISD HIV/AIDS and Development, UNRISD (United Nations Research Institute for Social Development), Geneva.

Shaikh, M. A., I. A. Shaikh, A. Kamal, and S. Masood. 2010. "Attitudes about Honour Killing among Men and Women: Perspective from Islamabad." *J Ayub Med Coll Abbottabad* 22 (3): 38–41.

Sharma, Nagendar. 2013. "A Disgrace: How Khap Panchayats Are Getting Away with 'Honour' Killings." *Hindustan Times*. http://www.hindustantimes.com/india-news/newdelhi/honour-killing-villains-find-friends-in-politicians/article1-1125802.aspx.

Siddiqi, Dina M. 2003. "The Sexual Harassment of Industrial Workers : Strategies for Intervention in the Workplace and Beyond." *CPD-UNFPA Paper* 26 (40).

———. 2012. "Blurred Boundaries: Sexuality and Seduction Narratives in Selected 'Forced Marriage' Cases from Bangladesh." In *Honour and Women's Rights: South Asian Perspectives*, eds. Manisha Gupte, Ramesh Awasthi and Shradda Chickerur. India: Mahila Sarvangeen Utkarsh Mandal (MSUM).

Silverman, Jay G., Michele R. Decker, Debbie M. Cheng, Kathleen Wirth, Niranjan Saggurti, Heather L. Mccauley, Kathryn L. Falb, Balaiah Donta, and Anita Raj. 2011. "Gender-Based Disparities in Infant and Child Mortality Based on Maternal Exposure to Spousal Violence." *American Medical Association* 165 (1): 22–27.

Silverman, Jay G., Michele R. Decker, Nitin A. Kapur, Jhumka Gupta, and Anita Raj. 2013. "Violence against Wives, Sexual Risk and Sexually Transmitted Infection among Bangladeshi Men." *Sexually Transmitted Infections* 83 (3): 211–15.

Silverman, Jay G., Anita Raj, Debbie M. Cheng, Michele R. Decker, Sharon Coleman, Carly Bridden, Manoj Pardeshi, Niranjan Saggurti, and Jeffrey H. Samet. 2011. "Sex Trafficking and Initiation-Related Violence, Alcohol Use, and HIV Risk among HIV-Infected Female Sex Workers in Mumbai, India." *The Journal of Infectious Diseases* 204 (Suppl 5): S1229–34.

Singh, Kirti, and Diviya Kapur. 2001. "Law, Violence, and the Girl Child." *Health and Human Rights* 5 (2): 8–29.

Skeldon, R. 2000. "Trafficking: A Perspective from Asia." *International Migration, Special Issue* 38 (3): 7–30.

Slugget, Cath. 2003. *Mapping of Psychosocial Support for Girls and Boys Affected by Child Sexual Abuse in Four Countries in South and Central Asia: Afghanistan, Bangladesh, Nepal and Pakistan.* Bangladesh: Save the Children Sweden Denmark Regional Office for South and Central Asia.

Sodhi, G., and M. Verma. 2003. "Sexual Coercion among Unmarried Adolescents of an Urban Slum in India." In *Towards Adulthood: Exploring the Sexual and Reproductive Health of Adolescents in South Asia*, eds. S. Bott et al. Geneva: World Health Organization, pp. 91–94.

Srinivas, M. N. 1984. "Some Reflections on Dowry." Centre for Women's Development Studies, Delhi.

Srinivasan, Sharada. 2005. "Daughters or Dowries? The Changing Nature of Dowry Practices in South India." *World Development* 33 (4) (April): 593–615.

Srinivasan, Sharada, and Arjun S. Bedi. 2007. "Domestic Violence and Dowry: Evidence from a South Indian Village." *World Development* 35 (5): 857–80.

Srivastava, Spriha. 2009. "Honour Killing: India's Continuing Shame." http://www.opendemocracy .net/openindia/spriha-srivastava/honour-killing-indias-continuing-shame.

Stark, N. 1993. "Gender and Therapy Management: Reproductive Decision Making in Rural Bangladesh." Dissertation, Southern Methodist University, Dallas.

Subramanian, P., and S. Sivayogan. 2001. "The Prevalence and Pattern of Wife Beating in the Trincomalee District in Eastern Sri Lanka." *Southeast Asian J Trop Med Public Health* 32 (1): 186–95.

Suran, Luciana, Sajeda Amin, Lopita Huq, and Kobita Chowdury. 2004. "Does Dowry Improve Life for Brides? A Test of the Bequest Theory of Dowry in Rural Bangladesh." Population Council, Dhaka.

UN News Centre. 2009. "UN Urges End to Nepalese Practice of Using Young Girls as Domestic Workers." *UN News Centre*, January 7, 2009. http://www.un.org/apps/news/story.asp?NewsID =29477&Cr=Nepal&Cr1=Human+rights#.UsPpHfttCSo.

UNAMA (United Nations Assistance Mission in Afghanistan). 2012. "Still a Long Way to Go: Implementation of the Law on Elimination of Violence against Women in Afghanistan." UNAMA, Kabul.

UNDP (United Nations Development Programme). 2013. *Human Development Report 2013, The Rise of the South: Human Progress in a Diverse World.* New York: UNDP.

UNFPA (United Nations Population Fund). 2012. "Marrying Too Young: End Child Marriage." UNFPA, New York.

UNICEF (United Nations Children's Fund). 2001. *Commercial Sexual Exploitation and Sexual Abuse of Children in South Asia.* Kathmandu: UNICEF Regional Office for South Asia. http:// www.unicef.org/rosa/commercial.pdf.

———. 2013. "Emerging Concerns and Case Studies on Child Marriage in Sri Lanka." UNICEF, New York. http://www.unicef.org/srilanka/Final_Uploaded_report_compress.pdf.

UNODC (United Nations Office on Drugs and Crime). 2007. "Afghanistan: Female Prisoners and Their Social Reintegration." UNODC, Vienna. https://www.unodc.org/pdf/criminal_justice /Afghanistan_Female_Prisoners_and_their_Social_Reintegration.pdf.

———. 2012. "Global Report on Trafficking in Persons." UNODC, Vienna. http://www.unodc.org /documents/data-and-analysis/glotip/Trafficking_in_Persons_2012_web.pdf.

Varma, D., M. Phil, P. Chandra, and Tinku Thomas. 2007. "Intimate Partner Violence and Sexual Coercion among Pregnant Women in India: Relationship and Post Traumatic Stress Disorder." *Journal of Affective Disorders* 102: 227–235.

Vasudevan, R. 2010. "India: Apex Court Upset at Increasing Cases of 'Honor Killings'." *Asian Tribune* (http://www.asiantribune.com/news/2010/06/22/india-apex-court-upset-increasing -cases-honor-killings).

Verma, Ravi, Tara Sinha, and Tina Khanna. 2013. "Asia Child Marriage Initiative: Summary of Research in Bangladesh, India and Nepal." UNICEF Global Database.

Venkatesan, J. 2011. "Stamp Out Khap Panchayats: Court." *The Hindu* (http://www.thehindu.com /news/national/article1710337.ece).

Volart, Berta. 2004. "Dowry in Rural Bangladesh: Participation as Insurance against Divorce." London School of Economics.

Welchman, L., and S. Hossain. 2005. "Naming the Crime: 'Honour', Rights and Wrongs." Abbreviated version, derived from *Honour: Crimes, Paradigms and Violence against Women*, eds. L. Welchman and S. Hossain. London: Zed Press.

Wijayatilake, Kamalini, and Camena Guneratne. 2002. "State and Community Responses to Domestic Violence in Sri Lanka." Study Series No. 28, CENWOR, Colombo.

World Bank. 2013. *Women, Business and the Law 2014: Removing Restrictions to Enhance Gender Equality—Key Findings*. London: Bloomsbury.

Yount, Kathryn M., Ann M. DiGirolamo, and Usha Ramakrishnan. 2011. "Impacts of Domestic Violence on Child Growth and Nutrition: A Conceptual Review of the Pathways of Influence." *Social Science & Medicine* 72 (9): 1534–54.

CHAPTER 4

Learning from Interventions to Address Violence against Women and Girls

A range of interventions across South Asia attempts to prevent and respond to violence against women and girls throughout their lives. In this chapter we analyze whether and how such interventions address some of the key risk factors for such violence, and what promising lessons emerge for future efforts. This review is based on an intensive effort over a span of six months to identify as many initiatives as possible. We do not aim to cover all such programs. Rather, this review's contribution is to scan across the many forms of violence and across all the countries in the region to distill some key promising approaches and to provide a common platform for discussion and next steps.

We consider two forms of "interventions." The first is the macro-level systemic economic, social, and policy "interventions" that may indirectly influence violence against women and girls at various points in their lives. These include economic development and patterns and shifts in other indicators across countries over time, such as female education and women's political participation. We broadly review these dynamics; however, reviewing or analyzing fully the large literature on the relationship between macro changes and violence is beyond the scope of this report. The second type of "intervention," which forms the bulk of our analysis, comprises targeted interventions designed to prevent or respond to violence against women and girls. We examine government policies and schemes, as well as programs, networks, media efforts, advocacy, campaigns, and other kinds of efforts.

Implications of Recent Economic, Political, and Social Changes for Violence

In much of South Asia, violence against women and girls is occurring against a backdrop of perhaps the most rapid economic and social changes the region has seen. Changes have also been notable in the realms of female education, fertility rates and women's political participation. These shifts, described in chapter 3, are likely to have implications for violence and for gender equality more broadly.

Fertility decline has had a direct effect on excess female child mortality in India. Das Gupta and Bhat (1997) and others have noted that son preference remained strong even as fertility was declining, motivating parents to ensure one son in a smaller family. Parents thus were likely to discriminate even more intensively against daughters. The lack of a decline in excess female child mortality in India may at least partially be explained by this "intensification" effect (Das Gupta and Bhat 1997). However, this dynamic has not occurred in Bangladesh, which has also experienced very rapid fertility decline and shows some evidence of son preference. While it is still unclear why Bangladesh's fertility decline did not exacerbate excess female child mortality in this country, some recent research suggests that government interventions focused on gender equality in education and employment, combined with a path of economic growth that favored women's employment, may have contributed to changing the value of girls relative to boys (Adams et al. 2013; Kabeer et al. 2013; see also box 4.3 below). The experience of the Republic of Korea provides an instructive example from outside of the region of the effect of such government interventions on excess female child mortality. Chung and Das Gupta (2007) and Das Gupta (2010) argue that economic modernization and the social and policy changes it wrought pushed South Korea's otherwise very patriarchal policy environment towards greater gender equality, thus accelerating the erosion of son preference.

Economic development can influence gender equality through its association with increased opportunities for women's labor force participation and education. There is a large literature that attests to the relationship between girls' secondary schooling and improved outcomes in a host of social, gender, and demographic characteristics. Higher levels of girls' secondary schooling and a smaller gender gap in secondary education should contribute also to a shift away from the low societal valuation of girls relative to boys that underlies much of the violence against women and girls. However, the persistence of violence in South Asia seems to suggest that while other indicators of gender equality may improve, violence is more resistant to change.

The role of female labor force participation is complex. Across all countries in the region except Sri Lanka, women are primarily employed in subsistence, informal, or agricultural sectors. As such, it is not clear that these forms of employment are necessarily empowering, though they may enhance the physical welfare of women and their families.

Women's employment in other sectors may not necessarily trigger a decline in violence, either. Analyses of the role of Bangladesh's garment industry—dominated by women workers—in empowerment and violence suggest that while such employment has changed women's lives in terms of their mobility and access to resources, it may be associated also with higher risks of violence. Working women face double risks of harassment: at work and on the street while getting to work (Siddiqi 2003). The specific conditions of work in this sector may contribute to an environment conducive to violence, such as the lack of formal contracts, which creates pressure on women to succumb to employers' sexual advances, or the necessity to work at night but without adequate oversight and other safeguards against sexual or physical harassment (Siddiqi 2003).

Whether or not female employment triggers violence may also depend on social acceptance of women working outside of the home. Traditional patriarchal norms dictate that women remain confined to domestic roles in the home. If a rise in female employment is not accompanied by a shift in these norms, then women who work may be viewed as breaking norms and thus "available" for harassment; this is indeed the experience documented by some studies from Bangladesh (Siddiqi 2003) and Sri Lanka (Hancock 2006). As one respondent in Hancock's (2006) qualitative study with women workers in Sri Lanka's export processing zones said: "*Society has a very bad perception of women factory workers. They look down on us and consider us as immoral people. We are not accepted and people disrespect us. We cannot walk on the road alone. Men think that we are playthings that can be used for their pleasure. Men fiddle and touch us on buses. They do not think of us as people working for a living*" (223).

This quotation illustrates well the ongoing clash between modernity and tradition as South Asian economies and societies continue to transform. As opportunities arise that open the doors to greater gender equality, women and girls may face a backlash, including increased violence, as they leave their homes to work or study. As women's greater participation in public life becomes the norm, violence may decrease, as chapter 3 explores in the context of women's participation in microcredit programs in Bangladesh (Schuler and Hashemi 1994; Koenig et al. 2003; Ahmed 2005).

This conflict between modernity and tradition is also exemplified by the role of women's political participation in redefining public and private spaces as women leaders bring into public debate issues that were earlier considered private, such as intimate partner or other forms of violence. India's experiment with mandating seats in local governance institutions or panchayats provides a good example. Studies have found that women panchayat leaders do tend to invest time and effort in issues that are of concern for women, such as health and water (Chattopadhyay and Duflo 2004). A recent examination of the role of the panchayati raj institutions in gender concerns also shows that as women move into leadership positions, they experience higher self esteem and are more valued by their households (ICRW and UN Women 2012). Yet, these developments have not necessarily translated into greater public discussion of domestic violence, which is still seen by and large as a private problem. At the same time, such political participation does provide a new space and opportunity for these concerns to be aired. The report by ICRW and UN Women (2012) notes that the responsibility of taking advantage of this space cannot be placed solely on women's shoulders. Rather, to make women's participation in panchayats truly gender transformative, governments and other stakeholders committed to gender equality in governance all need to make a collective effort.

Such collective effort is also necessary to directly address violence against women and girls. As the rest of this chapter illustrates, interventions need to occur at the level of individual women and girls, their immediate environments, their communities and institutions, and social norms. We turn next to an examination of such "targeted" interventions.

Methods to Identify and Definitions of Targeted Interventions

Through on-line and literature searches, and the help of organizations across the region that work to some degree on one or more forms of violence against women and girls, we identified approximately 700 organizations in the region with one or more interventions that aim to address one or more types of violence against women and girls (appendix S). We short-listed a total of 101 evaluated interventions for this analysis, across all the forms of violence considered, and across the eight countries of South Asia (appendixes C–K). Evaluations are largely clustered around interventions to prevent child marriage, interventions that explicitly aim to engage men and boys in preventing or responding to violence, and interventions that broadly address "violence against women," encompassing—but not solely focused on—intimate partner violence. Evaluation for all other forms of violence is spotty and of limited rigor.

METHODOLOGY AND PROCESS TO IDENTIFY INTERVENTIONS

Our methodology is illustrated in figure 4.1 and described in detail in appendix N. The team started with a broad literature review of research, policy, and program documents; consultations with various stakeholders in the region and elsewhere; and field trips in Bangladesh, Maldives, and Nepal. The initial reviews and discussions helped generate a preliminary list (List I) of organizations working on violence (appendix S). This master list was then used—in combination with follow-up rounds of consultation and interviews, as well as focused literature reviews—to generate a shortlist of evaluated interventions (List II). The team also selected four interventions as potential case studies (List III). Case studies were developed based on information from project documents as well as semi-structured key informant interviews. In addition, we identified evaluated interventions from other parts of the world that could help inform initiatives in South Asia (appendix T).

Our efforts were constrained by time, resources, the evolving nature of programs, and the limited pre-existing information on interventions and their evaluations. Follow-up

FIGURE 4.1 Methodology to Identify Interventions

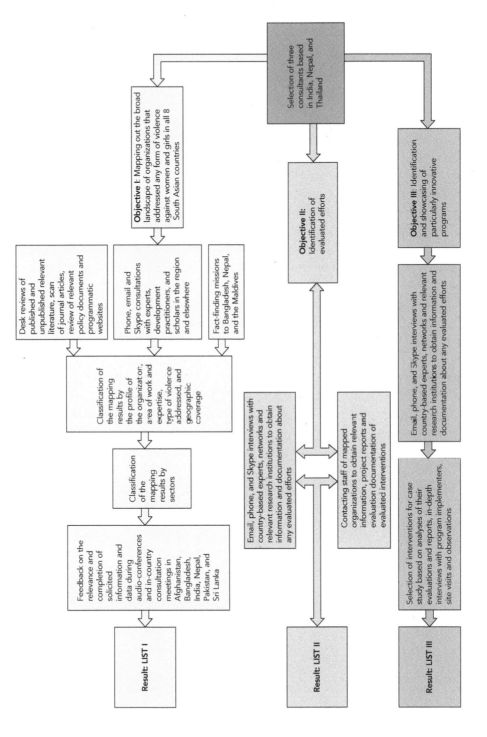

with the many individuals contacted was not always possible; in some cases, follow-up did not yield results as we did not have access to implementation or evaluation documentation. The research team did not have consultants based in some of the countries. While we attempted to minimize this constraint by reaching out to development actors from the countries other than those in which consultants were physically based, it is likely we did not capture the local nuances in some of these countries.

At the same time, we believe our approach has several strengths. A key strength of this exercise was its consultative nature. First, at each step of information gathering and analysis, the team in the field ensured ongoing and active collaboration and consultation with as many organizations as could be reached. This was especially true of the case studies. Second, the search was undertaken methodically, starting from the widest sweep of the landscape of programming and narrowing to evaluated and then innovative interventions. Key informant interviews for case studies followed a guide created by the study team for this purpose (appendix N). Finally, as described below, the analysis defined *"evaluation"* in ways that crossed the boundaries between academic rigor and field reality: while on the one hand, the attempt was to search for rigor, at the same time the realities of complex programs, field capacity, NGO goals, and peer considerations were taken into account when deciding whether to consider a program "evaluated."

EVALUATION DEFINITION AND CHALLENGES

We consider interventions to be evaluated if they have been assessed by any of several methods, described in figure 4.2. We draw conclusions for promising practices from the

FIGURE 4.2 The Continuum of Methods to Evaluate Interventions

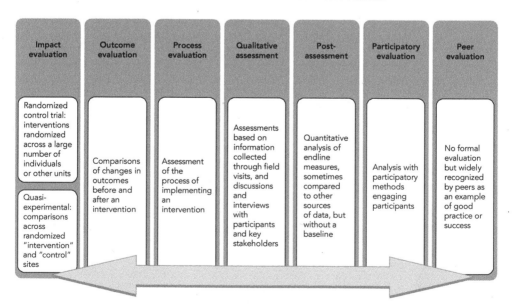

most rigorous evaluations available for each type of violence, drawing from less rigorous evaluations in the absence of rigorous ones. We define "promising" programs or practices as those that employ approaches that are shown to produce positive effects, and which can be used to inform design and implementation of other similar programs. Promising practices may also provide a basis for incorporating, replicating, or adapting select relevant strategies or elements into other programs to address particular forms of violence.

The most quantitatively rigorous form of impact evaluation is the randomized control trial (RCT), wherein the intervention is made available to randomly selected individuals, but withheld from others. Randomization statistically accounts for factors other than the intervention (background characteristics, for example) that may influence the outcome, thus allowing attribution of changes to the intervention. We found only three RCTs, of which one is completed (the RHANI wives intervention in India) and two are ongoing (the Kishori Konthaa and Dil Mil interventions in Bangladesh and India, respectively). In India, Breakthrough, an NGO that conducts campaigns against violence, has just completed baselines for two planned RCTs (Breakthrough n.d.).[1]

All other types of evaluations, which make up the bulk of our analyses, present certain methodological challenges (box 4.1). Nonetheless, such evaluations provide valuable information. Participatory qualitative evaluations can empower communities and provide important feedback from constituents of programs and policies on their effectiveness, accessibility, and acceptability. Quantitative evaluations that are not based on randomization still provide important information on program implementation processes, outputs, observed changes over time, and—in some cases—shifts in outcomes.

BOX 4.1 Methodological Challenges in Evaluating Interventions

1. *Selection bias:* When interventions are based on voluntary participation, typically those who agree to participate are unlikely to be representative of the general population. Program success or failure cannot therefore be attributed to the program alone, but is likely a combination of program elements and characteristics of participants.

2. *Quality and nature of data:* Available evaluation data are typically either cross-sectional or qualitative, or there is no baseline. In the absence of a baseline, or with cross-sectional data only, it is difficult to attribute change to an intervention. Similarly, it is difficult to attribute change to programs when evaluations are purely qualitative.

3. *Nature of interventions:* Many interventions that target different types of violence are multisectoral or multifaceted. This characteristic often contributes to success but also makes it hard to pinpoint in evaluations what exactly "works" to achieve documented success, and calls for more innovative or multiple methods of evaluation to assess attribution. It is also difficult to tease out the impact of a particular intervention when it is introduced over and above other existing programs by an organization, such that participants may already have been exposed to other ideas in ways that make them amenable to newly introduced interventions.

The Landscape of Evaluated Interventions in South Asia: A Summary

We identified a total of 101 interventions across types of violence—including interventions engaging men and boys—that were evaluated using any one of the approaches defined in figure 4.2. Figure 4.3 illustrates the distribution of identified evaluated interventions by type of violence, and interventions engaging men and boys.[2] The largest number of evaluated interventions comprised broad "violence against women" interventions that also addressed intimate partner violence (41). We also located 27 interventions to prevent child marriage that were evaluated in some manner, several of them as quasi-experimental studies (appendix E). The smallest number of evaluated interventions were those that addressed abuse specifically against girl children (3), custodial violence against women and girls (3), and honor crimes (3).

FIGURE 4.3 Evaluated Interventions by Violence Type (Number of Interventions)

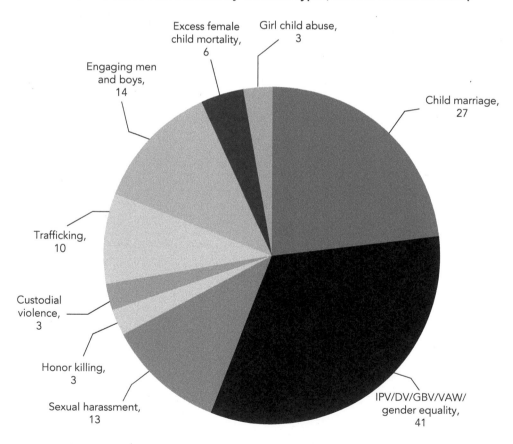

Note: DV = domestic violence; GBV = gender-based violence; IPV = intimate partner violence; VAW = violence against women.

FIGURE 4.4 Main Evaluation Methodology Used

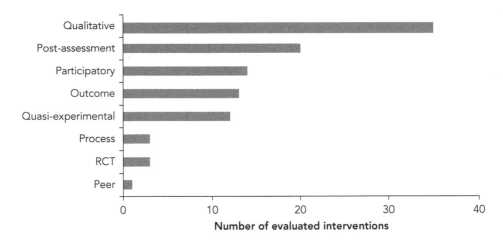

Note: RCT = randomized control trial.

Using our continuum of evaluation methods (figure 4.2), figure 4.4 describes the main evaluation methods used by these evaluated interventions. Of concern is the large number of evaluations that are conducted without a baseline, specifically all evaluations other than impact (RCT or quasi-experimental) or outcome evaluations. The largest number of evaluated interventions by far used what we define in this report as qualitative methods, that is, a combination of field visits, desk reviews, document reviews, and interviews (35). The use of such methods does not mean that these evaluations are weak. On the contrary, several of these evaluations use a multitude of qualitative methods, which allows them to triangulate their findings and provide rich nuance to our understanding of the program in question. However, the fact remains that observed changes cannot be attributed to the intervention, particularly since there is no baseline. Another concern is that only three of the evaluations explicitly included process evaluation. This is an unfortunate gap, as process evaluation and documentation are critical to understand the process of promising interventions to be able to replicate or scale them up. Twelve interventions used quasi-experimental methods. Most of these are either child marriage prevention interventions or interventions that aim to engage men and boys.

TYPOLOGY OF INTERVENTIONS RELATIVE TO THE LIFE CYCLE AND ECOLOGICAL FRAMEWORKS

While the interventions we identified map, by and large, to the different forms of violence for which women and girls may be at risk at different points in their life, they typically do not map cleanly to the ecological model in terms of the level at which they operate. Most interventions operate at multiple levels, recognizing that social change in a deeply engrained system, such as the patriarchy that underlies violence, necessitates such intervention. Risk and protective factors do map to levels of social ecology, as described in chapter 3.

Given this typology, we organize our analysis below primarily by form of violence across the life cycle, starting from birth and going through the different life stages. We analyze promising practices to prevent or respond to each form of violence and, where possible, identify which risk and protective factors at different levels of the social ecology are addressed.

Preventing Excess Female Child Mortality

Excess female child mortality starts at birth and continues through early childhood, contributing to what is referred to as a "daughter deficit." As the research in chapter 2 notes, this type of violence exists primarily in India, to a lesser degree (and with perhaps less known about it) in Pakistan and Nepal, and is reportedly diminishing in Bangladesh. Thus, it is perhaps not surprising that programs and policies directly addressing excess female child mortality and son preference are located mostly in India. Interventions focus, by and large, on shifting the relative value to parents of daughters and sons, providing financial incentives to parents to invest in daughters, and banning direct forms of postnatal daughter elimination such as female infanticide (figure 4.5).

We found six interventions that were evaluated in one of many ways. Most were post-intervention evaluations, but creatively addressed the lack of a baseline by using fortuitous natural experiment-scenarios of program introduction (e.g., Bedi and Srinivasan 2012), or else by using government program documentation and interviews (e.g., Sekhar 2012a).

SHIFTING THE RELATIVE VALUE OF SONS AND DAUGHTERS: LEGAL REFORM, MEDIA EFFORTS, AND EMPOWERING GIRLS

Government efforts to shift the relative value of sons and daughters focus largely on legal reform, while civil society efforts focus on changing parental and community attitudes about daughters using a range of media. One evaluated intervention in Pakistan worked directly with girls and their parents.

Government-led efforts at legal reform address two key reasons for the persistence of son preference: land inheritance through sons and the social norms that do not allow married daughters to be on hand for parents in old age. Legislative efforts in India have focused on the Hindu Succession (Amendment) Act (HSA) of 2005 and the Maintenance and Welfare of Parents and Senior Citizens Act (MWPSCA) of 2007 (Pande et al. 2009). The HSA legislates daughters as equal inheritors of ancestral or joint family property, while the MWPSCA makes it a legal obligation for sons, daughters, and other heirs to provide maintenance to parents and senior citizens from whom they inherit, in proportion to the share of any property inherited.

FIGURE 4.5 Evaluated Strategies to Prevent Excess Female Child Mortality

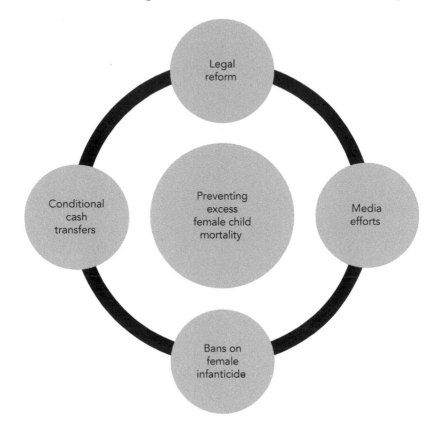

Recent research suggests that, while moving in the right direction, these reforms are either not enforced or continue to contain gender discriminatory clauses that dilute their effectiveness (Singh 2013). For example, while under the amended Hindu Succession Act daughters can inherit land, the manner in which they inherit in an extended family[3] is still not equal with brothers; nor is the manner in which women can bequeath property to heirs. Some of the states in northern and western India with the worst discrimination against girls are immune from the HSA under a provision preventing fragmentation of agricultural land. Finally, poor enforcement and the lack of protection from violence for women and girls who assert their inheritance rights have contributed to reluctance among women to claim this right.

Media interventions also attempt to address the underlying value of sons and daughters. We found two evaluated programs, the Meena campaign by UNICEF in Bangladesh, Nepal, India, and Pakistan, and Plan International's Let Girls Be Born campaign in India.[4] The Meena campaign comprised multi-media education-entertainment through fictional episodes on television and other media. Plan's campaign included media but also intensive community engagement. Both campaigns focused on promoting positive role models for girls and emphasizing girls as an asset, rather than a liability, to the family.

Both interventions were evaluated via qualitative participatory techniques with some quantitative elements. The evaluation reports of both campaigns report some success in promoting the message of gender equality, though the methods of evaluation make it difficult to attribute change to the campaigns per se. The Meena campaign evaluation noted that the campaign's power to change behavior in addition to attitudes was limited by the fact that there were no behavioral interventions to follow up on the attitude change triggered by the campaign (Chesterton 2004), an important lesson for other media interventions for this and other forms of violence. Another important lesson, this one from the draft evaluation report of Let Girls Be Born, is that maintaining community interest can be challenging and campaigns need to be prepared to innovate to do so (Dialectics 2014).

Television was viewers' main source of access to the Meena campaign content. The importance of television as a medium is also underscored by another study, albeit not a program evaluation. Jensen and Oster (2007) took advantage of the random spread of cable TV across India to use this "natural experiment" as a way to study the effect of cable TV on attitudes towards women. They found that access to such media was indeed associated with reduced son preference, and suggest that this was likely due to the portrayal in popular soap operas of women as professionals and leaders, thus challenging traditional views of acceptable roles for girls and women.

An innovative example of empowering girls themselves to change discriminatory behavior is the program of the Girl Guides Association in Pakistan, in conjunction with UNICEF, which reached girls in 800 schools across the country. An evaluation of the program in 2001 showed that the program contributed notably to changing parental and community perceptions of girls' value to the home and community (Croll 2001).

ENFORCING BANS ON FEMALE INFANTICIDE

Female infanticide is the only practice affecting the post-birth girl deficit that is explicitly banned.[5] Other practices contributing to post-birth girl deficits are likely impossible to ban, as they usually comprise familial neglect and discrimination related to feeding and health care use.

We found one evaluation of efforts to prevent female infanticide, from Tamil Nadu state in India, which has the highest reported prevalence of female infanticide in the country. This innovative evaluation used sharp changes in policies before and after 2001, as well as variations in policy intensity across districts, to conduct a quasi-experimental study (Bedi and Srinivasan 2012). Comparisons between 1996–99 and 2003 showed a drop of 46 percent in the female-to-male ratio of infant mortality rates (used as an estimate of female infanticide). The evaluation concluded that this success was due to the combination of government schemes providing incentives for families with daughters, and mass awareness-raising, community mobilization, and enforcement of laws and

---

BOX 4.2 Preventing Female Infanticide in Tamil Nadu, India

This intervention is a classic example of efforts that span multiple levels of the social ecology and included the following activities:

- *Cradle Baby Scheme:* provided cradles at government institutions where unwanted girl babies could be left, anonymously, and were then put up for adoption.

- *Girl Child Protection Scheme:* a conditional cash transfer scheme targeted to families below the poverty line with daughters ages 0–4 years and no son.

- *Social mobilization through the Tamil Nadu Area Health Care Project:* the project's platform was used for mass media, awareness campaigns, and street theater to promote the girl child and create awareness of the laws against female infanticide.

- *NGO initiatives in key "hot spot" districts:* self-help groups whose members vowed not to commit female infanticide were trained to prevent others from doing so; these groups engaged young couples, including providing them with economic support and enabling parents of daughters to access government schemes.

- *Vital Events Surveys:* systematically collected data on and regularly tracked births, deaths, and other vital demographic events for monitoring and planning purposes.

- *Death audit:* from 2001, deaths of all infants were investigated.

- *Legal action:* against those who committed or attempted female infanticide.

- *Pressure on local administrations to perform:* officials of high-risk districts were pressured by the state government to implement the laws and schemes.

Source: Bedi and Srinivasan 2012.

---

birth registration (box 4.2) (Bedi and Srinivasan 2012). At the same time, these efforts have been criticized for poor management and, for the Cradle Baby Scheme in particular, for uncertain success in fostering or adopting out abandoned babies. Civil society groups also argue that a scheme such as this does not change underlying son preference but, rather, may encourage parents to abandon unwanted girls (Srinivasan and Bedi 2010).

PROVIDING FINANCIAL INCENTIVES TO PARENTS TO INVEST IN DAUGHTERS: CONDITIONAL CASH TRANSFERS

Multiple efforts initiated by national and state governments in India attempt to increase the economic value of daughters by "rewarding" families who have girls. Even though the research is equivocal about the role of poverty in excess female child mortality, government programs often provide direct financial incentives to poor households with daughters, or subsidize the care and education of girls in poor households. Programs are typically structured as conditional cash transfers where the initial transfer occurs at the birth of a girl child. Subsequent transfers occur as a girl achieves different levels of schooling, serving as an incentive to invest in daughters; such incentives are sometimes also tied to immunization and other health care behaviors or outcomes. The final cashing in of the transfer occurs typically when the girl turns 18 or 20, provided she is unmarried, thus addressing child marriage (Sekhar 2010).

We found three evaluations of a cash transfer scheme in Haryana state, India (the *Apni Beti Apna Dhan* or ABAD program), and one study analyzing design and implementation of a set of such schemes across India. The evaluations are limited by the lack of a baseline, but try to circumvent this shortcoming in innovative ways (see appendix C). Sinha and Yoong (2009) suggest that the ABAD scheme succeeded in incentivizing poor households to bear daughters, as evidenced by less male-biased sex ratios of children over time, and increased investment in daughters' health care. Holla et al. (2007) also find that the program significantly contributed to changes in sex ratio at birth, increasing the likelihood of a girl's birth by 8–15 percent. However, they caution that the program may have merely shifted discriminatory practices to later years, as evidenced by no change in sex ratios of early childhood. Krishnan et al. (2014), in contrast, find no evidence of improvements in any indicators in their study villages.

While some of these mixed results are likely due to differences in samples, data sources, and econometric approaches, the lack of a demonstrable sustained impact may also reflect underlying design and implementation problems highlighted by several studies. Participation in cash transfer schemes is hampered by complicated criteria for eligibility, too many conditionalities attached to participation, and an onerous registration process to avail of benefits (Sekhar 2012b; Krishnan et al. 2014; Sharma et al. 2003). Often, even those tasked with implementing the schemes or policies may not fully understand all the eligibility criteria and conditions (Jaising et al. 2007), thus resulting in poor monitoring, coordination, and implementation.

Cash transfers also may not be appropriately targeted. Many are targeted specifically to poor households, though prenatal or postnatal discriminatory behavior to get rid of unwanted daughters occurs across levels of household wealth. Even for poor households, often the amounts offered by these schemes are too low to be attractive incentives for behavioral change (Krishnan et al. 2014; Holla et al. 2007). Similarly, schemes are often limited to first or second daughters, while the research shows that higher-birth-order girls are most at risk of discrimination and death (Das Gupta 1987; Pande 2003). The multiplicity of outcomes expected from each scheme further dilutes its effectiveness for addressing excess female child mortality (Sekhar 2012a; Krishnan et al. 2014).

LESSONS FROM SUCCESS IN ADDRESSING DAUGHTER DEFICIT

The review above suggests that policymakers in India are struggling to prevent excess female child mortality, with most evaluated efforts to date showing mixed success. In contrast, recent research from Bangladesh shows a sharp reversal in excess female child mortality and child sex ratios. The reasons for this success are not fully understood, but key elements distilled by some recent studies may prove instructive for efforts by other countries in the region. In particular, Bangladesh's experience suggests the importance of multisectoral yet selectively targeted efforts with an explicit gender focus that

---

BOX 4.3 "Scale, Speed, and Selectivity": Lessons from Bangladesh for Addressing Excess Female Child Mortality

Lessons for shifting the relative value of sons and daughters:

- *Improving basic health and survival for all children:* large-scale interventions addressed immunization, diarrheal disease, and other major contributors to childhood mortality and morbidity, with a gender focus that ensured girls benefited equally.

- *A development approach with an emphasis on opportunities for women:* examples range from microcredit and social protection to economic liberalization of the garment industry. This focus transformed women's lives and mobility, and contributed to changing families' and society's perceptions about women's capabilities.

- *Ubiquitous use of community mobilization, social marketing, demand creation, and intensive house-to-house delivery of programs:* intensive methods of delivery aimed to change deep-seated attitudes and beliefs about women and girls.

Lessons for encouraging parents to invest in daughters:

- *Economic development patterns encouraging women's labor force participation and earning potential:* expansion of microcredit and a focus on garment manufacturing-led growth contributed to greater availability of remunerative employment opportunities for young women, and provided economic incentives for parents to invest in daughters.

- *Large-scale subsidies for girls' education at primary and secondary levels:* these subsidies improved rates of girls' secondary schooling and addressed poverty constraints to schooling.

- *Commitment to investment in (some aspects of) women's health:* declines in maternal mortality and increased contraceptive use meant that girls and women were significantly more likely to survive childbirth.

Challenges remain:

- Weak governance and a failure to implement laws addressing other norms that discourage raising daughters, such as dowry and early marriage.

- Institutional constraints in workforce availability and management capacity of programs and policies.

- Persistent inability to reach the poorest, most disadvantaged, and hard-to-reach populations.

Sources: Adams et al. 2013; Kabeer et al. 2013.

---

simultaneously address risk factors at the individual, household, community, institutional, and structural levels of society (box 4.3).

Preventing and Responding to Abuse Faced by Girls throughout Childhood

There are a host of prevention and response efforts that address the other forms of physical and sexual violence girls face throughout childhood and into adolescence.

These efforts span levels of engagement including advocacy for legal reform, training of institutions that work with abused children, media, community mobilization, helplines and shelters, and empowering children themselves. Most are not evaluated, however. Among those that are, most do not separate out impact or other findings by gender. We identified 16 evaluated programs (appendix D), of which only three had a specific focus on girls: Plan International's regional Girl Power Program; Save the Children Fund's (SCF) program in partnership with TOLI, an NGO in Nepal; and, UNDP and the Bangladesh Government's ARISE project.

Plan International's Girl Power Program is implemented in multiple countries across the developing world. In South Asia, the program is ongoing in Bangladesh, Nepal, and Pakistan. It is too soon for any definitive lessons, yet the program is a promising example of a thoughtful comprehensive approach to address risk factors and enhance protective factors at the household, community, and macro levels, and support prevention and response efforts across levels of society. Mid-term outcome evaluations in all three South Asian countries document notable change in the willingness of parents and community members to oppose violence against girls and young women, and an increase in girls' capacity to protect themselves against violence, as well as to seek help and lodge formal cases when exposed to violence (Transition International 2014a, 2014b, 2014c).

The SCF-TOLI program, Safer Environment for Girls (2001–2011), aimed to support some of the key individual-level protective factors highlighted in chapter 3, in particular protective factors for sexual abuse vulnerability (Gautam 2012). Interventions worked across levels of the social ecology: empowering girls, making schools violence free, and training teachers. The largely qualitative evaluation suggests that these strategies succeeded in empowering girls and boys to recognize violence, and possibly increased girls' confidence through the program's child clubs; however, it is difficult to conclude from the report whether this "success" went beyond the girls included in the evaluation's focus group discussions. The ARISE project—with activities also spanning individual, household, and community factors that may increase violence, and also addressing prevention and response—focused on sexual vulnerability of girls on the street. However, a critical qualitative mid-term appraisal pointed out several key shortcomings: children were not engaged in any aspect of program planning, sexual abuse was rarely reported, and shelters meant for girls were found to mainly house boys (Sinha and Tapan 2001).

The mid-term and qualitative assessments of these programs do not allow attribution of observed positive changes to the intervention itself; Plan International's assessments of the Girl Power Projects note as much (Transition International 2014a, 2014b, 2014c). Clearly, more programs are needed that specifically focus activities *and* evaluation on outcomes for girls. Most programs that target child abuse position their interventions within a child's-rights framework that recognizes the vulnerability of all children—girls and boys. While this is indeed appropriate, the particular and persistent low valuation of girls in South Asia suggests that programs to address child abuse in the region need to explicitly inject a gender focus into what is a human rights concern. In fact, such a gender focus can be introduced into existing initiative types. Child clubs and peer groups can include groups specifically focused on girls' particular vulnerabilities; training of providers, such as police[6] and those running child helplines,[7] can likewise incorporate modules about girls' vulnerabilities. Groups working with children in conflict zones can provide special protection and services for girls, who may be especially vulnerable to sexual abuse.[8]

Preventing Child Marriage

South Asia has perhaps the heaviest concentration of programs worldwide to prevent child marriage.[9] These include both stand-alone life skills, schooling scholarships, or cash transfer programs by local and international NGOs focused specifically on delaying marriage, as well as multisectoral programs that combine individual-level approaches such as life skills or livelihoods programs with community involvement, media campaigns, and advocacy with government (figure 4.6).

Evaluations of child marriage prevention interventions have progressed much further than those for interventions to address other forms of violence against girl children. A review by Jain and Kurz (2007) of programs between 1992–2006 found three evaluated interventions in South Asia. A similar assessment of evaluated programs between

FIGURE 4.6 Evaluated Approaches to Prevent Child Marriage

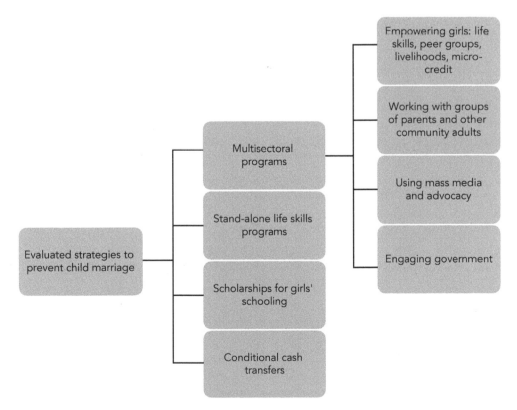

1997–2008 by Malhotra and colleagues (2011) found 14 in South Asia. For this study, we identified 27 efforts that we would consider evaluated according to the criteria outlined earlier in this chapter (appendix E). The majority are in Bangladesh and India, followed by Nepal. Despite the number of evaluations, rigor remains a concern, particularly in efforts to attribute observed declines in early marriage to programs. This is at least partly because of the very fact that there is so much activity around child marriage in the region's countries: the simultaneous nature of many of these programs makes it almost impossible to attribute change in preventing child marriage to any one program or strategy.

MULTISECTORAL PROGRAMMING TO PREVENT CHILD MARRIAGE

Evaluated multisectoral programs in Bangladesh, Nepal, and India report success in delaying marriage and in changing parental and community attitudes towards early marriage. Evaluations used quasi-experimental and/or baseline-endline quantitative methods combined with a range of qualitative methods. However, none of the evaluations teased out what elements of their programs were essential for success. An exception is the Prachar program in India, which asked respondents about what they considered critical. Research results indicated that the biggest motivators for delaying marriage were improved socio-economic status for households and a change in the perception of the value of schooling for girls (Pathfinder International 2011). While these changes could have occurred regardless of the Prachar intervention, sampled individuals remembered the messages of the Prachar program and felt that the program had contributed to the speed and sustainability of changed attitudes and behaviors.

To some extent it is possible to extricate common elements across Prachar and other multisectoral programs that are likely candidates contributing to program success. All these programs engaged adolescents and adults as "change makers" themselves. Examples include the EKATA groups in CARE's Shouhardo program in Bangladesh that engaged the community to stop violence against women, child marriage, and dowry (Tango International Inc. 2009); SCF's efforts in the KAISHAR program, also in Bangladesh, to train 1500 adolescent facilitators to take over program implementation (SCF 2009a, 2009b, 2009c, 2009d); and CARE's Chunauti program's peer groups in Nepal (CARE Nepal 2011). Many also used media to mobilize communities. Some sort of life skills curriculum formed a key part of all these programs. Beyond these few common strategies, however, each program used different additional approaches.

LIFE SKILLS PROGRAMS TO EMPOWER GIRLS

In addition to the life skills programming in the multisectoral interventions, there are examples also of evaluated stand-alone life skills programs. These conclude, by and large, that life skills programs are "effective" in raising girls' self-esteem and addressing antecedents to child marriage, such as the value of girls and parental and community attitudes towards early marriage. Some—most notably Cedpa's Better Life Options

Program (BLP) and the Institute of Health Management-Pachod's life skills program, both in India—also demonstrated success in delaying marriage.

The Institute of Health Management-Pachod (IHMP) evaluation is noteworthy as it provides a good example of methodological rigor in the absence of randomization. The pre-post case-control evaluation tracked changes in the program and control areas rather than among program participants only, thus addressing to some extent problems of selection into the program described in box 4.1 (Pande et al. 2006). The observed decline in proportions marrying early (80.7 percent to 61.8 percent in the treatment area and no change in control areas) and increased median age at marriage (from 16 to 17 years in the treatment area and unchanged in the control area) could be attributed to the intervention with more confidence. IHMP attributes its success to program intensity: engaging girls every day and parents on a monthly basis for a whole year immersed girls and parents, allowed sufficient time for changes to be cemented, and allowed time for ideas promoted in the life skills program to spread into the community at large.[10]

Even in ostensibly single-focus life skills programs, a huge range of activities is undertaken under the umbrella term *life skills,* including any combination of activities such as sexuality education, non-formal schooling, livelihoods training, peer support, sports, and safe spaces. This makes it difficult to isolate what exactly "works" to delay marriage. Evidence from across programs suggests that key elements for effectiveness include providing girls an opportunity to be exposed to new ideas, giving them access to a "safe space," and changing how others view girls. Still, more rigorous evaluation is needed to determine what exactly is required for effectiveness. Also, programs can run from being one day long, such as in the life skills component of the Girl Power Program in Nepal (Transition International 2014b) to a year long, such as the life skills program run by the IHMP in India (Pande et al. 2006). While it is unlikely that a one-day program can have a significant impact, still it is unclear how long a program has to run to be successful in delaying marriage.

INCREASING PARTICIPATION IN SECONDARY SCHOOLING

Several studies suggest that parents weigh the costs and benefits of delaying marriage and sending daughters to school against the costs and benefits of marrying their daughters early. Bajracharya and Amin (2013) also note that even mechanistically, a girl who is in school is not going to get married. Thus, it is not surprising that evaluations of schooling programs find an association between improved formal schooling and delay in marriage, particularly when financial incentives tilt parental cost-benefit assessments in favor of continuing their daughters' education.

Three of the evaluated programs we identified offered financial incentives to parents to keep girls in school. Programs by Pathfinder in Bangladesh and CARE in Nepal provided scholarships as one part of a larger community-based approach to preventing child marriage, while the World Bank's program, also in Bangladesh, focused solely on education stipends and scholarships.

The evaluation of Pathfinder's scholarship stipends reports that participating girls continued their education beyond the life of the program, as scholarships addressed the costs and parents saw the benefits of an education. Information collected from schools and marriage registration, though admittedly incomplete, suggests that rates of early marriage also dropped (Burket et al. 2006). Similarly, the World Bank's female secondary school stipend program in Bangladesh saw a strong and immediate effect on early marriage: between 1992 (pre-) and 1995 (one year after program introduction), the proportion of girls married between the ages of 13–15 years declined from 29 percent to 14 percent; for 16–18 year olds, this decline was from 79 percent to 64 percent (Amin et al. 1998; World Bank 2008). Qualitative findings from Phase II (Schurmann 2009) suggest, moreover, that the availability of this stipend did enter into parental calculations of marriage. These were not randomized programs; nonetheless, their scale—especially in the case of the World Bank program—makes it likely that at least part of the observed change was likely attributable to the program.

Such programs by themselves may not adequately and sustainably address the underlying poverty that is one of the key risk factors propelling early marriage, however. In Pathfinder's program in India, girls were afraid that parents would not be able to continue sending them to school once the scholarships stopped because they would be unable to afford doing so (Burket et al. 2006). The World Bank's stipend program in Bangladesh was unable to significantly increase schooling among the poorest. This was likely in part because it chose not to target poor or otherwise disadvantaged households (Amin et al. 1998; Schurmann 2009). However the poorest likely did not participate because the scholarships by themselves were not enough to overcome the poverty of their immediate environment: the areas where the poorest lived did not have suitable schools to which to send girls.

A range of conditional cash transfers in India also seeks to provide financial incentives to parents conditional on continuing girls' secondary school and delaying marriage. The largest and most carefully evaluated one is the same Apni Beti Apna Dhan (ABAD) program in Haryana state that also aims to prevent excess female child mortality (reviewed earlier in this chapter). An initial evaluation showed that participation in the ABAD program was significantly associated with girls' staying longer in school (Nanda et al. 2014). However, the endline survey for this evaluation was conducted before the first cohort of participating girls turned 18, which will occur in the second half of 2014. Researchers intend to conduct a follow-up at that point to examine effects of the program on delaying marriage; they will also examine marriage among younger sisters of ABAD participants to measure spillover effects.[11]

INCOME-GENERATING AND LIVELIHOODS ACTIVITIES

A recent review of adolescent livelihoods programs by Nanda et al. (2013) finds that livelihoods can empower young girls and improve their self-efficacy, increase their mobility and voice, and enhance their value to the family. Evaluations of livelihoods programs we identified also find such effects: as one participant of ICRW's DISHA program in India told an evaluator: "We can talk. Previously, we were scared to do anything. Now...we can go anywhere, do any work" (Kanesathasan et al. 2008, 18). The research reviewed in chapter 3 suggests that these transformations in girls and their immediate environment can help delay marriage. Increased confidence can empower girls to better negotiate marriage with their parents; effective livelihoods programs also provide parents and girls an alternative to marriage during adolescence and early adulthood. When girls earn, parents may also change their valuation of daughters and be willing to delay marriage.

At the same time, the Kishori Abhijan and ELA center programs in Bangladesh illustrate the real and perceived tensions between offering income generating opportunities on the one hand, and trying to encourage secondary schooling on the other. The Kishori Abhijan evaluation found that while working did not lead to school dropout, girls who were working were less likely to do school work outside of school at home (Amin and Suran 2005). Girls interviewed in the ELA centers noted that they were hesitant to join income-generating activities because they were anxious not to miss school. Although the quantitative evaluation did not show any impact on education, still the apprehension among girls affected their participation (Kashfi et al. 2012; Shahnaz and Karim 2008). Nanda et al's (2013) review suggests that programmers are indeed responding to this concern by encouraging girls who drop out to go back to school and scheduling livelihoods training sessions at times when school is not in session.

BOX 4.4 Beyond Livelihoods: Building Land and Non-Land Financial Assets for Girls in India

Landesa collaborated with the Indian government's Rajiv Gandhi Scheme for Empowerment of Adolescent Girls (RGSEAG) SABLA in West Bengal state. The Landesa-SABLA program taught girls about non-land assets such as savings accounts, life insurance policies and other financial savings instruments; encouraged parents to create assets for their daughters and to let daughters inherit land; and promoted land-based livelihoods through cultivation and sale of food crops by girls using household land. Comparing the more than 200 SABLA sites where this program was implemented with other SABLA sites and non-SABLA non-Landesa sites, the quasi-experimental case-control evaluation showed that:

- Participating girls were 15 percent more likely to have a financial savings asset in their name;

- Girls in the program were 20 percent more likely to earn their own income, cultivate household land, and keep part of the income earned for themselves;

- Parents were willing—at least in theory—to bequeath land to daughters;

- Participating girls married, on average, a year-and-a-half later than girls in control villages;

- Parents of participating girls paid a dowry 10 percent less than in control areas and were more likely to give marrying daughters a bequest that they could control post-marriage;

- Boys participating in program groups started to change their attitudes towards dowry and girls' rights to inherit land.

Sources: Landesa 2013 http://www.landesa.org/wp-content/uploads/Landesa-Girls-Poject-Baseline-Study.pdf and http://www.landesa.org/india-girls-project-study-shows-significant-benefits.

The Landesa program in India illustrates a particularly innovative way to use livelihoods to position girls as an asset rather than as a financial liability (box 4.4). The rigorous quasi-experimental evaluation demonstrates the possibility and power of encouraging parents to invest in non-land assets for girls in situations where land is scarce or inherited only by boys. The Landesa experience also shows that such an approach can simultaneously address early marriage, the underlying value of girls, household poverty, and dowry.

The Importance of Birth Registration to Address All Forms of Violence against Girls

Birth registration is critical to the prevention of and response to all forms of violence against girls. UNICEF (2013, 5) describes birth registration as children's "passport to protection." Without birth registration, girls can easily be married early or trafficked; birth registration is also essential for allowing governments to plan and budget for other forms of child abuse, such as sexual abuse or corporal punishment. Girls (and boys) can be prosecuted and charged as adults without proper birth registration, resulting in higher risks of custodial violence if incarcerated with adults.

Evaluations of efforts by Plan International, UNICEF, and the government of Bangladesh (described in appendix E) show that birth registration can be successfully universalized if (a) birth registration systems are decentralized; (b) local and national officials are trained in birth registration; and (c) birth registration is tied to essential services and is thus required to access those services (Muzzi 2010). Using these approaches, UNICEF's program was able to increase birth registration in Bangladesh from less than 10 percent in 2006 to over 50 percent by 2009. The evaluation cautions, however, that births will not be registered unless there are real deterrents put in place for those who fail to register. People do not voluntarily register births, at least to begin with, and thus campaigns exhorting people to do so need to continue until birth registration becomes a normal part of usual engagement with government services. Thus, for example, efforts to universalize birth registration in Bangladesh tied registration not to birth (since most women do not deliver in health centers) but to immunization programs, which have a national reach.

Opportunities, Gaps, and Challenges in Addressing All Forms of Violence against Girl Children

The review above shows that there are a huge number of efforts to address the multiple types of violence that girls face in South Asia. Still, there are several opportunities, gaps, and challenges that remain. Overall, a key challenge is to improve evaluation. This does not mean that all interventions have to undergo randomized control trials. The evaluations of the many child marriage interventions, and of the Girl Power Project, all provide innovative ways to evaluate rigorously even if RCTs are not possible. Some especially promising possibilities are to use mixed methods or external data sources and populations to triangulate results, or to match participants and non-participants on key characteristics to account for selection into a program.

There are some key risk and protective factors—particularly at the level of a girl's immediate environment, community, and institutions—that interventions don't address. For instance, we found only one intervention (the Landesa program) aimed at delaying marriage that addressed dowry. Interventions addressing excess female child mortality definitely need to pay more attention to the role of the sex composition of the household: a large body of research has convincingly proved its importance. Interventions aiming to prevent or respond to physical and sexual abuse of girls need to pay more attention to what goes on in the home—for example, violence between parents or parental substance abuse.

There are also some relatively clear opportunities to strengthen the effectiveness of interventions. For child abuse interventions, the need of the hour is for programs to better and more explicitly address the special vulnerabilities of girls, when relevant, and to map the influence of programs on participants by gender. A key opportunity for livelihoods interventions seeking to delay marriage is to include provision of non-land assets for girls in the portfolio of what is considered a livelihoods intervention. In fact, this focus could also be applied within conditional cash transfer programs that address excess female child mortality, and could be used to address dowry. There are, moreover, opportunities to learn across countries; for instance, it would be instructive to know how Bhutan, Maldives, and Sri Lanka achieved universal birth registration, or how Maldives achieved its low rates of child marriage.

Finally, we found that many interventions almost automatically focus on poverty and lack of education as key risk factors for the different types of violence against girls, even though the research in chapter 3 notes that girls face most kinds of violence across levels of household economic status, and that education is not unequivocally associated with better outcomes either. Interventions thus need to consider more carefully the circumstances under which these factors may be more or less critical to address than other, relatively ignored risk and protective factors within a girl's immediate environment.

Addressing Domestic and Intimate Partner Violence within Marriage

As young girls grow into adolescence and then adulthood, they move into the next phase of the South Asian life cycle, that of being a married adult. Within this life stage, programs address domestic or intimate partner violence. Programs that directly and solely focus on intimate partner violence are rare, however. Rather, intimate partner violence is covered either as part of broader programs to address overall "violence against women," incorporating multiple violence types that may exist in an implementing organization's geographical sphere; as part of programs in the health, education, legal/justice, or governance sectors, or in a combination of these four areas; as part of broad community development efforts wherein organizations respond to multiple gender-related needs and constraints of participating women; and/or where a community requests or needs intervention to address domestic or intimate partner violence (see appendix F).

Most of the program evaluations we identified are qualitative, with quantitative data used mainly to track output indicators. A few notable exceptions are mass campaigns such as the Bell Bajao! campaign in India and the regional We Can and Men's Action to Stop Violence Against Women (MASVAW) campaigns. Our analysis below thus supplements the few evaluations with field visits and consultations with experts and programmers.

Interventions tend to be separated into prevention or response efforts. Prevention efforts are primarily implemented through media, campaigns, awareness-raising, and the identification of "change makers" as role models for others. Several interventions also engage men and boys in efforts to change underlying gender norms and thereby decrease violence against women, including violence by intimate partners. Common response strategies include helplines, shelters, crisis centers, and various forms of legal aid.

PREVENTION STRATEGIES: THE USE OF MEDIA, CAMPAIGNS, AND CHANGE MAKERS

Media campaigns do not specifically target only intimate partner violence. Rather, they attempt to address underlying gender norms that impact all forms of violence that women may face, among which intimate partner violence is considered critical. As such, these efforts span different levels of society, working to engage individuals, involve communities, motivate legal action, and change social norms.

Partly because of this holistic approach, mass campaigns are difficult to formally evaluate. Still, the popular response to many of them suggests that they have contributed to opening up space for public discourse around violence against women, perhaps even hastening tipping points in public perception and acceptability of violence. They have also been successful in engaging men and boys. Evaluation findings suggest that key elements of success include utilizing existing community networks, using a range of deliberately selected and often innovative means of getting their message across to a wide audience, identifying change makers as important partners and messengers, and engaging a wide range of partners across the NGO, government, and private sectors.

The Bell Bajao! Campaign in India, launched in 2008, provides a good illustration of using existing community networks and a range of tailored communication methods. The campaign employs pop culture, media, the arts, and technology to promote awareness about domestic violence and engage men and boys; by mobilizing a large array of community mobilizers, it has reached millions of individuals. Multiple evaluations have found that its combination of activism, mass media, and community involvement have contributed to its success in raising awareness, especially about less well-known forms of intimate partner violence such as emotional violence. An evaluation by Breakthrough also notes that, as with evaluations of media interventions to address violence against children, television was the most effective and far-reaching tool (Breakthrough, n.d.).

In another example, the Suriya Development Organization in Sri Lanka developed a "clothesline" campaign (hanging clothes of survivors of violence along a clothesline for public view) to create awareness of intimate partner violence faced by women. An initial negative backlash, triggered by the perception of intimate partner violence as a private issue, transformed over time into more positive acceptance of such activities. Also as a result of such activities, intimate partner violence was gradually recognized as an issue of public concern.[12]

Finally, the regional We Can campaign, launched by Oxfam, has been evaluated multiple times. It provides several interesting lessons for the use of advocacy and campaigning as a tool to address attitudes toward and acceptance of not only intimate partner but in fact all forms of violence (box 4.5). Those leading the implementation of this

---

BOX 4.5 *We Can* **Campaign to End Violence against Women**

"Together, we can end all violence against women"—We Can Campaign in South Asia

The main goal of the We Can Campaign in South Asia, developed by Oxfam Great Britain, has been to reduce the social acceptance of gender discrimination and violence against women. First launched in 2004, the campaign aimed to reach 50 million individuals in Afghanistan, Bangladesh, India, Nepal, Pakistan, and Sri Lanka through the efforts of a somewhat collective and informal leadership shared among campaign alliance members ("allies"), including universities, civil society groups, corporate bodies, and private enterprises. The campaign has been largely driven by "change makers" who pledged to carry forward the campaign's message by initiating non-acceptance of violence against women in their own lives and in the lives of those around them (Rakib and Razan 2013; Oxfam GB 2012).

Promising strategies: The focus and method of implementation have varied by country, as has the success of the campaign. Still, a summary evaluation in September 2011 found that the campaign had been "relevant," "effective," and "efficient" (Raab 2011, 6) and had contributed to individual and institutional transformation and raising public awareness of issues related to violence against women. The following approaches and strategies are considered to have been key contributors to this success (Raab 2011; Williams and Aldred 2011; Aldred and Williams 2009):

- Early development of a well thought-out regional and country-specific implementation strategy, including an exit strategy that ensures sustainability of the program;

- Simple, culturally and contextually sensitive messaging, including in local languages;

- Provocation rather than education, with messages triggering discussion and action;

- Design that addresses an array of individuals, including both men and women, urban and rural dwellers, and different income levels;

- Informal structure with small national coordination bodies and activities;

- Decentralized programming, such that implementation ideas were left to local alliances, grassroots organizations, and individual change makers;

- Close collaboration between program staff, financers, and marketing members in sharing lessons learned, future plans, and mobilization of resources.

Sources: Published literature cited above, and interviews with Jinat Ara Haque, National Coordinator, We Can Campaign, Bangladesh; Dr. Noreen Khali, Regional Adviser on Gender and Governance, Oxfam; and Hajera Pasha, National Coordinator, We Can Pakistan.

campaign across countries attributed its success to the campaign's active engagement of partners, including government and other stakeholders.[13]

The Men's Action to Stop Violence Against Women (MASVAW) network of over 700 male activists in India has also been evaluated multiple times, with evaluations showing that men living in MASVAW areas as well as those directly exposed to MASVAW had more gender equitable attitudes than men in control groups (Das et al. 2012). As with Bell Bajao! and We Can, the MASVAW campaign also used a range of media and communication tools, together with individual mobilization and community involvement.

As noted earlier in this chapter, media and campaigns can start the process of social change but will likely not sustain behavioral change leading to lower intimate partner violence without additional input. Identifying and working with key change makers may be one such input. One interesting example in this regard is that of awareness-raising efforts in Afghanistan that have focused on religious leaders as change makers. UNDP's Gender Equality Program (GEP) established working groups within the Ministry of Hajj and Religious Affairs (MOHRA), trained religious leaders to raise awareness of Islamic interpretations of gender issues, and organized exposure visits to Malaysia and Turkey. According to the GEP's independent evaluation, MOHRA's newsletter was an effective outreach tool to reach and encourage mullahs to attend training on gender issues (Rodriguez and Anwari 2011). The Asia Foundation also conducted exposure visits with some 142 imams and traditional leaders to India, Malaysia, Turkey, and the United Arab Emirates, with positive results. Participants of the exposure visits were more tolerant and some used the experience and knowledge obtained from the visits to establish research centers and women's madrassas.[14] We could not find formal evaluations, however, that demonstrated the success of these and similar "change maker" efforts in preventing domestic or intimate partner violence.

PREVENTION STRATEGIES: ENGAGING MEN AND BOYS

The media campaigns discussed above successfully engage men and boys in reducing acceptance of violence against women, girls, and other men. In addition, impact evaluations of programs with young boys and men have shown that addressing gender inequality beliefs early in the life of boys and men can have important impacts on their attitudes towards intimate partner violence. Quasi-experimental evaluations of the Yaari Dosti and Engaging Men programs in India, and the Humqadam program in Pakistan, described in more detail in appendix F, showed success in using innovative and interactive sex education with young men to transform their notions of masculinity and attitudes about intimate partner and other forms of violence against women (Verma et al. 2008; Instituto Promundo 2012). A sports program by Saathi, in Nepal, and the Parivartan Program in India are examples of interventions that successfully use sports to connect with young men. The evaluation of the Parivartan program, for instance, illustrated the effectiveness of using sports as an entry point to trigger significant attitudinal and behavioral changes among coaches and athletes, including less support of physical abuse of girls among athletes and coaches, positive shifts in gender equitable attitudes, and a decline in sexually abusive behaviors among community athletes in program areas (Das et al. 2012).

The experience of these programs illustrates the importance and power of engaging young men and boys early in life. This is similar to the approach of life skills programs to prevent child marriage that seek to work with girls early to empower them. Programs that target young men and boys, or young women and girls (through life skills, for instance), all use a mix of sexuality education, life skills, sports, and some community engagement. All have the persons "at risk"—boys who may perpetrate violence or young girls who may be married early—at the center. And all address the relative value of girls and boys, women and men. As such there is tremendous scope for cross-learning between programs such as the ones highlighted in this section that try and engage young men and boys to prevent future violence against women and girls, and programs that involve girls in life skills efforts to prevent child marriage. The overlap in strategies also suggests that life skills programs could adapt curricula from men's and boys' programs to provide girls with skills—before they marry—to address risks of intimate partner violence they may encounter after they marry.

RESPONSE STRATEGIES: CRISIS CENTERS, SHELTERS, AND HELPLINES

Response strategies specifically address the individual woman and her needs, mostly without attempting to address risk or protective factors at other levels of the social ecology. Crisis centers and shelters are perhaps the most common forms of response to intimate partner violence, followed by helplines.

One approach increasingly held up as a promising practice is to provide in one place multiple related services that survivors of intimate partner violence may need, such as medical attention, shelter, crisis management, counseling, and legal aid. The Multi-Sectoral Programme on Violence against Women (MSPVAW) in Bangladesh, implemented since May 2000 with the Ministry of Women and Children Affairs as the lead coordinating agency, is one such example. The program, now in its third phase, engages ten other government ministries including the Ministry of Law, Ministry of Information, Ministry of Education, and Ministry of Health and Family Welfare. The program also involves NGOs, most notably by referring violence survivors to organizations that offer services for them.[15] The MSPVAW has been instrumental in the establishment and scale-up of hospital-based One-Stop Crisis Centers in tertiary-level medical college hospitals and One-Stop Crisis Cells in district and upazila hospitals that provide a range of services. Another far-reaching intervention set up by the MSPVAW is the National Helpline Centre for violence against women, a 24-hour helpline that can be accessed from land lines and mobile numbers using the short code 10921, and that has handled close to 18,000 calls since its opening in June 2012.[16]

Such a multisectoral approach does indeed have the potential to be a powerful and effective response mechanism and holds the promise of being a woman-friendly response system, enabling survivors to access all they need in one place. However, multisectoral programs that seek to respond to intimate partner violence also present

BOX 4.6 Nepal's One-Stop Crisis Management Centers

The One-Stop Crisis Management Centers (OCMC) are the first inter-ministerial, multisectoral, and hospital-based government initiative to address gender-based violence in Nepal. The OCMCs fall under the Ministry of Health and Population, and a central Coordination Committee administers the project. So far, 16 OCMCs have been established, each headed by a district coordination committee (Population Division 2013b). At an OCMC, a violence survivor can receive immediate medical treatment, psycho-social counseling, legal counseling, a safe home, and rehabilitation, services that were previously scattered across a number of organizations.

The OCMC initiative has had some success, and the basic treatment and psychosocial counseling are considered important services (Population Division 2013a). Some OCMCs, such as in Dang and Makwanpur, are examples of good practice and effective coordination, attributable at least in part to the personal commitment and leadership skills among OCMC staff, medical superintendents, and the district health office chief at these units. Still, the initiative as a whole faces a number of challenges:

1. *Weak information dissemination:* Many potential users and stakeholders at village, district, or sub-national levels may be unaware of OCMCs and their services and procedures. This lack of outreach has resulted in weak demand. Officials interviewed for this case study noted, "Even the police and village development committee members do not know about the OCMCs" (District-level official).

2. *Poor communication and coordination among stakeholders:* Due to the number of members on OCMC District Coordination Committees, convening meetings has proved difficult. Inadequate coordination between the committees responsible for OCMCs and for NGOs (Population Division 2013c) limits the OCMCs' effectiveness in linking survivors with NGOs for ongoing rehabilitation. Interviews with senior staff at the Nepal Health Sector Support Program revealed that the nature of police recruitment means a lack of adequate female police officers to place in OCMCs, making it difficult for OCMCs to link with the police for survivor security.

3. *Uncertain quality of service:* Many OCMCs have been unable to provide the planned 24-hour service because they are understaffed, with staff commitment undermined by the lack of long-term contracts; they also often do not have adequate medical and other supplies. Some centers are not easily accessible. Follow-up of individual cases is often weak; anecdotal evidence suggests that, in the case of hospital-based OCMCs, general hospital staff do not prioritize cases directed to them from the OCMCs. OCMCs have also not effectively provided the other services of linking victims with lawyers for legal guidance, NGOs for rehabilitation, and police for security.

4. *Limited treatment of severe cases:* No proper financial arrangements exist for severe cases that OCMCs refer to zonal hospitals. Government funds are available to reimburse victims, but the lengthy process and regulations make them difficult to access.

Sources: Published literature cited above; field visits; and interviews with government officials, OCMC staff, survivors, and community representatives.

many challenges in coordination and implementation, as illustrated by an assessment of Nepal's hospital-based One-Stop Crisis Management Centers (box 4.6).

Stand-alone crisis centers, shelters (with or without crisis centers), and helplines are also common forms of response to intimate partner violence. Yet we found no rigorous evaluations of programs providing these services. Several desk reviews, interviews by our report team, and process documentation do, however, give a picture of some key successes and challenges associated with these responses.

One example of an instructive process evaluation is the assessment of the Dilaasa "model," the first hospital-based crisis center in India for intimate partner violence survivors. The process documentation of this model (Deosthali et al. 2005) suggests a number of best practice approaches for implementing hospital-based crisis centers. Key among these are the importance of training health care professionals to accurately identify women and girls who might be at risk of, or already have suffered, violence in their homes; having a designated space within the hospital, near the casualty center, with well-trained counselors who can refer survivors to other services; and having the casualty centers in hospitals well set-up to screen survivors. Assessments of the Shahid Benazir Bhutto Centers for Women in Pakistan, based on desk reviews, site visits, and key informant interviews, add to these promising practices the importance of having a standard operating procedure across centers, as well as effective mechanisms to monitor such procedures (Zia 2010).

In Nepal, interviews conducted by our study's in-country consultant with the staff of Saathi's shelter house provide additional input that is likely instructive for both shelters and crisis centers. The interviews suggest that, at least in the Nepali context, there is a broad understanding of good practices needed to run shelters, including the need to create response systems that are centered on the needs of survivors. Still, space constraints, insufficient security, and long duration of stay in the shelters can hamper the delivery of services to women. Another problem faced in Nepal, highlighted in these interviews, is that survivors of domestic violence may be reluctant to stay in shelters that also house trafficked women or women with communicable diseases like HIV because they fear being stigmatized. Finally, staffing of shelters and follow-up by staff once the survivor leaves the shelter is of concern.[17] Shelter experiences in Afghanistan illustrate other issues: seeking help in shelters may require cumbersome paperwork, for instance (Vazirova 2011). Moreover, shelters may not guarantee protection: in Afghanistan, for example, even while she stays in a shelter, a woman can be vulnerable to abuse and attacks by her husband or husband's family.[18]

In part, these problems may reflect struggles with finances, capacity, and community commitment. For instance, the assessments of the Shahid Benazir Bhutto Centers for Women in Pakistan (Zia 2010, 2012) noted that though the centers were considered to provide a crucial service for survivors of intimate partner violence, half the centers were non-functional because of institutional and infrastructural flaws, and were in need of support from government and civil society stakeholders.

RESPONSE STRATEGIES: LEGAL AID, WORKING WITH JUSTICE SECTORS, AND MEDIATION

As with crisis centers and shelters, efforts to work with police, mediation, and legal aid are widespread, yet we could find few rigorous evaluations. However, qualitative and descriptive assessments suggest that these are areas of response where more work is needed.

The Rabta Program by Pakistani NGO Rozan developed its own model to train police in responding appropriately to survivors. A mixed-methods evaluation found that police who underwent the training were more sensitive to violence against women and more likely to be receptive to hiring women police officers. Many police inspectors had internalized the message of gender equality in their personal lives. Rozan's training module has been mainstreamed into regular police training curricula, but the scale-up has faced problems in maintaining a consistently high level of quality across police stations (Khalique et al. 2011). Other examples of police training to respond to intimate partner violence include special cells within police stations established in Afghanistan, India (Mahtani 2006), and Sri Lanka, frequently staffed by female police officers. However, understaffing, frequent turnover, lack of proper recording and ineffective training remain serious shortcomings in these endeavors.

Women are often distrustful of the formal police and judicial systems, as evidenced by data discussed in chapter 2 on low levels of disclosure of domestic and other forms of violence and care-seeking at formal institutions. Instead, the use of community-level mediation and re-integration are increasingly common approaches to settling cases of interpersonal violence, at least for intimate partner violence. Examples include Ain O Salish Kendra (ASK) and Bangladesh Legal Aid and Services Trust, both in Bangladesh, which provide legal aid through their own centers, accompany women to file complaints, follow up on cases, and provide mediation assistance. Some groups also try and engage community elders and councils to mediate, such as the Legal and Cultural Services for Women and Children of Afghanistan (LSWCA), which, among other activities, attempts to use the authority of community *shuras* to protect the violence survivors (Vazirova 2011). Community mediation can be a positive response approach, ensuring quick justice and perhaps contributing to normative change in the community as community members mete out justice. On the other hand, engaging *shuras* and other informal justice mechanisms may undermine the formal justice mechanisms that need to be strengthened.[19] Moreover, traditional mediation systems such as the *shuras* in Afghanistan often tend to see violence as a private conflict or dispute, rather than as a societal issue arising from gender inequality (Vazirova 2011), and thus may not actively promote long-term change. Once again, however, the above examples were not rigorously evaluated.

A more positive experience is illustrated by three examples of informal mediation in India (ICRW 2002). In three Indian states, pre-existing community-based activist groups and movements formed informal justice mechanisms specifically to address the issue of domestic and intimate partner violence. A participatory evaluation by ICRW

(2002) found that women and men in all three states favored these mediation mechanisms to other options. The intensive training of mediators—all women—in gender inequality, mediation, and violence were considered instrumental in creating a progressive forum. The group's base in broader community development, the openness to discussion, timeliness of judgment, and the involvement of all family members while keeping the woman's interest as the primary goal also contributed to mediation mechanisms' success and legitimacy. Further, these mediation groups engaged with formal systems as needed, rather than undermining them. These examples provide a road map for how to engage women, men, and communities in strengthening informal justice mechanisms.

Community-based paralegals are a potential middle ground between ineffective formal judicial systems and potentially worrisome local mediation efforts. Qualitative evaluations, such as of UNDP's GEP, show that training female members of community development committees as paralegals in Afghanistan has been accompanied by an increase in women's reporting of domestic violence cases (Rodriguez and Anwari 2011). Similarly, the Alternate Dispute Resolution Mechanism (Musalihat Anjuman) at the Union Council level in Pakistan is considered an innovative idea, although it has been plagued with implementation hurdles, frequent changes in management, and the Pakistan floods in 2010 that derailed the project (UNDP Pakistan 2011).

CHALLENGES AND OPPORTUNITIES IN PREVENTING AND RESPONDING TO INTIMATE PARTNER VIOLENCE

Our fieldwork revealed an impressive body of work across the region. A key challenge, however, is the lack of well-documented, rigorous evaluation. It is possible that we were unable to find some rigorous evaluations that may be part of broader multisectoral programs, for instance in the health sector. Also, many efforts to address interpersonal violence are nested within larger programs to address broad-based "violence against women" or "gender inequality." Assessments subsequently do not or cannot tease out the effect of interventions on the intimate partner aspect of violence versus other forms of violence addressed by the same program.

The lack of rigorous evaluations makes it difficult to unequivocally identify "promising approaches," whether at the level of providing services to the individual survivor or changing societal norms and attitudes. Still, campaigns, which are the most rigorously evaluated, show that using community networks, identifying change agents, and applying innovative media with provocative messages can at least bring intimate partner violence out of the private realm and into the public eye. Interventions with boys and men show that addressing unequal gender norms early through approaches similar to girls' life skills programs for early marriage can influence boys' perceptions of masculinity and gender norms.

While these are lessons for changing attitudes, however, there is little evidence of what works to change behavior. Some of the key risk factors for behavior identified in the research are not addressed, are poorly addressed, or are unavailable in evaluation documentation. A key example is alcohol abuse. In another example, while some research suggests that participation in microcredit or social groups may increase women's risks of violence, at least temporarily, none of the program evaluations we found discuss this relationship.

We also found no evaluated programs that address abuse by non-spousal perpetrators in the home. The research reviewed in chapters 2 and 3 identifies mothers-in-law as the second most common perpetrator of domestic violence after partners, particularly against young daughters-in-law. Yet, we found only one intervention that works specifically with mothers-in-law, the Dil Mil ("hearts together" in Hindi) program in Bengaluru, India. Results of the impact evaluation, structured as a randomized control trial, are forthcoming (Krishnan et al. 2012).

Finally, across most of the interventions we located, programs focused primarily on married women of reproductive age, or documentation did not specify the age of participants. Programs need to pay more attention and intervene also to prevent intimate partner violence encountered by women who never married and elderly women, and domestic violence faced by widowed or divorced women. Identified programs also did not define or address the particular constraints that married adolescent girls may face in trying to protect themselves from, or seek care for, domestic and intimate partner violence. This is a serious lacuna as research points out that married adolescents may have vulnerabilities that are somewhat different from those of married adult women; moreover, they face constraints that adult married women may not, ones that can hamper adolescents from accessing programs. There is a vast landscape of programming in South Asia on improving reproductive health for married adolescents, particularly in India and Bangladesh. These programs could provide a plausible entry point also for interventions to prevent marital domestic violence faced by adolescent girls.

Addressing Sexual Harassment in Public Spaces

Across the life cycle, whether married or unmarried, women and girls face sexual harassment in every public space they occupy. We identified 13 evaluated interventions that have some implication for sexual harassment, but few of these have been evaluated in any rigorous manner, with assessments based primarily on desk reviews or qualitative research only (appendix G). An exception is the Gender Equity Movement in Schools (GEMS) program, which was more rigorously evaluated and is discussed below.

This lack of evaluated interventions obscures the fact that there has been a recent upswing in public awareness and reaction across the region against sexual harassment of women and girls. Government efforts to improve institutional and legal responses to sexual harassment also have increased, and are at least in part influenced by the popular pressure generated through multiple civil society efforts. Five out of the eight countries in the region now have laws against sexual harassment, many of them recent. In February 2014, the Supreme Court of India ruled that a sexually harassed person could file complaints via post or email,[20] considerably easing the burden of filing complaints. As such, this is an opportune time to learn from interventions thus far and engage more actively in preventing and responding to sexual harassment in public places.

PREVENTING SEXUAL HARASSMENT THROUGH WORKPLACE LEGISLATION

The success of the Alliance against Sexual Harassment (AASHA) in Pakistan to promote workplace anti-sexual harassment legislation represents a strong example of the power of such recent activism. AASHA's success was based on its simultaneous use of engagement at all levels of the social ecology—from advocating with government and the private sector, to engaging individual volunteers, to using the media, as described in box 4.7.

PREVENTING SEXUAL HARASSMENT THROUGH STREET SAFETY, TRANSPORT, AND URBAN PLANNING

One recent example of efforts to improve street safety for women is the Safe Cities intervention in Delhi and several other cities in India. This intervention is part of UN Women's Safe Cities Global Initiative, the first-ever global comparative program to prevent and respond to sexual harassment and other forms of violence against women and girls in public areas. The program is ongoing and thus not yet evaluated (Jagori and UN Women 2011).

Another, smaller-scale but also innovative approach is the use of "safety audits," such as by Jagori in India, where women themselves collect, disseminate, and discuss data about, and solutions for, the persistence of violence on the street (Jagori 2010). This approach, which places those at risk at the center of identifying problems and solutions, is similar in its focus on the potential or actual survivor to the child-friendly approaches favored to address violence against girls. We found no evaluation of the success of such participatory safety audits in triggering action, however.

Efforts towards gender-sensitive urban planning are minimal (Viswanath and Mehrotra 2007; Phadke 2005; Khosla 2004), though organizations in India such as Jagori, INTACH, and CURE are starting to focus on such interventions. Still, larger schemes that could potentially have a significant impact, such as the Jawaharlal Nehru Urban Management Scheme in India, have been unable to mainstream gender concerns and create more gender-friendly urban spaces (UN Women 2012; Khosla 2009).

Finally, attention to safety in public transportation has been ad-hoc and sometimes regressive. Promising efforts have largely arisen from non-profit ventures, like the Safe Delhi Campaign and Blank Noise in India, and the SHOW You Care campaign in Sri Lanka, which have attempted to sensitize transport providers—in auto rickshaws and buses, for example—to sexual harassment issues. Other efforts are less progressive.

BOX 4.7 Alliance against Sexual Harassment in Pakistan (AASHA)

The Alliance against Sexual Harassment (AASHA) in Pakistan was an indigenous network of individuals and organizations instrumental in the passing of Pakistan's Protection against Harassment of Women at the Workplace Act, 2010, and the Criminal Law Amendment Act, 2009, which made sexual harassment of women a crime punishable by law. AASHA members voluntarily contributed their time and some finances. The overall core membership never exceeded ten organizations, thus keeping the alliance slim and accountable. Organizations such as the chamber of commerce, labor unions, and civil society organizations lent support by endorsing AASHA demands and mobilizing activities. Once legislation was passed, AASHA dissolved.

AASHA's process to achieve this legislation illustrates well how to engage multiple sectors for a common goal. First, AASHA developed guidelines to make work environments free of discrimination and harassment. When initially the government showed reluctance to adopt these guidelines as an employer, AASHA turned to the private sector while engaging with senior leadership in the government to keep them involved in the process. The government eventually came around to passing the laws, thanks to AASHA's persistent yet collaborative advocacy. Once laws were in place, AASHA focused on effective implementation and established support mechanisms for women victims at federal and provincial levels. AASHA was also instrumental in the appointment of the federal ombudsperson responsible for setting up support systems for redressal. Within the first year, over 1000 cases were resolved through three regional ombudsman offices in Sindh, Islamabad, and Lahore. Civil society organizations from other countries in the region, such as Maldives and Afghanistan, have turned to AASHA for advice on implementing similar legislation in their countries.

Factors key to AASHA's success

1. *Working as an alliance.* The mode of operation was nonhierarchical, allowing for a broad geographic spread, joint ownership, and bringing the strengths of different organizations together to deal with the issue at a national level. AASHA complemented this collaboration through persistent follow-up with stakeholders to ensure that promised action was taken.

2. *Inclusivity.* AASHA made it clear that their work was against a mode of behavior rather than against men, thus opening the door to involve men as allies.

3. *Bottom-up approach.* In order to prepare their proposed code for the workplace, AASHA conducted a great deal of research to identify the scope and dynamics of sexual harassment on the ground, supplemented by a knowledge of laws and sexual harassment prevention strategies from around the world.

4. *Flexibility towards existing norms.* AASHA was flexible, taking into consideration the request of some government officials to include quotations from the Koran in the code. AASHA explained that the code was totally congruent with the teachings of the Koran and fully supported the dignity of women. The neutral terminology employed—the "Code of Gender Justice"—allowed them to protect the content of the legislation.

5. *Engaging the media.* By building coalitions with various media groups, AASHA succeeded in getting over 200 programs aired on major television stations, numerous panel discussions conducted on radio stations, and more than 300 articles published in newspapers (Khaliq 2012, 9). All the material produced for AASHA's campaigns was open source, created primarily by volunteer professionals.

Sources: Interviews with Dr. Fouzia Saeed, founder of AASHA; Khaliq 2012.

One typical response in parts of India and Pakistan has been to promote gender-segregated transportation, be it on subways, trains, buses, or taxis. Recent surveys conducted by the World Bank (ALG and World Bank 2014) note that women feel safer on gender-segregated transportation. Still, such a focus, while perhaps a short-run palliative, can contribute to the persistence of gender-unequal norms in the long run by ghettoizing women, thereby reducing their access and diminishing their rights to the public space.

PREVENTING SEXUAL HARASSMENT IN EDUCATIONAL SETTINGS

We found one well-evaluated program to address sexual harassment in schools: the GEMS program in India. This program adds evidence to the growing understanding that intervening early is critical to changing gender equality norms and beliefs. The GEMS program addresses attitudes about sexual harassment inside and outside of schools and within a broader aim of transforming attitudes and behaviors related to intimate partner violence, child marriage, and gender norms (box 4.8).

GEMS is worth examining because of its success in introducing complex, creative, and participatory curricula to young boys and girls. It is also noteworthy in that it engaged not only young boys and young girls but also their mentors, teachers, and facilitators to examine and deconstruct attitudes on violence in their immediate environments. In part the GEMS program likely owed its success to the fact that teachers and school administrators alike were eager for a program that would address the acknowledged problem of harassment and violence in schools. Another factor contributing to success was program willingness to invest significantly in building capacity of teacher-facilitators, who were core to successful implementation. GEMS provides an opportunity for scale-up throughout public school systems, thus reaching a vast population of youth.

Evaluations from other regions of the world provide evidence for other good practices in the school setting. For example, the Population Council conducted a program to increase the financial literacy of adolescent girls in Zambia and use that as an opportunity to create safe spaces for girls. The evaluation suggests that building a savings account for girls, in addition to increasing self-esteem, knowledge of rights, and other skills, can be protective against sexual harassment (Austrian and Muthengi 2013). Another program in Tanzania found that having a female teacher act as a designated "guardian" was successful in getting students to report sexual harassment in schools (Mgalla et al. 1998).

ENGAGING MEN AND BOYS TO PREVENT SEXUAL HARASSMENT

The GEMS program, described above, is one exemplary model of how to engage young boys (and girls) to address underlying norms around violence against women, including sexual harassment. There have been other notable efforts to engage men and boys

BOX 4.8 Gender Equity Movement in Schools (GEMS) in India

The goal of the Gender Equity Movement in Schools (GEMS) program is gender-equitable behavior among adolescents, brought about through critical thinking and self-reflection about gender norms as experienced in daily life at home and at school. The program aims to contribute to greater self-confidence, assertiveness, independence, and involvement in the public sphere among girls; and less aggression, more sociability, and greater engagement in the private sphere among boys. A key strength of the model is its demonstrated adaptability to a range of contexts and populations.

FIGURE B4.8.1 Illustrations from the GEMS Training Manual

Source: ICRW 2011.

The GEMS training manual was developed in India by the International Center for Research on Women (ICRW) in partnership with the Tata Institute of Social Sciences and the Committee of Resource Organizations (CORO) for Literacy. In its first phase, GEMS was piloted in Mumbai public schools across two academic years (2008–09 and 2009–10). The GEMS activities focused on interactive group discussion and reflection with teachers trained to moderate. This structure allowed students the space to explore their own attitudes and feelings about the extent to which various potential daily interactions could be considered a form of violence, as illustrated in the excerpt above from one of the manuals.

The study used a quasi-experimental model with two intervention arms and one control arm to evaluate the intervention (Achyut et al. 2011). One experimental arm had the group education activities (GEA) and a school-based campaign; a second arm had only the campaign; and a third was a control arm. Data were collected through three

box continues next page

BOX 4.8 Gender Equity Movement in Schools (GEMS) in India *(continued)*

self-administered surveys, comprising one baseline and two follow-ups. Analysis revealed a significant shift in students' attitudes towards gender equality and roles, most of which occurred in the first year of the intervention. In contrast, students' comfort level with reporting sexual harassment took longer to achieve and was significantly different from the control arm only at the second follow-up. This shift was particularly notable among girls, suggesting success in breaking the taboo on girls' disclosure of such violence. Girls and boys opposed partner violence, attesting to the potential of transforming gender beliefs when intervening early. GEMS is currently being scaled up to over 250 schools in Mumbai and has been adapted for implementation in other parts of India.

Challenges for future replication and scale-up:

Identifying and maintaining relationships. It is essential to identify appropriate partners and create and maintain good relationships with government officials.

Wider dissemination of key messages. Thus far the focus has been on schools; a challenge lies in working with parents, health systems, community-based organizations, and others to integrate gender equity concepts into these forums.

Institutionalization. Building on current experience, further evolution is required to institutionalize and mainstream gender equity programs in national and state-level plans and budgets.

Budget constraints. Given the expense of high-quality gender equity programs, there is a need for more sustainable budgetary options.

Teacher involvement. Building the role of teachers as vital stakeholders in the process, while arming them with the skills to engage sensitively in gender issues and the strength to deal with potential controversy, is a key challenge.

Sources: Published literature cited above, and interview with Ravi Verma, Asia Regional Director, ICRW.

---

beyond school to prevent sexual harassment in other places and with other stakeholders. One is the intervention, *Mobilizing Men: A Transnational Effort to Challenge GBV in Local Institutions*, conducted in India. This program was part of a three-year initiative by Instituto Promundo, with support from the United Nations Trust Fund to End Violence Against Women (UNTF), that developed and piloted a multi-country project to engage men and boys in preventing violence against women—including sexual harassment in various settings—and promoting gender equality. The project took place in four countries and included the following interventions: (a) a community-based intervention in India; (b) a sports-based intervention in Brazil; (c) a health sector-based intervention in Chile; and (d) a workplace-based intervention in Rwanda.

In India the project, led by the Center for Health and Social Justice[21], worked with men in three contexts: universities, local governments, and the Dalit community. Male activists were trained in raising awareness around sexual violence and other forms of violence, how to appropriately document incidents of such violence, and how to develop and structure campaigns to change attitudes and practice around violence. *Mobilizing Men* established Anti-Sexual Harassment Committees on seven campuses of Pune University. Members also brought up the issue of violence against women and girls in *Panchayats* (village governments). While not formally evaluated, documentation of this intervention provides valuable lessons in how to simultaneously engage men in very different contexts to institutionalize discussions of sexual harassment and other forms of violence within educational settings, governance institutions, and among minority communities (McAllister et al. 2012; Greig and Jerker 2012).

INTERVENTIONS TO RESPOND TO SEXUAL HARASSMENT: POLICE TRAINING

Efforts to train police range from introducing women beat constables in New Delhi (Parivartan[22]) to programs on attitudinal change for police officials in Pakistan (Rabta program[23]). The available documentation does not clearly demonstrate their effect on improving responses to sexual harassment, however. Twenty-four-hour police helplines have also been introduced across the region, sometimes combined with efforts to make police forces respond more sensitively in cases of reported rape and assault. However, research on helpline effectiveness is sparse, and where it is available the results on effectiveness are mixed (Jagori and Marg 2013).

CONTINUING CHALLENGES AND OPPORTUNITIES

Our review suggests that while there may be growing awareness of the scope of sexual harassment and the importance of addressing sexual harassment in public places, interventions remain few and far between, and most are not evaluated in a manner that can provide promising lessons for what works.

Large gaps also remain in areas of intervention. One is the lack of anti-sexual harassment programs in the workplace. Another is to engage bystanders: the 2012 Nirbhaya rape case in India brought to the fore the potential role of bystanders, but we found only one program that tangentially addressed this concern. The Parivartan program in Mumbai, India, a sports-based program for young boys, trained them on how to respond to sexual harassment they may witness as bystanders; however, the evaluation did not examine the success of this aspect of the program (Das et al. 2012). Programs could glean lessons from the efforts to engage bystanders in the United States, which highlight successful practices in schools and universities that train and sensitize students to act if they observe sexual harassment (Banyard et al. 2007; Cissner 2009).

Finally, we found no evaluated programs to address the sexual pressure and coercion that young adolescent girls can face from partners in premarital romantic relationships, a situation of great vulnerability described in chapter 3.[24] Efforts to address such sexual coercion through "dating programs" in high schools and colleges in the United States are instructive. For example, impact evaluations find that peer activities engaging female and male students—such as through theater and campaigns—combined with special services for survivors of sexual harassment, can be effective in changing attitudes and reducing coercive behavior among school-going adolescents (Ricardo et al. 2011; Foshee et al. 1998, 2000, 2004). Although the cultural context between South Asia and the United States differs greatly, such examples can be adapted for use, especially in urban areas across South Asian countries.

Preventing and Responding to Honor Killings

Honor killings are another form of violence that spans the life course. Despite increases in recent awareness of honor killings, mostly thanks to news media vigilance and civil society advocacy efforts, we found few organized efforts that explicitly aim to prevent or respond to honor killings. Our literature and legal review uncovered 11 efforts of any kind, which took one of three forms: (i) legislation; (ii) online forums for advocacy or information exchange; and (iii) in-person programs aimed at preventing honor killing. With the exception of one international website—the Honour Based Violence Awareness (HBVA) Network—all of the efforts are based in India and Pakistan. Only two of the 11 interventions—both in Pakistan—were formally evaluated: the Public Private Partnership to End "Honour Crimes" in Pakistan through the Implementation of the 2004 Criminal Law (Amendment) Act underwent an impact assessment, and a pilot study by the Aurat Foundation (Lari 2011) assessed the influence of the law itself. One—the Love Commandos intervention in India—was not formally evaluated, but was considered a success by "peers" (appendix H).

In 2004 the Pakistan Criminal Law (Amendment) Act was passed, and in January 2005 it became law. An evaluation by the Aurat Foundation (Lari 2011) found, however, that communities at large, and even the justice sector and the police, were either completely unaware of the law or not familiar with its specifics. It also found that police who knew about the law were typically unwilling to implement it, due to the fear of undue influence from senior officials and because of society's overall acceptance of honor killing.

In India, legal developments have focused on dampening the power of extra-judicial decision-making bodies. Efforts include national-level legislation to eradicate honor killings and to allow leaders of extra judicial bodies (such as *khap panchayats*) to be prosecuted for sanctioning honor killings (Chesler and Bloom 2012). In 2010, India's Supreme Court directed seven state governments to take steps to protect potential victims of honor killings, declaring all honor killings ordered by *khap panchayats* illegal and barbaric (Chesler and Bloom 2012). We found no evaluations of these efforts, however, nor did we find evaluations of efforts that use online media.

Promising but non-evaluated efforts at the community level are those akin to the "change agent" interventions used to address other forms of violence. One example is a multi-partner Public Private Partnership to End Honour Crimes in Pakistan through the Implementation of the 2004 Criminal Law (Amendment) Act. Despite a cancelled evaluation due to floods, this program has been expanded to 56 districts (NCSW 2010). Another potentially promising intervention is a partnership between the United States Institute of Peace (USIP) and Islamabad-based Sustainable Peace and Development Organization (SPADO), which identified and trained local individuals as dispute mediators (Omestad 2012). India presents yet another intriguing program that should be assessed: the Love Commandos, which provides counseling, shelter, or other support to young couples who fear that their choice of marital partner will anger parents, or worse.

CHALLENGES AND OPPORTUNITIES

The increased awareness of the persistence and increasing violence of honor crimes, particularly in India and Pakistan, provides an opportunity for more systematic intervention. Media efforts are likely to be key. Lessons for designing, implementing, and evaluating such interventions can be extracted from the extensive evaluations of media campaigns that involve both men and women in addressing excess female child mortality, child marriage, and intimate partner violence. Media campaigns, however, may change attitudes but not necessarily affect behavior. Examples of school-based and community-based programs with young girls and boys, such as the GEMS, Yaari Dosti, or the myriad life skills programs to address child marriage, provide evaluated lessons for intervening early. Such early intervention could change the notions and meanings of "honor" in the same way as these programs currently attempt to change the notions and meanings of "gender" and "masculinity." Finally, experiences in engaging religious leaders to endorse preventing excess female child mortality or child marriage could be adapted also for honor killing prevention efforts.

Addressing Custodial Violence against Women and Girls

Custodial violence is the only form of violence included here that is constrained to a circumscribed environment—that is, one of "custody," whether in police stations or situations of war and conflict. Countries in the South Asia region are implementing myriad policy interventions to address custodial violence overall, including interventions in juvenile justice and advocacy, lobbying for human rights, training and collaboration with the armed forces, and broader efforts to change institutional and social structures in custodial situations to address issues related to gender-based violence. Most interventions have not, however, been gender-specific. The few examples that target women's vulnerabilities aim to address poor enforcement of laws and the lack of appropriate infrastructure, but evaluations are rare (we found only three). Existing evaluations relate to the execution of some components of the programs, such as whether inputs were delivered on time and in the proper condition, rather than to overall effectiveness or implications for replicability or scale-up (appendix I).

PREVENTION APPROACHES

The only prevention efforts focused on women that we were able to identify pertain to legal and procedural institutional constraints. One example is Afghanistan's special department to address the needs of women prisoners and enable their reintegration into society. Theoretically this is a positive move given the stigma surrounding any actual or suspected sexual abuse that women may have encountered in prison (UNODC 2007), but we were unable to find any evaluation. Another example is Sri Lanka's enactment of the 2005 Prevention of Domestic Violence (PDV) Act, No. 34, envisioned as an opportunity to renew and refocus efforts to address domestic violence, as well as custodial violence. This Act does not address the particular needs of women, however; they are grouped with children and disabled persons, despite the differing needs of each of these groups (Asian Center for Human Rights 2012a).

We found no evaluated prevention interventions engaging with actors at other levels of the social ecology, though our searches yielded a great deal of advocacy work in the region. Advocacy efforts using mass media and reaching broad audiences to prevent other types of violence offer lessons for evaluating existing advocacy efforts in preventing custodial violence.

RESPONDING TO CUSTODIAL VIOLENCE AGAINST WOMEN AND GIRLS

We found more examples of responses to custodial violence, though most of these also were not evaluated. One such approach that attends to a key institutional concern is to recruit, train, and place women custodians and police officers. However, this approach is open to the same criticism as the women-only transport efforts to address sexual harassment—that is, recruiting women police should not imply that men police are not trained and sensitized to violence against women. Furthermore, recruiting women police for women prisoners should not reduce violence against women to a "women's problem."

Making police stations more "women friendly" is critical, nonetheless. One example in India of efforts to do so is the Crimes against Women Cells program, initiated in 1983 at a Delhi police station. The program was the first police response meant specifically for women in India—and most likely anywhere in the world. An early assessment, however, found mixed results: the program was promising, but had difficulty in recruiting and training capable counselors, a challenge not only for this program, but a common problem for many other similar interventions (Deol 1983). A more recent intervention that has not yet been evaluated is India's initiative to create new All Women's Police Stations (Times of India 2014).

Shelters for women exposed to custodial violence are likely to be much needed, yet we found only one non-evaluated example, the Sarvodaya Sharamadana Movement Shelters in Sri Lanka. These shelters offer legal aid, support services, and counseling to women and children who experienced violence in conflict-affected areas (UNFPA-APWFD 2013).

Health interventions for women in custody also are likely to be important in providing services for abused women in custody. We found no interventions that do so, but other existing health interventions in prisons may provide an opportunity to also integrate treatment services for abuse. An example is a program by UNODC in Nepal that collaborates with the Government of Nepal and civil society organizations to reduce drug use and HIV-related high-risk behavior among female inmates in Kathmandu. Similar services are now provided in two other district prison sites in Nepal (UNODC 2011). Other health-related programs have taken the initiative to ban inhuman and demeaning custodial practices used against women and girls in South Asia, including the finger test of sexual assault victims, whereby the examining doctor notes the presence or absence of the hymen and the size and so-called laxity of the vagina (Human Rights Watch 2010).

Finally, there are a host of programs that monitor abuse against children in juvenile justice institutions. Most of those that have been evaluated are from India, though Pakistan has also made some progress in implementing similar programs (AGHS 2004). Most evaluations of such centers throughout India by the ACHR (2012a, 2012b, 2012c)—including in conflict-affected states of the country (ACHR 2013a and 2013b)—suggest that these homes do not function as per the statutory requirements, facilities are inadequate, and juveniles may be tortured or abused while in detention. Unfortunately results are not gender-disaggregated. Similarly, programs exist to prevent police violence against street children and to monitor children in prison, but either evaluations are not gender-disaggregated or they do not exist.

CHALLENGES AND OPPORTUNITIES

It is critical to increase the visibility of custodial violence against women and girls beyond the "silo" of those who work on it. This form of violence is perhaps the most hidden from the general public eye, as well as from programs that work on other forms of violence, but it is likely pernicious and persistent. Household acceptance of women who were abused in custody is also problematic and needs to be addressed. Examples of promising approaches in preventing and responding to other forms of violence offer some lessons. First of all, to influence social norms about custodial violence, many forms of media and advocacy could be successfully used to increase awareness and broaden the constituency to address such violence. The multiple campaigns against intimate partner violence are examples. At the institutional level, the example of AASHA in implementing and institutionalizing anti-sexual harassment laws for the workplace in Pakistan provides lessons in how to effectively create and use networks to strengthen legal and institutional responses. Finally, at the household level, child marriage efforts that seek to increase acceptance of unmarried adolescent girls in the home could perhaps be adapted to increase acceptance of abused women released from custody.

Preventing and Responding to Trafficking of Women and Girls

Programs to address trafficking of girls and women are concentrated in India, Bangladesh, Nepal, and, to a lesser degree, Sri Lanka. Pakistan and Afghanistan are seeing an increase in interventions arising from heightened risk of trafficking due to conflict in these countries. There are relatively few interventions in Maldives and Bhutan: while trafficking into Maldives is increasing, it appears to be a minor issue in Bhutan (Ahmed and Yoosuf 2012). Unlike with other forms of violence, national, regional, and international networks collaborate to combat trafficking. The South Asian Association for Regional Cooperation (SAARC) coordinates regional interventions, and Action against Trafficking and Sexual Exploitation of Children (ATSEC) operates in India and has a Bangladesh chapter. Many organizations work to address trafficking as a part of larger projects aimed at women's rights, natural disasters, health (including HIV/AIDS), and economic empowerment or development, partly because trafficking is linked to all these concerns. As with efforts to address other forms of violence, media and advocacy organizations play an important role.

Governments also have played an important role in combatting trafficking. In fact, India's Anti-Trafficking Cell has been hailed internationally as a best practice for its effectiveness—for example in coordinating, networking, and collecting feedback from police, judges, and NGOs, and building the capacity of police and the judiciary (UNODC 2013). Still, problems remain across the region, such as police corruption (Huntington 2001), weak prosecution because of judicial weaknesses (AIHRC 2011; United States Department of State 2013), and poor capacity of staff (Ayyub 2006). Some laws and policies, rather than addressing gender inequality, exhibit a lack of understanding of the realities of trafficking versus other forms of inter-state movement that can harm the very girls and women these laws are meant to protect. Examples include laws banning or otherwise restricting legitimate freedom of movement for women (Huntington 2001; Kapur 2001). The tendency to equate trafficking with sex work also hinders successful prosecution of traffickers (Kapur 2001).

We found no rigorous evaluations, but did identify 10 programs that are assessed via desk reviews or qualitative assessments (appendix J). Approaches used for trafficking prevention and response are often similar to those used for preventing child marriage, or for preventing or responding to intimate partner violence. As such, lessons from evaluations of child marriage and intimate partner violence interventions could be valuable.

APPROACHES TO PREVENT TRAFFICKING

Using media to raise awareness is widely accepted as an effective approach to disseminate information and otherwise address the problem of trafficking (Hameed et al. 2010; Dutta et al. 2010), but we found no evaluations of such efforts. Interventions for institutional reform include efforts to locate services near border points and offices responsible for migration, such as by the Women Rehabilitation Center (WOREC) in Nepal (UNDP 2003), Shakti Samuha, Maiti-Nepal and Saathi—all also in Nepal. Such strategies enable NGOs to reach and deter women planning to migrate on false documents; however, their effectiveness has not been evaluated.[25]

The Counter Trafficking Interventions (CTI) project implemented by the International Organization for Migration (IOM) in Bangladesh is an example of a promising community-level prevention intervention. This program engaged government leaders at all village council levels (Union Parishad). That trafficking is now discussed at monthly meetings of the Union Parishad and that the Union Parishads are mandated to investigate suspected trafficking activity is a testament to the success of this effort (IOM 2008, USAID 2009). That trafficking prevention has become part of official duties suggests that the approach also is sustainable.

At the individual level, in a notable departure from interventions to address other forms of violence, almost all the major anti-trafficking organizations identify and focus efforts specifically on high-risk groups, identified on the basis of age, socioeconomic indicators, and a profile built from historical trends. The approaches used by organizations to prevent trafficking of girls are similar to those used to prevent child marriage. Interventions include keeping girls in school and providing vocational and life skills training. In one example, the Rural Health Education Service Trust (RHEST) in Nepal provides scholarships for girls through grade 10; it combines this with activities in and out of school to raise awareness of trafficking among participating girls and their families. Though it is difficult to say how many girls have avoided being trafficked by staying in school, the research suggests that without this option, the poorest girls may well be trafficked (Hennink and Simkhada 2004). Including information about trafficking in school curricula would appear to be another promising role for the education sector, and such efforts exist in Bangladesh (Berman and Marshall 2011), Nepal—such as by the Rural Health Education Service Trust (RHEST)—and India. Similarly, several organizations provide vocational training to increase women's employability (Evans and Bhattarai 2000, Hameed et al. 2010; USAID 2009), microcredit schemes to at-risk women or girls (Huntington 2001), or employ at-risk women (Hameed et al. 2010). Most of these programs are not evaluated, however.

There are some evaluations of efforts to actively engage trafficking survivors themselves in awareness raising—such as by Maiti Nepal. Studies show that such an approach has the power to be effective because potential victims can relate to the messages delivered by trafficking survivors (Sijapati et al. 2011; Evans and Bhattarai 2000; Pandey et al. 2013). Such interventions also have the potential to empower survivors. Underscored by a similar logic, engaging sex workers can be effective in preventing sex trafficking while empowering participating sex workers. A well-known success story on both counts is the Durbar Mahila Samanwaya Committee in Kolkata (popularly known as the Sonagachi Project), which started the Self-Regulatory Board in Kolkata's red light areas and has been deemed effective in reducing the transmission of HIV/AIDS and the trafficking of minors into sex work (GAATW 2007). As a testament to its success,

CARE International has adopted this Self Regulatory Board model in Bangladesh (Ayyub 2006). Other NGOs in India, such as Prerna and STOP, have partnered with commercial sex workers to protect their rights and to reduce recruitment of minors and others forced into sex work. While not evaluated, reviews of anti-trafficking interventions that actively engage survivors highlight this approach as effective (UNDP 2003). It mirrors the child-centered and adolescent-centered programming to prevent and respond to abuse against girl children and adolescents, and to prevent child marriage.

APPROACHES USED IN RESPONSE AND REHABILITATION OF TRAFFICKED WOMEN AND GIRLS

Efforts to respond to and rehabilitate trafficked women and girls range from vocational skills development for trafficking survivors to the shelters and legal aid efforts familiar as response mechanisms for survivors of intimate partner violence. While we found no formal evaluations of any of these, there is a rich body of process documentation and research that points to promising practices and challenges.

Perhaps most promising are programs that provide non-traditional vocational skills for livelihood opportunities. Organizations such as Sanlaap, Prerna, and Sahas Kendra in India (Hameed et al. 2010) and Maiti-Nepal and Shakti Samuha in Nepal provide training on market-oriented employable skills. Others show the additional benefit of partnering with broader livelihoods programs or the private sector, such as the CAP-SARI/Q (South Asia Regional Initiative/Equity) project,[26] the PPVHTB program's Kafe Mukti in Bangladesh (Berman and Marshall 2011), and Maiti Nepal's collaboration with hotels in Nepal (Maiti Nepal 2012). In India, public-private partnerships range from collaborations with Microsoft to the Chhattisgarh Centre for Economic Development and the West Bengal Milk Federation Cooperative Society (Hameed et al. 2010). Organizations experimenting with non-traditional job skills need to also equip trafficking survivors to work in male-dominated workspaces and to deal with issues of confidence and safety (Richardson et al. 2013), including potential vulnerability to sexual harassment at work. It is unclear how successfully organizations address these issues, however.

Legal aid is minimally evaluated, but existing assessments point to several concerns. One major concern is the uncertainty about the extent to which cases that stretch over a long period are given careful attention; trafficking survivors also may not be kept adequately informed about their cases and legal procedures (USAID 2009). Legal assistance may not be easily accessible to all (Dutta et al. 2010), particularly in destination countries (Aurat Foundation 2012). Finally, lack of victim protection from the government may discourage victims from testifying against their traffickers (Tzvetkova 2002). As with intimate partner violence, efforts to obtain justice against trafficking increasingly reach for mediation outside the judicial system, but the effects and effectiveness of extra-judicial mediation for trafficking have not been studied.

The evidence on the efficacy and desirability of rescue operations is mixed. Some studies, such as by CESLAM, highlight rescue interventions as among the more successful interventions in Nepal (Sijapati et al. 2011; USAID 2009). Police raids with assistance from NGOs—such as the Rescue Foundation and Stop Trafficking and Oppression of Children and Women (STOP) in India—also are considered to be encouraging because they help victims receive enhanced protection and treatment (Hameed et al. 2010). Other research suggests that raids can be problematic: there is evidence that under the pretense of rescue raids, police have abused victims, taken bribes from brothel owners, or returned victims to families where they may be re-exposed to trafficking (Pandey et al. 2013; GAATW 2007). Victims "rescued" after a raid are given an option to file a case against the traffickers, yet inadequate government protection for trafficking victims discourages reporting.

As with intimate partner violence, shelters are a common form of response for trafficking victims, but inadequately evaluated. There are several unresolved concerns and questions. First, many shelter houses cater to women and girls who are victims of all forms of violence. On the one hand, segregating shelters for trafficking victims can lead to isolation and further stigmatization of trafficking victims (Huntington 2001). On the other hand, non-segregated shelters may dissuade survivors of domestic violence from fleeing abusive relationships because they do not want to access shelters that also house trafficking victims, as has been documented in Nepal. Second, while counseling services provided in shelter houses and rehabilitation centers are considered as an integral and appreciated service that can rejuvenate rescued women,[27] shelter infrastructure often is not appropriate for counseling—for example, where separate space for counseling is not available (MoHP 2013). There is also limited information on how severe trauma is treated (Tzvetkova 2002; Pandey et al. 2013). Third, the quality of the shelter homes varies and is rarely monitored. In Pakistan, for instance, government-run shelter houses do not permit women to leave without a male relative or a court order (Aurat Foundation 2012). Anecdotal evidence suggests that staff of government-run shelters may themselves traffic women (United States Department of State 2013). Fourth, resources are strained, affecting standard operating procedures (Evans and Bhattarai 2000) and raising concerns about the standards of long-term stay and services (Tzvetkova 2002).

A somewhat unique and promising, but not yet evaluated, approach to shelters is Maiti Nepal's halfway homes that aim to help trafficking survivors to gradually reintegrate into society. This concept merits further investigation because it encourages trafficking victims to venture out and rebuild their lives while ensuring protection and care.

IMPORTANT CHALLENGES IN ADDRESSING TRAFFICKING

Interventions to prevent or respond to and rehabilitate trafficked women and girls need to be systematically evaluated. In this regard, collaboration between those who work on trafficking and those who work on mitigating child marriage and intimate partner violence is likely to be fruitful as many of the approaches are similar. However, there are also challenges that are particular to trafficking.

The first such challenge is the confusion between trafficking and sex work. Trafficking is often equated with sex work, such that anti-trafficking interventions primarily target women who have been trafficked for sex work. Modern-day trafficking occurs for a range of circumstances where cheap labor is required, however. The continued strong association of trafficking with sex work creates undue stigma for women who have been trafficked for other reasons, such as for forced labor, adding an additional burden to their efforts to reintegrate. The lines are also blurred between trafficking and human smuggling,[28] as well as between trafficking or human smuggling on the one hand, and legitimate migration for employment on the other. The conflation of trafficking, migration, and human smuggling has some harmful consequences for approaches adopted to tackle trafficking (GAATW 2007; Huntington 2001; Sijapati et al. 2011; Evans and Bhattarai 2000). For instance, some organizations use scare tactics to discourage all migration (Evans and Bhattarai 2000). Concerns for human smuggling mean that many undocumented migrants are screened for illegal migration alone, ignoring the fact that they may have been trafficked and may thus need different interventions.

There is also a concern that the way awareness raising is conducted may intensify gender biases. Awareness raising materials tend to use fear to discourage women from leaving their homes, rather than providing the necessary information to enable women to make informed decisions (Evans and Bhattarai 2000). Such an approach infantilizes women. It also may dissuade women who are migrating for legitimate reasons like employment. Awareness raising activities also exacerbate the stigma associated with trafficking when programs equate trafficking with commercial sex work and HIV/AIDS (Huntington 2001).

Finally, repatriation and rehabilitation continue to be a challenge for all countries in the region, due in part to the lack of formal agreements or procedures between key source and destination countries, such as India and Nepal (Sijapati et al. 2011). The stigma attached to trafficking impedes reintegration as well, and it is unclear to what extent interventions maintain the confidentiality of trafficked victims to minimize such stigma and enable reintegration. Monitoring during reintegration is another challenge, and ineffective efforts can leave women and girls feeling unsupported (USAID 2009). Returned survivors may not have proper documents or may be minors. In such cases, their parents take responsibility, which poses risks for those who may have been trafficked by family members (Aurat Foundation 2012). Re-trafficking is a major concern also when viable alternative livelihood opportunities do not exist (Pandey et al. 2013), forcing women to succumb to trafficking once again.

Looking across Forms of Violence: Key Lessons and Challenges

Our mapping and analysis of interventions reveals that there is a commendable amount of action across forms of violence in the region. While the lack of rigorous evaluation prevents a definitive conclusion about "what works," there are clear indications of best practices and key challenges to strengthen intervention effectiveness, reach, and sustainability. We examine some of these below.

DO NO HARM

Interventions to address violence against women and girls are ultimately seeking to change deep-seated power relations between men and women. As such, it is perhaps inevitable that success will be accompanied, at least early on, by a spike in violence. Yet, the central non-negotiable requirement for all interventions across forms of violence and across levels of the social ecology has to be to do no harm. We did not find evaluations or other program documentation that specifically discussed how to effectively address potential backlash.

We did find examples of unexpected negative consequences, however. For instance, the Kishori Abhijan program found that parents who delayed marriage for their daughters ended up having to pay larger dowries. Thus, child marriage prevention programs working in areas where dowry is prevalent need to take this possibility into account when planning their interventions (Amin 2011). Other documentation of community involvement, especially by interventions working on child rights or child marriage, suggests that an overall good practice is to build time into program timelines to get a good pulse on a target population's norms and tolerance for change so as to better prepare for any unforeseen eventuality.

INCREASE THE FOCUS ON EVALUATING EXISTING AND FUTURE INTERVENTIONS

The most imperative challenge is that of competent evaluation. The astonishing array of programs, campaigns, advocacy, networking, and other forms of interventions we identified testifies to the commitment of actors at all levels of society to address violence against women and girls. Yet, the lack of competent evaluation means that a great deal of learning is lost and financial and human resources wasted. Competent evaluation does not have consist of randomized control experiments, though that does remain the most statistically rigorous way to attribute change to an intervention. For organizations that either do not wish to or cannot undertake such experiments, the evaluations we did find provide a multitude of methods that can be used more effectively than at present. A case in point is the evaluation of the Girl Power Project or the many evaluated child marriage prevention interventions.

Evaluations are particularly weak and thus need particular attention in the case of efforts to address sexual and physical violence against girls (as against all children), sexual harassment, honor killings, trafficking, and custodial violence. Shelters, helplines, and crisis centers critically need evaluation since these approaches are used everywhere. Finally, evaluated interventions—such as those for vocational training, life skills, and other similar strategies—require more nuanced study to assess not just whether and how they work, but also to extract the minimum critical elements of these interventions necessary for success.

ENGAGE MEN AND BOYS

The systematic and evaluated engagement of men and boys that we were able to identify in connection with violence prevention and response for South Asia were clustered in the domain of intimate partner violence or interventions addressing norms of masculinity. Examples include school-based programs such as GEMS and campaigns such as MASVAW and We Can.

Men and boys, however, need to be engaged at all levels and across all forms of violence for several reasons. First, such violence is primarily a result of underlying gender norms and structures, and "gender" includes women and men. Trying to change gender norms therefore must also include both women and men. This is all the more important when one recognizes that rigid norms related to gender and power differentials mean that many men feel pressure to prove their manhood by using violence against women or other men. Second, the nature of violence is an interactive exchange between a woman or girl who experiences the violence and the perpetrator. A focus solely on women and girls places the onus of responsibility of addressing violence on them, leaving the perpetrator out of the equation. While perpetrators are not always men, for the types of violence considered in this book they are mainly men and boys. Including them in any effort to address such violence is essential. Men and boys themselves have many motivations for ending men's use of violence against women and girls and promoting gender equality: the women who face violence are often, after all, their mothers, daughters, or partners (Katz 2003).

We identified 14 evaluated interventions that engage men and boys in addressing intimate partner violence, gender-based violence more broadly, and gender equality and norms of masculinity (appendix K). This set offers many examples of rigorous evaluations, lessons for campaigns, school-based programming to shift gender norms, and efforts to improve partner communication.

CONTINUE TO RAISE AWARENESS, BREAK TABOOS, AND EXPOSE VIOLENCE

Evaluations across several forms of violence demonstrate the power of campaigns and media to engage actors at all levels of society. Campaigns have raised awareness, started to break taboos, and attempted—often with success—to expose the extent of certain forms of violence, such as excess female child mortality, child marriage, domestic and intimate partner violence, and sexual harassment. The promising approaches identified by evaluations of media and advocacy efforts in these realms need to be transferred and adapted to raise awareness and break taboos also for forms of violence such as child sexual abuse, honor killings, trafficking, and custodial violence. If used strategically with other programming, as demonstrated by campaigns to prevent child marriage, media can be an even more powerful agent of change across forms of violence.

CONTINUE TO REFORM LAWS AND INSTITUTIONS FOR AN ENABLING ENVIRONMENT

While laws alone are not sufficient to prevent violence, they are necessary, as discussed in chapter 3. Various institutional mechanisms need to be in place across the system, however, to enable laws to be implemented and enforced; together these create a necessary enabling environment within which to prevent and respond to violence. Successful examples of how to do so include the AASHA experience in Pakistan and the experience of the Tamil Nadu government in enforcing bans on female infanticide in India. One key institutional reform that affects all forms of violence against children but that still requires attention is birth registration. Given that this is a logistical rather than philosophical or value-laden intervention, it should be considered relatively "low-hanging fruit," and, as such, addressed in the short term. Finally, a higher level of political commitment and adequate funding is necessary to give teeth to laws, institutional reform, or other policies.

EMPHASIZE TRAINING

Intensive and—as needed—repeat training needs to be emphasized in programs, and needs to be rigorously evaluated. As the GEMS experience illustrates, good training is essential to the success of efforts to change norms (and behavior) around violence and gender. Other programs—such as the Rabta intervention in Pakistan—illustrate the challenges of good training. Most programs have some training element, but we found minimal evaluation. All interventions need to ensure a strong emphasis on training implementers, and an equally strong emphasis on rigorously evaluating and modifying training, so that they are as effective as possible.

TAP INTO COMMUNITY OPPORTUNITIES AND ACCOMMODATE COMMUNITY CONSTRAINTS

Almost all prevention and some response efforts across forms of violence engage with community members; however, one strategic approach that could be explored and specifically evaluated is to engage potential opponents as allies. One clear candidate is religious and other "thought leaders" who set norms. These guardians of patriarchy can also be engaged in promoting a more progressive agenda, if approached in a non-antagonistic way. Other such potential allies include community resources such as wedding caterers (for child marriage prevention interventions) and transport operators (for trafficking or anti-sexual harassment). Examples of interventions to address child marriage and intimate partner violence illustrate how to involve such stakeholders as "change agents," but further evaluation is needed to determine which approaches are likely to be successful and why.

Another community engagement strategy often used and considered successful is engaging young women and adolescent girls in groups, some of which may include income generation activities as well. While this approach can empower women by offering a route for collective support from other women or alternate means of income, the research reviewed in chapter 3 also cautions that group participation may, at least initially, trigger a spike in violence. Programmers need to pay attention to this possibility as they implement such interventions.

Bystanders also need to be better engaged. The experiences of the Bell Bajao! campaign in India illustrate an effective means of engagement, as do evaluated interventions with university students in the United States (Gidycz et al. 2011; Banyard et al. 2007).

In experimenting with these and other means of community engagement, community-based interventions need to tread carefully when trying to shift gender norms. Efforts to address any form of violence need to be cognizant of the strength of community norms so as to minimize harm and maximize impact. Process evaluation from child marriage interventions in India also points to the importance of gauging community infrastructure and capacity before designing a program, so as to incorporate constraints therein in program design.

ENGAGE KEY HOUSEHOLD MEMBERS AND ADDRESS KEY FACTORS AT THE HOUSEHOLD LEVEL

Interventions have not focused very much on engaging household members other than husbands; however, other members of a woman's or girl's family may also increase vulnerability or provide support. An important example is that of mothers-in-law; engaging other household members such as parents, other in-laws, and siblings is likely also critical, but we found no evaluated interventions that do so. There are also important household-level factors that interventions do not address, or address very minimally. Key among these is alcohol abuse, parent-child interaction, and intergenerational transmission of violence.

INTERVENE EARLY AND ENGAGE SURVIVORS AND THOSE AT RISK AS ACTIVE PARTICIPANTS

Evaluations of interventions with young girls and adolescents and anti-trafficking programs point to two key lessons: the imperative to intervene early and the importance of engaging survivors and those at risk as active participants. However, these lessons need to be adopted and adapted by interventions to address other forms of violence.

BE SENSITIVE TO PARTICULAR VULNERABILITIES AND NEEDS OF ADOLESCENTS

The research reviewed in chapters 2 and 3 clearly demonstrates that adolescents—whether married or unmarried—have certain constraints, vulnerabilities, and opportunities for intervention that differ from those of adult women. We found little evidence of attention to these differences in interventions that consider violence among adult women (that is, intimate partner violence) or interventions for violence that cuts across life stages. Given that young people increasingly form the bulk of the population across South Asia, such a perspective is even more critical.

Notes

1. These are school-based programs to decrease excess female child mortality in Haryana state, and another on delaying early marriage in Bihar and Jharkhand states. (Interview with Sonali Khan, Breakthrough India Country Director and Vice President. February 7, 2014.)

2. Some interventions are counted more than once in figure 4.3 if they explicitly addressed more than one type of violence; however, each intervention is only counted once for figure 4.4.

3. An extended family refers to a family that extends beyond the nuclear family, and includes grandparents, aunts, uncles, and/or other relatives, who all live in one household.

4. At the time of writing this chapter, Plan was finalizing the draft evaluation report for the Let Girls Be Born campaign in India. Any comments in this book are based on the draft.

5. Bans exist also for prenatal sex-selective abortion, but an analysis of these is outside the scope of this study, as explained in chapter 1.

6. Several organizations develop such training modules, including Rozan and the Konpal Child Abuse Prevention Society in Pakistan; the HAQ Center, Arpan, and Jagori in India; the Samanata Institute for Gender Equality in Nepal; and the Afghanistan Independent Human Rights Commission.

7. Examples are the toll free helplines institutionalized across the region by the South Asian Association of Child Helplines, as well as helplines for sexual abuse provided by organizations in India such as RAHI and TARSHI.

8. Evaluated programs such as UNICEF's Protective Learning and Community Emergency Services (PLaCES) and the School as Zones of Peace Initiative, both in Nepal and both featured in appendix D, may provide lessons that can be adapted to identify and respond to girls' particular needs and vulnerabilities in situations of conflict or natural disasters.

9. Many evaluated programs address also the consequences of child marriage; however, these interventions do not, by and large, address violence faced by married adolescents. Rather, their focus is on ensuring access for married adolescent girls and young women to appropriate, high-quality reproductive and sexual health services, contraception, and delaying the first birth. As such, these are outside the scope of our book. It must be noted, however, that these programs provide a key point of entry for responding to and preventing violence against married adolescents.

10. Conversations with IHMP director, Dr. Ashok Dyalchand, and with IHMP program and research staff.

11. Conversation with Dr. Priya Nanda, ICRW program director for ABAD evaluation.

12. In-person interviews with the Suriya Development Organization in Sri Lanka. Interviews and conversations were conducted as part of a USAID-funded project that explored the effectiveness of interventions to address gender-based violence in pre-crisis, crisis, and post-crisis settings (April–May 2013, Sri Lanka).

13. Interviews with Jinat Ara Haque, national coordinator of the We Can Campaign, Bangladesh; Dr. Noreen Khali, Regional Adviser on Gender and Governance, Oxfam; and Hajera Pasha, National Coordinator, We Can Pakistan.

14. http://asiafoundation.org/country/overview/afghanistan.

15. MSPVAW program website, http://ww.mspvaw.org.bd. Accessed February 10, 2014.

16. Ibid.

17. Interview with staff of Saathi's shelter: Pramila Shah, Renu Shah, Samjhana K.C.

18. Interview with Selay Ghaffar, Executive Director, HAWCA.

19. Interview with Selay Ghaffar, Executive Director, HAWCA.

20. http://timesofindia.indiatimes.com/india/Women-can-email-post-complaints-to-SC-sexual-harassment-cell/articleshow/30686877.cms Last accessed: 26th February 2014.

21. http://www.chsj.org/mobilising-men-against-sgbv.html.

22. http://www.delhipolice.nic.in/parivartan/parivartan.htm.

23. http://www.rozan.org/rabta.php.

24. A life skills and parental engagement program with unmarried adolescent girls in Tigri, Delhi, did include empowering girls to say "No" to such pressure. However, the evaluation did not discuss program success in doing so (Pande et al. 2006).

25. Interview with Sunita Dhanuwar, president of Shakti Samuha.

26. http//www.capfoundation.in/?p=358.

27. Interview with Selay Ghaffar, executive director, HAWCA, 25th January 2014.

28. The United States Department of State defines human smuggling as "...the facilitation, transportation, attempted transportation or illegal entry of a person(s) across an international border, in violation of one or more countries' laws, either clandestinely or through deception, such as the use of fraudulent documents. ...Human smuggling is generally with the consent of the person(s) being smuggled, who often pay large sums of money." http://www.state.gov/m/ds/hstcenter/90434.htm

References

Achyut, P., N. Bhatla, S. Khandekar, S. Maitra, and R. K. Verma. 2011. *Building Support for Gender Equality among Young Adolescents in School: Findings from Mumbai, India*. New Delhi, India: International Center for Research on Women.

Adams, A. M., A. Rabbani, S. Ahmed, S. Mahmood, A. Al-sabir, S. F. Rashid, and T. G. Evans. 2013. "Explaining Equity Gains in Child Survival in Bangladesh: Scale, Speed, and Selectivity in Health and Development." *Lancet* 382: 2027–37.

Afghanistan Independent Human Rights Commission (AIHRC). 2011. "Summary Report on Investigation of Causes and Factors of Trafficking in Women and Children." AIHRC, Kabul.

AGHS Child Rights Unit. 2004. http://aghscru.org.pk/About%20us.html.

Ahmed, Syed M. 2005. "Intimate Partner Violence against Women: Experiences from a Woman-focused Development Programme in Matlab, Bangladesh." *Journal of Health, Population and Nutrition* 23 (1): 95–101.

Ahmed, A. and R. Yoosuf. 2012. "Maldives NGO Shadow Report to the Committee on the Elimination of Discrimination against Women." Hope for Women, Malé, Maldives.

Aldred, A. and S. Williams. 2009. *We Can: The Story So Far.* New Delhi, India: We Can South Asia Regional Secretariat.

ALG and World Bank. 2014. "Exploring the Demand and Viability of Women Only Bus Services in Dhaka: Final Report."

Amin, S. 2011. "Empowering Adolescent Girls in Rural Bangladesh: Kishori Abhijan." Transitions to Adulthood Brief Number 13. The Population Council, New York.

Amin, S., G. Sedgh, R. Magnani, E. Seiber, E. Z. Gutierrez, D. Vereau, and N. Alonso. 1998. "Incentive Schemes for School Attendance in Rural Bangladesh." *Journal of Developing Areas* 32 (3): 77–99.

Amin, S. and L. Suran. 2005. "Program Efforts to Delay Marriage through Improved Opportunities: Some Evidence from Rural Bangladesh." Presented at the 2005 Annual Meeting of the Population Association of America, Philadelphia, Pennsylvania, March 31–April 2.

Asian Center for Human Rights. 2012a. "Assam: The State of Juvenile Justice." http://www.achrweb.org/reports/india/JJ-Assam-2012.pdf.

———. 2012b. "The State of Juvenile Justice in Himachal Pradesh." http://www.achrweb.org/reports/india/JJ-HP-2012.pdf.

———. 2012c. "Madhya Pradesh: Snail Speed on Implementation of Juvenile Justice." http://www.achrweb.org/reports/india/JJ-MP-2012.pdf.

———. 2013a. "India's Hell Holes: Child Sexual Assault in Juvenile Justice Homes." ACHR, New Delhi, India.

———. 2013b. "Nobody's Children: Juveniles of Conflict Affected Districts of India." ACHR, New Delhi, India.

Aurat Foundation. 2012. "Internal Trafficking of Women and Girls in Pakistan: A Research Study." Aurat Publication and Information Services Foundation, Islamabad.

Austrian, K. and E. Muthengi. 2013. "Safe and Smart Savings Products for Vulnerable Adolescent Girls in Kenya and Uganda: Evaluation Report." Population Council, Nairobi.

Ayyub, R. 2006. "Trafficking and HIV and AIDS Prevention Project." Project Completion Report. CARE International, Bangladesh.

Bajracharya, A. and S. Amin. 2013. "Microcredit and Domestic Violence in Bangladesh: An Exploration of Selection Bias Influences." *Demography* 50 (5): 1819–43.

Banyard, V. L., M. M. Moynihan and F. G. Plante. 2007. "Sexual Violence Prevention Through Bystander Education: An Experimental Evaluation." *Journal of Community Psychology* 35 (4): 463–481.

Bedi, A. S., and S. Srinivasan. 2012. "Bare Branches and Drifting Kites: Tackling Female Infanticide and Foeticide in Tamil Nadu, India." In *Development, Freedom and Welfare: Essays Presented to Amartya Sen by Young Scholars.* Oxford University Press.

Berman, J. and P. Marshall. 2011. "Evaluation of the International Organization for Migration and its Efforts to Combat Human Trafficking." Norwegian Agency for Development Cooperation, Norway.

Breakthrough. n.d. "Bell Bajao! Campaign: A Report." New Delhi: Breakthrough.

Burket, M., M. Alauddin, A. Malek, and M. Rahman. 2006. "Raising the Age of Marriage for Young Girls in Bangladesh." Pathfinder International.

CARE Nepal. 2011. "Addressing Child Marriage in Nepal through Behavior Change Communication and Social Mobilization: Chunauti." Project Final Report, CARE Nepal, Kathmandu.

Chattopadhyay, R. and E. Duflo. 2004. "The Impact of Reservation in Panchayati Raj: Evidence from a Nationwide Randomized Experiment." *Economic and Political Weekly* 39 (9): 979–86.

Chesler, P. and N. Bloom. 2012. "Hindu vs. Muslim Honor Killings." *Middle East Quarterly*: 3–11.

Chesterton, Paul. 2004. "Evaluation of the Meena Communication Initiative." UNICEF Regional Office for South Asia, Kathmandu, Nepal.

Chung, W. and M. Das Gupta. 2007. "The Decline of Son Preference in South Korea: The Roles of Development and Public Policy," *Population and Development Review* 33(4): 757–783.

Cissner, A. B. 2009. *Evaluating the Mentors in Violence Prevention Program: Preventing Gender Violence on a College Campus.* U.S. Department of Education.

Croll. E. 2007. "The Girl Child Shield Project Pakistan: Assessment Report." School of Oriental and African Studies, University of London, London.

Das, M., S. Ghosh, F. Miller, B. O'Conner, and R. Verma. 2012. "Engaging Coaches and Athletes in Fostering Gender Equity: Findings from the Parivartan Program in Mumbai, India." New Delhi: ICRW & Futures Without Violence.

Das Gupta, M. 2010. "Family Systems, Political Systems and Asia's 'Missing Girls.'" *Asian Population Studies* 6 (2) (July): 123–52.

Das Gupta, M. 1987. "Selective Discrimination against Female Children in Rural Punjab, India." *Population and Development Review*: 77–100.

Das Gupta, M. and P. N. M. Bhat. 1997. "Fertility Decline and Increased Manifestation of Sex Bias in India." *Population Studies* 51: 307–15.

Deol, K. 1983. *Crimes Against Women Cells—The Delhi Police Experience.* Resource Material Series No. 69: 77–84.

Deosthali, P., P. Maghnani, and S. Malik. 2005. *Establishing Dilaasa: Documenting the Challenges.* Mumbai, India: CEHAT.

Dialectics. 2014. "Evaluation of Let Girls Be Born Project of Plan India." Draft evaluation submitted by Dialectics to Plan India.

Dutta, M., B. Zutshi, and A. Vajpeyi. 2010. "UNIFEM Regional Anti-Trafficking Programme in South Asia (2000–2009) - Evaluation Report." UNIFEM, India.

Evans, C. and M. P. Bhattarai. 2000. *A Comparative Analysis of Anti-Trafficking Intervention Approaches in Nepal.* Kathmandu: Asia Foundation and Population Council.

Foshee, V. A., K. E. Bauman, X. B. Arriaga, R. W. Helms, G. G. Koch, and G. F. Linder. 1998. "An Evaluation of Safe Dates, an Adolescent Dating Violence Prevention Program." *American Journal of Public Health*, 88: 45–50.

Foshee, V. A., K. E. Bauman, W. F Greene, G. G Koch, G. F Linder, and J. E. MacDougall. 2000. "The Safe Dates Program: 1-Year Follow-up Results." *American Journal of Public Health* 90 (10): 1619–22.

Foshee, V. A., K. E. Bauman, S. T. Ennnett, G. F. Linder, T. Benefield, and C. Suchindran. 2004. "Assessing the Long-Term Effects of the Safe Dates Program and a Booster in Preventing and Reducing Adolescent Dating Violence Victimization and Perpetration." *American Journal of Public Health* 94: 619–24.

Global Alliance Against Traffic in Women (GAATW). 2007. *Collateral Damage: The Impact of Anti-Trafficking Measures on Human Rights around the World*. Bangkok: Global Alliance Against Traffic in Women (GAATW).

Gautam, I. P. 2012. "Final Evaluation of Safer Environment for Girls (TOLI) in Kaski and Tanahun District." Save the Children Fund Nepal Country Office, Bagdurbar, Sundhara, Kathmandu.

Gidycz, C. A., L. M. Orchowski, and A. D. Berkowitz. 2011. "Preventing Sexual Aggression among College Men: An Evaluation of a Social Norms and Bystander Intervention Program." *Violence Against Women* 17: 720–42.

Global Alliance Against Traffic in Women (GAATW). 2007. *Collateral Damage: The Impact of Anti-Trafficking Measures on Human Rights around the World*. Bangkok: Global Alliance Against Traffic in Women (GAATW).

Greig, A. and E. Jerker. 2012. *Mobilising Men in Practice: Challenging Sexual and Gender-based Violence in Institutional Settings*. Brighton: Institute of Development Studies.

Hancock, P. 2006. "Violence, Women, Work and Empowerment: Narratives from Factory Women in Sri Lanka's Export Processing Zones." *Gender, Technology and Development* 10: 211–28.

Hameed, S., S. Hlatshwayo, E. Tanne, M. Turker, and J. Yang. 2010. "Human Trafficking in India: Dynamics, Current Efforts, and Intervention Opportunities for the Asia Foundation." Report by Stanford University for The Asia Foundation.

Hennink, M., and P. Simkhada. 2004. "Sex Trafficking in Nepal: Context and Process." Opportunities and Choices Working Paper No. 11. University of Southampton, UK, Division of Social Statistics, Southampton.

Holla, A., R. Jensen, and E. Oster. 2007. "Daughters as Wealth? The Effects of Cash Incentives on Sex Ratios." Brown University Working Paper. Brown University, Rhode Island.

Human Rights Watch. 2010. "'Dignity on Trial': India's Need for Sound Standards for Conducting and Interpreting Forensic Examinations of Rape Survivors." http://www.hrw.org/sites/default /files/reports/india0910webwcover.pdf.

Huntington, Dale. 2001. "Anti-Trafficking Programs in South Asia: Appropriate Activities, Indicators and Evaluation Methodologies." Summary Report of a Technical Consultative meeting held on September 11–13, 2001, in Kathmandu, Nepal, coordinated by UNIFEM, Population Council/HORIZONS, USAID, and PATH.

Instituto Promundo. 2012. "Engaging Men to Prevent Gender-Based Violence: A Multi-Country Intervention and Impact Evaluation Study." Report for the UN Trust Fund. Promundo, Washington, D.C.

ICRW (International Center for Research on Women). 2002. "Women-Initiated Community Level Responses to Domestic Violence: Summary Report of Three Studies." Report Number 5, Domestic Violence in India: Exploring Strategies, Promoting Dialogue. ICRW, Washington, DC and New Delhi.

———. 2011. "Gender Equity Movement in Schools: Training Manual for Facilitators." ICRW, New Delhi.

———. and UN Women. 2012. *Opportunities and Challenges of Women's Political Participation in India: A Synthesis of Research Findings from Select Districts in India*. New Delhi: ICRW.

International Organization for Migration (IOM). 2008. "Counter-Trafficking Interventions in Prevention, Protection and Prosecution for Victims of Trafficking in Persons in Bangladesh." End Project Evaluation Report. IOM, Dhaka.

Jagori and Multiple Action Research Group (Marg). 2013. *Safe Cities Free of Violence Against Women & Girls Initiative: A Study of Delhi Police Helplines (100 & 1091)*. New Delhi, India: Jagori, Marg and UN Women.

Jagori. 2010. *Understanding Women's Safety: Towards a Gender Inclusive City. Research Findings Delhi 2009–10*. New Delhi: Jagori.

Jagori, and UN Women. 2011. *Safe Cities Free of Violence against Women and Girls Initiative*. New Delhi, India: Jagori and UN Women.

Jain, S. and K. Kurz. 2007. *New Insights on Preventing Child Marriage: A Global Analysis of Factors and Programs*.Washington, DC: International Center for Research on Women.

Jaising, I., C. Sathyamala, and A. Basu. 2007. *From the Abnormal to the Normal: Preventing Sex Selective Abortions through the Law*. New Delhi: Lawyers Collective (Women's Rights Initiative).

Jensen, R. and E. Oster. 2007. "The Power of TV: Cable Television and Women's Status in India." NBER Working Paper Series, Working Paper 13305. http://www.nber.org/papers/w13305.

Kashfi, F., S. Ramdoss, and S. MacMillan. 2012. "BRAC's Empowerment and Livelihood for Adolescents: Changing Mind-sets and Going to Scale with Social and Financial Skills for Girls." *Child Policy Insights*. New York: UNICEF.

Kabeer, N., L. Huq, and S. Mahmud. 2013. "Diverging Stories of "Missing Women" in South Asia: Is Son Preference Weakening in Bangladesh?" *Feminist Economics* DOI: 10.1080/13545701.2013.857423.

Kanesathasan, A., L. J. Cardinal, E. Pearson, S. Das Gupta, S. Mukherjee, and A. Malhotra. 2008. *Catalyzing Change: Improving Youth Sexual and Reproductive Health through DISHA: An Integrated Program in India*. Washington, DC: International Center for Research on Women.

Kapur, Ratna. 2001. "Tricks and the Law: Legal Regulation of Trafficking, Sex Work and Migration." Paper presented at the technical consultative meeting on Anti-trafficking Programmes in South Asia, September, Kathmandu.

Katz, J. 2003. *Building a "Big Tent" Approach to Ending Men's Violence: Building Partners Initiative*. Washington, DC: Building Partners Initiative, United States Department of Justice.

Khalique, H., Z. N. Christopher, E. Sadiq, H. Mir, J. Sultan, S. Abro, A. Hussain, and S. Zafar. 2011. "Evaluation Report Rabta Programme, Rozan. 1999–2010." Submitted to Rozan by Harris Khalique and Team.

Khaliq, B. 2012. "External Assessment of the Implementation of Anti-Sexual Harassment Legislation." Lahore: WISE and Islamabad: AASHA.

Khosla, R. 2009. *Addressing Gender Concerns in India's Urban Renewal Mission*. New Delhi: United Nations Development Program (UNDP).

Khosla, R. 2004. "Women and Sanitation: The Urban Reality experience of Government Programmes, NGOs and CBOs," in M.D. Asthana and S. Ali, eds. *Urban Poverty in India: Issues and Policies*. New Delhi: Uppal Publishing House.

Koenig, M. A., S. Ahmed, M. B. Hossain, and A. B. M. Khorshed Alam Mozumder. 2003. "Women's Status and Domestic Violence in Rural Bangladesh: Individual- and Community-Level Effects." *Demography* 40 (2): 269–88.

Krishnan, A., R. Amarchand, P. Byass, C. Pandav, and N. Ng. 2014. ""No One Says 'No' to Money"—A Mixed Methods Approach for Evaluating Conditional Cash Transfer Schemes to Improve Girl Children's Status in Haryana, India." *International Journal for Equity in Health* 13: 11.

Krishnan, S., K. Subbiah, S. Khanum, P. S. Chandra, and N. S. Padian. 2012. "An Intergenerational Women's Empowerment Intervention to Mitigate Domestic Violence: Results of a Pilot Study in Bengaluru, India." *Violence against Women* 18 (3): 346–70.

Landesa Rural Development Institute (RDI). 2013. *Security for Girls through Land. Pilot Evaluation 2012–2013*. New Delhi: Landesa.

Lari, M. Z. 2011. *A Pilot Study on 'Honor Killings' in Pakistan and Compliance of Law*. Islamabad: The Aurat Foundation.

Mahtani, R. P. 2006. "Executive Summary Report of "Strategy Planning for the Special Cells for Women and Children: an Action Research Project (2002–2005)." Draft working paper, Tata Institute of Social Studies, TISS, Mumbai.

Maiti Nepal. 2012. "Annual Report 2012." Kathmandu, Nepal.

McAllister F., A. Burgess, J. Kato, and G. Barker. 2012. *Fatherhood: Parenting Programmes and Polcy. A Critical Review of Best Practice*. Fatherhood Institute/Promundo/MenCare, London and Washington, DC.

Malhotra, A., A. Warner, A. McGonagle, and S. Lee-Rife. 2011. *Solutions to End Child Marriage: What the Evidence Shows*. Washington, DC: International Center for Research on Women.

Mgalla, Z., D. Schapink, and J. T. Boerma. 1998. "Protecting School Girls against Sexual Exploitation: A Guardian Programme in Mwanza, Tanzania." *Reproductive Health Matters* 6 (12): 19–30.

MoHP. (Population Division) 2013. *Assessment of the Performance of Hospital-Based One Stop Crisis Management Centres*. Kathmandu: Ministry of Health and Population.

Muzzi, M. 2010. *UNICEF Good Practices in Integrating Birth Registration into Health Systems (2000–2009): Case studies: Bangladesh, Brazil, the Gambia and Delhi*. New York: UNICEF.

Nanda, P., N. Datta, and P. Das. 2014. *Impact of Conditional Cash Transfers on Girls' Education*. New Delhi: International Center for Research on Women.

Nanda, P., P. Das, A. Singh, and R. Negi. 2013. *Addressing Comprehensive Needs of Adolescent Girls in India: A Potential for Creating Livelihoods*. New Delhi: International Center for Research on Women.

National Commission on the Status of Women (NCSW) and Government of Pakistan. 2010. "Impact Assessment Report: Public Private Partnership to End 'Honour Crimes' in Pakistan through the implementation of Criminal Law (Amendment) Act 2004." National Commission on the Status of Women, Islamabad.

Omestad, T. 2012. "'Honor' Killings Averted: How a USIP-Trained Pakistani Helped Save Lives." United States Institute of Peace, Washington, DC. http://www.usip.org/publications/honor-killings-averted-how-usip-trained-pakistani-helped-save-lives.

Oxfam Great Britain (GB). 2012. "Enhancing Effectiveness through Evidence-Based Learning: The We Can Campaign, Bangladesh, 2011–12. Project Effectiveness Review." http://www.alnap.org/pool/files/er-we-can-bangladesh-effectiveness-review-081012-full-report-en.pdf.

Pande, Rohini. 2003. "Selective Gender Differences in Childhood Nutrition and Immunization in Rural India: The Role of Siblings." *Demography* 40 (3): 395–418.

Pande, R., P. Nanda, S. Kapoor, A. Mukherjee, S. Lee-Rife, L. Tan, and F. Wu. 2009. "Counting Girls: Addressing Son Preference and Daughter Discrimination in India and China." Paper presented at the Population Association of America meetings, Detroit, April 30th–May 2nd, 2009.

Pande, R., K. Kurz, S. Walia, K. MacQuarrie, and S. Jain. 2006. *Improving the reproductive health of married and unmarried youth in India: evidence of effectiveness and costs from community-based interventions. Final report of the Adolescent Reproductive Health Program in India.* Washington, D.C.: International Center for Research on Women.

Pandey, S., H. R. Tewari, and P. K. Bhowmick. 2013. "Antecedents and Reintegration of Sex Trafficked Victims in India: A Conceptual Framework." *International Journal of Criminal Justice Sciences* 8 (1): 47–62.

Pathfinder International. 2011. *PRAGYA—Multisectoral, Gendered Approach to Improve Family Planning and Sexual and Reproductive Health for Young People: A Research Study.* Watertown, MA: Pathfinder International.

Phadke, S. 2005. "'You Can Be Lonely in a Crowd'—The Production of Safety in Mumbai." *Indian Journal of Gender Studies* 12 (1): 41–62.

Population Division. 2013a. *Assessment of the Performance of Hospital-Based One-Stop Crisis Management Centres.* Kathmandu: Ministry of Health and Population.

———. 2013b. *District Population Management Programme Operational Guidelines.* Kathmandu: Ministry of Health and Population.

———. 2013c. *Process Report on National Workshop on Review and Future Direction of OCMC.* Kathmandu: Ministry of Health and Population.

Raab, M. 2011. "The 'We Can' Campaign in South Asia (2004–2001)." External Evaluation Report. Oxfam GB. http://policy-practice.oxfam.org.uk/publications/the-we-can-campaign-in-south-asia-2004-2011-external-evaluation-report-146189.

Rakib, M. A., and A. Razan. 2013. *"We Can"—A Model of Behavioral Change Concerning Violence against Women: An Assessment Report of We Can Campaign. Bangladesh Report (2010–11).* Dhaka: Oxfam GB.

Ricardo, C., M. Eads, and G. Barker. 2011. *Engaging Boys and Young Men in the Prevention of Sexual Violence: A Systematic and Global Review of Evaluated Interventions.* Washington, DC: Promundo-US.

Richardson, D., N. Laurie, M. Poudel, and J. Townsend. 2013. *Making Return Safe Post-Trafficking.* Newcastle: Newcastle University, School of Geography, Politics and Sociology.

Rodriguez, F., and H. Anwari. 2011. *United Nations Development Program—Afghanistan: Independent/External Evaluation Report.* Kabul: UNDP.

Save the Children Fund (SCF). 2009a. Adolescent Reproductive and Sexual Health Program Overview: Narsirnagar, Bangladesh. Westport, CT: SCF.

———. 2009b. Adolescent Reproductive and Sexual Health Update. Westport, CT: SCF.

———. 2009c. Empowered Youth, Supportive Community: ARSH Results from Bangladesh. Westport, CT: SCF.

———. 2009d. Involving Religious Leaders to Promote Adolescent Reproductive and Sexual Health in Bangladesh. Westport, CT: SCF.

Schuler, S. R., and Syed M. Hashemi. 1994. "Credit Programs, Women's Empowerment, and Contraceptive use in Rural Bangladesh." *Studies in Family Planning* 25 (2): 65–76.

Schurmann, A. T. 2009. "Review of the Bangladesh Female Secondary School Stipend Project Using a Social Exclusion Framework." *Journal of Health, Population, and Nutrition* 27 (4): 505–17.

Sekhar, T. V. 2010. "Special Financing Incentive Schemes for the Girl Child in India: A Review of Select Schemes." Background paper for The Planning Commission, Govenrment of India. In collaboration with the United Nations Population Fund, New Delhi.

———. 2012a. "Skewed Sex Ratios, Conditional Cash Transfers and Promotion of Girl Children: The Indian Experience." Study commissioned by United Nations Population Fund (UNFPA)– India at the request of the Planning Commission, Govt. of India. UNFPA, New Delhi.

———. 2012b. "Ladlis and Lakshmis: Financial Incentive Schemes for the Girl Child." *Economic and Political Weekly* xlvii (17): 58–65.

Shahnaz, R. and R. Karim. 2008. *Providing Microfinance and Social Space to Empower Adolescent Girls: An Evaluation of BRAC's ELA Centres*. BRAC Research and Evaluation Division Working Paper No. 3. Dhaka: BRAC.

Sharma, R., R. Goel, and H. Gupta. 2003. "Rajalakshmi—An Initiative for Improving the Status of Girl Child in Rajasthan." *The Journal of Family Welfare* 29 (1): 66–72.

Siddiqi, D. M. 2003. *The Sexual Harassment of Industrial Workers: Strategies for Intervention in the Workplace and Beyond*. Paper Number 26. Dhaka: Center for Policy Dialogue.

Sijapati, B., A. Limbu, and M. Khadka. 2011. *Trafficking and Forced Labour in Nepal: A Review of the Literature*. Kathmandu: Centre for the Study of Labour and Mobility and Himal Books.

Singh, K. 2013. *Laws and Son Preference in India: A Reality Check*. New Delhi: UNFPA.

Sinha, I., and S. M. Tapan. 2001. *The Mid-Term Evaluation of Appropriate Resources for Improving Street Children's Environment (ARISE) Project*. Department of Social Services, Ministry of Social Welfare. Dhaka: Government of Bangladesh.

Sinha, N., and J. Yoong. 2009. *Long-Term Financial Incentives and Investment in Daughters: Evidence from Conditional Cash Transfers in North India*. World Bank Policy Research Working Paper 4860. Washington, DC: The World Bank.

Srinivasan, S., and A. Bedi. 2010. "Daughter Elimination: Cradle Baby Scheme in Tamil Nadu." *Economic & Political Weekly* xiv (23): 17–20.

Srinivasan, Sharada, and Arjun Bedi. 2009. "Girl Child Protection Scheme in Tamil Nadu: An Appraisal." *Economic & Political Weekly* xliv (48): 28–30.

Tango International Inc. 2009. "Shouhardo: A Title II Program of USAID—Final Evaluation Report." USAID, CARE International, Bangladesh.

Times of India. 2014. "Women Can Email, Post Complaints to SC Sexual Harassment Cell." *Times of India*, February 19.

Transition International. 2014a. *Girl Power Programme Mid-Term Evaluation. Country Report-Bangladesh*. The Netherlands: Girl Power Alliance.

———. 2014b. *Girl Power Programme Mid-Term Evaluation. Country Report-Nepal*. The Netherlands: Girl Power Alliance.

———. 2014c. *Girl Power Programme Mid-Term Evaluation. Country Report-Pakistan*. The Netherlands: Girl Power Alliance.

Tzvetkova, M. 2002. "NGO Responses to Trafficking in Women." *Gender & Development* 10 (1): 60–68.

United Nations Children's Fund (UNICEF). 2013. *Every Child's Birth Right: Inequities and Trends in Birth Registration*. New York: UNICEF.

United Nations Development Program (UNDP) Pakistan. 2011. "Mid-term Evaluation of the Gender Justice through Musalihat Anjuman Project (GJTMAP)." http://erc.undp.org /evaluationadmin/manageevaluation/viewevaluationdetail.html?evalid=5248.

United Nations Development Program (UNDP). 2003. *From Challenges to Opportunities: Responses to Trafficking and HIV/AIDS in South Asia*. New Delhi: UNDP Regional HIV and Development Programme, South and North East Asia.

United Nations Office on Drugs and Crime (UNODC). 2013. *India Country Assessment Report: Current Status of Victim Service Providers and Criminal Justice Actors on Anti Human Trafficking*. New Delhi: UNODC Regional Office for South Asia.

United Nations Office on Drugs and Crime (UNODC). 2007. *Afghanistan: Female Prisoners and Their Social Reintegration*. New York: United Nations.

The United Nations Population Fund and the Asia-Pacific Women, Faith, and Development Alliance (UNFPA-APWFD). 2013. "A Mapping of Faith-based Responses to Violence against Women and Girls in the Asia-Pacific Region." Breakthrough, World Vision and UNFPA. http:// www.unfpa.org/webdav/site/global/shared/documents/publications/2013/UNFPA-WVA -FBO-VAWG-AP-2012.pdf.

Unites States Agency for International Development (USAID). 2009. "USAID Anti-Trafficking in Persons Programs in Asia: A Synthesis." Report submitted to Unites States Agency for International Development by Chemonics International.

UN Women. 2012. *Critical Gender Concerns in Jawaharlal Nehru National Urban Renewal Mission*. India: UN Women.

United States Department of State. 2013. "Trafficking in Persons Report 2013." U.S. Department of State, Washington, DC.

Vazirova, A. 2011. *The Assessment of Services Provided to Victims of Gender Based Violence (GBV) by State and Non-state Agencies in Pilot Areas*. Kabul: United Nations Population Fund.

Verma, R., J. Pulerwitz, V. Sharma Mahendra, S. Khandekar, A. K. Singh, S. S. Das, S. Mehra, A. Nura, and G. Barker. 2008. "Promoting Gender Equity as a Strategy to Reduce HIV Risk and Gender-based violence among Young Men in India." Horizons Final Report. Population Council, Washington, DC.

Viswanath, K., and S. Tandon Mehrotra. 2007. "'Shall We Go Out?' Women's Safety in Public Spaces in Delhi." *Economic and Political Weekly* 42 (17): 1542–48.

Williams, S., and A. Aldred. 2011. *Change-Making: How We Adopt New Attitudes, Beliefs and Practices. Insights from the We Can Campaign*. Oxford: We Can Campaign.

World Bank. 2008. *Female Secondary School Assistance Project II. Implementation Completion and Results Report (IDA-36140-BD)*. Washington, DC: World Bank.

Zia, A. 2012. *Crisis Centers and Gender Crime Cell: An Investigative Study.* Islamabad: National Commission on the Status of Women.

Zia, A. 2010. *External Evaluation for Rozan's 3 Year Collaborative Project "Strengthening Government and Civil Society Response to Gender-Based Violence."* Islamabad: Rozan.

CHAPTER 5

Where Do We Go from Here?

Heightened public awareness, continuous advocacy and programs by civil society groups, and significant political and legal reforms contribute to the efforts to address violence against women and girls in South Asia. Although we do not definitively know what works to prevent and to respond to the various forms of violence against women and girls, there are a number of promising approaches that merit further attention and resources. On the whole, these suggest that addressing the entrenched gender norms that define masculinity and femininity and that underlie the risk factors for violence described in the previous chapters require coordinated and continuous efforts.

As described in chapters 2 and 3, violence against women and girls occurs in different forms throughout their lives, and a range of risk factors influence vulnerability to these forms of violence. As illustrated in chapter 4, interventions to address violence against women and girls in the region attempt to address these types of violence at macro (social norms), institutional, household, and individual levels. This chapter draws from the research findings in chapters 2 and 3, and the intervention stocktaking and lessons learned from interventions analyzed in chapter 4. It aims to synthesize these findings into tangible recommendations for different actors—governments in South Asia; local and international civil society organizations; research institutions; the media, entertainment, and communications sectors; the private sector; and donors. We start with recommendations that are common across the different actors and follow these with recommendations that are specific to an actor. The recommendations include short- and medium-term actions as well as long-term goals. There is, inevitably, some overlap between the general recommendations and those that are specific to a particular actor.

Recommendations for All Actors

The recommendations that follow are grouped into two broad categories: (a) those that call for more work in under-researched areas; and, (b) those that indicate ways of bolstering existing efforts. Some actions can be undertaken immediately, in the short term. Others require a little more time, but can still be achieved within the medium term. Still others, which require some form of integration or institutionalization of practices, will need a long-term perspective to be achieved fully (table 5.1).

EXPLORE POTENTIAL LINKS BETWEEN EFFORTS TO ADDRESS DIFFERENT TYPES OF VIOLENCE

Our interactions with organizations in the field, our vast literature search, and our analysis of interventions reveal little overlap or meaningful exchange between interventions that address the various types of violence that women face as children and

TABLE 5.1 Recommendations for All Actors

Actions	Time frame		
	Short-term actions	Medium-term actions	Long-term goals
Explore links between efforts to address different types of violence.	√	√	
Pilot programs and research that address risk factors.	√		
Integrate a focus on risk factors in all prevention and response programs.		√	√
Engage men and boys and strengthen existing alliances.	√	√	
Broaden policies so that they include a focus on men and boys.		√	√
Strengthen capacity for monitoring and evaluation, ensure that data is disaggregated by gender, and separate outcomes for different types of violence.	√	√	
Develop better techniques to accurately measure violence.	√	√	√
Conduct more rigorous impact evaluations.	√	√	√
Link violence programs with STI or HIV prevention programs.	√	√	√
Use antenatal care and family planning programs to screen for violence and provide support and information for victims.	√	√	√
Design interventions that focus on under-researched forms of violence.	√	√	
Emphasize training and its evaluation	√	√	

Note: STI = sexually transmitted infections; HIV = human immunodeficiency virus.

as adults. Yet, linking those who work on violence against girls and adolescents with those who work on violence against adult women is important: there are mutual lessons—and meeting points—that would benefit both constituencies.

One example is the use of media. Efforts to address violence—be it in childhood, adolescence, or adulthood—have made use of innovative and often revolutionary media and advocacy to break the silence around violence and to motivate stakeholders to act. Joining forces for media and advocacy could enable all interventions to reach a broader range of stakeholders with the message that any form of violence against women and girls is unacceptable.

A second example of mutual lessons is that of approach. Child rights programs and adolescent life skills programs illustrate well how to engage girls and boys as partners, rather than merely as program recipients. These programs also provide lessons on how to present policies and basic understanding of rights in ways that are accessible to those suffering or at risk of violence. Child-centered programming that is core to child rights and child marriage prevention efforts can thus provide valuable lessons to violence-against-women prevention programs on how to make such programs more woman centered or couple centered. Similarly, efforts in trafficking interventions that engage trafficking survivors as implementers illustrate how survivors can play a central role in advocacy and raising awareness. This important lesson must be shared, given the need for extensive efforts to rehabilitate and reintegrate survivors of other forms of violence into their communities in ways that do not exacerbate any stigma against them or disempower them as they reenter the very milieu from which the violence they suffered arose.

Child rights and child marriage interventions or anti-trafficking interventions, however, do not seem to engage men and boys as systematically as do efforts to address intimate partner violence. In particular, campaigns to prevent girl child abuse and excess female child mortality can learn from successful campaigns against domestic violence and broader violence against women, such as the We Can and Men's Action to Stop Violence Against Women (MASVAW) campaigns, on how to best engage men and boys. These campaigns also illustrate how to evaluate a mass media or campaign-centered program.

Approaches that address violence faced by girls and adolescents and those that address violence faced by women also have similar points of difficulty. Those points include (a) evaluations that are limited in number and of limited rigor; (b) training that is badly needed but is ad hoc, especially for police; and (c) lack of documentation that makes clear what approaches—and under what circumstances—are most effective for community involvement. Sharing experiences and learning across programs could help fill all of these gaps.

INTEGRATE A FOCUS ON RISK FACTORS IN PREVENTION AND RESPONSE PROGRAMS

We found little evidence that interventions to prevent and respond to violence against women and girls have systematically taken into account the different risk factors across all levels of the social ecology identified in chapter 3. We were only able to identify one intervention that was working with mothers-in-law, and minimal evaluated interventions that addressed alcohol abuse. We also found no evaluated interventions that explicitly addressed the intergenerational transmission of violence. Outside of child marriage interventions, we were not able to find interventions that addressed violence by enhancing a girl's or a woman's ownership of assets. Only one intervention explicitly addressed and measured any effect on dowry, a key factor influencing child marriage and intimate partner violence.

Across most of the interventions we located, programs did not identify the particular constraints that married adolescent girls might face in protecting themselves from or in seeking care for domestic violence. These are serious lacunae; research points out that adolescents may have vulnerabilities that are different from those of adult women because of their lower status in the familial and social hierarchy. Adolescents face constraints that prevent them from accessing programs to the extent that adult women might. Extensive programming now exists to provide reproductive health to married adolescents, particularly in Bangladesh and India. These programs could provide plausible entry points for interventions to prevent marital domestic violence among married adolescents.

Integrating specific attention to risk factors across all levels of the social ecology will improve targeting of interventions; however, it will most likely entail substantial programmatic shifts. Needed actions in this regard include (a) funding for pilot programs that address ignored risk factors; (b) improving targeting, training, monitoring and evaluation efforts; and (c) conducting rigorous research that more accurately measures and analyzes potential risk factors or causes of violence against women and girls so that programs and policies know where to focus attention in specific contexts.

SCALE UP EFFORTS TO ENGAGE MEN AND BOYS

There is an urgent need to deepen the involvement of men and boys in addressing all forms of violence faced by women and girls; to bring existing, promising approaches to work with men and boys to scale; and to invest in sustainability to ensure long-lasting impact. Until now, interventions involving men and boys have focused largely on boys and men in general, or on husbands, with fewer evaluated efforts illustrating how to engage them in other roles, such as brothers, fathers, or fathers-in-law.

In the short term, scaling up interventions that work with men as change makers and partners in efforts to address violence against women and girls can be aided by strengthening existing alliances, such as the MenEngage South Asia Alliance. In addition, such interventions can be strengthened and scaled up through greater collaboration between existing alliances and other civil society organizations and networks, women's rights organizations, local religious and community leaders, and other decision makers. Interventions also need to experiment, over the short and medium terms, with engaging men in other roles, as brothers (supporting their sisters for all forms of violence), as fathers (supporting girls and preventing violence against their daughters), and as future and current fathers-in-law (in efforts to prevent child marriage and domestic violence). While some efforts in these directions exist (see, for example, McAllister et al.'s 2012 review of fatherhood initiatives), these need to be mainstreamed and evaluated more rigorously. In the medium and longer terms, policy discussions with all stakeholders are important to ensure that existing policy frameworks on violence against women and girls are broadened to focus on men and boys—not just as perpetrators of such violence, but also as supporters of women who survive violence. Such discussions will pave the way for the long-term broadening of such policies. They also will provide opportunities to consider even more comprehensive policies to address gender-based violence—those that acknowledge men's own gender-specific needs, realities, and cultural contexts as survivors of violence themselves.

CONDUCT MORE AND BETTER EVALUATION AND OTHER RESEARCH

Later in this chapter we include specific recommendations for researchers in the region, yet all actors have a role to play in ensuring that data are collected (and disaggregated by gender when feasible), analyzed, and communicated. The very first imperative in this regard is evaluations. More rigorous evaluations—although not necessarily randomized control trials (RCTs)—are needed across the region. Governments, donors, and other stakeholders who help finance these evaluations must ensure that funds and timelines are sufficient to enable reliable and complete evaluations, that implementing organizations have or can build the capacity to conduct meaningful evaluations, and that findings are made readily available and are acted upon. Better techniques to accurately measure violence are also imperative: a large body of research points out that existing techniques can incorrectly estimate many forms of violence, such as child and adult sexual abuse, sexual harassment, or trafficking.

More research is also needed to understand when and how intervening will be most effective. For instance, the research on addressing intimate partner violence faced by married adolescent and adult women suggests that early intervention is key to preventing marital intimate partner violence. That is, married girls and women need to develop the skills and awareness to protect them from violence *before* they marry. Life skills programs are one way to do so, but longer-term follow-up of girls who go through these programs is essential to establish whether and how exposure to such programs can be protective for girls later in life. Similarly, the research indicates that gender norms are formed at a young age; thus, programs targeted to increasing gender-equitable attitudes among young boys and girls are crucial interventions (Naved et al. 2006; Santhya et al. 2007; IIPS and Population Council 2009; Jejeebhoy et al. 2013). Successful evaluated efforts—such as the GEMS program described in chapter 4—need funding and effort to sustain the training required for successful implementation and to continue evaluating impact over the longer term, such that successful interventions can be replicated and scaled up. Other critical early intervention areas that have largely been ignored include intervening with parents and children in households where there is alcohol abuse and where spousal violence is prevalent so that the inter-generational cycle of violence can be broken (Martin et al. 2002).

IMPROVE ATTENTION TO VIOLENCE AGAINST WOMEN AND GIRLS IN HEALTH SECTOR INTERVENTIONS

The health sector is an important entry point for prevention and response efforts. Much research points to the need to better use health service delivery points to respond to violence. This is especially the case for reproductive health services that reach large numbers of young and adolescent married women, such as basic services for sexual and reproductive health (Santhya et al. 2007; Jejeebhoy et al. 2010; Chibber and Krishnan 2011), family planning (Stephenson et al. 2008), and antenatal care (Fikree et al. 2006). Health care providers should be trained to identify, screen, and work with women who seek care (Martin et al. 1999; Kumar et al. 2005; Naved et al. 2006; Jejeebhoy et al. 2010).

Research suggests that enhanced screening for intimate partner violence and referral services through health interventions are effective in enabling survivors of domestic violence to end abusive relationships (Miller et al. 2011); those who participate in such services also report significantly fewer threats of abuse (McFarlane et al. 2006). Screening for mental health is abysmal, however. Despite evidence that survivors of domestic violence are at increased risk of suffering from depression and other health issues, few health-related violence response interventions address depression or provide mental health counseling. Serious effort is needed to expand and evaluate the provision of such services.

Linking efforts to prevent marital violence with human immunodeficiency virus (HIV) prevention interventions is also important and logical because repeat violence—especially sexual violence—may place women at heightened risk of HIV and other sexually transmitted infections (STIs) (Stephenson et al. 2006; Jejeebhoy et al. 2010; Puri et al. 2011). Engaging men and boys via such programs is also an important violence prevention strategy. Programs across the developing world have shown that men participating in comprehensive HIV-related interventions that also had a violence-prevention module showed significant changes in perpetrating physical or sexual intimate partner violence (Jewkes et al. 2008) and a shift toward more gender-equitable norms (Pulerwitz et al. 2006; Pulerwitz et al. 2010).

DESIGN INTERVENTIONS THAT FOCUS ON UNDERRESEARCHED FORMS OF VIOLENCE

As mentioned previously in this book, there is little research and work on violence against never-married, divorced, widowed, and elderly women. Yet, the minimal research available on these subgroups of women, reviewed in chapter 2, suggests that these groups will increase in size in the near future and that they face significant degrees and particular types of violence that need targeted intervention.

Similarly, while research and some interventions recognize the importance of addressing intimate partner violence among unmarried adolescents, the taboo around intimate relationships before marriage has prevented proper attention to this form of violence. Research outside the region on interventions to prevent intimate partner sexual violence against unmarried adolescents, however, points to successful interventions that can potentially be adapted and tested in South Asia. The Safe Dates program is an example of a school-based intervention developed in the United States that helped students understand the difference between supportive and abusive relationships. The program evaluation, an RCT, revealed positive short-term behavioral effects. Adolescents in the treatment group were less accepting of intimate partner violence, perceived more negative consequences from engaging in such violence, reported using less destructive responses to anger, and were more aware of victim and perpetrator services (Foshee et al. 1998; Foshee et al. 2000). Moreover, they reported significantly less physical and sexual intimate partner violence perpetration and victimization four years after the program (Foshee et al. 2004). Programs working with men and women in universities, research has shown, increase knowledge of sexual assault and decrease acceptance of cultural rape myths (Lanier et al. 1998; Lonsway and Kothari 2000; Potter et al. 2009).

EMPHASIZE TRAINING AND ITS EVALUATION

Sufficient and appropriate training is critical to the success of interventions, as the evaluations in chapter 4 suggest. Given that, at their foundation, successful efforts need to transform gendered beliefs and behaviors, the need for careful training is not surprising.

All actors have a role to play in ensuring that this key input is emphasized. Governments and NGOs need to build in enough time in program planning and implementation for in-depth and meaningful training of staff at all levels; donors need to provide funds and space in timelines for implementers to conduct effective training; and researchers need to emphasize evaluations of trainings when they partner with implementing organizations for monitoring and evaluation research.

Recommendations for Governments

As evidenced by the recommendations that follow, governments in South Asia have a critical role to play to ensure that existing policies protecting women and girls from violence are implemented effectively and that government services—such as crisis centers and shelters—reach the intended populations. Moreover, governments have a crucial role to play in ensuring adequate funding for policies and programs that address specific forms of violence and in incentivizing improved efforts to address violence against women and girls across ministries or departments. For example, governments can more effectively use conditional cash transfers to combat son preference and delay

TABLE 5.2 Recommendations for Government

Actions	Time frame		
	Short-term actions	Medium-term actions	Long-term goals
Coordinate across all ministries and with different actors to ensure there is coherent policy focused on girl child and women's rights.	√	√	
Improve data collection on all forms of violence in surveys measuring prevalence and crime records systems and increase monitoring and oversight of case registration for police.	√	√	√
Conduct technical assessments of government-run shelters and crisis centers.	√		
Integrate violence screening and support in antenatal care, family planning programs, and STI and HIV prevention programs.	√	√	√
Improve training of police and establish an effective and independent complaints system in prisons to report incidents of torture and abuse.	√	√	
Increase the number of female officers in police departments and post female officers to decision-making roles.		√	√
Enforce witness protection and address capacity constraints in the judiciary.		√	√
Ramp up efforts to register births and marriages.	√	√	
Expand or enact legislation to protect against all forms of violence, and clarify laws and policies pertaining to trafficking.		√	√
Dedicate funding to programs preventing and responding to violence against women and girls, and establish clear parameters for disbursement of such funds.	√	√	√

Note: STI = sexually transmitted infections; HIV = human immunodeficiency virus.

marriage of adolescent girls, as in the case of the *Apni Beti, Apna Dhan* (Our Daughter, Our Wealth) scheme in India, if known conceptual and implementation problems are corrected. Finally, governments already have in place systems for service provision that have great reach and potential to make a large, positive impact, but that often are bypassed by donors and civil society programs because of inefficiencies and other problems. Such systems need to be better designed, managed, monitored, and funded, for all of which government commitment is essential. Table 5.2 summarizes the recommendations for government action that are feasible in the short term, and that governments need to address in the medium and longer terms.

FACILITATE GREATER COORDINATION AND COMMUNICATION

As both implementers and donors of violence prevention and response programs, governments across the region should call for and facilitate dialogue among all stakeholders to develop methods to improve coordination, communication, and sharing of policies and program results. This undertaking should include short-term actions such as support for regional learning initiatives, strategies to work with men and boys, and collection of good practices that have not yet been fully examined or evaluated but show promising results.

Governments across the region also need to work with researchers, donors, and civil society organizations to improve data collection on all forms of violence against women and girls. In particular, data collection can be improved in surveys, such as the Demographic and Health Surveys and others that measure prevalence, and in crime records systems that track incidents of legally criminalized forms of violence. In general, all South Asian countries need to come up with more reliable methods to gather evidence of crimes against women. Currently, most countries rely on handwritten First Information Reports (FIR) that do not give an accurate picture of reported crime trends. India's National Crime Records Bureau (NCRB) is the most comprehensive system for collecting data on violence against women. However, the NCRB's methodology in collecting records of rapes can be questioned because it only takes into account "principal offences" as recorded in the FIRs, which leads to systematic underrepresentation of crimes against women (*The Hindu*, September 2013).

Greater government collaboration with civil society organizations can strengthen support services offered to victims. The large number of nongovernmental organizations (NGOs) that provide legal, medical, and other services to women prisoners, for example, can be mobilized to help monitor the conditions of prisoners and assist with their reintegration (UNODC 2007). Similarly, there is scope to improve the services offered to women in government-run shelters. Such improvements should be guided by a detailed assessment of the shelters that lists services offered and to whom (for instance: Are women and children allowed? Are women with communicable diseases allowed?), guidelines for length of stay, assessment of support services offered, and mechanisms and efficacy of reintegration and mediation efforts. Finally, governments need to pay attention to evaluate these services.

VIOLENCE AGAINST WOMEN AND GIRLS IS NOT THE PURVIEW OF A SPECIFIC MINISTRY

Efforts to address violence against women and girls often are pigeonholed into ministries that focus on "women's affairs" or reproductive health. Violence pervades all realms of women's lives, however, as we demonstrate throughout this book. Thus, in order to successfully address violence, governments must institutionalize their efforts within all ministries that deal with various realms of life, rather than relegate and isolate such efforts to one or a few specific ministries. Bangladesh's Multi-Sectoral Programme on Violence against Women (MSPVAW), described in chapter 4, is a good example of successful collaboration across ministries.[1]

Following the example set in Bangladesh, other governments in the region need to coordinate across all departments (including those with responsibility for finance, trade, employment, security, tourism, housing, transport, and urban planning) to ensure coherent policies focused on girl child and women's rights. For instance, as explored in chapter 4, early marriage interventions in Bangladesh, India, and Nepal highlight the potentially transformative power of life skills education. Yet, governments in South Asia largely have failed to comprehensively institutionalize curricula on life skills in the education sector; where they do, they miss opportunities to include strategies that arm children with a knowledge of their rights. Another missed opportunity is to work in the transport sector. Violence prevention activities in transportation can include (a) tamper-proof global positioning systems in buses that would allow police to quickly respond to complaints of violence and harassment on public transport, and (b) citizen watch committees that raise awareness of harassment in different modes of transport and that could be trained to step in to stop cases of harassment. Similarly, ministries responsible for environmental issues can work with those responsible for home affairs to develop plans to address gender violence concerns in situations of natural disasters or communal ethnic violence.

IMPROVE PROVIDER SENSITIVITY AND ATTENTION TO SURVIVORS

Violence is already highly stigmatized, as a result of which women, girls, and sometimes their families fear reporting or seeking services or justice. The stigma combines with an overall lack of trust in the ability or motivation of providers and justice systems to provide redress and further discourages women. Any response-based intervention must address women's trust of and access to the service provider and be sensitive to the possibility that reporting may induce further violence. This is especially relevant for police, judicial systems, and related authorities. In particular, police often do not display appropriate gender sensitivity when working with survivors of violence and may engage in misconduct, such as improperly recording incidences of violence (Sri Lanka, evidenced by Wijayatilake and Guneratne 2002; Pakistan, evidenced by Lari 2011).

Attention to the needs of survivors can be improved by, first, incorporating in police trainings some instruction on the dynamics of violence in the marital home. The training programs already taking place need to be better evaluated. Emphasis needs to be placed on the actual content, quality, and increased monitoring and oversight of case registration to measure the effect of these trainings. Such programs also need to be institutionalized and not just part of ad hoc general police training sessions.

Second, all countries should seek to increase the number of female officers in their departments, and, in particular, female officers should be posted to decision-making roles. For instance, an almost universally recommended solution to the problem of custodial violence against women and girls in South Asian countries that goes beyond individual programs is the implementation of laws mandating that women custodians take care of and oversee women prisoners. This approach has occurred on a small scale in India's all-women's police stations. In Afghanistan, a special department to deal with women offenders was established—a positive move to address the needs of women prisoners and enable their reintegration into society given the stigma surrounding any actual or suspected sexual abuse the women may have faced in prison (UNODC 2007). At the same time, as noted in chapter 4, such initiatives need to be undertaken carefully, so that having women law enforcement officers or departments does not reduce violence to a women's issue and does not result in male law enforcement officials neglecting their responsibilities.

Third, medical professionals need to receive training to treat abuse cases. Such training is particularly lacking in cases of custodial violence suffered by women and children. Those being treated require immediate access to reproductive and sexual health services and treatment for post-traumatic stress disorder and other psychological conditions that survivors of such violence experience (Human Rights Watch 2011). Raising the awareness of medical personnel so that they can provide necessary protection and work more effectively with survivors of custodial violence is critical (Srinivasan 2011).

Finally, all countries need to enforce witness protection for survivors of any form of violence (Heiberg and Thukral 2013). In the majority of cases, survivors of violence live in close proximity to their attackers, or the violence was perpetrated by an acquaintance or someone with whom the victim has a relationship. These situations can lead to threats, intimidation, and obstruction of justice during the legal process; children are especially vulnerable because they are minors.

ADDRESS CAPACITY CONSTRAINTS IN THE JUDICIARY

South Asian courts have a demonstrated lack of capacity for cases of violence against women and girls, as evidenced by the severe backlog of cases across the region. Additionally, the negative impact that low rates of female participation in judicial mechanisms and processes—ranging from the ability to stand before courts to serving as lawyers, judges, and other judiciary staff—have on women's access to justice is an outstanding issue. In Afghanistan and Pakistan, for instance, women often face a pro-male bias in the courtroom as a result of such low participation (Amnesty International 1999; Choudhury 2007).

Governments should work toward enhancing overall court capacity by increasing staffing where needed and by improving facilities and access to legal materials, where possible. Preexisting low rates of literacy among women throughout much of the region, combined with the poor general dissemination of laws, have contributed to a lack of legal literacy in South Asia. Legal ministries should continue to invest in legal literacy programs for women and work toward disseminating legal materials in local languages. Simultaneously, judiciary bodies and officials, including lawyers, must be apprised of updates in local and national laws pertaining to women.

TACKLE PERSISTENT LEGAL CHALLENGES

Addressing the lack of clarity in laws is an urgent need. Laws and policies should have clear definitions. One outstanding example is the case of trafficking, where such clarity means distinguishing between trafficking for sex work, for forced labor, for unsafe migration, and for human smuggling. For instance, the South Asian Association for Regional Cooperation's (SAARC) Convention on Preventing and Combating Trafficking in Women and Children for Prostitution conflates trafficking with prostitution. Other limitations include the following: (a) the convention does not consider consent in sex work and encompasses voluntary prostitution; (b) the convention does not delve into consent of trafficked persons during repatriation; and (c) the convention lists prevention mechanisms that encourage the surveillance of a broad range of female workers without the active involvement of trafficked persons, vulnerable groups, or the community (GAATW 2007; Evans and Bhattarai 2000). Governments also need to strengthen prosecution of traffickers and government officers who comply with traffickers and to review policies and practices that may involve prosecuting trafficking victims.

Another persistent legal challenge that needs to be addressed is registration of births and marriages. Improving registration rates takes time, but can and must be initiated in the short term. Keeping gender-specific records of children is crucial so that governments, child protection agencies, and NGOs have identity information for girls—and boys—who go missing from being on the streets, through commercial sexual exploitation, through bonded labor, and so forth. Moreover, such information holds parents and guardians accountable for the safety and protection of children. Birth and marriage registration are also key to monitoring and preventing child marriage. Bhutan, Maldives, and Sri Lanka have achieved almost universal birth registration. In Bangladesh, UNICEF and the Government of Bangladesh have achieved a considerable measure of success in increasing birth registration. Further analysis of how these countries have succeeded could aid efforts to make registration universal in other countries in the region.

EXPAND OR ENACT LEGISLATION TO PROTECT AGAINST ALL FORMS OF VIOLENCE

Most countries in South Asia have enacted legislation protecting women and girls from many forms of violence. Bangladesh recently enacted legislation criminalizing torture and custodial violence (International Press Agency 2013). Legal actions include suspension of suspected violators and the possibility of fines and imprisonment for life.

Across the region, however, there remains a pressing need to amend, harmonize, or enact laws protecting women and girls from all forms of violence (see tables 3.4 and 5.3). In Sri Lanka, the Prevention of Domestic Violence Act does not protect women independently; instead, its umbrella protection treats women together with children and disabled persons, despite the differing needs of these populations. In Pakistan, important contradictions exist between the various laws related to children and child rights, starting with the definition of and age of the child. Furthermore, as described in chapter 3, systems of personal law are utilized in many South Asian countries, which often demonstrate a visible imbalance between the rights offered by personal laws for majority groups and personal laws governing minority communities.

Specific state-sanctioned legal protections do not exist for (a) sexual harassment in Afghanistan and Maldives; (b) custodial violence in Afghanistan, Bhutan, India,

TABLE 5.3 Country-Specific Recommendations for Legal Changes Where Laws Are Missing or Inadequate

	Afghanistan	Bangladesh	Bhutan	India	Maldives	Nepal	Pakistan	Sri Lanka
Enact protections against sexual harassment.	√				√			
Enact protections against custodial violence.	√		√	√	√	√	√	
Enact protections against abuse of elderly women.	√	√	√		√		√	
Criminalize marital rape.	√	√		√	√		√	√
End prosecution of extramarital relationships.	√				√		√	
Correct imbalances in systems of personal law.		√		√			√	√

Maldives, Nepal, and Pakistan; or (c) elder abuse in Afghanistan, Bangladesh, Bhutan, Maldives, and Pakistan. Rape, when it occurs within marriage, is not a criminal offense in Afghanistan, Bangladesh, India, Maldives, Pakistan, and Sri Lanka. Legislative frameworks in Afghanistan, Maldives, and Pakistan currently enable to varying degrees the prosecution of crimes pertaining to extramarital sexual relations. Penalties are typically considered inhumane by the international community and may range from prison sentences in Afghanistan to public lashings in Maldives.

As described by Kapur (2013), laws in South Asia may be designed around the logic of protectionism or paternalism—more concerned with preserving a woman's modesty and other sociocultural norms than with promoting equal rights between women and men. With regard to the design of new laws as well as the reform of existing laws, legislators instead should seek to focus on women and girls as equal citizens to men and boys.

DEDICATE FUNDING FOR PROGRAMS THAT ADDRESS VIOLENCE AGAINST WOMEN AND GIRLS

Support services in South Asia typically face a dearth of material resources needed to properly serve those facing violence. Programming budgets cannot rely on donor support alone. Financial support from the government is imperative to help reduce gaps in the availability and quality of services. Some countries in South Asia have made recent positive strides in including gender-responsive budgeting into their budget plans. The government of India's budget for 2013–2014 has been recognized, for instance, for its focus on gender security and sensitivity. However, reporting on the gender budget merely touches on certain proportions of funds for women and children (Kaul and Shrivastava 2013). More targeted funding for specific policies, laws, and programs that address violence is necessary to enable their implementation. Funding for the Protection of Women against Domestic Violence Act in India, for instance, needs to be reassessed to allow for flexibility in the use of funds by states (Jhamb 2011). In other cases, existing targeted funds need to be effectively and transparently managed and used. Government funding mechanisms should also support more research and program impact evaluations, focusing on themes that are ripe for scaling up and for which other actors may not have the reach or financial muscle of governments.

Recommendations for Donors

Bilateral and multilateral donors support the bulk of programs and research addressing violence against women and girls. These organizations have a continued role to play in (a) supporting cross-learning between programs that address different forms of violence; (b) research; and (c) efforts to bring promising interventions to scale (table 5.4). Moreover, donor agencies, in collaboration with governments and civil society organizations, are in a position to promote gender-transformative programs that not only address the immediate tangible outputs of various interventions, but also have another measurable layer of transforming gender relations.

As illustrated in chapter 4, few interventions have been rigorously evaluated and fewer still have been scaled up. Donors can support both of these immediate and long-term needs by (a) providing adequate funding and technical support—where needed—for effective and adequate training, and for rigorous evaluation; (b) supporting and engaging in the development of frameworks to identify interventions that can be sustainable and scaled up; (c) identifying effective methods of delivery, including provision of dedicated funding; and (d) developing more comprehensive multisectoral initiatives that take advantage of links within and across different sectors. Improved harmonization across programs supported by donors as well as greater use of existing systems that reach the grassroots level (including those established by governments) is needed to accomplish the above-mentioned activities.

Donors need to send a clear message about the importance of monitoring and evaluation research. The United Nations Trust Fund to End Violence against Women, for example, emphasizes evidence-based programming; however, it seems to place an arbitrary cap (10 percent) on costs for monitoring and evaluation. Although such a cap helps to promote the need for monitoring frameworks even in small interventions, thereby increasing institutional capacity for monitoring and evaluation, the cap does not give teams the

TABLE 5.4 Recommendations for All Donors

Actions	Time frame		
	Short-term actions	Medium-term actions	Long-term goals
Develop frameworks to identify interventions that can be scaled up.	√		
Allocate reasonable budgets for training, and for monitoring and evaluation, including for rigorous impact evaluations.	√	√	
Fund longitudinal studies that look at the costs and consequences of violence and allow for identification of long-term program impacts.	√	√	√
Support comprehensive and multisectoral interventions, where feasible.	√	√	√
Promote greater harmonization across programs and donor agencies.	√	√	√

scope to use more rigorous evaluation techniques, which can be costly. At the same time, evaluations need to be designed in ways that take into account the current and potential capacity of implementing organizations. Unless program organizations can take ownership of and successfully integrate monitoring and evaluation into their primary mandate of program implementation, evaluation research will not be institutionalized into program work.

In addition to rigorous evaluations, donors need to fund data collection and research on the costs and consequences of violence. In particular, estimates of the costs of violence against women and girls are few and far between, and methods of estimation suffer from multiple flaws and limitations, including the lack of reliable data. Donors also need to expand their time horizons for research and programs in order to address attitudes and behavior underlying violence against women and girls. Sustained attitudinal and behavioral changes take time. Dedicated, relatively long-term funding for interventions that motivate such changes allow time and space for such efforts to be more transformative than current three- to five-year-funding horizons permit. Donor willingness to dedicate funding for research programs that measure such changes can vastly improve our understanding of what works to address violence against women and girls—not just a year after the intervention ends, but in the years that follow.

Recommendations for Nongovernmental Organizations

NGOs are at the front lines of violence prevention and response programs. Table 5.5 lists several key ways in which NGOs can use their position in the short, medium and long terms.

TABLE 5.5 Recommendations for NGOs

Actions	Time frame		
	Short-term actions	Medium-term actions	Long-term goals
Improve documentation of the implementation process, including by improving monitoring frameworks.	√		
Engage men and boys better by collaborating with the vast networks of men and boys that are working on efforts to stop violence against women.	√	√	√
Increase dialogue and work across NGOs to share best practices and to standardize services.	√	√	√
Address risk factors in interventions.	√	√	√
Increase awareness and knowledge about violence against widows and the elderly and divorced or never-married women.	√		

Note: NGO = nongovernmental organization.

NGOs provide the strongest examples of rights-based approaches to addressing violence against women and girls. NGOs that have found success from such approaches have designed programs that place survivors of violence at the center of programmatic efforts. As discussed in chapter 4, survivor-centered programs can be critical to preventing child sexual abuse by involving children who have suffered abuse and encourage others to speak out. Similarly, by identifying risks and procedures associated with trafficking, survivors have been seminal to trafficking prevention programs in India and Nepal. These experiences suggest that it would be worthwhile for NGOs that have not internalized such a survivor-centric philosophy to engage with those that have. Other actors—governments and donors, for example—can also learn from these efforts in their planning, policies, and funding decisions.

As is the case with the other stakeholders working on violence prevention and response, there is much scope for growth to improve delivery of services. This can be achieved by, first, improving documentation of processes followed during program implementation. Such documentation will allow for comparisons of the merits or benefits of different program components within and across NGOs and interventions. Second, among themselves, NGOs need to have greater dialogue, sharing of experiences, and collaboration. These actions will allow for at least some standardization in the services offered (for example, all support programs implemented by NGOs could include counseling and psychosocial support), as well as the identification of means to increase awareness and knowledge about under-researched forms of violence, such as violence against widows or elderly women. Such engagement can also facilitate the practice of empowering survivors to engage fully in all stages of programming, as mentioned in several parts of this book. Third, NGOs need to better engage not just survivors but also other members of their households. For instance, interventions addressing intimate partner violence can involve mothers-in-law; those addressing violence against children need to more actively and explicitly involve fathers, mothers, and siblings. All these individuals in a girl's or women's immediate environment can be either perpetrators of violence or supporters of women's safety and growth. It is incumbent on interventions to do their best to engage them as supporters. Finally, as noted in chapter 4, NGOs need to better identify potential unintended consequences of their interventions. Those running programs that seek to delay marriage, for example, need to ensure that their efforts do not inadvertently trigger an increase in dowry size. NGOs that engage women by forming groups—some of them with financial activities—need to take into account the possibility of violence as group participation (especially when combined with financial benefits) starts to empower women.

Monitoring and evaluation is another area in which NGOs need to improve their capacities. They will need to work closely with researchers to ensure that monitoring frameworks include gender-disaggregated indicators, capture information on perpetrators as well as victims, include evaluations of training programs, and allow for assessments of impact and outcome indicators. Such monitoring and evaluation frameworks will more strongly support mid-course corrections to improve the sustainability of an intervention, and allow for a better understanding of which factors work to address which forms of violence against women and girls.

Recommendations for the Research Community

As this report has illustrated, there are many gaps in knowledge, in particular to establish a causal effect of many putative risk and protective factors. Some of the links for specific types of violence that beg more rigorous testing include the links between sexual abuse and insecure working conditions, the links between trafficking and HIV/ AIDS, and the links between domestic violence and participation in micro-credit and other social and political groups. More broadly, and across multiple forms of violence, research needs to better establish the positive role of factors such as female education, and the negative role of factors such as alcohol abuse by caretakers or intimate partners and the inter-generational nature of violence. Similarly, researchers focusing on different forms of violence need to collaborate to better understand and document the coexistence of various types of violence; such information could vastly improve violence prevention planning. A better understanding of the links between positive role models and more gender-equitable attitudes and practices would also be tremendously useful in program and policy design. Additionally, researchers should coordinate to collect data that are more comparable across countries. This is especially lacking in the case of trafficking (Dutta et al. 2010). Another key gap concerns the disparity in research across different countries; research on most forms of violence is extremely limited for Bhutan and the Maldives, and limited also—though slightly less so—for Afghanistan, Pakistan, and Sri Lanka. Finally, across all countries, certain forms of violence have been particularly neglected by research: child sexual abuse, honor killings, and custodial violence. Researchers need to pay attention to analyzing and disseminating results of such analysis for these forms of violence.

There is no question that more rigorous evaluations are needed. In our research, we found 101 evaluated interventions, of which only three were randomized control trials. We also found glaring gaps in evaluations of shelters, help lines, and interventions addressing custodial violence, honor crimes, and trafficking (see figures 4.3 and 4.4). The lack of competent evaluations indicates that a great deal of learning is lost, and financial and human resources wasted. Collaboration between researchers and NGOs is critical for more rigorous evaluation, as is dissemination of results in the short term and more cross-country—and even cross-regional—collaborations among researchers in the long term.

Media

Throughout this book, we have discussed the use of media as a tool to strategically influence norms on a large scale. Media messaging must be gender transformative, targeted in its form and content to specific audiences, and connected to interventions to increase exposure to alternative ideas, to increase knowledge, and to influence behavior and practices. In order to fulfill all these criteria, as noted in chapter 4, media efforts need to engage also with behavioral interventions so that their impact on norms and awareness of violence can be sustained and can feed into behavior change efforts.

We have not touched as extensively on the communication sector, although many organizations have worked directly with media professionals to improve coverage of cases of violence against women and girls. One example is the White Ribbon Campaign in Pakistan (box 5.1), which collaborated with media professionals to develop a code of conduct and recognizes members of the media for exemplary efforts. Another example,

---

BOX 5.1 White Ribbon Campaign in Pakistan

The White Ribbon Campaign in Pakistan (WCRP) has been working with print and television journalists and other media personnel in its Nationwide Journalists Engagement Program. The objective of the program is to sensitize media professionals on violence against women. The various training and awareness-raising events with more than 200 members of the media in Pakistan's largest cities have resulted in developing a code of ethics for the media that includes guidelines for fair and balanced coverage of gender inequality and violence against women, for protecting the identities and personal information of survivors so that they are not put at risk of further harm, for using gender-sensitive language, and for developing policies against sexual harassment in the work place, among others. The campaign launched the WRCP Media Awards in 2013 to recognize efforts by Pakistani media to provide gender-balanced portrayals.

Source: White Ribbon Campaign in Pakistan, http://www.whiteribbon.org.pk.

also in Pakistan, is Uks, the first non-governmental organization in South Asia to compile and disseminate a *Gender Sensitive Code of Ethics for Print Media* (Uks Research Center and UNFPA 2010). Such approaches need to be tried in other South Asian countries to ascertain whether they can be replicated. Similarly, the use of TV is a powerful tool, as evidenced by evaluations of programs to address son preference. On the whole, the entertainment industry has immense power and potential to reach people and influence attitudes in South Asia, which strongly suggests the need also to assess which entertainment-based interventions are effective and how they work.

Recommendations for the Private Sector

The private sector needs to be more involved in efforts to address violence against women and girls. Companies need to be proactive in recruiting and hiring women, making their workforces more diverse, and encouraging talent. As illustrated by the experience of AASHA in Pakistan (see box 4.7), the private sector can play a key role in adopting anti-sexual harassment codes to make workplaces more secure.

The private sector can also be engaged in preventing child marriage and other forms of violence against women. For instance, it can support and contribute to school-to-work transition and life skills programs for adolescent girls and young women, employment programs for women, and help lines, shelters, and crisis centers that are being implemented by various donors and local organizations. We found few evaluated lessons on how to constructively engage the private sector, however. Perhaps investing in pilot programs that test and evaluate different approaches to private sector engagement would be a wise investment for donors, governments, and NGOs.

Concluding Remarks

Throughout this book, we have described how violence against women and girls is a serious gender, development, and human rights issue. The current heightened focus on this issue in South Asia is an opportunity for all actors to make concerted efforts to understand what works to prevent and respond to the various forms of violence that South Asian women and girls face throughout their lives. Now is the time to understand the link between risk factors and violence, to institutionalize promising approaches, and to improve data collection and evaluation.

Our recommendations point to the need to address the individual, household, institutional, and social norms and other macro-level risks by supporting parental and societal investment in girls, clarifying and enforcing laws to protect against all forms of violence, working more effectively with all members of households and communities, and engaging men and boys in efforts to change gender norms. Dedicated funding and political commitment at all levels is needed to scale up promising approaches. The recognition of women and girls as equal citizens, not victims, should be central in these efforts.

Note

1. For more information about the MSPVAW crisis centers and help line, see the MSPVAW website at http://www.mspvaw.org.bd.

References

Amnesty International. 1999. "Pakistan: Honour Killings of Girls and Women." http://www.amnesty.org/en/library/asset/ASA33/018/1999/en/9fe83c27-e0f1-11dd-be39-2d4003be4450/asa330181999en.pdf.

Chibber, K., and S. Krishnan. 2011. "Confronting Intimate Partner Violence: A Global Health Priority." *Mount Sinai Journal of Medicine* 78: 449–57.

Choudhury, N. 2007. "Constrained Spaces for Islamic Feminism: Women's Rights and the 2004 Constitution of Afghanistan." *Yale Journal of Law and Feminism* (19): 155–99.

Dutta, M., B. Zutshi, and A. Vajpeyi. 2010. "UNIFEM Regional Anti-Trafficking Programme in South Asia (2000–2009)." Evaluation report, UNIFEM, India.

Evans, C., and M. P. Bhattarai. 2000. *A Comparative Analysis of Anti-Trafficking Intervention Approaches in Nepal.* Kathmandu: Asia Foundation and Population Council.

Fikree, F. F., S. N. Jafarey, R. Korejo, A. Afshan, and J. M. Durocher. 2006. "Intimate Partner Violence Before and During Pregnancy: Experiences of Postpartum Women in Karachi, Pakistan." *Journal of Pakistan Medical Association* 56 (6): 252–57.

Foshee, V. A., K. E. Bauman, X. B. Arriaga, R. W. Helms, G. G. Koch, and G. F. Linder. 1998. "An Evaluation of Safe Dates, An Adolescent Dating Violence Prevention Program." *American Journal of Public Health* 88: 45–50.

Foshee, V. A., K. E. Bauman, W. F. Greene, G. G. Koch, G. F. Linder, and J. E. MacDougall. 2000. "The Safe Dates Program: 1-Year Follow-Up Results." *American Journal of Public Health* 90 (10): 1619–22.

Foshee, V. A., K. E. Bauman, S. T. Ennnett, G. F. Linder, T. Benefield, and C. Suchindran. 2004. "Assessing the Long-Term Effects of the Safe Dates Program and a Booster in Preventing and Reducing Adolescent Dating Violence Victimization and Perpetration." *American Journal of Public Health* 94: 619–24.

GAATW (Global Alliance Against Traffic in Women). 2007. *Collateral Damage: The Impact of Anti-Trafficking Measures on Human Rights around the World.* Bangkok: GAATW.

Heiberg, T., and E. G. Thukral, eds. 2013. *The South Asian Report: On the Child-Friendliness of Governments.* Terre des Hommes, Germany, Save the Children, HAQ: Centre for Child Rights, Plan International, and CRY: Child Rights and You.

The Hindu. 2013. "India Officially Undercounts all Crimes Including Rape." *The Hindu,* September 13.

Human Rights Watch. 2011. *Just Don't Call It a Militia: Impunity, Militias, and the Afghan Local Police.* Washington, DC: Human Rights Watch.

IIPS (International Institute for Population Sciences) and Population Council. 2009. "Violence within Marriage among Young People in Tamil Nadu." *Youth in India: Situation and Needs 2006–2007, Policy Brief No. 12.* Mumbai: IIPS.

International Press Agency. 2013. "Watershed Legislation Criminalizing Torture and Custodial Violence Enacted in Bangladesh." *Pressenza*, October 26, 2013. https://www.pressenza.com/2013/10/watershed-legislation-criminalising-torture-custodial-violence-enacted-bangladesh/.

Jejeebhoy, S. J., K. G. Santhya, and R. Acharya. 2010. *Health and Social Consequences of Marital Violence: A Synthesis of Evidence from India*. New Delhi: Population Council and UNFPA.

Jejeebhoy, S. J., K. G. Santhya, and S. Sabarwal. 2013. *Gender-Based Violence: A Qualitative Exploration of Norms, Experiences, and Positive Deviances*. New Delhi: Population Council.

Jewkes, R., M. Nduna, J. Levin, N. Jama, K. Dunkle, A. Puren, and N. Duvvury. 2008. "Impact of Stepping Stones on Incidence of HIV & HSV-2 and Sexual Behaviour in Rural South Africa: Cluster Randomised Controlled Trial." *British Medical Journal* 337: a506.

Jhamb, B. 2011. "The Missing Link in the Domestic Violence Act." *Economic and Political Weekly* 46 (33): 45–50.

Kapur, R. 2013. "Violence against Women in South Asia and the Limits of Law." Background paper for current report, World Bank, Washington, DC.

Kaul, K., and S. Shrivastava. 2013. "How Well Does Union Budget 2013–14 Address Gender-Based Challenges?" September, Center for Budget and Governance Accountability, New Delhi.

Kumar, S., L. Jeyaseelan, S. Suresh, and R. C. Ahuja. 2005. "Domestic Violence and Its Mental Health Correlates in Indian Women." *The British Journal of Psychiatry: The Journal of Mental Science* 187: 62–67.

Lanier, C. A., M. N. Elliott, D. Martin, and A. Kapadia. 1998. "Evaluation of an Intervention to Change Attitudes toward Date Rape." *College Teaching* 46 (2): 76–8.

Lari, M. Z. 2011. "'Honour Killings' in Pakistan and Compliance of Law." Aurat Publication and Information Service Foundation, Islamabad.

Lonsway, K. A., and C. Kothari. 2000. "First Year Campus Acquaintance Rape Education: Evaluating the Impact of a Mandatory Intervention." *Psychology of Women Quarterly* 24: 220–32.

Martin, S. L, A. O. Tsui, K. Maitra, and R. Marinshaw. 1999. "Domestic Violence in Northern India." *American Journal of Epidemiology* 150 (4): 417–26.

Martin, S. L., K. E. Moracco, J. Garro, A. O. Tsui, L. Kupper, J. L. Chase, and J. C. Campbell. 2002. "Domestic Violence across Generations: Findings from Northern India." *International Epidemiological Association* 31: 560–72.

McAllister, F., A. Burgess, J. Kato, and G. Barker. 2012. *Fatherhood: Parenting Programmes and Policy. A Critical Review of Best Practice*. London and Washington, DC: Fatherhood Institute /Promundo/MenCare.

McFarlane J. M., J. Y. Groff, J. A. O'Brien, and K. Watson. 2006. "Secondary Prevention of Intimate Partner Violence: A Randomized Controlled Trial." *Nursing Research* 55 (1): 52–61.

Miller E., M. R. Decker, H. L. McCauley, D. J. Tancredi, R. R. Levenson, J. Waldman, P. Schoenwald, and J. G. Silverman. 2011. "A Family Planning Clinic Partner Violence Intervention to Reduce Risk Associated with Reproductive Coercion." *Contraception* 83 (3): 274–80.

Naved, R. T., S. Azim, A. Bhuiya, and L. A. Persson. 2006. "Physical Violence by Husbands: Magnitude, Disclosure and Help-Seeking Behavior of Women in Bangladesh." *Social Science & Medicine* 62 (2006): 2917–29.

Potter, S. J., M. M. Moynihan, J. G. Stapleton, and V. L. Banyard. 2009. "Empowering Bystanders to Prevent Campus Violence against Women: A Preliminary Evaluation of a Poster Campaign." *Violence Against Women* 15 (1): 106–21.

Pulerwitz, J., G. Barker, M. Segundo, and M. Nascimento. 2006. "Promoting More Gender-Equitable Norms and Behaviors among Young Men as an HIV/AIDS Prevention Strategy." In *Horizons Final Report*. Washington, DC: Population Council.

Pulerwitz J., S. Martin, M. Mehta, T. Castillo, A. Kidanu, F. Verani, and S. Tewolde. 2010. *Promoting Gender Equity for HIV and Violence Prevention: Results from the Male Norms Initiative Evaluation in Ethiopia*. Washington, DC: PATH.

Puri, M., J. Tamang, and I. Shah. 2011. "Suffering in Silence: Consequences of Sexual Violence within Marriage among Young Women in Nepal." *BMC Public Health* 11: 29. doi:10.1186/1471-2458-11-29.

Santhya, K. G., N. Haberland, F. Ram, R. K. Sinha, and S. K. Mohanty. 2007. "Consent and Coercion: Examining Unwanted Sex among Married Young Women in India." *International Family Planning Perspectives* 33 (3): 124–32.

Stephenson, R., M. A. Koenig, and S. Ahmed. 2006. "Domestic Violence and Symptoms of Gynecologic Morbidity among Women in North India." *International Family Planning Perspectives* 32 (4): 201–8.

Stephenson, R., M. A. Koenig, R. Acharya, and T. K. Roy. 2008. "Domestic Violence, Contraceptive Use, and Unwanted Pregnancy in Rural India." *Studies in Family Planning* 39 (3): 177–86.

Uks Research Center and UNFPA. 2010. "Through the Gender Lens: Motivating Youth to Analyze and Develop Gender-Sensitive Media Content on Gender Based Violence." http://www.uksresearch.com/PublicationsPDFs/Through%20The%20Gender%20Lens.pdf.

UNODC (United Nations Office on Drugs and Crime). 2007. *Afghanistan: Female Prisoners and Their Social Reintegration*. Vienna: UNODC.

White Ribbon Campaign Pakistan, online resources retrieved from http://www.whiteribbon.org.pk.

Wijayatilake, K., and C. Guneratne. 2002. "State and Community Responses to Domestic Violence in Sri Lanka." Study Series No. 28, CENWOR, Colombo.

Data Sources Available and Used for Descriptive Analysis

Life stage	Type of violence	Data sources
Unmarried girl children and adolescents	Excess female child mortality	DHS
	Child abuse and maltreatment	GOI 2007; Central Bureau of Statistics 2012; CSO and UNICEF 2012
	Child sexual abuse	GOI 2007
	Nonmarital intimate partner violence: unmarried adolescents	—
	Child marriage	DHS
	Forced marriage	—
Married girls and adult women	Dowry violence	NCRB India
	Domestic intimate partner and nonpartner violence	DHS; Nijhowne and Oates, 2008; WHO et al. 2013
	Violence against never-married women	—
	Violence against elderly women	—
Violence that crosses life stages	Sexual harassment in public spaces	Mayhew et al. 2009
	Rape	—
	Trafficking	United Nations 2012
	Custodial violence	—
	Honor crimes	—

Note: — = Reliable data not available; DHS = Demographic and Health Surveys; GOI = Government of India; NCRB = National Crime Records Bureau; UNODC = United Nations Office of Drugs and Crime.

References

Central Bureau of Statistics. 2012. *Nepal Multiple Indicator Cluster Survey 2010, Mid- and Far Western Regions, Final Report.* Kathmandu: Central Bureau of Statistics and UNICEF Nepal.

CSO (Central Statistics Organisation) and UNICEF. 2012. *Afghanistan Multiple Indicator Cluster Survey 2010–2011: Final Report.* Kabul: CSO and UNICEF.

DHS (Demographic and Health Survey) for each country as noted: Bangladesh, 2011, 2007; Benin, 2006; Burkina Faso, 2010, 2003; Cameroon, 2004; Chad, 2004; Democratic Republic of Congo, 2007; Arab Republic of Egypt, 2005; Ethiopia, 2011; Ghana, 2008; Guinea, 2005; Haiti, 2005–06; India, 2005–06; Jordon, 2007; Kenya, 2008–09; Madagascar, 2008–09; Malawi, 2010, 2004; Maldives, 2009; Mali, 2006; Mauritania, 2001; Mexico, 1987; Nepal, 2011; Nicaragua, 2001; Niger, 2006; Pakistan 2012–13; Peru 2007–08; São Tomé and Príncipe, 2008–09; Sierra Leone, 2008; Sri Lanka, 1987; Sudan, 1989–90; Swaziland, 2006–07; Tajikistan, 2012; Uganda, 2011; Zambia, 2009; Zimbabwe, 2005–06.

GOI (Government of India). 2007. "Study on Child Abuse: INDIA 2007." Ministry of Women and Child Development, GOI, New Delhi.

Mayhew, S., M. Collumbien, A. Qureshi, L. Platt, N. Rafiq, A. Faisel, N. Lalji, and S. Hawkes. 2009. "Protecting the Unprotected: Mixed-Method Research on Drug Use, Sex Work, and Rights in Pakistan's Fight Against HIV/AIDS." *Sexually Transmitted Infections* 63 (1): S21–S27.

NCRB (National Crime Records Bureau). 2001–2012. Government of India.

Nijhowne, D., and L. Oates. 2008. *Living with Violence: A National Report on Domestic Abuse in Afghanistan.* Washington, DC: Global Rights: Partners for Justice.

United Nations. 2012. *Global Report on Trafficking in Persons 2012.* Vienna: United Nations Office on Drugs and Crime.

WHO, Department of Reproductive Health and Research, London School of Hygiene and Tropical Medicine, South African Medical Research Council. 2013. Global and Regional *Estimates of Violence against Women: Prevalence and Health Effects of Intimate Partner Violence and Non-Partner Sexual Violence.* Geneva: World Health Organization.

World Bank Projects Addressing Gender-Based Violence, Active in 2008 or Later

GBV as exclusive or primary focus

Project ID and title	Sector	Region	In analysis	In activities	In monitoring and evaluation	In impact evaluation	Financing	Amount (US$)	Approval CY
Breaking the cycle of violence, Honduras	SD	LAC	Y	Y	Y		IF	10,000	2012
LAC Hackathon	PSG	LAC	Y	Y	NA		IF	200,000	2012
P110728 Protection from GBV in Côte d'Ivoire	SD	AFR	Y	Y	Y	Y	ERL	732,759	2008
P115562 Learning for Equality, Access, and Peace Program (LOGiCA)	SD	AFR	Y	Y	Y	Y	GP	431,000	2009
P117558 Addressing GBV in South Kivu	SD	AFR	Y	Y	Y		SPF	1,984,787	2010
P127249 Bangladesh: Gender, Social Protection and Human Rights	SP	SAR	Y	Y	NA		NTF	460,869	2011
P128403 Women and Girls in Haiti's Reconstruction: Addressing and Preventing GBV	PREM	LAC	Y	Y	Y		RSR	584,828	2011
P129617 Procuradoria Especial da Mulher, Brazil	GED	LAC	Y	Y	N		IDF	300,000	2012
P130819 Safer Municipalities	SD	LAC	Y	Y	Y		SIL	17,000,000	2012
P131462 PNG Women in Mining and Petroleum	Energy	EAP	Y	Y	Y		JSDF	180,000	2012
P132325 Brazil Social Inclusion and Gender Equity	PREM	LAC	Y	Y	N		NLTA	50,000	2012
P143772 Improving Services for Victims of Gender-Based and Domestic Violence Project (Kiribati)	GED	EAP	Y	Y	Y		IDF	400,000	2013
P143773 Improving Services for Victims of Gender-Based and Domestic Violence Project (Solomon Islands)	GED	EAP	Y	Y	Y		IDF	130,000	2013
P145412 Gender-Based Violence Conference in South Asia and Nepal Hackathon	SD	SAR	Y	Y	NA		IF	225,000	2013
Total:								**22,689,243**	

GBV component in larger projects

Project ID and title	Sector	Region	In analysis	In activities	In monitoring and evaluation	In impact evaluation	Financing	Amount (US$)	Approval CY
P003248 Zambia National Response to HIV/AIDS (ZANARA)	HD	AFR	Y	Y	N		SIL		2002
P051306 Colombia Peace and Development	SD	LAC	N	Y	N		APL		2004
P073438 Justice Services Improvement Project, Peru	PSG	LAC	Y	Y	N		TAL		2004
P077513 Republic of Congo HIV/AIDs and Health	HD	AFR	N	Y	Y		APL		2004
P081516 HN Judicial Branch Modernization	PSG	LAC	Y	Y	Y		TAL		2005
P083904 Justice Services Strengthening Colombia	PSG	LAC	Y	N	N		APL		2009
P088319 Barrio Ciudad, Honduras	Urban	LAC	Y	Y	N	Y	SIL		2005
P088751 Congo, Dem. Rep. Health Sector Rehab Support	HD	AFR	Y	Y	N		SIL		2005
P091299 Inner City Basic Services, Jamaica	Urban	LAC	Y	N	N		SIL		2006
P091299 Jamaica Violence Observatory (Cofinancing for Jamaican Inner City Basic Services)	Urban	LAC	Y	Y	NA		JSDF		2009
P091472 Strengthening Uruguay's Justice Institutions for Equitable Development	PSG	LAC	Y	Y	N		IDF		2004
P101504 Bolsa Familia Brazil	SP	LAC	N	N	N	Y	APL		2010
P102396 PNG Second Mining Sector Institutional Strengthening TAL	Energy	EAP	Y	Y	N		TAL		2008
P110571 AGI Liberia	GED	AFR	Y	Y	Y	Y	SIL		2008

table continues next page

Project ID and title	Sector	Region	In analysis	In activities	In monitoring and evaluation	In impact evaluation	Financing	Amount (US$)	Approval CY
P111250 Philippines—Country Assessment on Gender and Peacebuilding	SD	EAP	Y	Y	NA		NLTA		2008
P116360 AGI Rwanda	SD	AFR	N	Y	N		TAL		2011
P116636 AGI South Sudan	GED	AFR	Y	Y	N	Y	TAL		2009
P117214 Nepal: Adolescent Girls Employment Initiative (AGEI)	GED	SAR	N	N	N	Y	SIL		2010
P123483 Haiti AGI	GED	LAC	Y	Y	N		NLTA		2012
P124157 HN Employment Generation in Poor Urban Neighborhoods	Urban	LAC	Y	Y	NA		JSDF		2010
P124761 Social Promotion and Protection Project—Lebanon	SP	MNA	N	Y	N		SIL		2013
P125285 AF Burkina Faso, Health Sector/AIDS Project	HD	AFR	Y	Y	N		SIML		2011
P126088 Congo, Dem. Rep. AF Primary Health Care	HD	AFR	Y	Y	N		SIL		2012
P126158 AF Nutrition and Social Protection—Honduras	SP	LAC	N	Y	NA		SIL		2011

Source: Willman, A. M., and C. Corman. 2013. "Gender-based Violence: What Is the World Bank Doing and What Have We Learned?" Strategic Review, annex 1, World Bank Social Development Department, Washington, DC.

Note: AF = Additional Financing; AFR = Africa; AGI= Adolescent Girls Initiative; CY = calendar year; EAP = East Asia and Pacific; GBV = gender-based violence; HN = Honduras; LAC = Latin America and the Caribbean; MNA = Middle East and North Africa; N = no; NA = not available; PNG = Papua New Guinea; SAR = South Asia Region; Y = yes.

Sector: GED = Gender and Development; HD = Human Development; PREM = Poverty Reduction and Economic Management; PSG = Public Sector Governance; SD = Social Development; SP = Social Protection.

Financing: APL = Adaptable Program Loan; ERL = Emergency Recovery Loan; GP = Global Programs and Partnerships; IF = Institutional Financing; IDF = Institutional Development Fund; JSDF = Japan Social Development Fund; NTF = Nordic Trust Fund; NLTA = Non-lending Technical Assistance; RSR = Rapid Social Response; SIL = Specific Investment Loan; SIML = Sector Investment and Maintenance Loan; SPF = State and Peace-Building Fund; TAL = Technical Assistance Loan.

Evaluated Interventions to Address Excess Female Child Mortality[1]

Program and organization. Sources.	Country	Program description	Focus areas	Evaluation description and findings
Meena Communication Initiative 1991–2003 UNICEF Chesterton 2004	Bangladesh, India, Nepal, Pakistan	A campaign that aimed to influence attitudes toward the girl child and to address discrimination against girls. The campaign was based on a multimedia, education-entertainment approach, with stories of a 9-year-old girl named Meena and her family and community. Messages covered gender equity, value of the girl child, health, education, and freedom from abuse.	A, B	**Methodology:** Quantitative and qualitative data collection, desk reviews, key informant interviews. **Findings:** The TV character Meena contributed to shifts in understanding of gender relations and aspirations among young girls and boys. Behaviors did not change, either because parents could not relate messages to their lives, or girls did not feel empowered to act on discrimination.
Apni Beti, Apna Dhan (ABAD) 1994–98 Haryana State Government Holla, Jensen, and Oster 2007; Sinha and Yoong 2009	India	The program offered an immediate cash grant upon birth of a daughter and a long-term savings bond redeemable upon the girl's 18th birthday if she was still unmarried. Bond amounts increased by level of daughters' schooling. The scheme was expanded in 1995 offering a higher amount for girls willing to delay redeeming their maturities and offering credit loans for entrepreneurial activities.	A, B	**Methodology:** No baseline. Evaluations used National Family Health Survey rounds to approximate baselines and participation criteria to create treatment and control groups. **Findings:** Sinha and Yoong (2009) found that the scheme was successful in incentivizing poor households to bear daughters, although there was no change in son preference. Holla, Jensen, and Oster (2007) also found evidence of less masculine sex ratios at birth, but no improvement in sex ratios in early childhood.
ABAD and Ladli 1994–present Haryana State Government Krishnan et al. 2014	India	This is an evaluation of the ABAD program, which led to the Ladli program. The Ladli scheme restricted benefits to the second daughter, removed targeting by poverty, and increased the monetary amount of financial incentives offered.	A, B	**Methodology:** Demographic surveillance database in 28 villages of 2 districts that had been maintained since 1992; key informant interviews. **Findings:** No quantitative evidence of significant improvements was found in either sex ratios or immunization differentials, although interviewed officials claimed that the programs were successful.
Financial incentive programs Multiple years National and state governments Sekhar 2010	India	This study was a program assessment of the implementation and effectiveness of multiple conditional cash transfers and other financial incentive programs for the girl child's survival and health.	A, B	**Methodology:** Desk reviews and key informant interviews. **Findings:** The schemes have unnecessarily complex eligibility criteria, and registration requirements that inhibit participation. Schemes are mostly poorly implemented with limited coordination between line ministries involved and limited understanding of the guidelines for implementation even among implementers and other administrative officials.

Focus area codes: A = Efforts to change the relative value of girls and boys; B = Financial incentives to parents to bear and invest in girls; C = Efforts to enforce laws and policies.

Program and organization. Sources.	Country	Program description	Focus areas	Evaluation description and findings
Basket of schemes to address female infanticide 1992–ongoing Government of Tamil Nadu Bedi and Srinivasan 2012; Srinivasan and Bedi 2009, 2010.	India	From 1992 to present, the state of Tamil Nadu created a number of schemes and policies to tackle female infanticide, which have been evaluated together as a packet of interventions. These are (a) the Cradle Baby Scheme, (b) law enforcement, (c) cash transfer scheme, (d) community awareness, (e) birth registration, and (f) a death audit to investigate infant deaths.	A, B, C	**Methodology:** No baseline data. Authors used discrete policy changes before and after 2001 as a natural experiment scenario, variations in policy intensity across districts, and census and sample data to create treatment and control villages. **Findings:** Comparisons between 1996–99 and 2003 show a drop of 46% in the female-to-male ratio of infant mortality rates (estimate of female infanticide). Econometric analysis suggests that post-birth deficit decline may be attributed to the basket of interventions, but not so for the prebirth deficit decline.
Let A Girl Be Born 2010–ongoing Plan International Dialectics 2014	India	The campaign aimed to ensure the right of a girl to be born, named, and registered; to change the value of girls; to decrease sex-selective abortion and female infanticide; and to improve implementation of the PCPNDT Act. Activities included community-based advocacy groups, support to newly married couples against pressure to bear sons, and media and other means to raise awareness.	A, C	**Methodology:** A qualitative, participatory assessment of intervention and control sites and a quantitative survey with government and NGO individuals. No baseline. **Findings:** Gender-based discrimination, dowry and domestic violence, and sex-selective abortion were the main concerns cited by respondents. The three most recognized post-campaign changes were increased spaces for women's concerns, recognition of the need for gender equality, and attention to girls' and women's education and health needs. Key problems included maintaining community interest, engaging men and boys, and engaging couples.
Girl Child Shield Project 1997–2001 Girl Guides Association Pakistan, UNICEF Croll 2001	Pakistan	The program operated in 800 schools in rural and urban areas across the country, working with girls ages 11–16. Girl Guides earned a series of six badges that focused on rights of the girl child, health, education, and survival.	A	**Methodology:** Desk reviews, key informant interviews, direct observation. **Findings:** Participating girls showed high awareness of discriminatory attitudes and behavior against girls in the home and tried to negotiate some rights with their parents. Some change in parental and community perceptions of girls was observed.

Note: NGO = nongovernmental organization; PCPNDT = Pre-Conception and Pre-Natal Diagnostic Techniques.

Focus area codes: A = Efforts to change the relative value of girls and boys; B = Financial incentives to parents to bear and invest in girls; C = Efforts to enforce laws and policies.

Note

1. Criteria used in this list are from Guo, Das Gupta, and Li 2013.

References

Bedi, A. S., and S. Srinivasan. 2012. "Bare Branches and Drifting Kites: Tackling Female Infanticide and Foeticide in Tamil Nadu, India." In *Development, Freedom and Welfare: Essays Presented to Amartya Sen by Young Scholars*, edited by A. Sharma and A. Prakash. New Delhi: Oxford University Press.

Chesterton, Paul. 2004. *Evaluation of the Meena Communication Initiative*. Kathmandu: UNICEF Regional Office for South Asia.

Croll, E. 2001. "The Girl Child Shield Project Pakistan: Assessment Report." School of Oriental and African Studies, University of London, London.

Dialectics. 2014. "Evaluation of Let Girls Be Born Project of Plan India." Draft, Plan India internal document, received through personal communication with Plan India program staff.

Guo, Z., M. Das Gupta, and S. Li. 2013. "Missing Girls in China and India: Trends and Policy Impacts." Maryland Population Research Center Working Paper PWP-MPRC-2013-001, University of Maryland, College Park, MD.

Holla, A., R. Jensen, and E. Oster. 2007. "Daughters as Wealth? The Effects of Cash Incentives on Sex Ratios." Working Paper, Department of Economics, Brown University, Providence, RI.

Krishnan, A., R. Amarchand, P. Byass, C. Pandav, and N. Ng. 2014. "'No One Says 'No' to Money'—A Mixed Methods Approach for Evaluating Conditional Cash Transfer Schemes to Improve Girl Children's Status in Haryana, India." *International Journal for Equity in Health* 13:11. doi:10.1186/1475-9276-13-11.

Sekhar, T. V. 2010. "Special Financial Incentive Schemes for the Girl Child in India: A Review of Select Schemes." Background paper for the Planning Commission, Government of India, in collaboration with the United Nations Population Fund, New Delhi.

Sinha, N., and J. Yoong. 2009. "Long-Term Financial Incentives and Investment in Daughters: Evidence from Conditional Cash Transfers in North India." World Bank Policy Research Working Paper 4860, World Bank, Washington, DC.

Srinivasan, S., and A. Bedi. 2009. "Girl Child Protection Scheme in Tamil Nadu: An Appraisal." *Economic and Political Weekly*, November 28.

———. 2010. "Daughter Elimination: Cradle Baby Scheme in Tamil Nadu." *Economic and Political Weekly*, June 5.

Evaluated Interventions to Address Abuse against Girl Children

Program and organization. Sources.	Country	Program description	Focus areas	Evaluation description and findings
Evaluated interventions that explicitly address and separately evaluate the effect of intervention on girl children.				
ARISE (Appropriate Resources for Improving Street Children's Environment) 2001 UNDP and Government of Bangladesh Sinha and Tapan 2001	Bangladesh	ARISE built a referral network between street children and various nongovernmental organizations; organized training of trainers for counseling; and offered educational opportunities, shelters, and vocational and life skills training. Focused on the most vulnerable street children, including girls.	B, C, D	**Methodology:** Secondary reports and data; focus group discussions with the target population. **Findings:** Drop-in centers and shelter homes were identified as crucial but needed to be made more child friendly; street children were not involved in project planning at all; project did not address root causes of problems faced by street children; training and materials were not tailored to individual children's needs; and training was not timely.
Safer Environment for Girls 2001–11 Save the Children Fund and TOLI (Team Organizing Local Institute) Gautam 2012	Nepal	This project focused on child protection with special emphasis on protection from sexual abuse and violence, especially for girl children. Key activities included (a) child networks and protection committees in schools and communities and (b) school infrastructure maintenance such as drinking water and building toilets for girls.	A, C	**Methodology:** A qualitative study using participatory techniques. **Findings:** The evaluation reported an increase in children's awareness of good touch and bad touch. There were anecdotal reports of girls feeling empowered and confident through child clubs. Collaboration with various government and nongovernmental agencies improved. However, participants expressed the need to allocate more money for child protection.
Girl Power Program (GPP) 2011–15 Girl Power Alliance Transition International 2014a, 2014b, 2014c	Bangladesh, Nepal, and Pakistan	GPP is a multisectoral program to build awareness and capacity to empower girl children and adolescents and to address violence against them. GPP includes a range of prevention and response activities ranging from girls' schooling and child clubs to helplines and legal aid.	A, B, C	**Methodology:** Midterm quantitative and qualitative outcome evaluation. **Findings:** No observed decline in prevalence of violence against girls, although reports note that it may be too early to expect such change. In all countries, girls and adolescents are more empowered to say "no," and young survivors are more likely to seek help via help lines and legal aid. There is a change in attitudes toward girls' education, although this cannot be attributed solely to this program. Religious and other leaders support the intervention, and there is a strong sense of ownership in participating communities. Partner organization capacity has been improved, helping sustainability. Boys and men are not adequately engaged.

Focus area codes: A = Using a child-centered approach; B = Training, advocacy, and media; C = Engaging schools and communities in child protection; D = Addressing abuse among street children.

Evaluated interventions for prevention and response to child abuse whose evaluations do not explicitly consider effect on girls' exposure to violence.

India	Khanna, R. 2008. *Assessing the Conditions and Quality of Counseling Related to Sexuality and Sexual Health. A Review of the TARSHI Helpline, 1996–2009.* New Delhi: WHO, KIT. http://www.kit.nl/kit/Publication?item=2492.
India	Chuppi Todo Campaign. Ongoing. Sanjay Singh (documentary filmmaker) and Plan India. http://thealternative.in/education/chuppi-todo-go-tell-mom/.
India	Deloitte. 2011. *Evaluation of Gender Sensitization and People Friendly Police Initiative, Karnataka. Karnataka State Police and UNICEF.* http://www.unicef.org/evaldatabase/files/2010-15_Evaluation_of_GSPP_Karnataka_Final_Report_-June_2011.pdf.
Maldives	UNICEF. 2009. "Children and the 2004 Indian Ocean Tsunami: Evaluation of UNICEF's Response in the Maldives, 2005–2008." Country Synthesis Report, UNICEF, New York. http://www.unicef.org/evaldatabase/files/Maldives_Final_for_Print_20_Jan.pdf.
Nepal	Shrestha, B. 2008. "A Mapping of SZoP Programs in Nepal." Partnership Nepal and Save the Children Fund, for Children as Zones of Peace (CZoP) Coalition, Nepal. http://www.protectingeducation.org/sites/default/files/documents/a_mapping_of_szop_programs_in_nepal.pdf. Naylor, R., and B. Koirala. 2010. "Rewrite the Future Global Evaluation, Nepal Country Report." Save the Children Norway, Oslo. http://www.norad.no/en/tools-and-publications/publications/publication?key=381051.
Pakistan	Rozan–Aangan program. 2003. "The Roshan School Project: Teacher Training on Life Skills." Rozan, Islamabad. http://www.rozan.org/uploads/22The_Roshan_School_Project.pdf.
Pakistan	Naz, S. 2012. "External Evaluation of Aangan's Interventions of Rehmatabad Community, Aangan, Rozan, 2006–11." Evaluation funded by the Finland Embassy.
Pakistan	H and H Consulting. 2012. "Evaluation of Social Reintegration of Street Children Project, 2005–11." UNICEF, Azad Foundation in Karachi and Mehran Welfare Trust in Larkana. http://www.unicef.org/evaldatabase/files/CP_Street_Children_Evaluation_Report_Final.pdf.
Pakistan	UNICEF. 2013. "2013 Pakistan: Evaluation of UNICEF Programmes to Protect Children in Emergencies: Pakistan Country Case Study." UNICEF, New York. http://www.unicef.org/evaldatabase/ ndex_71771.html.
Sri Lanka	Samarajeeva, H. 2010. "2010 Sri Lanka: Qualitative Evaluation of Child Friendly Schools (CFS) in Badulla and Batticaloa." Evaluation report, AusAid, Canberra. http://www.unicef.org/evaldatabase/index_59807.html.
Bangladesh, Nepal, Pakistan, Sri Lanka	O'Kane, C., and K. Moore. 2012. "Lessons for Protection: A Comparative Analysis of Community-Based Child Protection Mechanisms Supported by Plan in Asia." Summary Report, Plan Asia, Bangkok. http://childprotectionforum.org/wp/wp-content/uploads/downloads/2013/03/Plan-ARO-CBCPM-Comparative-Analysis-Summary-Report.pdf.
Global	Plan. 2012. "The Campaign to Stop Violence in Schools: Third Progress Report." Report, Learn without Fear campaign, Plan Limited, Woking, UK. http://plan-international.org/learnwithoutfear/files/third-progress-report.
Global	UNICEF. 2012. *Protecting Children From Violence: A Synthesis of Evaluation Findings.* New York: UNICEF. http://www.unicef.org/evaldatabase/files/Protecting_Children_from_Violence_A_synthesis_of_Evaluation_Findings_2012.pdf.

References

Gautam, I. P. 2012. "Final Evaluation of Safer Environment for Girls (TOLI) in Kaski and Tanahun District." Save the Children, Nepal Country Office, Kathmandu.

Sinha, I. and S. M. Tapan. 2001. "The Mid-Term Evaluation of Appropriate Resources for Improving Street Children's Environment (ARISE) Project." Department of Social Services, Ministry of Social Welfare, Government of Bangladesh: Dhaka.

Transition International. 2014a. *Girl Power Programme Mid-Term Evaluation. Country Report-Bangladesh*. Girl Power Alliance: The Netherlands.

———. 2014b. *Girl Power Programme Mid-Term Evaluation. Country Report-Nepal*. Girl Power Alliance: The Netherlands.

———. 2014c. *Girl Power Programme Mid-Term Evaluation. Country Report-Pakistan*. Girl Power Alliance: The Netherlands.

Evaluated Interventions to Prevent Child Marriage[1]

Program and organization. Sources.	Country	Program description	Focus areas	Evaluation description and findings
Community-based rural livelihoods program 2003–06 Oxfam–Great Britain Gandhi and Krijnen 2006	Afghanistan	A broad community-based program that included challenging gender stereotypes by training women to be community health workers, community veterinarians, and traditional birth attendants. Male and female *shuras* (councils) were established as spaces in which to discuss and raise awareness about gender issues, girls' education, and early marriage.	B, C, D	**Methodology:** Post-intervention assessment based on project records, field visits, interviews with staff, and discussions with project participants. **Findings:** Male and female *shura* participants were more likely to understand the negative consequences of early marriage and were able to link early marriage with pregnancy complications. Women reported stopping some early marriages in their villages.
Gender Quality Action Learning Program (GQAL) 2005–06 BRAC Alim 2007	Bangladesh	This rural women's empowerment project addressed villagers' knowledge, perceptions, and attitudes toward men and women, violence against women, and child marriage related issues. Activities included courtyard meetings, videos on gender equality, and street theater.	B	**Methodology:** Baseline–endline surveys and in-depth interviews. **Findings:** Some limited change seen in knowledge and attitudes toward child marriage; author concludes that such ingrained attitudes take time to change.
Kishori Abhijan 2001–03 Government of Bangladesh, Population Council, and partners Amin and Suran 2005; Amin 2011	Bangladesh	Three-arm intervention that comprised (a) an Adolescent Peer Organized Network (APON), which provided information to girls about health, legal rights, early marriage, and dowry, and created a library and space for games; (b) microcredit to qualified members of APON; and (c) education and awareness programs with microcredit. The intervention as a whole aimed to raise median age at marriage by at least 2 years. Activities included various life skills and livelihoods training.	A, C, D	**Methodology:** Quasi-experimental analysis combined with qualitative data. Used propensity score matching to address selectivity of program participants. **Findings:** No significant increase in age at marriage when comparing matched participants and nonparticipants. However, participants who did not have a nonparticipant match showed significant delay in marriage, possibly because they were more likely to be poorer, younger, and more motivated. An important side effect was that delaying marriage contributed to higher dowry.

Focus area codes: A = Empowering girls with information, skills, and support networks; B = Educating and mobilizing parents and community members; C = Enhancing accessibility and quality of formal schooling for girls; D = Offering economic support and incentives for girls and families; E = Fostering and enabling legal and policy frameworks.

Program and organization. Sources.	Country	Program description	Focus areas	Evaluation description and findings
Adolescent Development Program (ADP) 1993–ongoing BRAC Kabir, Afroze, and Aldeen 2007	Bangladesh	The program aimed to empower girls to participate in key life decisions including marriage, and to create an enabling environment for adolescent development at home and in the community. Established reading centers as safe spaces, supplemented by APON to provide life skills training.	A, B	**Methodology:** Quantitative and qualitative, post-intervention follow-up. There was no baseline, so survey data was used to establish a pseudo-control group. **Findings:** Significantly higher knowledge of negative consequences of early marriage and of legal age at marriage among APON girls compared to control site.
Employment and Livelihood for Adolescents (ELA) Centers 2005–ongoing BRAC Shahnaz and Karim 2008	Bangladesh	This program combined preexisting adolescent centers under BRAC's Adolescent Development Program with girls' groups called Employment and Livelihood for Adolescents (ELA). The combined intervention was called "ELA centers" and provided a combination of life skills, safe spaces, financial literacy, and access to income through microcredit.	A, B, C, D	**Methodology:** Quantitative and qualitative comparisons of outcomes between different intervention and control groups. **Findings:** Participants were more likely to stay in school, take part in income generating activities, and have better communication with parents about life choices. ELA centers have been replicated in six countries in Asia, Africa, and Central America.
Kishori Konthaa 2006–10 Save the Children USA, Bangladesh Development Society (BDS), JPAL Poverty Lab MIT Scales et al. 2013	Bangladesh	Girls in 307 villages were randomized into one of four intervention arms. In the 'basic package', peer educators led interactive information-giving, skill-building, and discussion sessions on life skills, reproductive health and nutrition, effects of early marriage, child rights, and violence against women. The centers also provided a space for socializing and play, with dancing and singing and other recreation for participating girls. The 'livelihoods package' added livelihoods training. The 'full package' further added a direct financial incentive to delay marriage till age 18 that was higher than anticipated dowry at that age. The final arm, the 'delayed marriage package', provided only the financial incentive.	A, D	**Methodology:** Randomized-control design with four intervention packages and a comparison group. **Findings:** Full evaluation is forthcoming.

table continues next page

Focus area codes: A = Empowering girls with information, skills, and support networks; B = Educating and mobilizing parents and community members; C = Enhancing accessibility and quality of formal schooling for girls; D = Offering economic support and incentives for girls and families; E = Fostering and enabling legal and policy frameworks.

Program and organization. Sources.	Country	Program description	Focus areas	Evaluation description and findings
Asia Child Marriage Initiative Ongoing Plan International Plan and ICRW 2013	Bangladesh	Multipronged program with awareness-raising activities, life skills training for adolescents, promotion of peer leaders, and advocacy efforts. Program aims to increase the mean age of girls at marriage from age 15 to 18 by 2015 and to strengthen the online birth registration system and enforcement of the Child Marriage Restraint Act (1929).	A, B, E	**Methodology:** Qualitative evaluation with key informant interviews. **Findings:** Child marriage awareness was high but the practice continued to be firmly entrenched and few marriages were prevented. However, efforts did identify "positive deviant" role models who delayed marriage, and Plan's model provided opportunities for girls to explore possibilities other than early marriage.
Innovation through Sport: Promoting Leaders, Empowering Youth (ITSPLEY) 2009–11 CARE USA Kendall and Miske 2012	Bangladesh	Used sports to empower girls and instill leadership qualities. Boys and girls were also engaged in life skills and civic action on a range of topics, including violence against women, early marriage, and harassment of girls. Included 9,000 girls and about 8,000 boys.	A	**Methodology:** Post-study, quantitative, and qualitative evaluation. **Findings:** Participating girls had high levels of self-confidence. Data were found to be of mixed quality, but suggested that sports are a good medium to involve girls and boys in addressing gender concerns, including early marriage, although it was more challenging to engage men and boys.
Raising the Age of Marriage for Young Girls 2003–06 Pathfinder and Swarnirvar Burket et al. 2006	Bangladesh	Provided financial incentives for secondary schools in the 5 poorest upazilas—or subdistricts—of Bangladesh. Discussed the negative consequences of child marriage in stakeholder and community meetings. Provided training and jobs for secondary school graduates along with scholarships.	A, B, C, D	**Methodology:** Post-intervention quantitative and qualitative interviews. **Findings:** Increase in girls' secondary school enrollment in project areas by 16%; also increase in primary school enrollment. Increase in community awareness and involvement (including involvement of religious leaders) in preventing early marriage. Participating girls wanted to delay marriage. However, the extent to which changes were attributable to project was unclear.

Focus area codes: A = Empowering girls with information, skills, and support networks; B = Educating and mobilizing parents and community members; C = Enhancing accessibility and quality of formal schooling for girls; D = Offering economic support and incentives for girls and families; E = Fostering and enabling legal and policy frameworks.

Program and organization. Sources.	Country	Program description	Focus areas	Evaluation description and findings
Female Secondary School Stipend Program (Two phases) 1993/4–2006 World Bank, Government of Bangladesh, and partners Amin et al. 1998; World Bank 2008; Schurmann 2009	Bangladesh	Paid tuition fees and provided monthly stipends for unmarried rural girls up to class 10 who attended recognized institutions, remained unmarried, maintained at least 75% attendance, and secured at least 45% marks in the annual examinations (a pass requires 35%). In 2002, extended to high school. Stipend was not targeted by poverty or other disadvantage-based criteria. Aimed to delay marriage and childbearing by increasing school enrollment and retention.	C, D	**Methodology:** Outcome evaluation with qualitative data in second phase. **Findings:** Phase I analysis showed a strong shift in child marriage, with the proportion of girls married between ages 13–15 declining from 29% to 14%; for ages 16–18, from 79% to 64%. Qualitative data suggested the stipend did enter into parental calculations of marriage. Huge increases in girls' secondary schooling, but poorest may not have benefited. Hard to attribute changes to program as there were many other efforts simultaneously to increase secondary schooling and delay marriage.
Shouhardo: Exploring and addressing community norms 2004–10 CARE Tango International Inc. 2009	Bangladesh	Large multisectoral project based on EKATA (Empowerment, Knowledge, and Transformative Action) groups, each with 20 women and 10 adolescent girls. Groups engaged the community to address violence against women, child marriage, dowry, and other social issues, and provided adolescent girls with life skills and reproductive health education.	A, B	**Methodology:** Quantitative: 2 baselines, 6 monitoring surveys, 2 endlines. In-depth interviews and focus group discussions. **Findings:** Adolescents reported increased awareness of consequences of early marriage. Women appreciated the needs and vulnerabilities of girls and committed to protecting them from violence; girls have positive adult role models. However, girls still need tools to act on their increased self-reliance.
KAISHAR adolescent program 2003–08 Save the Children Fund (SCF) SCF 2009a, 2009b, 2009c, 2009d	Bangladesh	Youth-friendly reproductive health services with community education, workshops on adolescent development for parents and other adults, and advocacy and media. Reached more than 6,000 girls in more than 13 unions of the country. Trained 1,500 adolescent facilitators and transferred program implementation to communities.	A, B, E	**Methodology:** Baseline–endline comparisons of surveys. Qualitative interviews with community. **Findings:** Showed a 0.6% increase in delayed marriage. Qualitative interviews showed changes in perceptions of girls, increased reproductive health knowledge and confidence among the girls, and greater discussion of taboo subject of adolescent sexuality.

table continues next page

Focus area codes: A = Empowering girls with information, skills, and support networks; B = Educating and mobilizing parents and community members; C = Enhancing accessibility and quality of formal schooling for girls; D = Offering economic support and incentives for girls and families; E = Fostering and enabling legal and policy frameworks.

Program and organization. Sources.	Country	Program description	Focus areas	Evaluation description and findings
Universalizing birth registration 1996–2009 UNICEF, Plan International, Government of Bangladesh Muzzi 2009	Bangladesh	Supported Government of Bangladesh in enacting the Birth and Death Registration Act of 2004 and a Universal Birth Registration Strategy. Helped set up an electronic birth registration system and tied it to several other government services. Special initiatives to reach vulnerable groups and raise awareness.	E	**Methodology:** Impact evaluation by comparing birth registration in UNICEF national surveys (MICS) in 2006 and 2009. **Findings:** Increase in birth registration nationally from 9.8% in 2006 to 53.0% in 2009.
Deepshikha: part of Adolescent Girls and Gender Empowerment (AGG) program 2008–ongoing UNICEF, Government of Maharashtra, and partners Patil et al. 2008	India	Potential group leaders or *prerikas* are identified by village committees and trained on child rights, health, and gender issues. They form a *deepshikha* group, which, after 40 meetings, can form a self-help group with a revolving loan fund for members. There are currently more than 2,400 deepshikhas in Maharashtra state, reaching more than 50,000 adolescent girls.	A, B, D	**Methodology:** Qualitative assessment based on primary and secondary data. **Findings:** Parents allow participation but are not involved or aware of program benefits or issues raised, thus girls attend sporadically. This is likely to affect program impact on issues such as child marriage. However, participating girls are enthusiastic and actively involved, including in promoting later marriage.
Maharashtra Life Skills Program 1998–99 ICRW, Institute for Health Management-Pachod (IHMP), Rockefeller Foundation Pande et al. 2006	India	Program objectives were to: (a) improve the social and health status of adolescent girls, (b) promote self-esteem, and (c) raise the age at marriage. Unmarried adolescent girls ages 12–18 were enrolled in an intensive life skills course taught by trained village women; the course met for an hour each weekday for one year. IHMP held monthly meetings for parents.	A, B	**Methodology:** Quasi-experimental evaluation combined with annual data on age at marriage to examine trends over time. **Findings:** Decrease in the proportion of married girls (ages 11–17) in the treatment area, from 80.7% to 61.8% from 1997 to 2001. No change occurred in the control area. Similarly, the median age at marriage of young girls in the program area increased from age 16 in 1997–2000 to age 17 in 2001 and remained unchanged in the control area. Girls who fully attended the life skills course were 4 times less likely to marry young (before age 18) than those in the control villages.

Focus area codes: A = Empowering girls with information, skills, and support networks; B = Educating and mobilizing parents and community members; C = Enhancing accessibility and quality of formal schooling for girls; D = Offering economic support and incentives for girls and families; E = Fostering and enabling legal and policy frameworks.

Program and organization. Sources.	Country	Program description	Focus areas	Evaluation description and findings
Development Initiative for Supporting Healthy Adolescence (DISHA) 2005–07 ICRW, Packard Foundation, and partners Kanesathasan et al. 2008	India	Program aimed to enhance youth skills and capacity, provide an enabling environment for youth, and make sexual and reproductive health services more youth friendly. The program also specifically sought to delay marriage and childbearing. The program supported the creation of youth groups, training of volunteer peer educators, and livelihoods training. Adult groups for men and women were also organized by the project.	A, B, D	**Methodology:** Quasi-experimental evaluation using quantitative and qualitative data. Tested extent of change attributable to program by analyzing matched pairs of participants and nonparticipants. **Findings:** Participating youth were 14% more likely to know the legal age at marriage for girls than nonparticipants. Participating adults were 7% more likely to support delaying marriage than nonparticipating adults. Average age at marriage increased by nearly two years between baseline and endline. Difficult to evaluate full effect on age at marriage because at the end of the program, all participating girls were not married. Unmarried girls were significantly more likely at endline to report being able to talk to parents about marriage.
Better Life Options Program (BLP) 1996–99 CEDPA CEDPA 2001	India	Program aimed to improve the economic and social empowerment of adolescent girls. The program included a combination of life skills development, with literacy and vocational training; support to enter and stay in formal school; family life education; and leadership training.	A, C	**Methodology:** Post-intervention program-control assessment. Analyses controlled for girls' education and parents' education and occupation. **Findings:** A significantly higher percentage of BLP alumnae married after the legal age of marriage (37%) compared to the control group (26%) and had a say in the selection of their husbands.
Asia Child Marriage Initiative Ongoing Plan International Plan International and ICRW 2013; Digantar 2003	India	Program aims to promote knowledge, attitudes, and practices with regard to child marriage and children's rights. Activities include residential education camps for girls who drop out of school or have never enrolled to help them get back into school.	A, B, C	**Methodology:** Key informant interviews, desk reviews, quantitative assessment of girls' learning. **Findings:** Program staff noted an increased willingness by parents to send girls to school and have them continue education, and increased participation of girls in social issues. Parents observed and appreciated changes in their daughters such as increased confidence and eagerness to continue schooling.

table continues next page

Focus area codes: A = Empowering girls with information, skills, and support networks; B = Educating and mobilizing parents and community members; C = Enhancing accessibility and quality of formal schooling for girls; D = Offering economic support and incentives for girls and families; E = Fostering and enabling legal and policy frameworks.

Program and organization. Sources.	Country	Program description	Focus areas	Evaluation description and findings
Prachar 2001–12 Pathfinder International Daniel and Nanda 2012; Pathfinder International 2013	India	The program aimed to delay marriage for girls until age 18, and for boys until age 21. Activities included a range of community-based activities designed to increase nongovernmental organization (NGO) capacity to work on youth sexual and reproductive health, to address underlying gender norms, and to empower girls.	A, B	**Methodology:** Pre-post intervention and comparison sites with a quasi-experimental design for Phase II. **Findings:** Program participants married about 2.6 years later (at age 22) than nonparticipants. Adjusting for differences in education and caste, young women in the intervention area were 44% less likely to be married than young women in the comparison areas.
Pragya: Study of gender transformative success of Prachar program Pathfinder International Pathfinder International 2011	India	This study was undertaken after Prachar ended, to examine longer term effects and whether Prachar's gender transformative approaches had made a difference in gender norms in the communities as a whole.	A, B	**Methodology:** Quasi-experimental design combined with qualitative data. **Findings:** Participants were less likely to want to marry early, more likely to discuss marriage with parents, and more aware of gender-related information on sexual and reproductive health. Qualitative analysis shows that deep-seated norms about masculinity and femininity were slower to change, as was behavior. Dowry, poverty, and the lack of punitive action for child marriage were key persistent risk factors.
Security for Girls Through Land 2013 Landesa, Government of India Landesa 2013	India	Program aimed to change parental and community attitudes about girls, to change marriage and dowry practices, and to empower girls. Parents and girls were encouraged to create assets for girls such as a fixed deposit, savings account, recurring deposit, or life insurance policy. Other issues addressed included life skills, dowry, girls' secondary schooling, early marriage, and laws on dowry, inheritance, and marriage.	A, B, C, D	**Methodology:** Quasi-experimental with 3 groups, key informant interviews, program monitoring data, community feedback, and participant diaries. **Findings:** Participating girls married a year and a half later than girls in control villages. Participants were more likely to have a financial asset in their name and to earn and keep income; parents were willing to bequeath land to daughters; parents of participating girls paid less dowry than in control areas; participating girls demonstrated greater legal knowledge and were less likely to drop out of school; participating boys' attitudes toward dowry and girls' rights to inherit land started to change.

Focus area codes: A = Empowering girls with information, skills, and support networks; B = Educating and mobilizing parents and community members; C = Enhancing accessibility and quality of formal schooling for girls; D = Offering economic support and incentives for girls and families; E = Fostering and enabling legal and policy frameworks.

Program and organization. Sources.	Country	Program description	Focus areas	Evaluation description and findings
Girls Gaining Ground (GGG) 2005–09 Bhavishya Alliance (Hindustan Unilever, UNICEF Maharashtra, the Synergos Institute) Baker et al. 2009	India	This program sought to delay marriage through empowering girls to negotiate with parents. Activities included safe spaces to discuss girls' legal rights to refuse early marriage and various life skills. The program provided tools to access government services and empowered girls to take community action and be vocal stakeholders in their communities.	A, D	**Methodology:** Qualitative stakeholder interviews and discussions; field visits. **Findings:** Respondents credited the work between adult facilitators and adolescent girls as breaking the culture of silence around sexuality, menstruation, and early marriage. Girls felt empowered to discuss early marriage with their parents and negotiate their own marriages. Respondents suggested including boys in their role as the future husbands.
Chunauti 2008–11 CARE Nepal CARE Nepal 2011	Nepal	Program aimed to strengthen the enabling environment to combat child marriage and other forms of gender-based violence through a range of multisectoral activities. These included community awareness raising, scholarships for girls' education, engaging boys, public hearings on child marriage, and establishing codes of conduct for government officials on child marriage and dowry.	A, B, C, E	**Methodology:** Program assessment using program documentation and baseline-endline quantitative data. **Findings:** Four-fold increase in knowledge of legal age at marriage between baseline and endline among girls, boys, and parents. Large increases also in awareness of legal punishment for child marriage and the harmful consequences of child marriage. The assessment concludes that a "holistic" comprehensive approach is needed to address child marriage.
Choose Your Future (CYF) 2008–11 UNFPA Wilkinson et al. 2011	Nepal	Program for out-of-school girls focused on life skills, education, empowerment, sexual and reproductive health, and child marriage. Implemented through the Nepal government's Women in Development office.	A, C	**Methodology:** Post-intervention, with desk reviews, field visits, and key informant and group interviews. **Findings:** Indicators were weak, but some evidence describes increased confidence among girls to make decisions about their lives, including marriage. The government has incorporated the groups into its adolescent program, Kishori Bikash.

table continues next page

Focus area codes: A = Empowering girls with information, skills, and support networks; B = Educating and mobilizing parents and community members; C = Enhancing accessibility and quality of formal schooling for girls; D = Offering economic support and incentives for girls and families; E = Fostering and enabling legal and policy frameworks.

Program and organization. Sources.	Country	Program description	Focus areas	Evaluation description and findings
Asia Child Marriage Initiative Ongoing Plan International Plan and ICRW 2013	Nepal	Program aimed to build capacity and commitment to eliminate child marriage through awareness building, child-centered mobilization, life skills, and community involvement. Used CEDPA's Better Life Options Program (BLP) training curriculum for life skills through girls' groups.	A, B	**Methodology:** Qualitative, with young girls and boys, parents, local leaders, and government officers. **Findings:** Children who participated in BLP or children's club activities reported that participation helped them to better express themselves and enhanced their self-confidence.
Youth Reproductive Health in Nepal 1998–2003 ICRW and EngenderHealth, with New Era Foundation and multiple other Nepali NGO partners Mathur, Mehta, and Malhotra 2004	Nepal	Program tested the effectiveness of participatory approaches to address youth reproductive and sexual health concerns and child marriage. Activities included the provision of youth reproductive and sexual health services in two sites; participatory sites had 8 additional activities, including peer education, youth clubs, life skills, and livelihood skills.	A, B, D	**Methodology:** Quantitative baseline and endline, supplemented by qualitative and participatory methods. **Findings:** Proportion of married girls ages 14–21 declined between baseline and endline significantly more in urban (but not rural) program than control areas. The program also noted an increase in girls' schooling, girls' mobility, and participation in the group activities in program versus control areas, particularly in rural sites.
Promoting Gender Justice in Pakistan Norwegian Church Aid 2013.	Pakistan	See appendix F	A, D	

Focus area codes: A = Empowering girls with information, skills, and support networks; B = Educating and mobilizing parents and community members; C = Enhancing accessibility and quality of formal schooling for girls; D = Offering economic support and incentives for girls and families; E = Fostering and enabling legal and policy frameworks.

Note

1. Approach categories from Lee-Rife, Malhotra, and Warner 2012.

References

Alim, M. A. 2007. "Change in Knowledge, Perception, and Attitudes of the Villagers Towards Gender Roles and Gender Relations: An Evaluation of Gender Quality Action Learning Programme." BRAC Research Report, BRAC, Dhaka, Bangladesh.

Amin, S. 2011. "Empowering Adolescent Girls in Rural Bangladesh: Kishori Abhijan." Transitions to Adulthood Brief Number 13, Population Council, New York.

Amin, S., G. Sedgh, R. Magnani, E. Seiber, E. Z. Gutierrez, D. Vereau, and N. Alonso. 1998. "Incentive Schemes for School Attendance in Rural Bangladesh." *Journal of Developing Areas*, 32 (3): 77–99.

Amin, S., and L. Suran. 2005. "Program Efforts to Delay Marriage through Improved Opportunities: Some Evidence from Rural Bangladesh." Presented at the 2005 Annual Meeting of the Population Association of America, Philadelphia, PA, March 31–April 2.

Baker, A., M. Nakagami, T. Noronha, K. Potaski, and E. Puckart. 2009. *A Qualitative Assessment of Girls Gaining Ground: Working Towards Female Empowerment in Maharashtra, India.* Bhavishya Alliance, Maharashtra, India.

Burket, M., M. Alauddin, A. Malek, and M. Rahman. 2006. *Raising the Age of Marriage for Young Girls in Bangladesh.* Watertown, MA: Pathfinder International.

CARE Nepal. 2011. *Addressing Child Marriage in Nepal through Behavior Change Communication and Social Mobilization: Chunauti.* Project Final Report, CARE Nepal, Kathmandu.

CEDPA (Centre for Development and Population Activities). 2001. *Adolescent Girls in India Choose a Better Future: An Impact Assessment.* India: CEDPA.

Daniel, E. E., and R. Nanda. 2012. "The Effect of Reproductive Health Communication Interventions on Age at Marriage and First Birth in Rural Bihar, India: A Retrospective Study." Pathfinder International Research and Evaluation Working Paper, Pathfinder International, Watertown, MA.

Digantar. 2003. "Creating Possibilities: A Report on the Study of Balika Shivirs." Rajasthan, India: Digantar.

Gandhi, K., and J. Krijnen. 2006. "Evaluation of Community-Based Rural Livelihoods Programme in Badakhshan, Afghanistan." Commissioned by Oxfam Great Britain, Oxford, UK.

Kabir, M. M., R. Afroze, and M. Aldeen. 2007. "Impact Assessment of Adolescent Development Programme (ADP) of BRAC." BRAC Research Report, BRAC, Dhaka, Bangladesh.

Kanesathasan, A., L. J. Cardinal, E. Pearson, S. Das Gupta, S. Mukherjee, and A. Malhotra. 2008. *Catalyzing Change: Improving Youth Sexual and Reproductive Health through DISHA: An Integrated Program in India.* Washington, DC: International Center for Research on Women.

Kendall, N., and S. Miske. 2012. "Innovation through Sport: Promoting Leaders, Empowering Youth (ITSPLEY) Strategic Objective 2." Final Cross-Country Evaluation Report for CARE USA. Saint Paul, MN: Miske Witt & Associates Inc.

Landesa Rural Development Institute (RDI). 2013. *Security for Girls through Land. Pilot Evaluation 2012–2013.* New Delhi: Landesa.

Lee-Rife, S., A. Malhotra, and A. Warner. 2012. "What Works to Prevent Child Marriage: A Review of the Evidence." *Studies in Family Planning* 43 (4): 287–303.

Mathur, S., M. Mehta, and A. Malhotra. 2004. *Youth Reproductive Health in Nepal: Is Participation the Answer?* Washington, DC, and New York: International Center for Research on Women (ICRW) and EngenderHealth.

Muzzi, M. 2009. "UNICEF Good Practices in Integrating Birth Registration into Health Systems (2000–2009): Case studies: Bangladesh, Brazil, the Gambia and Delhi." Working paper, UNICEF, New York.

Norwegian Church Aid. 2013. "Promoting Gender Justice in Pakistan." Final report for grants from the Norwegian Ministry of Foreign Affairs, Oslo.

Pande, R., K. Kurz, S. Walia, K. MacQuarrie, and S. Jain. 2006. *Improving the Reproductive Health of Married and Unmarried Youth in India: Evidence of Effectiveness and Costs from Community-Based Interventions. Final Report of the Adolescent Reproductive Health Program in India.* Washington, DC: International Center for Research on Women.

Pathfinder International. 2011. *PRAGYA—Multisectoral, Gendered Approach to Improve Family Planning and Sexual and Reproductive Health for Young People: A Research Study.* Watertown, MA: Pathfinder International.

———. 2013. *PRACHAR: Advancing Young People's Sexual and Reproductive Health and Rights in India.* India: Pathfinder International.

Patil, B. A., P. Dudeja, S. P. Mendhapukar, M. T. Mohammed, and M. Pratap. 2008. *Gender in Development: Adolescent Girls' Life-Skills Education.* India: Tata Institute of Social Sciences and UNICEF.

Plan Asia Regional Office and ICRW (International Center for Research on Women). 2013. *Asia Child Marriage Initiative: Summary of Research in Bangladesh, India and Nepal.* New Delhi: Plan and ICRW.

Save the Children Fund (SCF). 2009a. *Adolescent Reproductive and Sexual Health Program Overview: Narsirnagar, Bangladesh.* Westport, CT: SCF.

———. 2009b. *Adolescent Reproductive and Sexual Health Update.* Westport, CT: SCF.

———. 2009c. *Empowered Youth, Supportive Community: ARSH Results from Bangladesh.* Westport, CT: SCF.

———. 2009d. *Involving Religious Leaders to Promote Adolescent Reproductive and Sexual Health in Bangladesh.* Westport, CT: SCF.

Scales, P., P. Benson, L. Dershem, K. Fraher, R. Makonnen, S. Nazreen, A. Syvertsen, and S. Titus. 2013. "Building Developmental Assets to Empower Adolescent Girls in Rural Bangladesh: Evaluation of Project *Kishoree Kontha.*" *Journal of Research on Adolescence* 23 (1): 171–84.

Schurmann, A. T. 2009. "Review of the Bangladesh Female Secondary School Stipend Project Using a Social Exclusion Framework." *Journal of Health, Population, and Nutrition* 27 (4): 505–17.

Shahnaz, R., and R. Karim. 2008. "Providing Microfinance and Social Space to Empower Adolescent Girls: An Evaluation of BRAC's ELA Centres." BRAC Research and Evaluation Division Working Paper No. 3, BRAC, Dhaka, Bangladesh.

Tango International Inc. 2009. *Shouhardo: A Title II Program of USAID—Final Evaluation Report.* Bangladesh: USAID, Care International.

Wilkinson, D., S. Acharya, B. Devkota, P. Singh, and R. A. Uprety. 2011. "Evaluation of UNFPA's Sixth Country Programme in Nepal (2008–2012)." Report prepared for United Nations Population Fund (UNFPA), Nepal.

World Bank. 2008. "Female Secondary School Assistance Project II. Implementation Completion and Results Report (IDA-36140-BD)." World Bank, Washington, DC.

Evaluated Interventions to Address Intimate Partner Violence

Program and organization. Sources.	Country	Program description	Focus areas	Evaluation description and findings
Gender Equity Project (GEP) 2009–11 United Nations Development Programme (UNDP) Rodriguez and Anwari 2011	Afghanistan	GEP works to enhance access to justice initiatives, sensitize religious leaders and media centers, train community development council members on the Elimination of Violence Against Women law, provide income generation training for women, and provide support through legal centers. The program created a Women's Policy Development Center in the Ministry of Women's Affairs, and strengthened state capacity for gender-responsive budgeting.	**A, B, C, E, F**	**Methodology:** Desk review, key informant discussions, field visits. **Findings:** Trained 500 religious leaders and established a working group at the Ministry of Hajj and Religious Affairs, which was seen as a best practice. Eight legal help centers were established, which addressed more than 100 cases of violence against women a month.
Services Provided to Victims of Gender-Based Violence (GBV) by State and Nonstate Agencies in Pilot Areas 2010–13 United Nations Population Fund (UNFPA) Vazirova 2011	Afghanistan	Part of the Gender Component of the 2010–2013 Country Program Action Plan of the Government of Afghanistan and UNFPA, comprising service provision, working with communities, and interagency coordination. The report assesses formal and informal agencies in the health sector, law enforcement, judiciary, Ministry of Women Affairs, Afghanistan Independent Human Rights Commission, and nongovernmental organizations.	**B, C, D, E, F**	**Methodology:** Key informant interviews. **Findings:** Local health care facilities are convenient entry points for victims seeking help, although staff tends to be fearful of identifying and assisting survivors. There is no unit to address special needs of survivors; staff does not promote services; there is a lack of regulations; and engaging communities is a challenge.
UN Women Afghanistan Country Programme 2010–13 Taylor and Anwari 2013	Afghanistan	UN Women programs include policy and legal reform, a paralegal program, and a database on violence against women.	**C, D, E, F**	**Methodology:** Key informant interviews and field visits. **Findings:** The program was successful in establishing a database and training partner organizations in its use. The paralegal programs are considered effective in preventing violence. However, resources are limited, and there is little coordination among involved agencies.

Focus area codes: A = Changing gender norms, attitudes, behaviors; B = Use of advocacy, networking, and media; C = Providing services for violence survivors; D = Addressing violence through different sectors; E = Strengthening law enforcement and policy framework; F = Capacity building of service providers.

Program and organization. Sources.	Country	Program description	Focus areas	Evaluation description and findings
Grameen Bank, BRAC, and Association for Social Advancement (ASA) Microcredit Programme Impact 1980s–ongoing Schuler et al. 1996; Develtere and Huybrechts 2002	Bangladesh	The microcredit approach developed by Grameen Bank, BRAC, and ASA offers small loans to poor women who are deprived of access to credit offered by regular private banks.	D	**Methodology:** Economic impact assessment, supplemented by qualitative data. **Findings:** Women participating in the microcredit program were somewhat protected against domestic violence by having a more public social role through their program participation. The entrance of women in public life when joining a microcredit institution is the most important factor in explaining the reduction in domestic violence.
Joint UN Program to Address Violence against Women in Bangladesh 2010–13 MDG Fund 2013a, 2013b	Bangladesh	The intervention was designed to address violence against women, including domestic violence, by strengthening policy and legal implementation, raising awareness to change community attitudes, and providing and improving services to survivors.	A, C, D, E, F	**Methodology:** Quantitative surveys and qualitative data. **Findings:** The program enhanced government and civil society capacity, increased awareness of gaps in laws and of lesser-known forms of violence such as workplace harassment and violence against sex workers, improved response services, and piloted a database on violence against women to monitor progress.
Promoting Rights of the Disadvantaged by Preventing Violence Against Women (PROTIRODH) 2007–10 Care Bangladesh Mannan 2010	Bangladesh	The PROTIRODH project aimed to reduce violence against women and improve women's rights in 4 unions of rural Dinajpur and among female sex workers in Dhaka, Khulna, and Tangail. The program established a range of services for survivors at the local and union level, created and strengthened women's groups, and provided legal aid.	A, B, C, F	**Methodology:** Literature review, surveys, and qualitative methods. **Findings:** Women reported increased self-confidence and a stronger ability to mitigate, control, and prevent violence. The project has helped women and female sex workers to protest violence and to access services.

table continues next page

Focus area codes: A = Changing gender norms, attitudes, behaviors; B = Use of advocacy, networking, and media; C = Providing services for violence survivors; D = Addressing violence through different sectors; E = Strengthening law enforcement and policy framework; F = Capacity building of service providers.

Program and organization. Sources.

Program and organization. Sources.	Country	Program description	Focus areas	Evaluation description and findings
We Can campaign Oxfam–Great Britain 2004–11 Raab 2011	Afghanistan, Bangladesh, India, Nepal, Pakistan and Sri Lanka	The campaign focuses on addressing the problem of domestic violence and promoting equal and violence-free relationships. In 2008, the campaign was implemented by more than 2,400 organizations (campaign alliances), collectives, and individuals in 6 countries of South Asia.	A, B	**Methodology:** A summative evaluation, using desk review, prior internal evaluations of the program, country assessments, and stakeholder interviews and discussions. **Findings:** We Can reportedly recruited some 3.9 million "change makers" across South Asia, that is, almost four-fifths of the original target. Although exact findings vary by country, the assessments conclude that the campaign was relevant and effective.
Respect Educate Nurture and Empower Women (RENEW) 2005–present RENEW and UNFPA RENEW and UNFPA 2011	Bhutan	This program provided information on alcohol and drug abuse and laws for divorce, inheritance, and child custody, and networked with local authorities and advocated for prevention of domestic violence through campaigns and rallies. The program also provided a range of response activities including counseling, shelters, and legal aid.	A, B, C, E, F	**Methodology:** Desk review, field visits, and stakeholder discussions. **Findings:** The cadre of community-based volunteers created by this program helped preventive services to reach remote areas. More than 50% of volunteers are men.
Bell Bajao! Campaign 2008–present Breakthrough Breakthrough n.d.	India	Bell Bajao! is a media campaign that seeks to reduce domestic violence by calling on men and boys to take a stand against this form of violence. Breakthrough works with survivors and trains young men and women to become "agents of change." Activities also include a multimedia campaign and community mobilization initiatives.	A, B	**Methodology:** Baseline and endline surveys, qualitative tools, secondary data analysis. **Findings:** The campaign reached an estimated 230 million people through various media platforms, with TV being the most effective and far-reaching. The campaign raised awareness of violence, but perceptions of what constitutes sexual violence were hard to change.

Focus area codes: A = Changing gender norms, attitudes, behaviors; B = Use of advocacy, networking, and media; C = Providing services for violence survivors; D = Addressing violence through different sectors; E = Strengthening law enforcement and policy framework; F = Capacity building of service providers.

Program and organization. Sources.	Country	Program description	Focus areas	Evaluation description and findings
Dilaasa 2001–ongoing Centre for Enquiry into Health and Allied Themes (CEHAT) Deosthali, Maghnani, and Malik 2005	India	This program established the first hospital-based crisis center in India for survivors of domestic violence.	C, D, F	**Methodology:** In-depth interviews, shelter observation, review of medical records. **Findings:** The assessment highlighted several problems in providing proper services to survivors of violence in the health care setting, including that women had little faith in the police and the judiciary and that health professionals were overburdened, understaffed, and did not see domestic violence as a health priority, but as a private matter.
Staying Alive—Yearly Evaluation of the Protection of Women from Domestic Violence Act (PWDVA) 2005–12 Lawyers Collective Lawyers Collective 2012	India	The Staying Alive series documents the implementation of the PWDVA with data and inputs from all states. Findings reported here are from the most recent (2013) report.	E, F	**Methodology:** Analysis of 42.8% of court orders in study year from 27 states and union territories. **Findings:** The main finding was that the PWDVA might fail to address the consequences of violence within a marriage or a domestic relationship if the act becomes secondary to personal laws governing women's rights in the family. Courts still show a bias against women in judgments, and protection officers file cases with delay.
Rhani Wives Intervention 2010–11 Population Council Raj et al. 2013	India	The Rhani Wives Intervention targeted wives in Mumbai who are at risk of HIV infection from their husbands. The program focused on marital communication, sexual negotiation, and condom use. This study assessed the program's effect on safer sex and the extent of marital violence.	A, D	**Methodology:** Two-arm cluster randomized control trial. **Findings:** Among women who are at risk of HIV infection from their husbands, the risk of infection and marital violence was significantly reduced for program participants.

table continues next page

Focus area codes: A = Changing gender norms, attitudes, behaviors; B = Use of advocacy, networking, and media; C = Providing services for violence survivors; D = Addressing violence through different sectors; E = Strengthening law enforcement and policy framework; F = Capacity building of service providers.

Program and organization. Sources.	Country	Program description	Focus areas	Evaluation description and findings
Improving services for Center for Social Research's (CSR) crisis intervention centers Ongoing CSR Mukherjee n.d.	India	This program, undertaken in different low-income neighborhoods of Delhi, provided counseling services, legal advice, access to medical services, and men's support committees and created women's collectives.	A, C, D, F	**Methodology:** Field visits, participatory qualitative data and case studies. **Findings:** The crisis centers are well known in the community, network effectively with law enforcement and the judiciary, and are able to engage men to work with other men in preventing violence. Counselors noted the lack of private rooms for counseling services.
Women's Resource Centers 2006–ongoing Seva Mandir Cavas 2013	India	Seva Mandir's Women's Resource Centers provide mediation to stop domestic violence and potentially prevent future violence through challenging cultural norms that perpetuate violence. The centers also create and strengthen women's groups, conduct awareness campaigns, and build capacity through training.	A, C, F	**Methodology:** Observations and interviews with community implementers. **Findings:** Women leaders who implement the conflict mediation centers are self-confident and effective. Challenges included the need for a new physical space and confusion about fee structures. Women needed to leave their house to report violence, which was not always feasible.
The Dil Mil trial 2010–13 RTI International Krishnan et al. 2012	India	This intervention engages young daughters-in-law and mothers-in-law to mitigate domestic violence and related adverse health outcomes.	A	**Methodology:** Randomized control trial, supplemented by focus group discussions and in-depth interviews. **Findings:** Results are forthcoming.
Action for Equality 2009–ongoing Equal Community Foundation Equal Community Foundation 2011	India	Action for Equality is a model for engaging men to end violence against women in Pune, India, and works through group training.	A, D, F	**Methodology:** Outcome assessment interviews with female partners of participating men and other women in the community. **Findings:** A majority of respondents reported a positive change in attitudes and violent behavior by their partners after participation, and almost half reported increased partner support in domestic work.

Focus area codes: A = Changing gender norms, attitudes, behaviors; B = Use of advocacy, networking, and media; C = Providing services for violence survivors; D = Addressing violence through different sectors; E = Strengthening law enforcement and policy framework; F = Capacity building of service providers.

Program and organization. Sources.	Country	Program description	Focus areas	Evaluation description and findings
Special Cell for Women and Children with the Maharashtra State Police System 2002–05 Resource Center for Violence against Women (RCI-VAW), Tata Institute of Social Sciences Mahtani 2006	India	This study aims to understand the nature of interventions, nature of expectations from, and the perceptions of the special cell for women and children	**C, E, F**	**Methodology:** Interviews with clients of a sample of police system–based crisis centers. **Findings:** Overall, 57.4% reported satisfaction with the services, 31.4% were somewhat satisfied, and 9.6% were not satisfied at all. Notably, 41.9% of women said they felt confident to notify the police, and knew what steps to take if the police did not listen to them. Respondents also expressed the need for police assistance and said that visiting crisis centers was helpful.
Western India Gender Justice Program 2010–13 Oxfam India Kaarak 2013	India	This program seeks to address attitudes and norms through women's political empowerment, and to ensure easy access to justice for violence survivors.	**A, B, C, F**	**Methodology:** Desk review, key informant interviews, focus group discussions, case studies, workshops, and small survey. **Findings:** The program has been effective in improving understandings of gendered power relations and of laws against domestic violence and has increased capacity among partner organizations. It has also been able to reach vulnerable minorities, but has had less success in engaging men.
Zero Violence Zone 2003–05 MAMTA and United Nations Development Fund MAMTA n.d.	India	The aim of this pilot project was to create a "zero violence zone" in project communities. Objectives included raising awareness, sensitizing government bodies and others, encouraging community-based redress through community support groups, and developing links between support groups and other institutions.	**A, B, C, D, F**	**Methodology:** Literature review, qualitative data collection, case studies, participatory observation. **Findings:** Meetings were organized to help men reflect on their behavior, and there was significant change in understanding women's rights among both men and women. Younger girls were also made aware of their legal rights and reported increased self-confidence.

table continues next page

Focus area codes: A = Changing gender norms, attitudes, behaviors;. B = Use of advocacy, networking, and media; C = Providing services for violence survivors; D = Addressing violence through different sectors; E = Strengthening law enforcement and policy framework; F = Capacity building of service providers.

Program and organization. Sources.	Country	Program description	Focus areas	Evaluation description and findings
Center for Vulnerable Children and Women Society for Nutrition Education and Health Action (SNEHA) 1999–ongoing SNEHA and Center for Vulnerable Women and Children 2009	India	This report covers the first 6 years of the Center for Vulnerable Women and Children in Dharavi, Mumbai. Records were available for 701 primary clients, most of whom were women (5 were men and 35 were children). Services offered were counseling, legal, medical, and psychiatric support.	**C, F**	**Methodology:** Analysis of client cases. **Findings:** Referrals were successful in getting women to come to the crisis center, and about one-third of users reported satisfaction with the services. The project did not have much success in preventing alcohol abuse. Less than 2% of women reported wanting assistance to contact the police.
Sharamajibee Mahila Samity (SMS) Shalishi 1990–? SMS, Gujarat state ICRW 2002	India	The SMS is a community-based organization that adapted the traditional village dispute resolution system—shalishi—to address violence against women, including intimate partner and domestic violence. Facilitators of the SMS shalishis try to negotiate a resolution of the dispute, ask each party to sign it, and then call on the community to enforce the resolution. The SMS also provides emotional support to women and referrals to the local health center. Police are asked to intervene only if the shalishi fails. Case loads had grown to more than 400 cases a year by 2002.	**C, D**	**Methodology:** Participatory and multimethod. Survey of 151 women users of the shalishi and analysis of 1,671 SMS organization records. **Findings:** The evaluation found an increase in women's willingness to disclose violence and seek and gain redress, and a decline in spousal violence. 90% of women surveyed were satisfied with the SMS shalishi process. Women prefer to refer other women to these shalishi rather than other organizations. The SMS's follow-up, pressure on the perpetrator to change behavior, resolution of family life, use of persuasion, consensus, and impartiality are considered critical. The community now perceives shalishi—traditionally male dominated—as a suitable venue to engage women and to discuss concerns such as violence.

Focus area codes: A = Changing gender norms, attitudes, behaviors; B = Use of advocacy, networking, and media; C = Providing services for violence survivors; D = Addressing violence through different sectors; E = Strengthening law enforcement and policy framework; F = Capacity building of service providers.

Program and organization. Sources.	Country	Program description	Focus areas	Evaluation description and findings
Sahara Sangh (SS) and Nari Adalat (NA) 1996–? Mahila Samakhya program, Uttar Pradesh state ICRW 2002	India	These two local conflict resolution mechanisms were formed by women's collectives initiated through the Mahila Samakhya program, and aimed specifically to address issues of violence and related concerns for women. Both are federations of women and village collectives that adjudicate cases of domestic and intimate partner violence against women.	C, D	**Methodology:** Participatory, multimethod. **Findings:** Existing program documentation from the Mahila Samakhya program did not lend itself to analyzing the effect of the SS/NA models nor to tracking trends in their spread or extent of participation. Participatory methods reveal that the SS and NA are considered legitimate because of their transparency, neutrality, and timeliness. Respondents noted positive changes in women's confidence, husbands' violence, and community attitudes toward violence against women.
Nari Adalat (NA) and Mahila Panch (MP) 1998–? Mahila Samakhya program, Gujarat state ICRW 2002	India	The NA and MP were formed by women members of Mahila Samakhya groups. These are independent, conflict resolution forums, specifically to address domestic and intimate partner violence. Cases are brought by village councils or by individual women.	C, D	**Methodology:** Participatory, multimethod, with 27 case studies. **Findings:** The NA/MP groups consider reestablishing rights of women in their marriages a key goal. The NA/MP's timeliness, transparency, and positive engagement in other community concerns contribute to their legitimacy. Most women and men respondents expressed satisfaction with the NA/MP. Women participating in the NA/MP reported increased confidence and ability to negotiate in their family and community.
Engaging Men in GBV Prevention via Community Leadership Councils	India	See appendix K.	A	

Focus area codes: A = Changing gender norms, attitudes, behaviors; B = Use of advocacy, networking, and media; C = Providing services for violence survivors; D = Addressing violence through different sectors; E = Strengthening law enforcement and policy framework; F = Capacity building of service providers.

table continues next page

Program and organization. Sources.	Country	Program description	Focus areas	Evaluation description and findings
Cultural, community, and clinical approaches to preventing HIV transmission and sexually transmitted infections among men	India	See appendix K.	A	
Men's Action for Stopping Violence Against Women (MASVAW)	India	See appendix K.	A, B	
Yaari-Dosti: Promoting Gender-Equitable Norms and Behaviors	India	See appendix K.	A	
Integrated Development Programme of Women Cooperatives to Reduce Gender Based Violence 2010–present Ministry of Women, Children and Social Welfare/United Kingdom Department for International Development (UK DFID) UK DFID 2013; Grandjean 2010	Nepal	The program has four components: (a) awareness raising and legal empowerment; (b) referrals; (c) monitoring, reporting, and follow-up support to the survivors; and (d) supporting transition of paralegal committees to violence watch groups.	A, B, C, F	**Methodology:** An output evaluation based on desk reviews and field visits. **Findings:** As of February 2012, a total of 1,026 Paralegal Committees (PLCs) had been established and were operating in 59 districts. Of all PLCs, members of 732 PLCs had completed the compulsory 18-day training. Approximately 12,075 cases of violence against women and children were recorded by PLCs. A National Monitoring System was developed and implemented.

Focus area codes: A = Changing gender norms, attitudes, behaviors; B = Use of advocacy, networking, and media; C = Providing services for violence survivors; D = Addressing violence through different sectors; E = Strengthening law enforcement and policy framework; F = Capacity building of service providers.

Program and organization. Sources.	Country	Program description	Focus areas	Evaluation description and findings
Support to Office of the Prime Minister and Council of Ministers (OPMCM)/GBV Unit 2010–13 UK DFID Robertson and Chapagain 2012	Nepal	The project provided technical advice to support the OPMCM/GBV unit. A special high-level planning meeting reviewed the National Plan of Action on GEV. A separate GBV elimination fund was established. Standard operationa procedures for shelters were developed. A GBV legal fast track system is being developed with United Nations Development Programme support.	C, E, F	**Methodology:** An output evaluation based on a desk review, semistructured and in-depth interviews, and focus group discussions with partners and stakeholders. **Findings:** A mapping study showed improved knowledge on violence issues, actors, and interventions in project areas. The project provided key technical expertise and outreach to the unit on violence within OPMCM, and identified gaps in existing laws.
Women's Rights Helpline 2003–05 Legal Aid and Consultancy Centre (LACC) LACC 2005	Nepal	Provides legal information and counseling via a help line, followed by in-person appointments, free legal aid, counseling, mediation, court representation, and financial assistance. Focuses on poor, disadvantaged women and all forms of violence.	C	**Methodology:** Document review and key informant interviews. **Findings:** The report notes increased awareness about women's rights and help line services. Counseling, mediation, and referral to quasi-judicial mechanisms were found to be more effective than lawsuits and legal procedures in assisting survivors of violence. 68% of cases were resolved through mediation.
Breaking the silence on sexual abuse, trafficking and domestic violence towards children and women in rural Nepal 2000–present Aawaaj Comas and Despature 2008	Nepal	Program objectives are to raise awareness on domestic violence and sexual abuse, mobilize community members, decision makers, and local authorities, and to support women and children who are survivors. Activities include community and private sector engagement, advocacy and networking with government, and supporting community mediation.	A, B, C, E	**Methodology:** Qualitative. **Findings:** The community support mechanisms are seen as an effective approach to engage community members in preventing violence against women and to provide support to survivors. Counseling provided by Aawaaj has helped survivors feel more confident. Mediation services have helped survivors feel that they are heard and have contributed to decreasing instances of physical violence.

table continues next page

Focus area codes: A = Changing gender norms, attitudes, behaviors; B = Use of advocacy, networking, and media; C = Providing services for violence survivors; D = Addressing violence through different sectors; E = Strengthening law enforcement and policy framework; F = Capacity building of service providers.

259

Program and organization. Sources.	Country	Program description	Focus areas	Evaluation description and findings
One-Stop Crisis Management Centres (OCMC) 2011–present Ministry of Health and Population (MoHP) MoHP Population Division 2013	Nepal	These centers provide health services, psychosocial counseling to survivors and perpetrators, legal counseling, referrals to safe homes, security, and rehabilitation.	C, D	**Methodology:** Document review, key informant interviews, and case studies. **Findings:** Knowledge of the centers and services was limited among officials and the public. Necessary coordination among multiple stakeholders was weak. The OCMCs suffered from inadequate infrastructure, insufficient human resources, and a lack of capacity building.
Gender-based violence among Afghan refugees 2009–? International Medical Corps (IMC) IMC 2010	Pakistan	This program aims to raise awareness about and to reduce the incidence of violence, as well as to improve the health of violence survivors in four Afghan refugee camps in the North-West Frontier Province. IMC also conducted trainings for community health workers, doctors, and others in the identification, appropriate counseling, and medical management of violence cases.	C, F	**Methodology:** Quantitative outcome evaluation. **Findings:** Data collection was problematic. Still, data revealed an 11-percentage point increase post-intervention in women's knowledge of their rights in Islam and a greater understanding that they could refuse sex with their husbands. One-third reported an increase in knowledge of services. Women did not report violence because of stigma, shame, and the belief that reporting such matters would cause additional problems.
Promoting Gender Justice in Pakistan 2009–12 Norwegian Church Aid Norwegian Church Aid 2013	Pakistan	This program aimed to enhance women's rights to inheritance and promote choice in marriage. Activities include negotiation training for adolescents, training community organizers, strengthening religious leaders to promote consensual marriages and rights to inheritance.	A, E, F	**Methodology:** Qualitative data and a quantitative baseline. **Findings:** In target communities, the program reported a 10% increase in women receiving their share of inheritance according to personal laws. The project also improved clarity with regard to the legal and procedural aspects of inheritance and land holding, while partner organizations assisted in preventing forced marriages.

Focus area codes: A = Changing gender norms, attitudes, behaviors; B = Use of advocacy, networking, and media; C = Providing services for violence survivors; D = Addressing violence through different sectors; E = Strengthening law enforcement and policy framework; F = Capacity building of service providers.

Program and organization. Sources.	Country	Program description	Focus areas	Evaluation description and findings
Rabta Programme, Rozan 1999–2010	Pakistan	See appendix G.	**C, D, E**	
Gender Justice through Musalihat Anjuman 2009–13 UNDP UNDP Pakistan 2011	Pakistan	Musalihat Anjuman (MA) is a formal microlevel dispute resolution mechanism that uses informal procedures to resolve disputes of all kinds at the local level. This program aimed to assist implementing MAs and to make them gender sensitive. The project helped establish 1,063 MAs in 4 provinces, and trained more than 15,000 stakeholders.	E, F	**Methodology:** A midterm evaluation, using desk reviews, field work, and key informant interviews. **Findings:** Free, flexible services are the strength of the MA mechanism. Three-quarters of cases brought forward by the time of the midterm evaluation had been successfully addressed or resolved. There is an urgent need for defined physical spaces to ensure confidentiality for women, and MAs must be more effectively linked with existing judicial and police systems. The politicization of MAs must also be addressed.
Comprehensive Skills Training and Empowerment of Afghan Refugees in Baluchistan 2010–11 SEHER, CARE, U.S. Department of State Ibadat 2011	Pakistan	This project aimed to improve safeguards against sexual and gender based violence by empowering Afghan refugees through the enhancement of skills and literacy, as well as by providing access to legal services and health care. The project has four components: raising awareness, building the capacity of state institutions, facilitating access to service delivery, and empowering refugees.	A, B, C, D, F	**Methodology:** Desk reviews, key informant and stakeholder interviews and discussions, field visits, and observations. **Findings:** 75% of identified violence survivors reported satisfaction with the services offered. Women who received skills training were supporting their families, contributing to household income, participating in family decisions, and engaging in improved spousal relations and communication. Women reported male participants as being less aggressive toward them as the project ended. The program's radio programs reached a wide audience.

table continues next page

Focus area codes: A = Changing gender norms, attitudes, behaviors; B = Use of advocacy, networking, and media; C = Providing services for violence survivors; D = Addressing violence through different sectors; E = Strengthening law enforcement and policy framework; F = Capacity building of service providers.

Program and organization. Sources.	Country	Program description	Focus areas	Evaluation description and findings
The Equal Access to Justice Project 2004–08 (Phase I) and 2009–13 (Phase II) Samaranayake and Saparamadu 2012	Sri Lanka	The program sought to decrease barriers to accessing the legal system; to better promote and effectively protect human rights, including those of violence survivors; and to train judges and lawyers on interpreting laws and handling domestic violence cases.	B, C, E, F	**Methodology:** Output evaluation with desk reviews, stakeholder and participant interviews, and staff self-assessments. **Findings:** The program trained 35 high court judges on relevant laws, held multiple awareness and training sessions with survivors, and increased the reporting of violence by survivors.
Engaging Fathers for Children's Education and Family Well-Being April 2012 World Vision Sri Lanka and Instituto Promundo World Vision and MenCare 2012	Sri Lanka	The mission of the fathers' groups is to promote gender equality in the home and to improve the overall well-being of families. Group education sessions covered gender equality and nonviolence in the home, healthy sexuality and its relationship to a happy marriage, couples' communication and family planning, corporal punishment and children's rights, alcohol and drug abuse, and nonviolent approaches to parenting, among other topics.	A	**Methodology:** Interviews with stakeholders and participants. **Findings:** There were several reports of a decrease in use of alcohol and drugs—both strongly associated with the use of violence against women in Sri Lanka. The review noted that working with fathers is a critical intervention to address violence in the home.
Promoting Active Citizenship in the Hill Country in Sri Lanka 2011–12 Search for Common Ground, Sri Lanka (SFCG|SL) Senanayake, Manivanan, and Hillary 2013	Sri Lanka	The intervention sought to empower Indian-origin Tamil minority youth in Sri Lanka's plantation economy to participate fully in civic life, increase awareness of their rights and responsibilities, and engage youth and communities. The program responded to the vulnerability of minority youth in the country's postwar transition.	A, B, D	**Methodology:** Primarily qualitative, with some quantitative data. **Findings:** Participants took the initiative to address domestic violence in their community. The project helped create awareness of rights and entitlements, including those regarding violence against women and girls.

Focus area codes: A = Changing gender norms, attitudes, behaviors; B = Use of advocacy, networking, and media; C = Providing services for violence survivors; D = Addressing violence through different sectors; E = Strengthening law enforcement and policy framework; F = Capacity building of service providers.

References

Breakthrough. n.d. "Bell Bajao! Campaign: A Report." Breakthrough India, New Delhi.

Cavas J. 2013. "Voices Against Violence: Empowering Women to Access Informal Justice in Rural India." Master's thesis, University of Oregon, Eugene. https://scholarsbank.uoregon.edu /xmlui/bitstream/handle/1794/13415/Cavas_oregon_0171N_10792.pdf?sequence=1.

Comas, E., and I. D. Asociación (EXIL). 2008. "Evaluation Report." Aawaaj, Kathmandu.

Deosthali, P., P. Maghnani, and S. Malik. 2005. "Establishing Dilaasa: Documenting the Challenges." Centre for Enquiry into Health and Allied Themes, Mumbai, India.

Develtere, P., and A. Huybrechts. 2002. "Evidence on the Social and Economic Impact of Grameen Bank and BRAC on the Poor in Bangladesh." University of Leuven, Leuven, Belgium.

Equal Community Foundation. 2011. "Action for Equality Programme: Outcome Assessment Data." Pune, India. http://ecf.org.in/wp-content/uploads/Impact-Stories.pdf.

Grandjean, A. 2010. "No Rights Without Accountability: Promoting Access to Justice for Children." Legal Empowerment Working Papers No. 10, International Development Law Organization, Rome.

Ibadat, G. 2011. "Comprehensive Skills Training and Empowerment of Afghan Refugees in Baluchistan." SEHER, Quetta, Pakistan.

ICRW (International Center for Research on Women). 2002. "Women-Initiated Community Level Responses to Domestic Violence: Summary Report of Three Studies." Report Number 5, *Domestic Violence in India: Exploring Strategies, Promoting Dialogue*. Washington, DC, and New Delhi: ICRW.

IMC (International Medical Corps). 2010. "Gender-Based Violence among Afghan Refugees: Summary of Post-intervention Survey Findings in Three Camps in Northwest Frontier Provinces." IMC, Santa Monica, CA.

Kaarak. 2013. "End Impact Evaluation for Oxfam India Western India Gender Justice Report." Draft Report, Oxfam India, New Delhi.

Krishnan, S., K. Subbiah, P. Chandra, and K. Srinivasan. 2012. "Minimizing Risks and Monitoring Safety of an Antenatal Care Intervention to Mitigate Domestic Violence among Young Indian Women: The Dil Mil Trial." *BMC Public Health* 12 (1): 943.

LACC (Legal Aid Consultancy Center). 2005. "Evaluation Report." LACC, Lalitpur, Nepal.

Lawyers Collective. 2012. "Staying Alive: 5th Monitoring and Evaluation on the Protection of Women from Domestic Violence Act." Lawyers Collective and International Centre for Research on Women, Delhi.

Mahtani, R. P. 2006. "Executive Summary Report of Strategy Planning for the Special Cells for Women and Children: An Action Research Project (2002–2005)." Draft working paper, Tata Institute of Social Studies, Mumbai, India.

MAMTA Health Institute for Mother and Child. n.d. "Impact Assessment Report—Zero Violence Zone." MAMTA, New Delhi.

Mannan, M. A. 2010. "The Final Evaluation of CARE Bangladesh's PROTIRODH Project." Final Report, Bangladesh Institute of Development Studies (BIDS), Dhaka. http://www.bids.org.bd /files/final_report_on_protirodh.pdf.

MDG (Millennium Development Goals) Achievement Fund. 2013a. "Final Evaluation: Bangladesh, Gender Equality and Women's Empowerment." http://www.mdgfund.org/sites /default/files/Bangladesh%20-%20Gender%20-%20Final%20Evaluation%20Report.pdf.

———. 2013b. "Bangladesh Country Fact Sheet." http://www.mdgfund.org/sites/default/files /Bangladesh%20Joint%20Programmes%20Fact%20Sheet.pdf.

MoHP (Ministry of Health and Population), Population Division. 2013. *Assessment of the Performance of Hospital-Based One-Stop Crisis Management Centres.* Kathmandu: Ministry of Health and Population.

Mukherjee, A. n.d. "Creating a Supportive and Violence Free Environment by Enabling Economic Self-Sufficiency amongst Community Members in CSR's Crisis Intervention Centers." Centre for Social Research, New Delhi.

Norwegian Church Aid. 2013. "Promoting Gender Justice in Pakistan." Final Report for grants from the Norwegian Ministry of Foreign Affairs, Norwegian Church Aid, Oslo.

Raab, M. 2011. "The We Can Campaign in South Asia, 2004–2011: External Evaluation Report." Oxfam -Great Britain. http://policy-practice.oxfam.org.uk/publications/the-we-can-campaign -in-south-asia-2004-2011-external-evaluation-report-146189.

Raj, A., N. Saggurti, M. Battala, S. Nair, A. Dasgupta, D. D. Naik, D. Abramovitz, J. Silverman, and D. Balaiah. 2013. "Randomized Controlled Trial to Test the RHANI Wives HIV Intervention for Women in India at Risk for HIV from Husbands." *AIDS and Behavior* 17 (9): 3066–80.

RENEW (Respect, Educate, Nurture, and Empower Women) and UNFPA (United Nations Population Fund). 2011. "Community Based Support System (CBSS) Program Assessment." RENEW, Thimphu.

Robertson, G., and Y. Chapagain. 2012. "Project Cluster Evaluation: Enabling State Fund and Social Inclusion Action Fund Report." Enabling State Programme, Kathmandu.

Rodriguez, F., and H. Anwari. 2011. "United Nations Development Program (UNDP)–Gender Equality Project Independent/External Evaluation Report." UNDP, Kabul.

Samaranayake, M. R., and C. D. Saparamadu. 2012. "Evaluation of Outcome 5: Greater and More Diverse Access to Justice Redress Mechanisms (A2J)." Under the UNDP Sri Lanka CPAP 2008–2012, United Nations Development Programme, New York.

Schuler, S. R., S. M. Hashemi, A. P. Riley, and S. Akhter. 1996. "Credit Programmes, Patriarchy, and Men's Violence against Women in Rural Bangladesh." *Social Science & Medicine* 43: 1729–42.

Senanayake, D. R., N. Manivanan, and N. Hillary. 2013. "Final Evaluation Report: Promoting Active Citizenship in the Hill Country in Sri Lanka." Search for Common Ground Sri Lanka (SFCG|SL), Sri Lanka.

SNEHA (Society for Nutrition Education and Health Action). 2009. "Empowering Survivors of Violence: Every Woman and Child Counts." Center for Vulnerable Women and Children, SNEHA, Mumbai.

Taylor, A. J., and H. Anwari. 2013. "Mid-term Review of Assistance to the UN Women Afghanistan Country Programme in the Planned Period 2010–2013." UN Women and UNICEF, Kabul.

UK DFID (Department for International Development). 2013. "Integrated Development Programme of Women Cooperatives to Reduce Gender Based Violence." Annual review, UK DFID, London. http://iati.dfid.gov.uk/iati_documents/3898751.doc.

UNDP (United Nations Development Program) Pakistan. 2011. "Mid-term Evaluation of the Gender Justice through Musalihat Anjuman Project (GJTMAP)." UNDP, Pakistan.

Vazirova, A. 2011. "The Assessment of Services Provided to Victims of Gender Based Violence (GBV) by State and Non-state Agencies in Pilot Areas." United Nations Population Fund, Kabul.

World Vision and MenCare. 2012. "Engaging Fathers for Children's Education and Family Well-Being." MenCare Global Fatherhood Campaign, Sri Lanka.

APPENDIX G

Evaluated Interventions to Address Sexual Harassment

Program and organization. Sources.	Country	Program description	Focus areas	Evaluation description and findings
Protibadi 2013–present Protibadi Ahmed et al. 2014	Bangladesh	Protibadi is a web and mobile application intended for use by college-going women in Dhaka to fight sexual harassment. It has a "save me" button that women can press when feeling unsafe, which generates sound and sends an emergency text message. Users can also go to the website to report incidents.	C	**Methodology:** Online survey and user interviews before the application was introduced and user interviews post-introduction. **Findings:** Help on the spot, reaching friends, and sharing experiences were identified as key priorities by women. Women noted they would be embarrassed to use the "save me" button.
Joint UN Programme to Address Violence against Women in Bangladesh	Bangladesh	See appendix F	A, D	
Care and Support for Rape Survivors at First Point of Contact Population Council Khan et al. 2008	Bangladesh, India	This study was undertaken to analyze service provision for rape survivors.	B, D	**Methodology:** Data collected from medical practitioners and nurses from public hospitals as well as from police personnel located near the hospitals. **Findings:** There is no uniform service provision protocol, services supposed to exist according to particular protocols are not in place, and police officers are not aware of protocols for service provision. Police stations and hospitals had minimal services and were not sensitized to survivors' trauma.
A study of Delhi Police Helplines (100 and 1091) 1996–present Jagori, UN Women, UN Habitat, Government of India Jagori and MARG 2013	India	This research study surveyed the effectiveness and patterns of the Delhi Police Helplines (100 and 1091).	D	**Methodology:** Desk review, surveys, focus group discussions, and direct observation. **Findings:** Call takers see their job as receiving data and transferring calls to the police station. There is a lack of standard operating procedures, cases are not tracked, and there is no follow-up. No women were on the staff in the control centers.
Parivartan Program 2009–10 International Center for Research on Women and Futures Without Violence Das et al. 2012	India	The Mumbai-based program engaged cricket coaches and mentors in schools and the community to (a) raise awareness about abusive and disrespectful behavior; (b) promote gender-equitable, nonviolent attitudes; and (c) teach skills for speaking up and intervening when witnessing harmful and disrespectful behavior.	C	**Methodology:** Quasi-experimental design with intervention and comparison arms in schools and community. Supplemented by interviews of 15 female relatives of participants. **Findings:** The school and community athletes participating in the program demonstrated a greater positive shift in gender attitudes compared to nonparticipants.

Focus area codes: A = Addressing sexual harassment in public places; B = Addressing sexual harassment in institutional settings and at work; C = Addressing sexual harassment in schools; D = Working with the police to address sexual harassment in public spaces.

Program and organization. Sources.	Country	Program description	Focus areas	Evaluation description and findings
Action Research Project on Women's Rights and Access to Water and Sanitation in Asian Cities 2009–11 Women in Cities International, Jagori, Action India Travers et al. 2011	India	The project tested and adapted the women's safety audit methodology to generate a model for engaging poor women with local governments and other partners. The action research aimed to (a) assess the link between sexual harassment and the lack of access to basic services and (b) explore what changes can be made in local governance to meet the water and sanitation needs of poor urban women and girls.	A	**Methodology:** Detailed literature review, key informant interviews, and participatory methodology. **Findings:** Families could not build toilets because of limited living space and thus resorted to open defecation, which increased perceptions of a general lack of safety. Sexual harassment is severe near water collecting pumps. The project created a safe space for dialogue about women's safety, which decreased hesitation in addressing matters such as defecation and menstruation.
Adolescent Education Program (AEP) 2006–09 Government of India and United Nations Population Fund Jaya et al. 2014	India	AEP worked with three national school systems to empower young people to respond to real life situations. The program trained teachers to facilitate student training, organized advocacy sessions with principals of participating schools, and had sensitization sessions with parents.	C	**Methodology:** Quantitative surveys and in-depth interviews with participating students and teachers on their attitudes related to gender stereotypes and adolescent girls' education. **Results:** Girls in program schools were better able to challenge gender stereotypes. The program had a statistically significant role in improving teachers' attitudes.
Project Parivartan[1] 2003–08 Bill and Melinda Gates Foundation, Avahan India AIDS Initiative Biradavolu et al. 2009	India	This study aims to assess the strategies used by female sex workers in Southern India to modify police behavior. The project organized sensitization meetings with local police officials and established sex workers as "social change agents." The program's crisis intervention team of sex workers, lawyers, and activists addressed police violations.	B, D	**Methodology:** Ethnographic observations over a two-year period and key informant interviews. **Findings:** After the program, sex workers were able to organize and speak collectively and were more willing to challenge police. Police officers ensured basic rules, such as having women officers available at the time of arrest.
Program H Population Council	India	See appendix K	A	
Gender Equality Movement in Schools (GEMS)	India	See appendix K	C	

Focus area codes: A = Addressing sexual harassment in public places; B = Addressing sexual harassment in institutional settings and at work; C = Addressing sexual harassment in schools; D = Working with the police to address sexual harassment in public spaces.

table continues next page

Program and organization. Sources.	Country	Program description	Focus areas	Evaluation description and findings
Yaari-Dosti	India	See appendix K	A	
Rabta Programme 1999–2010 Rozan Khalique et al. 2011	Pakistan	Rozan initiated Rabta with the aim to develop the capacity of police forces to effectively deal with violence against women. The program provides various training modules and also seeks to enhance police-community relationships.	D	**Methodology:** Literature review, surveys, focus group discussions, and key informant interviews. **Findings:** Police who underwent the training were more sensitive about violence against women and were more likely to be receptive to hiring female police officers. Unfortunately, many participants did not take the training seriously, there is minimal follow-up, and police have not assumed responsibility for the program.
From Fear to Safety: Harassment Response and Awareness 2012 Blue Veins Blue Veins 2012	Pakistan	The project established Sexual Harassment Inquiry Committees in 30 educational institutes in the central zone of Khyber Pakhtunkhwa. Aims included increasing knowledge about sexual harassment, developing a code of conduct, creating a web-based reporting tool, and providing free counseling and legal aid to survivors.	C	**Methodology:** Output assessment. **Findings:** The evaluation noted that there were many challenges because university administrations in Khyber Pakhtunkhwa needed to be convinced of the value of the project.

Focus area codes: A = Addressing sexual harassment in public places; B = Addressing sexual harassment in institutional settings and at work; C = Addressing sexual harassment in schools; D = Working with the police to address sexual harassment in public spaces.

Note

1. Project Parivartan is different from the Parivartan program, which addresses changing attitudes among men and boys.

References

Ahmed, S. I., S. Jackson, N. Ahmed, H. S. Ferdous, R. Rifat, A. Rizvi, S. Ahmed, and R. Mansur. 2014. "Protibadi: A Platform for Fighting Sexual Harassment in Urban Bangladesh." Proceedings of the SIGCHI Conference on Human Factors in Computing Systems, Toronto, April 26–May 1. doi: 10.1145/2556288.2557376.

Biradavolu, M., S. Burris, A. George, A. Jena, and K. M. Blankenship. 2009. "Can Sex Workers Regulate Police? Learning from an HIV Prevention Project for Sex Workers in Southern India." *Social Science and Medicine* 68 (8): 1541–47.

Blue Veins. 2012. "From Fear to Safety: Harassment Response and Awareness." Final Report, Blue Veins, Peshawar, Pakistan.

Das M., S. Ghosh, E. Miller, B. O'Conner, and R. Verma. 2012. *Engaging Coaches and Athletes in Fostering Gender Equity: Findings from the Parivartan Program in Mumbai, India.* New Delhi: International Center for Research on Women and Futures Without Violence.

Jagori and MARG (Multiple Action Research Group). 2013. *Safe Cities Free of Violence Against Women and Girls Initiative: A Study of Delhi Police Helplines (100 and 1091).* New Delhi: Jagori, MARG, and UN Women.

Jaya, J., P. Dhillon, and S. Kumar. 2014. "Challenging Gender Stereotypes and Sexual Harassment in Schools: Evidence from Adolescent Education Programs in India." Paper presented at the Population Association of America 2014 Annual Meeting, May 1–3, Boston, MA.

Khalique, H., Z. N. Christopher, E. Sadiq, H. Mir, J. Sultan, S. Abro, A. Hussain, and S. Zafar. 2011. "Evaluation Report: Rabta Programme, Rozan 1999–2010." Report prepared for Rozan by Harris Khalique and Team, Islamabad.

Khan, M. E., A. Bhattacharya, I. Bhuiya, and A. Aeron. 2008. "A Situation Analysis of Care and Support for Rape Survivors at First Point of Contact in India and Bangladesh." U.S. Agency for International Development, Washington, DC, and Frontiers in Reproductive Health, Population Council, India and Bangladesh offices.

Travers, K., M. Canuto, P. Khosla, A. Ali, S. Dhar, and S. T. Mehrotra. 2011. *Gender and Essential Services in Low Income Communities.* New Delhi: Women in Cities International.

Evaluated Interventions to Address Honor Killings

Program and organization name. Sources.	Country	Program description	Focus areas	Evaluation description and findings
Love Commandos 2010–Ongoing	India	This national organization helps couples combat harassment so that they may marry the partners of their choice. The organization offers hot lines and other services through its website (see the References section) and also provides shelter to such couples.	B	No formal evaluation, but has been featured and positively reviewed by more than 100 local, national, and international media sources, as well as on social media.
Public-private partnership to implement the Criminal Law (Amendment) Act, 2004

National Commission on the Status of Women (NCSW), Government of Pakistan, Rozan, and National Rural Support Program (NRSP)

NCSW 2010 | Pakistan | Program aimed to increase use of the law through participation of the media, police, lawyers, and political and religious leaders, as well as by improving data. Activities included training, media, and advocacy. | A, B, C | **Methodology:** Qualitative, supplemented by secondary data and community checklists. **Findings:** Because of floods in Sindh, the assessment could not be conducted. NRSP still expanded the project to 56 districts. |
| Follow-up pilot study of the Criminal Law (Amendment) Act, 2004

Aurat Foundation and Legislative Watch Group

Lari 2011 | Pakistan | This pilot study aimed to assess awareness of the Criminal Law (Amendment) Act of 2004 among communities and law enforcement. | C | **Methodology:** Analysis of registered police cases and key informant interviews. **Findings:** The report found little to no awareness of the law. Police are reluctant to implement the law because of the influence of power holders and society's overwhelming acceptance of honor killing. |

Focus area codes: A = Developing materials for prevention responses; B = Providing training for prevention or direct support to those at risk; C = Fostering an enabling legal and policy framework.

References

Lari, M. Z. 2011. *A Pilot Study on: "Honour Killings" in Pakistan and Compliance of Law.* Islamabad: Aurat Publication and Information Service Foundation.

Love Commandos. http://lovecommandos.org/.

NCSW (National Commission on the Status of Women) and Government of Pakistan. 2010. *Impact Assessment Report: Public Private Partnership to End 'Honour Crimes' in Pakistan through the implementation of Criminal Law (Amendment) Act 2004.* Islamabad: National Commission on the Status of Women.

Evaluated Interventions to Address Custodial Violence against Women and Girls

Program and organization. Sources.	Country	Program description	Focus areas	Evaluation description and findings
Evaluated interventions that explicitly address and separately evaluate the effect of intervention on women and girls.				
Social and Legal Protection of Women/Girls at Risk and Children Detained with their Mothers 2009–2013 Medica Afghanistan Women Support Organization, Women for Afghan Women, Medica Mondiale Saporte 2012	Afghanistan	The project's overall objective is to address the vulnerability of women and girls who are at risk of custodial violence because of family disputes and who are held in police or transitional detention centers, victims of criminal offences, and children older than five years of age who are detained with their mothers. The project provides legal counseling and mediation services; care for children whose mothers are in prison through a child support center; and trainings to the police, prison personnel, social service providers, and Mullahs (Muslims who are learned in Islamic theology and sacred law, usually holding official posts).	B, C	**Methodology:** Desk studies, focus group discussions, interviews, and observations. **Findings:** Awareness raising and legal advice empowered women to defend their positions in front of judges. Despite the fact that the quality of mediation can be improved, mediation between different parties has often led to the successful reintegration of women with their families. Women are more aware of their rights and are more self-confident.
Crimes against Women Cells 1983–present Delhi Police Deol 1983	India	The Crimes against Women Cell was developed in 1983 in the Delhi Police Department. The program was the first police response meant specifically for women in India. The program included a help line, crisis management, and self-defense training and counseling for women, as well as training for police on how to treat women.	B, C	**Methodology:** Review by then Joint Commissioner of Police, Delhi Police. **Findings:** Effectiveness is of mixed quality. The report notes that police officers think the government might have used these cells to reduce the issue of violence against women to a problem to be addressed just by the police force, when the issue needs to be addressed by multiple institutions.
HIV Prevention Programs for Female Prisoners in Nepal United Nations Office on Drugs and Crimes (UNODC) and Government of Nepal UNODC 2011	Nepal	UNODC is helping to reduce drug use and HIV-related high-risk behavior among female inmates in four Nepali jails and two district prisons through training on HIV/AIDS, STIs, and drug use prevention, treatment, and care.	A, C	**Methodology:** Project review report that shows outputs. **Findings:** The project has conducted behavioral change communication programs, trained inmates as peer educators, and established voluntary counseling and testing sites for HIV and STIs.

Note: HIV/AIDS = human immunodeficiency virus/acquired immune deficiency syndrome; STI = sexually transmitted infections.

Focus area codes: A = Health interventions in prisons; B = Responding and providing services for survivors of custodial violence; C = Training and awareness building.

Evaluated interventions for prevention and response to custodial violence whose evaluations do not explicitly consider women and girls.	
Afghanistan	Human Rights Watch. 2011. "Just Don't Call It a Militia: Impunity, Militias, and the "Afghan Local Police."" Governments of Afghanistan and the United States. http://www.hrw.org/reports/2011/09/12/just-don-t-call-it-militia.
India	Asian Centre for Human Rights. 2013. *Nobody's Children: Juveniles of Conflict Affected Districts of India.* New Delhi: Asian Centre for Human Rights. http://achrweb.org/reports/india/JJ-Nobodys_Children2013.pdf.
India	Asian Centre for Human Rights. 2012. *Madhya Pradesh: Snail Speed on Implementation of Juvenile Justice.* New Delhi: Asian Centre for Human Rights. www.achrweb.org/reports/india/JJ-MP-2012.pdf.
India	Asian Centre for Human Rights. 2012. "The State of Juvenile Justice in Himachal Pradesh." October 16, Asian Centre for Human Rights, New Delhi. http://www.achrweb.org/reports/india/JJ-HP-2012.pdf.
India	Asian Centre for Human Rights. 2013. *State of Juvenile Justice in Mizoram.* Asian Centre for Human Rights: New Delhi. http://achrweb.org/reports/india/JJ-Mizoram-2013.pdf.
Nepal	UNICEF. 2007. "Improving the Protection of Children in Conflict with the Law in South Asia." UNICEF, New York. http://www.ipu.org/PDF/publications/chil_law_en.pdf.

References

Deol, K. 1983. "Crimes against Women Cells: The Delhi Police Experience." 130th International Training Course Visiting Experts Papers, Resource Material Series, No. 69: 77–84. http://www.unafei.or.jp/english/pdf/RS_No69/No69_11VE_Deol1.pdf.

Saporte, L. 2012. "Final Evaluation: Social and Legal Protection of Women/Girls at Risk and Children Detained with their Mothers." Medica Mondiale, Cologne, Germany.

UNODC (United Nations Office on Drugs and Crimes). 2011. "Promoting Health, Justice, and Rule of Law." http://www.unodc.org/documents/southasia/reports/UNODC_ROSA_BROCHURE_2011.PDF.

Evaluated Interventions to Address Trafficking of Women and Girls[1]

Program and organization name. Sources.	Country	Program description	Focus areas	Evaluation description and findings
Counter-Trafficking Interventions in Bangladesh 2005–08 International Organization for Migration (IOM) Government of Bangladesh and IOM 2008	Bangladesh	The program was implemented in 18 districts. Activities included community awareness; capacity building of officers-in-charge of police stations, land port immigration officials, inspector-level police officials, and lawyers from the selected districts; and provision of legal, medical, and psychosocial support. Trafficking victims were also given vocational skill training and business support. The program conducted research and study tours to observe shelter homes in India and Nepal. It supported those affected by Cyclone Sidr. It also included Trafficking in Persons in a disaster reconstruction and rehabilitation effort and established the Community Information Center.	B, D, E	**Methodology:** Literature review, key informant and stakeholder interviews, and input from U.S. Agency for International Development (USAID)/Bangladesh. **Findings:** The report notes a decline in the incidence of trafficking because of increased awareness of trafficking and engagement of Union Parishads (UP). UP members discuss trafficking-related issues in monthly meetings in all the project districts, and committees have been set up to protect district areas against traffickers. As a result, police and the local administration have been more supportive of trafficking victims. The Bar Council has also set up a legal aid clinic.
Prevention and Protection for Victims of Human Trafficking in Bangladesh 2007–10 IOM Berman and Marshall 2011	Bangladesh	Focused on children, the project designed activities to screen for child trafficking, ensure children's rights, and provide shelter, as well as rehabilitation and reintegration services. For women over age 18, IOM has a livelihood support initiative. The project also includes initiatives in the private sector and on generating awareness, with a focus on partnerships with local artists and producing films and documentaries.	C, D, E	**Methodology:** Desk review, site visits, key informant interviews, case studies, and an online survey of implementing staff. **Findings:** IOM has supported the government to develop national action plans and collaborate with nongovernmental organizations (NGOs) to combat trafficking. Other successes include cooperation among multiple ministries, capacity building for counter-trafficking committees, awareness raising, and viable income generation. However, short funding and project cycles have had adverse effects.

Focus area codes: A = Empowering women and girls with information; B = Building awareness and engaging community members; C = Addressing vulnerabilities (livelihoods, jobs, and security); D = Assisting victims from rescue to rehabilitation; E = Strengthening law enforcement and policy frameworks.

Program and organization name. Sources.	Country	Program description	Focus areas	Evaluation description and findings
Trafficking and HIV and AIDS Prevention 2005–06 Care Bangladesh Ayyub 2006	Bangladesh	The project worked toward reducing the spread of HIV and AIDS. It aimed to build the capacity of self-help groups to prevent trafficking, disseminate information, establish a referral system for trafficking victims, and strengthen collaboration among organizations working to end trafficking.	A, B, E	**Methodology:** Project completion report. **Findings:** The project set up three information booths, which became the center of awareness and training activities. The project also established a multiorganizational, coordinated system of referrals, as well as three community watchdog committees to address trafficking of young girls into sex work.
Anyay Rahit Zingadi (ARZ) Programs 1997–ongoing ARZ Raghavan and Pawar-Kate 2009	India	This organization aims to increase community understanding of trafficking; to prevent entry of traffickers into Goa; to rescue, rehabilitate, and reintegrate trafficking victims; and to support the state government of Goa and other source states to implement anti-trafficking interventions including legal action. Activities include prevention and response actions with youth, police, NGOs, and trafficked victims.	B, C, D, E	**Methodology:** Literature review, field visits, and key informant interviews to evaluate the organization. **Findings:** ARZ was able to initiate action against traffickers and brothel keepers and to rescue minors and women forced into sex work. ARZ has contributed to the implementation of certain sections of the Immoral Traffic (Prevention) Act (TIPA). It has been successful in rescue, return, and rehabilitation of those rescued.
Prevention of Child Trafficking in the Northeast States of India 2007–09 United Nations Development Fund for Women (UNIFEM) Kilsby 2009	India	The program aimed to build capacity and networks of individuals, community-based organizations, NGOs, and government bodies to share data, raise public awareness, and advocate for the implementation of standard operating procedures. The program also set up rehabilitation centers in participating states.	B, C, D, E	**Methodology:** Interviews of member and partner organizations. **Findings:** The program trained border security forces and police. As a result, a specialized human trafficking police unit has been established. It has strengthened interagency collaboration and police protocols and has raised awareness through multiple means.

table continues next page

Focus area codes: A = Empowering women and girls with information; B = Building awareness and engaging community members; C = Addressing vulnerabilities (livelihoods, jobs, and security); D = Assisting victims from rescue to rehabilitation; E = Strengthening law enforcement and policy frameworks.

Program and organization name. Sources.	Country	Program description	Focus areas	Evaluation description and findings
Preventing and combating the trafficking of girls in India 2010–11 Sanlaap Pramod and Liberaloto 2011	India	The program was a short-term pilot project to ensure that girls and women had access to legal and regulatory systems and services. It worked to build the capacity of lawyers and paralegal experts to provide legal assistance, networked with law enforcement agencies, and created legal awareness among girls and community members.	A, B, E	**Methodology:** Semistructured qualitative interviews and focus group discussions with implementing organizations and participants, supplemented by a "polling booth survey." **Findings:** Training for lawyers and paralegals, and networking with judges, improved the timeliness and availability of legal counseling and assistance in this pilot phase.
Scholarship program 1996–present Rural Health Education Service Trust (RHEST) Arnaoudova 2010	Nepal	The program aims to keep girls from disadvantaged households in school by providing financial aid and to raise awareness on human trafficking. It provides education to girls and adolescents from grades 1 through 10, provides financial support for higher education and undergraduate studies, and trains students on managing individual finances. RHEST works with students and parents to raise awareness on human trafficking, among other human rights–oriented topics.	B, C	**Methodology:** Interviews with staff and other stakeholders and a small household survey. **Findings:** As of 2010, RHEST supported 6,266 students from 365 schools in rural Nepal. Dropout rates are low, and the percentage of girls who pass grade 10 national exams is higher among RHEST students than for the national average. Beneficiaries of the scholarship program demonstrate strong interest in their studies and performance.
Community-based project to enhance the protection of women and children against trafficking 2011–present Shakti Samuha Bhatt 2013	Nepal	The objective of this project is to create a community mechanism to protect women and children from trafficking. Project activities include nonformal education (NFE), savings and credit groups, protection committees, and formation of adolescent groups for girls age 12–18.	A, B, C, D	**Methodology:** Participant interviews and focus group discussions, and direct observation. **Findings:** The NFE classes, women's savings and credit groups, and protection and response committees have been established. Adolescent girl groups have increased girls' confidence and have helped to raise awareness on human trafficking, child rights, violence against women, domestic violence, and various prevention measures.

Focus area codes: A = Empowering women and girls with information; B = Building awareness and engaging community members; C = Addressing vulnerabilities (livelihoods, jobs, and security); D = Assisting victims from rescue to rehabilitation; E = Strengthening law enforcement and policy frameworks.

Program and organization name. Sources.	Country	Program description	Focus areas	Evaluation description and findings
Anti-Trafficking in Persons Programs in Asia Bangladesh, India: 2000–present Nepal: 2001–present USAID USAID 2009	Bangladesh, India, Nepal	Activities vary somewhat across countries, but the core support includes legal assistance, assistance in rescue, repatriation and shelter, awareness raising through various mechanisms, and linking with government authorities for advocacy.	A, B, C, D, E	**Methodology:** Desk review of programs. **Findings:** Some of the many key promising practices identified include strengthening community and police capacity to monitor and respond to trafficking (Bangladesh); promoting a code of conduct in the tourism industry to combat child sex tourism (India); and involving employers to expand market-driven employment opportunities for those vulnerable to trafficking (Nepal).
Regional Anti-Trafficking Programme in South Asia UNIFEM 2000–09 Dutta, Zutshi, and Vajpeyi 2009	Bangladesh, India, Nepal, Sri Lanka	Program activities spanned the spectrum of research, information systems, and databases; regional collaboration; policy and advocacy with governments; legal assistance and counseling of refugees; and other community-based prevention and response actions. The program also engaged the South Asian Association for Regional Cooperation to implement the Convention on Trafficking of Women and Children.	B, C, E	**Methodology:** Key informant interviews, desk review, case studies, field visits, and a stratified random survey. **Findings:** The report noted improvements in government engagement and regional collaboration, increased awareness and community involvement, changes in attitudes toward trafficked persons, and improved shelter services. However, legal support was not widely available or easily accessible.

Focus area codes: A = Empowering women and girls with information; B = Building awareness and engaging community members; C = Addressing vulnerabilities (livelihoods, jobs, and security); D = Assisting victims from rescue to rehabilitation; E = Strengthening law enforcement and policy frameworks.

Note

1. Approach categories from USAID (2009).

References

Arnaoudova, I. 2010. "Changing Lives: The Impacts of RHEST's Scholarship Program on Girls in Nepali Rural Communities." Master's thesis, Utrecht University, Utrecht, Netherlands. http://dspace.library.uu.nl/handle/1874/179462.

Ayyub, R. 2006. "Trafficking and HIV and AIDS Prevention Project." Project Completion Report, Care International, Bangladesh.

Berman, J., and P. Marshall. 2011. *Evaluation of the International Organization for Migration and its Efforts to Combat Human Trafficking.* Oslo: Norwegian Agency for Development Cooperation.

Bhatt, G. 2013. "Community Based Project to Enhance the Protection of Women and Children Against Trafficking." A Project Evaluation Report, Shakti Samuha, Nepal.

Dutta, M., B. Zutshi, and A. Vajpeyi. 2010. "UNIFEM Regional Anti-Trafficking Programme in South Asia (2000–2009)." Evaluation Report, UNIFEM, India.

Government of Bangladesh and IOM (International Organization for Migration). 2008. "Counter-Trafficking Interventions in Prevention Protection and Prosecution for Victims of Trafficking in Persons in Bangladesh." End Project Evaluation Report, IOM, Dhaka.

Kilsby, R. 2009. "Impulse NGO Network's Final Evaluation of Project A: Prevention of Child Trafficking in the Northeast States in India and Project B: Cross Border Anti Trafficking Initiative in North East India." Report, Impulse NGO Network, Shillong, Meghalaya, India.

Pramod, V. R., and S. Liberalato. 2011. "Preventing and Combating the Trafficking of Girls in India Using Legal Empowerment Strategies." Report, International Development Law Organization Monitoring and Evaluation Unit, India.

Raghavan, V., and A. Pawar-Kate. 2009. "Evaluation Report of ARZ-Anyay Rahit Zindagi, Goa." Report, Anyay Rahit Zindagi, Goa, India.

USAID (Unites States Agency for International Development). 2009. "USAID Anti-Trafficking in Persons Programs in Asia: A Synthesis." Report submitted to USAID by Chemonics International, Washington, DC.

Evaluated Interventions That Engage Men and Boys in Addressing Violence against Women and Girls

Program and organization. Sources.	Country	Program description	Focus areas	Evaluation description and findings
We Can campaign 2004–ongoing	Afghanistan, Bangladesh, India, Nepal, Pakistan and Sri Lanka	See appendix F.	B, C, D	
Engaging Men in GBV Prevention via Community Leadership Councils 2010–12 Instituto Promundo Instituto Promundo 2012	India	*Grameen Vikas Jan Sahbhagita Trust Jaunpur and Ujala Welfare Society* engaged local male leaders of the local leadership councils—Panchayats—to promote change in attitudes and behaviors related to violence among male youth and adult community leaders. Main activities were youth groups, advocacy campaigns, and community outreach.	C, D	**Methodology:** Quasi-experimental design and community-wide pre- and post-intervention survey with women and men. **Findings:** Men self-reported participating more equally in household responsibilities and boys self-reported advocating for their sisters' right to an education as a result of workshops. Participants developed individual plans to address the violence against women in their own lives, and the group devised community education plans. Participants reported increased knowledge of women's property rights, abortion laws, and more gender-equitable attitudes toward violence and household relationships.
Cultural, community, and clinical approaches to preventing HIV transmission and sexually transmitted infections among men 2008–12 Horizons program, Population Council Verma, Schensul, and Saggurti 2007	India	This program used a community and service-based model and focused on questioning social norms and multiple issues including gender-based violence (GBV). The program provided counseling, education, service provider training, referrals, and links to providers; undertook community outreach, activities and mobilization; and worked on clinical infrastructure.	A, D	**Methodology:** Quantitative and qualitative data. **Findings:** Six-month data showed improved attitudes and behavior among participating men. Changes in attitudes included lower hyper-masculinity and improved assessment as a sexual partner. Behavior change included lower self-reported spousal abuse.

Focus area codes: A = Engaging men and boys in sexual and reproductive health; B = Addressing gender socialization; C = Promoting nonviolence, gender equitable norms, and behavior; D = Influencing men's behavior and attitudes toward violence.

Program and organization. Sources.	Country	Program description	Focus areas	Evaluation description and findings
Program H 2004–05 Population Council Pulerwitz et al. 2006	India	The program addressed sexual and reproductive health, violence (against women and men), substance use and fatherhood. Activities included interactive group education, videos, social marketing campaigns, focus groups with youth, and a community-level mass-media campaign.	B, C, D	**Methodology:** Quantitative pre- and post-evaluation using the Gender-Equitable Men (GEM) Scale. **Findings:** A significantly smaller proportion of respondents supported inequitable gender norms at endline compared to baseline, and changes were maintained at the one-year follow-up in both intervention sites.
Men's Action for Stopping Violence Against Women (MASVAW) 2009–ongoing Sahayog Singh et al. 2011	India	The aim of the intervention was to enhance awareness of gender-based nondiscriminatory behavior and nonviolence against women. Main activities comprised group education sessions and campaigns. One district included men and women combined; a second, only men; and a third was a comparison district with no program activities.	C, D	**Methodology:** Quasi-experimental treatment-control with key informant interviews and community surveys. **Findings:** The combined community demonstrated positive shifts on some issues, but not on others. Men from the men-only community also showed mixed results and continued to justify wife beating in 1 of 4 domains. However, reported violence against any women by participating and other men in program districts declined, as reported by both men and women.
Yaari-Dosti: Promoting Gender-Equitable Norms and Behaviors 2004–05 Population Council, Horizons, CORO, MAMTA, and Instituto Promundo Verma et al. 2008	India	An adaptation of Program H, this intervention attempted to stimulate critical thinking about the rigid gender norms that promote risky behavior and to create support for young 'gender equitable' men[1] to promote care and better communication.	B, C, D	**Methodology:** Quasi-experimental design using the GEM scale. **Findings:** Participants reported less support for inequitable gender norms than control groups. Self-reported violence against a partner declined in the intervention sites.

Focus area codes: A = Engaging men and boys in sexual and reproductive health; B = Addressing gender socialization; C = Promoting nonviolence, gender equitable norms, and behavior; D = Influencing men's behavior and attitudes toward violence.

table continues next page

Program and organization. Sources.	Country	Program description	Focus areas	Evaluation description and findings
Gender Equality Movement in Schools (GEMS) 2008–09 and 2009–10 Committee of Resource Organizations for Literacy, Tata Institute for Social Sciences, International Center for Research on Women Achyut et al. 2011	India	Engaged young school-going girls and boys, ages 12–14, to discuss and critically reflect on the issues related to inequitable gender norms and violence. The intervention builds on previous successful efforts (e.g., Yaari Dosti). The program was carried out in a randomly selected sample of 45 schools in Mumbai City, with two intervention arms and one control arm.	B, C	**Methodology:** A quasi-experimental design. The schools were randomly and equally distributed across the three arms. **Findings:** Evaluation suggests a positive shift in students' attitudes toward gender equality. The number of students willing to take action in response to sexual harassment increased, as did the proportion believing that girls should be at least age 18 at marriage.
Improving services for Center for Social Research's crisis intervention centers Mukherjee n.d.	India	See appendix F.	C, D	
Parivartan Program 2009–10 Das et al. 2012	India	See appendix G.	B, C, D	
Action for Equality 2009–ongoing Equal Community Foundation 2011	India	See appendix F.	C	

Focus area codes: A = Engaging men and boys in sexual and reproductive health; B = Addressing gender socialization; C = Promoting nonviolence, gender equitable norms, and behavior; D = Influencing men's behavior and attitudes toward violence.

Program and organization. Sources.	Country	Program description	Focus areas	Evaluation description and findings
Promoting Gender Justice in Pakistan Norwegian Church Aid 2013	Pakistan	See appendix F.	C	
Comprehensive Skills Training and Empowerment of Afghan Refugees in Baluchistan 2010–11 Ibadat 2011	Pakistan	See appendix F.	C	
Engaging Men to Empower and Redefine Gender Equality (EMERGE) 2012–ongoing CARE International Fulu et al. 2013 CARE International, Sri Lanka 2012	Sri Lanka	This initiative engages and encourages men and other stakeholders to play a positive role in their homes, workplaces, and communities. It aims to address violence against women and contribute to women's lives more broadly, to promote collective decision making within households by husbands and wives, and to enhance services for women through a nationwide communication and advocacy campaign. Activities also include training of trainers on gender issues and research on men and boys in addressing GBV.	B, C, D	**Methodology:** Quantitative output assessment through a survey; no baseline. **Findings:** The project has created a pool of gender specialists who can deliver training programs for other organization staff. The project launched the "WE" campaign, which resulted in the development of communication materials that were widely disseminated. The project also included the first research study on knowledge, attitudes, and perceptions of men and boys on gender and GBV in Sri Lanka.
Engaging Fathers for Children's Education and Family Well-Being April 2012–May 2012 World Vision and MenCare 2012	Sri Lanka	See appendix F.	C, D	

Focus area codes: A = Engaging men and boys in sexual and reproductive health; B = Addressing gender socialization; C = Promoting nonviolence, gender equitable norms, and behavior; D = Influencing men's behavior and attitudes toward violence.

Note

1. This report defines a gender-equitable man as one who supports relationships based on respect, equality, and intimacy rather than on sexual conquest; is or seeks to be an involved domestic partner and father, both in terms of child care and household activities; assumes or shares with his partner the responsibility for sexual and reproductive health and disease prevention; and, finally, opposes intimate partner violence and homophobia (Verma et al. 2008).

References

Achyut, P., N. Bhatla, S. Khandekar, S. Maitra, and R. K. Verma. 2011. "Building Support for Gender Equality among Young Adolescents in School: Findings from Mumbai, India." New Delhi: International Center for Research on Women.

CARE International, Sri Lanka. 2012. "Engagingmen.net, A Gender Justice Information Network." http://www.engagingmen.net/content/mid-term-evaluation-engaging-men-project-care-international-sri-lanka.

Das M., S. Ghosh, E. Miller, B. O'Conner, and R. Verma. 2012. *Engaging Coaches and Athletes in Fostering Gender Equity: Findings from the Parivartan Program in Mumbai, India.* New Delhi: International Center for Research on Women and Futures Without Violence.

Equal Community Foundation. 2011. "Action for Equality Programme: Outcome Assessment Data." Pune, India. http://ecf.org.in/wp-content/uploads/Impact-Stories.pdf

Fulu, E., X. Warner, S. Miedema, R. Jewkes, T. Roselli, and J. Lang. 2013. *Why Do Some Men Use Violence Against Women and How Can We Prevent It? Quantitative Findings from the UN Multi-country Study on Men and Violence in Asia and the Pacific.* Bangkok: United Nations Development Programme, United Nations Population Fund, UN Women, and United Nations Volunteers.

Ibadat, G. 2011. "Comprehensive Skills Training and Empowerment of Afghan Refugees in Baluchistan." SEHER, Quetta, Pakistan.

Instituto Promundo. 2012. "Engaging Men to Prevent Gender-Based Violence: A Multi-Country Intervention and Impact Evaluation Study." Report for the United Nations Trust Fund, Promundo, Washington, DC.

Mukherjee, A. n.d. "Creating a Supportive and Violence Free Environment by Enabling Economic Self-Sufficiency amongst Community Members in CSR's Crisis Intervention Centers." New Delhi: Centre for Social Research.

Norwegian Church Aid. 2013. "Promoting Gender Justice in Pakistan." Final Report for grants from the Norwegian Ministry of Foreign Affairs, Norwegian Church Aid, Oslo.

Pulerwitz, J., G. Barker, M. Segundo, and N. Nascimento. 2006. "Promoting More Gender-Equitable Norms and Behaviors among Young Men as an HIV/AIDS Prevention Strategy." Population Council, New York. http://www.popcouncil.org/pdfs/horizons/brgendernorms.pdf.

Singh, A. K., V. Pandey, S. Singh, A. Das, G. Barker, and R. K. Verma. 2011. "Engaging Men to End Gender-Based Violence: An Evaluation Study." International Center for Research on Women (ICRW), Washington, DC.

Verma R., S. Schensul, and N. Saggurti. 2007. "Cultural, Community and Clinical Approaches to HIV/STI Prevention among Men: Results from Five Year Male Sexual Health Intervention Study in Urban India." Mumbai, Research and Intervention in Sexual Health: Theory to Action (RISHTA).

Verma, R., J. Pulerwitz, V. S. Mahendra, S. Khandekar, A. K. Singh, S. S. Das, S. Mehra, A. Nura, and G. Barker. 2008. "Promoting Gender Equity as a Strategy to Reduce HIV Risk and Gender-Based Violence among Young Men in India." Horizons Final Report, Population Council, New York.

World Vision and MenCare. 2012. "Engaging Fathers for Children's Education and Family Well-Being." MenCare Global Fatherhood Campaign, Sri Lanka.

Online Appendixes

The following appendixes can be found online at
http://www.worldbank.org/southasia/gbv/report

ECO-AUDIT
Environmental Benefits Statement

The World Bank is committed to preserving endangered forests and natural resources. The Publishing and Knowledge Unit has chosen to print *Violence against Women and Girls: Lessons from South Asia* on recycled paper with 100 percent postconsumer fiber in accordance with the recommended standards for paper usage set by the Green Press Initiative, a nonprofit program supporting publishers in using fiber that is not sourced from endangered forests. For more information, visit www.greenpressinitiative.org.

Saved:
• 13 trees
• 6 million Btu of total energy
• 1,077 pounds of net greenhouse gases
• 5,845 gallons of waste water
• 391 pounds of solid waste